AMERICAN BATTLE MONUMENTS

AMERICAN BATTLE MONUMENTS:

A Guide to Military Cemeteries and Monuments Maintained By the American Battle Monuments Commission

Elizabeth Nishiura
Editor

Omnigraphics, Inc.
Penobscot Building • Detroit, Michigan 48226

Bibliographic Note

All text, photographs, and maps in this publication originate from a series of booklets issued by the American Battle Monuments Commission and are published by Omnigraphics, Inc. with the consent and cooperation of the Commission.

Elizabeth Nishiura
Editor

Margaret Mary Missar
Editorial Associate

Annie M. Brewer
Vice President/Research

James A. Sellgren
Vice President/Operations

Frederick G. Ruffner, Jr.
Publisher

Library of Congress Catalog Card Number 89-61537
ISBN 1-55888-812-8

Printed in the United States of America

CONTENTS

UNITED KINGDOM:

UNITED STATES:

Part Three: World War II Cemeteries and Memorials

BELGIUM:

FRANCE:

Suresnes American Cemetery and Memorial
(Commemorates both World War I and World War II.
See Part Two, pages 105-13.)

ITALY:

LUXEMBOURG:

NETHERLANDS:

PACIFIC ISLANDS:

PHILIPPINES:

TUNISIA:

UNITED KINGDOM:

UNITED STATES:

Part Four: Cemeteries and Memorials of Other American Military Efforts

MEXICO:

PANAMA:

UNITED STATES:

Foreword

On behalf of the membership of the Veterans of Foreign Wars of the United States, it is a distinct honor that I commend this long overdue volume to the reader. The American Battle Monuments Commission, in a quietly magnificent way, has beautifully commemorated those who have fallen in the defense of our nation, as evidenced by the cemeteries and memorials depicted in this book.

The VFW has for years supported ABMC efforts overseas and in this country and is quite proud of the affiliation.

These pages do not honor war, for there is no glory in armed conflict. Instead, these scenes and places honor those who gave their last full measure participating in events that hopefully shall come no more.

Howard E. Vander Clute, Jr.
Adjutant General
Veterans of Foreign Wars
of the United States
June 1989

Preface

For over 65 years the American Battle Monuments Commission (ABMC) has been carefully preserving America's overseas military cemeteries as well as many battle monuments located in the U.S. and abroad. During these years, the ABMC has been committed to making its memorials accessible to the public, and as part of that project they have printed a series of informational pamphlets about the sites. *American Battle Monuments* was compiled from these pamphlets. Spanning four continents, five wars and nearly 150 years of American military history, *American Battle Monuments* is intended to be used both as a guide to the general work of the American Battle Monuments Commission, and as a source for information about particular cemeteries and memorials.

The Organization

There are four main divisions in the text of *American Battle Monuments*. The first section, "American Memorials and Overseas Military Cemeteries," provides an overview of the ABMC and its mission. Descriptions of the individual memorials are found in Parts Two through Four. Part Two describes World War I sites; Part Three covers World War II cemeteries and monuments; and in Part Four all of the memorials which commemorate other American military efforts are included.

Within each of the latter three sections, the descriptions of the sites are presented in alphabetical order, first by country name, and then, if necessary, by site name within the individual countries.

The only exceptions to this alphabetical arrangement occur when the history of a monument (or monuments) is very closely related to that of a neighboring cemetery. In these instances the descriptions of the cemetery and the related monument are grouped together, with their place within the section's alphabetical order determined by the name of the cemetery. This design follows the arrangement of the original ABMC pamphlets, and while I regret that these exceptions to the general organizational scheme occur, I felt that it was more important to maintain the coherence of the text than it was to prevent a few deviations from a strictly alphabetical order. If the reader has any doubt about where the description of a particular memorial can be found in *American Battle Monuments*, he or she should turn to the Index for illumination.

The Index

The Index adds a new dimension of accessibility to the original texts of the Commission's booklets. For example, many of the descriptions in the booklets contain information about particular military units, including where the units' feats and sacrifices are commemorated, and with the addition of the Index this information is quickly retrieved.

Also included in the Index are the names of all of the artists and architects involved in the construction of the memorials, as well as the names of the battles, historical figures, and locations which are described in the text. Every effort has been made to avoid errors and omissions. Any mistakes which may occur, however, result from my oversights, and do not reflect the judgment of the American Battle Monuments Commission.

Acknowledgements

American Battle Monuments would not have been possible without the generous cooperation of the entire American Battle Monuments Commission. The text, photos, and maps all originate from the Commission, and I am indebted to the ABMC for sharing this wealth of materials. Except for a very few instances in which irrelevant, outdated, or duplicated information has been removed, the text that appears in this book is exactly that which was printed in the original pamphlets, and the American Battle Monuments Commission deserves full credit for its prose and illustrations.

I would especially like to thank Colonel William E. Ryan, Jr., director of Operations and Finance at the American Battle Monuments Commission, for his patience and willingness to answer questions; and Martha Sell, chief of the Commission's Operations division, who dedicated months to the collection of photographs, maps and other materials from the Commission's archives in Washington, D.C. Ms. Sell was also my faithful contact for all types of information regarding the ABMC and this project, and I am extremely grateful for her help.

Thank you, also, to Howard E. Vander Clute, Jr., Adjutant General of the Veterans of Foreign Wars of the United States, for kindly providing the Foreword for this book. His words eloquently pay tribute to the American Battle Monuments Commission and its work.

Finally, the current addresses of the ABMC offices in the U.S. and abroad appear on page 13 of this book, and I strongly urge the reader to contact these offices for further information about the Commission and its memorials. I can testify from personal experience that the American Battle Monuments Commission is extraordinarily willing to assist the public with its inquiries.

Elizabeth Nishiura

INTRODUCTION:

AMERICAN MEMORIALS AND
OVERSEAS MILITARY CEMETERIES

Cambridge American Cemetery and Memorial

AMERICAN MEMORIALS and OVERSEAS MILITARY CEMETERIES

The AMERICAN BATTLE MONUMENTS COMMISSION was created by act of Congress in March 1923 to erect and maintain memorials in the United States and foreign countries where the United States Armed Forces have served since 6 April 1917, and to control as to design and provide regulations for the erection of monuments, markers and memorials in foreign countries by other United States citizens and organizations, public or private. It was later given responsibility for establishing or taking over from the Armed Forces permanent burial grounds in

ABMC Cemeteries and Monuments in Europe

foreign countries and designing, constructing and maintaining permanent cemetery memorials at these burial sites; controlling as to design and materials, providing regulations for and supervising erection of all monuments, memorials, buildings and other structures in permanent United States cemetery memorials on foreign soil; and cooperating with American citizens, states, municipalities, or associations desiring to erect war memorials outside the continental limits of the United States. It is not responsible for construction, maintenance or operation of cemeteries in the continental United States or its territories and possessions.

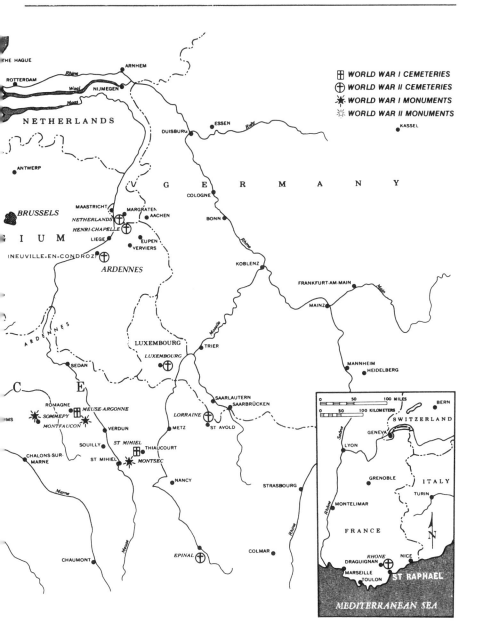

After World War I the American Battle Monuments Commission erected a memorial chapel in each of the eight military cemeteries overseas already established by the War Department, as well as eleven monuments and two bronze tablets on the battlefields and elsewhere, to record the achievements of our Armed Forces. In 1934 the World War I oversea cemeteries were transferred to the Commission by Executive Order.

The names and locations of these World War I cemetery memorials, the number of burials and the number of Missing recorded at their memorials are:

World War I	Burials		Missing
	Known	Unknown	Commemorated
Aisne-Marne, Belleau, France	2,039	249	1,060
Brookwood, England	427	41	563
Flanders Field, Waregem, Belgium	347	21	43
Meuse-Argonne, Romagne, France	13,760	486	954
Oise-Aisne, Fere-en-Tardenois, France	5,415	597	241
St. Mihiel, Thiaucourt, France	4,036	117	284
Somme, Bony, France	1,707	137	333
Suresnes (See WW II also), France	1,535	6	974
Totals	29,266	1,654	4,452

World War I monuments erected by the Commission are located at or near: Audenarde, Belgium; Bellicourt, France; Brest, France; Cantigny, France; Chateau-Thierry, France; Gibraltar; Kemmel, Belgium; Montfaucon, France; Montsec, France; Sommepy, France; and Tours, France. World War I tablets are at Chaumont and Souilly, France.

By the end of World War II several hundred temporary cemeteries had been established by the American Graves Registration Service of the United States Army. During the years 1947 to 1954 that Service, complying with the expressed wishes of the next of kin, and by authority of law, repatriated the remains of some 172,000 recovered bodies. The remainder were given final interment in the permanent military cemeteries on foreign soil, in private cemeteries overseas and in the national cemeteries in Honolulu, Sitka and Puerto Rico (which are now administered by the National Cemetery System, Veterans' Administration). As was the case after World War I, some remains were left in isolated graves outside of the cemeteries by request of the families who then became responsible for their maintenance.

Fourteen sites in foreign countries were selected as permanent cemeteries in 1947 by the Secretary of the Army and the American Battle Monuments Commission in concert. Their locations reflect the progress of the military operations and were selected with consideration of their accessibility, aspect, prospect, drainage and other practical factors. The World War II cemeteries with numbers of burials, including Unknowns, and the numbers of Missing recorded at their memorials and at three separate memorials on United States soil are:

World War II	Burials		Missing
	Known	Unknown	Commemorated
Ardennes, Neupre (Neuville-en-Condroz) Belgium	4,536	791	462
Brittany, St. James, France	4,313	97	497
Cambridge, England	3,787	24	5,126
Epinal, France	5,186	69	424
Florence, Italy	4,189	213	1,409
Henri-Chapelle, Belgium	7,895	94	450
Lorraine, St. Avold, France	10,338	151	444
Luxembourg, Luxembourg City, Luxembourg	4,975	101	370
Manila, Republic of the Philippines	13,462	3,744	36,280
Netherlands, Margraten, Holland	8,195	106	1,722
Normandy, St. Laurent-sur-Mer, France	9,079	307	1,557
North Africa, Carthage, Tunisia	2,601	240	3,724
Rhone, Draguignan, France	799	62	293
Sicily-Rome, Nettuno, Italy	7,372	490	3,095
Suresnes (See WW I also), France	. . .	24	. . .

East Coast Memorial, New York City, New York . . .	. . .	. . .	4,596
Honolulu Memorial, Honolulu, Hawaii	. . .	. . .	18,094
West Coast Memorial, San Francisco, California	. . .	. . .	413
Totals	86,727	6,513	78,956

World War II cemeteries maintained by the National Cemetery System, Veterans' Administration

National Memorial Cemetery of the Pacific			(See
Honolulu, Hawaii	11,597	2,079	Honolulu
			Memorial)
Puerto Rico	69	. . .	. . .
Sitka, Alaska	67	5	. . .

Other Missing in Action Commemorated by ABMC

Korean War, Honolulu Memorial,			
Honolulu, Hawaii	. . .	. . .	8,195
Vietnam War, Honolulu Memorial,			
Honolulu, Hawaii	. . .	. . .	2,489

In every case, use of the permanent cemetery sites on foreign soil was granted in perpetuity by the host government to the United States free of cost, rent and taxation. The temporary cemetery sites not selected as permanent cemeteries reverted to the landowners.

In 1947, an outstanding American architect was selected to design each of the World War II cemeteries, conceiving its grave plots, a chapel and a museum as complementary elements of an integral memorial to the services and sacrifices of the American Armed Services who fought in the particular region. Upon approval of their general schemes by the Commission and by agreement with the Secretary of the Army, the architects' plans of the grave plots were followed by the American Graves Registration Service in making the permanent burials of those remains which by decision of the next of kin were to be interred overseas. The timely cooperation between these two agencies contributed appreciably to the coherence of the development of the cemetery designs.

Beginning in the latter half of 1949, the permanent interments having been virtually completed, the World War II overseas cemeteries were progressively transferred for construction and maintenance to the American Battle Monuments Commission by Presidential Executive Order. Thereupon the remaining portions of the architects' designs were carried out, step by step — grading; installation of a system of reinforced concrete beams on piles to maintain the levels and alignments of the headstones; fabrication and installation of the headstones; construction of water supply and distribution systems, utilities buildings, roads and paths; plantings; and erection of the memorials, visitors' buildings and flagpoles.

For design of the various memorials, no specific limitations were imposed upon the architects other than budgeted cost and a requirement that each was to embody these features:

A small devotional chapel;

inscription of the names and particulars of the Missing in the region;

a graphic record, in permanent form, of the services of our troops (WW II only; however, Oise-Aisne, Meuse-Argonne and St. Mihiel WW I American Cemeteries also have battle maps).

These requirements have been interpreted in a wide and interesting variety of forms.

An important motive for the construction of the memorials is the implied undertaking by our Govern-

St. Mihiel American Cemetery and Memorial

ment to record by monuments the achievements of our Armed Services, since the erection of memorials by the troops (which in the past unfortunately had all too often been found to be poorly designed, poorly constructed and lacking provision for maintenance) was expressly forbidden by the military services. The permanent graphic record takes the form of military maps, usually large murals, amplified by descriptive texts in English as well as in the language of the country in which the cemetery is located. The historical data for these maps were prepared by the American Battle Monuments Commission. The maps themselves were rendered by experienced artists in tasteful presentation using various media: layered marbles, fresco, bronze relief, mosaic concrete or ceramics. Another feature of interest at each memorial is the two sets of ''key-maps'': ''The War

Against Germany'' and ''The War Against Japan.'' Each set consists of three maps, each covering about one-third of the period of our participation in the war. By these key-maps any major battle may be related to the others in time and space.

With each architect, an American landscape architect, an American sculptor and an American muralist or painter usually collaborated. Their combined talents produced the beauty and dignity of the memorials, all of which are dedicated to the memory of the achievements of those who served and of the sacrifices of those who died. The construction of the cemeteries and memorials and the execution of most of the works of art, were performed by local contractors and artists under the supervision of the Commission.

At each cemetery there is a visitors' building or room, with comfortable furnishings. Here visitors

View of Suresnes Cemetery and Memorial

Detail from memorial at Rhone American Cemetery

may learn the grave locations (or inscriptions of the Missing) at any of the oversea cemeteries.

Each grave in the oversea cemeteries is marked by a headstone of white marble—a Star of David for those of Jewish faith, a Latin cross for all others. Each headstone bears the deceased's name, rank, service, organization, date of death and state or territory from which he entered the military service.

In the World War I cemeteries, headstones of the Unknowns, i.e., those remains which could not be identified, bear the inscription:

HERE RESTS IN HONORED GLORY AN AMERICAN SOLDIER KNOWN BUT TO GOD.

In the World War II cemeteries, the inscription reads:

HERE RESTS IN HONORED GLORY A COMRADE IN ARMS KNOWN BUT TO GOD.

Tablets of the Missing (which also include the names of those whose remains could not be identified and those lost or buried at sea) give name, rank, organization and state; the circumstances under which death occurred often precluded the possibility of determining the exact date.

These cemeteries are open every day of the year. Photography is permitted without special authorization, except when it is to be used for commercial purposes—in such cases, permission must be obtained from the Commission.

Unlike National cemeteries under jurisdiction of the Veterans Administration, there can be no further burials in the American military cemeteries overseas except of those remains which may, in the future, be found on the battlefields. Essentially, these graves with their memorials constitute inviolable shrines.

ABMC Cemeteries and Monuments along the Mediterranean

ADDITIONAL INFORMATION

Further information regarding cemeteries and memorials may be obtained at the Commission's offices in Washington, Garches (near Paris), Rome or Manila. Visitors passing through these cities are invited to call. The Commission's representatives there may be of assistance in verifying travel routes and schedules and also in furnishing information concerning overnight accommodations. These offices are not open on Saturdays, Sundays or holidays, but essential information may be obtained overseas through our Embassy telephone operators.

FLORAL DECORATIONS

In the oversea cemeteries, the decoration of graves or the Tablets of the Missing with natural cut flowers only is permitted. The Commission is always ready to help arrange with local florists in foreign countries for placement of such decorations. Requests should be mailed so as to arrive at the appropriate Commission office at least thirty days before the date of decoration and should be accompanied by check or U. S. Postal Money Order in dollars. Deposits may be made for a single decoration on a particular day—birthday, Memorial Day, Christmas Day, for example—or for several decorations on particular dates within a year or over a period of years. Checks should be made payable to "ABMC Flower Fund," money orders to "The American Battle Monuments Commission." Requests should be addressed to the Commission's European office, except in the case of Florence, Sicily-Rome and North Africa cemeteries, where the Mediterranean office is responsible and Manila cemetery, where the Philippine office is responsible.

Orders for flowers for all cemeteries may also be placed through any local florist who is a member of the "Florists Telegraph Delivery Association." In such cases, the name of the deceased, his rank, service number, name of the cemetery, country in which located and the location by plot, row and grave should be provided, if known.

SERVICES TO THE PUBLIC
AVAILABLE THROUGH
THE AMERICAN BATTLE MONUMENTS COMMISSION

Name, location, and general information concerning the cemetery or memorial; plot, row, and grave number if appropriate; best routes and modes of travel in-country to the cemetery or memorial; general information about the accommodations that may be available in the vicinity; escort service within the cemetery memorial for relatives; letters authorizing fee-free passports for members of the immediate family traveling overseas to visit a grave or memorial site; black and white photographs of headstones and sections of the Tablets of the Missing on which the servicemen's names are engraved; large color lithographs of World War I and II cemeteries and memorials to which the appropriate headstone or section of the Tablets of the Missing photographs are affixed; and arrangements for floral decoration of grave and memorial sites. Photographs of graves in the National Memorial Cemetery of the Pacific (in Honolulu) are not available through the Commission.

THE AMERICAN BATTLE MONUMENTS COMMISSION

ESTABLISHED BY CONGRESS MARCH 1923

Membership

Andrew J. Goodpaster *Chairman*	Armistead J. Maupin *Vice Chairman*
Francis J. Bagnell	William E. Hickey
Kitty D. Bradley	Preston H. Long
Joseph W. Canzeri	John C. McDonald
Aubrey O. Cookman	Freda J. Poundstone
Rexford C. Early	A. J. Adams, *Secretary*

UNITED STATES OFFICE
Casimir Pulaski Building
20 Massachusetts Ave., N.W.
Washington, D.C. 20314-0300
Telephone: (202) 272-0533
272-0532

MEDITERRANEAN OFFICE
Street Address:
American Embassy
Via Veneto 119a
Rome, Italy
Mailing Address:
APO New York 09794-0007
Telephone: 4674, Ext. 2033
482-4157

EUROPEAN OFFICE
Street Address:
68, rue du 19 Janvier
92380 - Garches, France
Mailing Address:
APO New York 09777
Telephone: 4795-4976

PHILIPPINE OFFICE
Street Address:
American Military Cemetery
Manila, R. P.
Mailing Address:
APO San Francisco 96528
Telephone: Manila 88-02-12

Decorated Gravesite of an "Unknown"

WORLD WAR I
CEMETERIES AND MEMORIALS:

BELGIUM

Flanders Field American Cemetery and Memorial

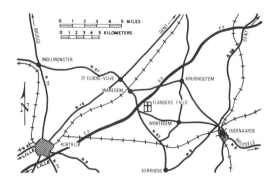

LOCATION

Flanders Field American Cemetery and Memorial is located on the south-eastern edge of the industrial commune of Waregem, Belgium, about 1.5 miles/2.5 km. from the center of town, on the road to Audenarde (Oudenaarde).[1]

Waregem may be reached by train from Brussels via Ghent (Gent) in approximately one hour; from the Gare du Nord in Paris in about 5 hours via Lille (Rysel) and Courtrai (Kortrijk) and 5½ hours via Brussels and Ghent. Taxi service to the cemetery is available at the railroad station in Waregem. Road distances to Waregem from various cities are: Brussels — 46 miles/74 km., Mons — 50 miles/80 km., Ghent — 21 miles/34 km., Bruges (Brugge) — 29 miles/47 km., Courtrai — 10 miles/16 km., Audenarde — 8 miles/13 km., Ypres (Ieper) — 28 miles/45 km., Lille — 29 miles/47 km., and Paris — 175 miles/280 km.

Adequate hotel accommodations may be found in Waregem and in

[1] Parenthetical references show Flemish spelling.

Entrance Gates

Chapel Interior

most of the surrounding cities and towns.

HOURS

The cemetery is open daily to the public as shown below:

SUMMER (16 March–30 September)
 9:00 a.m.–6:00 p.m. — weekdays
 10:00 a.m.–6:00 p.m. — Saturdays, Sundays and holidays
WINTER (1 October–15 March)
 9:00 a.m.–5:00 p.m. — weekdays
 10:00 a.m.–5:00 p.m. — Saturdays, Sundays and holidays

When the cemetery is open to the public, a staff member is on duty in the Visitors' Building to answer questions and to escort relatives to grave and memorial sites (except between the hours of noon and 3:00 p.m. on weekends and holidays).

HISTORY

The Flanders Field American Cemetery is situated on a battlefield where the U.S. 91st Division suffered many casualties in securing the wooded area called "Spitaals Bosschen," a few hundred yards to its east.

Before advancing into Belgium, the U.S. 91st and U.S. 37th Divisions had been engaged in heavy fighting in the Meuse-Argonne region. Both divisions received orders in October 1918 to join the French Army in Belgium and assist in the operations launched there on 28 September 1918 by the Group of Armies of Flanders under the command of Albert I, King of Belgium.

The two divisions joined the Ypres-Lys offensive on 30 October; the U.S. 37th, along the railroad at Olsene, and the U.S. 91st just south of Waregem. A French division separated them in the lines when the general attack eastward toward the Escaut River (also known as the Schelde River) began at 5:30 a.m. on 31 October 1918.

The U.S. 91st Division quickly drove forward despite intense artil-

Garden with Chapel in Background

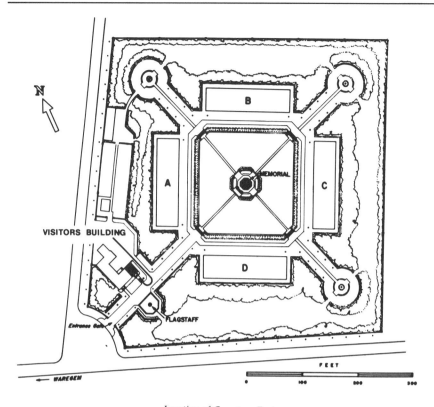

Location of Cemetery Features

lery and machine gun fire and captured the "Spitaals Bosschen" a short distance in front of its line of departure. The division was then delayed by severe enfilade fire from its right, as the French Division on that flank had been unable to make a corresponding advance. Meanwhile, the U.S. 37th Division advanced under heavy enemy fire about 2½ miles to the western outskirts of Cruyshautem (Kruishoutem) where it dug in for the night. The following day, it being evident that the Germans were retreating, both divisions advanced rapidly to the Escaut River. The U.S. 91st occupied part of Audenarde on 2 November and the remainder of it the next day. Early on 2 November under heavy fire the U.S. 37th Division forced a crossing of the Escaut south-

east of Heurne. A German counterattack against the bridgehead on 4 November was repulsed. Both divisions were relieved during the night of 4 November to prepare for another general offensive and returned to the front lines on 10 November. The following day, both divisions were able to advance with little opposition. The Armistice became effective at 11:00 a.m. on that date (11 November 1918).

SITE

Smallest of the permanent American military cemeteries on the European continent, the Flanders Field American Cemetery occupies 6 acres. It was dedicated on 8 August 1937, and is the only American World War I cemetery

Visitors' Building

in Belgium. The use of the land on which it rests has been granted by the Belgian Government free of charge or taxation in perpetuity, as an expression of its gratitude to the United States.

Charles A. Lindbergh flew over the cemetery in the *Spirit of St. Louis* on 30 May 1927 to salute his fallen countrymen and drop poppies on the Memorial Day ceremonies being held below. He did this just 9 days after he completed his historic solo trans-Atlantic flight.

For many Americans, the cemetery has special significance because of John McCrae's poem, "In Flanders Field." The poem, however, was not written about the fighting which occurred there. Lt. Col. John McCrae, M.D., a Canadian physician, wrote it while serving at a medical station in Ypres. On 8 December 1915, the poem was published anonymously in *Punch* magazine. Colonel McCrae died of pneumonia on 28 January 1918, 9 months prior to large-scale fighting in the Flanders area. In 1919, his verses were collected and published under the title *In Flanders Field and Other Poems.*

IN FLANDERS FIELD

In Flanders fields, the poppies blow
Between the crosses, row on row,
    That mark our place; and in the sky
    The larks, still bravely singing, fly.
Scarce heard amid the guns below.

We are the Dead. Short days ago
We lived, felt dawn, saw sunset glow,
    Loved and were loved, and now we lie
        In Flanders fields.

Take up our quarrel with the foe:
To you from failing hands we throw
    The torch; Be yours to hold it high.
    If ye break faith with us who die
We shall not sleep, though poppies grow
        In Flanders fields.

It was due to the poem "In Flanders Field" that Miss Moina Michael originated the Flanders Field Memorial Poppy which has raised millions of dollars for veterans and their families.

Miss Michael is known to millions of World War I veterans as the "Poppy Lady" and on 9 November 1918 she wrote the poem "We Shall Keep the Faith" in answer to the "In Flanders Field" poem.

WE SHALL KEEP THE FAITH

Oh! You who sleep in "Flanders Fields,"
    Sleep sweet — to rise anew!
    We caught the Torch you threw
And, holding high we keep the Faith
        With all who died.

We cherish, too, the poppy red
That grows on fields where valor led:
    It seems to signal to the skies
    That blood of heroes never dies.
But lends a lustre to the red
Of the flower that blooms above the dead
        In Flanders Fields.

And now the Torch and Poppy red
We wear in honor of our dead.
    Fear not that ye have died for naught;
    We've learned the lesson that ye taught
        In Flanders Fields.
                                Moina Michael

ARCHITECT

Dr. Paul P. Cret of Philadelphia, Pennsylvania was the architect of the cemetery and the memorial. The landscape architect was J. Greber of Paris, France.

GENERAL LAYOUT

From the wrought-iron entrance gates on the Waregem/Audenarde road, a short gravelled lane bordered by linden trees on a carpet of grass leads past the Visitors' Building on the left and the flagpole terrace on the right to the memorial chapel and graves area beyond. The American flag flies daily from the 50-foot flagpole on the terrace near the entrance gate. The pole's cast bronze base is ornamented with Acanthus leaves, butterflies, sea-shells, oak leaves and acorns with a circle of poppies at the point where the staff is inserted in the base. The flagpole was designed by Egerton Swartwout, New York City, N.Y.

Mosaic Ceiling in Chapel

and cast by Susse Freres, Paris, France. Other architectural ornaments in the cemetery were created by L. Bottiau of Paris, France.

Steps lead down from the end of the gravelled lane directly to the corner of a square-shaped sunken garden in the center of which is an interdenominational chapel where visitors may pause for meditation and prayer. Paralleling each side of the sunken garden is one of the cemetery's four rectangular grave plots. Flagstone paths lead from the chapel to steps at the three other corners of the sunken garden beyond which small secluded recesses enclosed with trees are located, each containing a decorative urn on a pedestal and stone benches on which to rest. The insignia of the four American divisions which fought in Belgium (27th, 30th, 37th and 91st) are shown on the urns in sculptured form.

MEMORIAL CHAPEL

At the center of the cemetery is the small memorial chapel of white Pouillenay stone. Above its bronze entrance door is engraved:

GREET THEM EVER WITH
GRATEFUL HEARTS

to remind the visitor that those buried there died for their freedom.

On three of the outer walls, the dedicatory inscription appears in French, Flemish and English:

THIS CHAPEL HAS BEEN ERECTED BY THE UNITED STATES OF AMERICA IN MEMORY OF HER SOLDIERS WHO FOUGHT AND DIED IN BELGIUM DURING THE WORLD WAR. THESE GRAVES ARE THE PERMANENT AND VISIBLE SYMBOL OF THE HEROIC DEVOTION WITH WHICH THEY GAVE THEIR LIVES TO THE COMMON CAUSE OF HUMANITY.

Wall of the Missing in Chapel

Flanders Field Memorial Chapel

Beneath the three versions of the inscription, sculptured bas-relief figures symbolizing Grief, Remembrance and History respectively appear.

CHAPEL INTERIOR

Inside the chapel, one's attention is drawn to the altar of Grand Antique (black and white) marble. On the front of the altar is inscribed:

I WILL RANSOM THEM FROM THE POWER OF THE GRAVE, I WILL REDEEM THEM FROM DEATH (Hosea, XIII, 14).

Above it carved on a rose-tinted marble panel is a Crusader's sword outlined in gold. On either side of the altar stands a bronze candelabrum and flagstaffs supporting flags of the United States, Belgium, France, Great Britain and Italy. On the side walls of the chapel, panels of rose St. George marble enframed in bronze molding carry the names of 43 American soldiers who lost their lives in Belgium and sleep in unknown graves. Above the names is the Great Seal of the United States and the inscription:

IN MEMORY OF THOSE AMERICAN SOLDIERS WHO FOUGHT IN THIS REGION AND WHO SLEEP IN UNKNOWN GRAVES.

The beauty of the interior is enhanced by the mosaic ceiling, which depicts a lighted oil lamp under the stars of Heaven with doves of peace flying toward the light, and a large ornamental window over the door through which comes a subdued golden light.

The furniture of the chapel is of carved oak, stained black with veining in white to harmonize with the black and white marble altar.

GRAVES AREA

The graves area consists of four rectangular plots. Each plot contains 92 graves marked with white marble headstones set in stately rows on a carpet of green grass. Stars of David mark the graves of those of Jewish faith and Latin Crosses mark all others. Each grave plot is enframed by an English yew hedge and dense massifs of colorful trees and shrubs. Twenty-one of the 368 graves in the cemetery are of Unknowns.

VISITORS' ROOM

Near the cemetery entrance a comfortably furnished room is provided where visitors may pause to refresh themselves or obtain information from the cemetery staff. A register is maintained there, and all visitors are encouraged to sign it before leaving the cemetery. Burial locations and sites of memorialization in all of the overseas American military cemeteries of both World War I and World War II, plus other information of interest concerning the overseas cemeteries or local history, may be obtained from the Superintendent or the cemetery staff.

PLANTINGS

Behind the linden trees bordering the lane, a currant hedge sets off dense massifs of trees and colorful shrubs of rhododendron, lilac, azalea, birch, ash, oak, elm, holly, maple, osmanthus, hydrangea, magnolia, spirea and Japanese prune.

Visitors' Room

Flanders Field Memorial Chapel

Audenarde
Monument

In 1936, the American Battle Monuments Commission erected a small monument in Audenarde (Oudenaarde), Belgium to the 40,000 American troops who participated in operations in that area during World War I. The monument of yellow Cruchaud stone is located in a small park at Tacambaro Place in the center of the city. It was designed by Mr. Harry Sternfeld of Philadelphia, Pennsylvania.

On the front of the monument above a sculptured shield of the United States is engraved the inscription:

37TH DIVISION — 91ST DIVISION — 53RD FIELD ARTILLERY BRIGADE.

Below the shield and flanked by two sculptured American eagles is the inscription:

ERECTED BY THE UNITED STATES OF AMERICA TO COMMEMORATE THE SERVICES OF AMERICAN TROOPS WHO FOUGHT IN THIS VICINITY, OCT 30 — NOV 11, 1918.

A French version of the inscription is repeated on the right side of the monument and a Flemish version on the left.

𝕶𝖊𝖒𝖒𝖊𝖑 𝕸𝖔𝖓𝖚𝖒𝖊𝖓𝖙

In 1929, the American Battle Monuments Commission erected a small monument commemorating the achievements of the 27th and 30th Divisions which fought in the Ypres-Lys offensive with the British Army from 18 August to 4 September 1918. The monument of clear Rocheret stone is located near the hamlet of Vierstraat on the road to Mont Kemmel (Kemmelberg) about 4 miles/6.5 km. south of Ypres. It was designed by Mr. George Howe of Philadelphia, Pennsylvania.

Engraved on the front of the monument is the inscription:

27TH DIVISION — 30TH DIVISION.

ERECTED BY THE UNITED STATES OF AMERICA TO COMMEMORATE THE SERVICES OF AMERICAN TROOPS WHO FOUGHT IN THIS VICINITY AUGUST 18–SEPTEMBER 4, 1918.

The inscription is flanked on either side by a sculptured American bayonet. Below the inscription is a sculptured American helmet resting upon a wreath. A French version of the inscription is engraved on the left side of the monument and a Flemish version on the right. The insignia of the 27th and 30th Divisions are engraved on the back side of the monument with their respective numerical designations beneath them.

WORLD WAR I
CEMETERIES AND MEMORIALS:

FRANCE

Aisne-Marne American Cemetery and Memorial

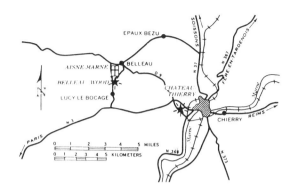

LOCATION

The Aisne-Marne American Cemetery and Memorial is located 6.5 miles/10.5 kilometers northwest of Chateau-Thierry, just southwest of the village of Belleau, Aisne, France. Travel by train from the Gare de l'Est in Paris to Chateau-Thierry takes about one hour. Taxi service to the cemetery is available at the Chateau-Thierry railroad station. The cemetery may also be reached by automobile from Paris via autoroute A-3 east by taking the Montreuil-aux-Lyons exit and following the cemetery signs to Lucy-le-Bocage and proceeding through Belleau Woods to the entrance to the cemetery. The distance from Paris to the cemetery by automobile is approximately 50 miles/80 kilometers. Hotel accommodations are available in the cities of Chateau-Thierry, Meaux, Soissons and Reims.

Entrance to the Cemetery

Apse in Chapel

HOURS

The cemetery is open daily to the public as shown below:
SUMMER (16 March – 30 September)
    9:00 a.m. – 6:00 p.m. — weekdays
    10:00 a.m. – 6:00 p.m. — Saturdays, Sundays, and holidays
WINTER (1 October – 15 March)
    9:00 a.m. – 5:00 p.m. — weekdays
    10:00 a.m. – 5:00 p.m. — Saturdays, Sundays, and holidays

When the cemetery is open to the public, a staff member is on duty in the Visitors' building to answer questions and to escort relatives to grave and memorial sites (except between the hours of noon and 3:00 p.m. on weekends and holidays).

HISTORY

On the morning of 27 May 1918, the Germans attacked in force on the Aisne front between Berry-au-Bac and Anizy-le-Chateau. Reserves were rushed there by the Allies from every quarter. The French were able to stem the onslaught with the help of American troops, but only after a large salient had been driven into Allied lines roughly defined by the triangle of Reims, Chateau-Thierry and Soissons. On 9 June, two German armies attacked from the salient toward Compiegne in an attempt to widen it and secure use of the railroad from Compiegne to Soissons; the attack was unsuccessful.

The Germans then began preparations for a major offensive on either side of Reims in the general direction of Epernay and Chalons-sur-Marne. Its objective was the capture of Reims and the high ground south of it to obtain use of an additional trunk line railroad. Three German armies totaling 47 divisions and a large quantity of artillery were assembled for the offensive. Meanwhile, the Allies were doing everything they could to discover when and where the next offensive would take place. They were completely successful in their efforts, as they not only learned the line of attack, but the exact day and hour that the German offensive was scheduled to commence.

On 15 July, the date of the German offensive, there were 26 American divisions in France, of which 12 were available for combat. Because of their large size, 12 American divisions were equivalent in fire power to 24 French, British or German divisions. With so many fresh American troops available and knowing that soon there would be more, Marshal Foch, the Allied Commander, incorporated an attack by U.S. troops on the western face of the Aisne-Marne salient in his counterattack plans, as it was considered the most vulnerable part of the German lines. Shortly before the German attack was scheduled to begin, the Allies reduced the manning of their front lines to weak detachments with orders for them to retire under heavy bombardment. This tactic proved exceptionally successful as the Germans wasted much of their preparatory fire on newly abandoned positions.

To capitalize further on knowing the exact hour that the Germans were to attack, the Allies began bombarding the German assembly areas for the planned offensive 30 minutes before the preparatory fire by the Germans was scheduled to begin. This caused much confusion in the assault forces, and they took many casualties. Two days later, after sustaining heavy losses, the Germans halted their offensive without attaining the important results they had expected to achieve.

The following day, 18 July, the Allies launched their counterattack against the western face of the Aisne-Marne salient. Although the Germans resisted stubbornly, they quickly realized that their position was untenable and began a gradual withdrawal from the salient. Reduction of the Aisne-Marne salient be-

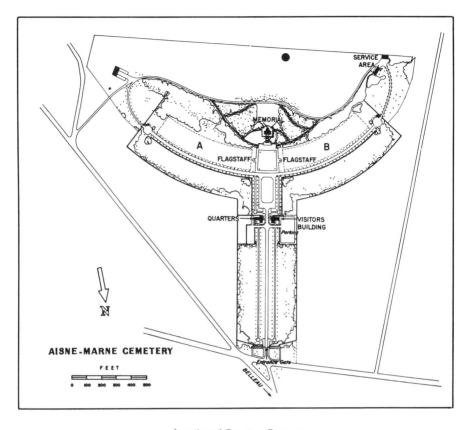

Location of Cemetery Features

came a fact on 4 August, when Allied troops reached the south bank of the Vesle. On 6 August, the counterattack was officially terminated. Not only had a serious threat to Paris been removed, but important railroads were freed once again for Allied use. Marshal Petain, who drew up the Allied plans for meeting the German offensive, said that the counterattack could not have succeeded without American troops.

During the fighting, the church in the village of Belleau was destroyed by American artillery fire. It was restored after the war by a veterans' association of the 26th Division. Located opposite the entrance of the Aisne-Marne American Cemetery, it is still known as the 26th Division Memorial Church of Belleau.

SITE

The Aisne-Marne Cemetery Memorial, 42.5 acres in extent, is situated at the foot of the hill on which stands Belleau Wood where many of those buried in the cemetery lost their lives. During World War I, it was one of the temporary wartime cemeteries established by the Army's Graves Registration Service, and was known as the American Expeditionary Forces' Cemetery No. 1764-Belleau Wood. A photograph of the temporary cemetery hangs in the superintendent's office in the Visitors' building. In 1921, Congress authorized retention of the cemetery as one of eight permanent World War I military cemeteries on foreign soil. The following year an agreement

Superintendent's Quarters and Visitors' Building on Entrance Road

was signed with the Government of France granting its use as a military cemetery in perpetuity free of charge or taxation. The permanent cemetery is named for the World War I campaign area in which it is located.

The memorial chapel, the Visitors' building, the superintendent's quarters, and the service area facilities were constructed by the American Battle Monuments Commission as part of its program of commemorating the achievements of U.S. Armed Forces in the Great War. The Commission also landscaped the grounds. In 1934, The President, by Executive Order, gave the Commission the added responsibility of operating and maintaining this and other permanent military cemeteries overseas.

ARCHITECTS

Cram and Ferguson of Boston, Massachusetts were the architects of the cemetery's memorial features.

GENERAL LAYOUT

The cemetery is laid out generally in the form of a "T." A long avenue leads from the entrance gate past the Visitors' building and parking area on the right (west) and the superintendent's quarters opposite on the left to the mall and the memorial chapel beyond. The chapel which crowns the "T" sits on high ground to the south. The cross bar of the "T" is formed by the cemetery's two grave plots, each projecting in a slightly convex arc from opposite sides of the mall. A flag pole, centered on each side of the mall, overlooks each grave plot.

MEMORIAL CHAPEL

The memorial chapel was erected over front line trenches dug by the 2nd Division as part of the defense of Belleau Wood, following capture of Belleau Wood by the division on 25 June 1918. Rising more than 80 feet

Memorial Chapel

above the hillside overlooking the cemetery, the chapel is a striking example of French Romanesque architecture. Its exterior walls, steps and terrace are of native St. Maximin, Savonnieres and Massangis limestone.

The decorative embellishments on the outside of the chapel were designed by William F. Ross and Company, East Cambridge, Massachusetts and were executed by Alfred Bottiau, Paris, France. The carvings on the captials of the three columns which flank each side of the chapel entrance depict scenes from the trenches of World War I. Carved on the columns on the right side are soldiers preparing for a bayonet charge, automatic riflemen and riflemen; carved on the columns on the left are artillery observers, a machine gun crew and soldiers launching grenades. In the tympanum over the entrance is carved the figure of a crusader in armor, defender of right, flanked by the shields of the United States and France intertwined with branches of oak to symbolize the traditional unity of the two countries. Around the top of the chapel on stone shields are carved the insignia of American corps and divisions which fought in the area and the U.S. coat of arms. On the north face are the insignia of I Corps, the U.S. coat of arms and III Corps; on the west face are the insignia of the 1st, 2d and 3d Divisions; on the south face those of the 4th, 26th and 28th Divisions; and on the east face those of the 32d, 42d and 77th Divisions. Decorative embellishments are also carved on the capitals of the belfry columns. The following eleven carvings appear: bayonets for the Infantry, cannon for the Artillery, tanks for the Tank Corps, crossed heavy machine guns for Machine Gun units, propellers for Aviation units, artillery rounds for both the Artillery and Ordnance, a plane-table for the Engineers, the Greek cross and caduceus for Medi-

cal units, airplane engines for Aviation repair units, a mule's head over which is engraved "8 Chev" for the French boxcar used to transport 40 men or 8 horses, and oak leaves for the Judge Advocate General Corps. Seven of these carvings appear on each side of the chapel. On the north face are a mule's head, bayonets, plane-table, crossed machine guns, Greek cross and caduceus, airplane engines and cannon; on the east face are artillery rounds, mule's head, bayonets, oak leaves, Greek cross and caduceus, cannon, propellers and tanks; on the south face are a plane-table, crossed machine guns, oak leaves, Greek cross and caduceus, cannon, propellers and tanks; on the west face are artillery rounds, bayonets, plane-table, airplane engines, cannon, propellers and tanks. The arches of the belfry openings are embellished with carvings of small arms ammunition, the front view of a machine gun and projectile, field packs with entrenching tools attached, and selected officer and enlisted insignia. Engraved on the sills are orientation arrows with distances to points of historic interest. Below the belfry openings are sculptured heads representing the men and women of the Allied armed forces in World War I as follows: a French soldier, a French nurse, an American aviator, a Scottish soldier, a Russian soldier, a Portuguese soldier, a Canadian aviator, and a British Women's Army Corps driver. The same figures appear on each side of the chapel but in different order.

To the right of the chapel entrance is a hole in the stonework made in 1940 by a German anti-tank gun which was firing at French tanks passing in the vicinity of the cemetery. Other minor damage to the stonework occurred but was repaired. This particular shell hole was left untouched as evidence of combat action in the region during World War II.

Inside of Chapel Entrance

CHAPEL INTERIOR

The Chapel is entered through a large double door of oak, ornamented with wrought iron which opens onto the vestibule. Above the inside of the entrance is inscribed: THE NAMES RECORDED ON THESE WALLS ARE THOSE OF AMERICAN SOLDIERS WHO FOUGHT IN THIS REGION AND WHO SLEEP IN UNKNOWN GRAVES.

To the right and left of the vestibule are small alcoves with benches where many of the names of the 1,060 Missing in the region whose remains were never recovered, or if recovered never identified, are engraved on the walls. The remainder of the names are engraved on the walls of the vestibule and the apse. Each alcove has one of the chapel's five beautiful stained-glass windows by Reynolds, Francis and Rohnstock

of Boston, Massachusetts. The window in the alcove on the left contains the coats of arms of some of the Allied nations of World War I: the United States, France, Great Britain, Italy, Belgium, Serbia and Romania. The window of the alcove on the right contains the coats of arms of the United States, the insignia of I and II Corps and the insignia of the 1st, 2d, 3d, 4th, 26th, 28th, 32d, 42d and 77th Divisions; these are the same insignia which are engraved on the stone shields around the top of the tower.

On entering the chapel, one's eyes are drawn to the apse with its exquisitely carved and gilded altar of Italian marble, the color of peach blossoms. At the top of the altar back are carved, respectively, an owl for wisdom, a crusader whose shield bears a lion device for fortitude, and scales

Interior of Chapel

Stained Glass Window over Altar

for justice. Below these figures the six virtues appear in two lines — WISDOM, FORTITUDE, JUSTICE and FAITH, HOPE, CHARITY. Lower on the altar back in five circles are carved respectively a Gallic rock, symbolic of France; a pommee cross on an apple blossom with a serpent representing the Garden of Eden; a fouled anchor and lily, symbolic of lasting peace; a poppy, representing valor; and a passion flower, symbolic of the Crucifixion and Resurrection. Across the face of the altar is inscribed: PEACEFUL THEY REST IN GLORY EVERLASTING.

Sprigs of olive and oak are carved on the altar front, symbolizing peace and life. Carved in the center of the altar front is a bird feeding her young, symbolic of Christ feeding his flock.

Inscribed on the wall to the left of the altar are the words: IN GRATEFUL REMEMBRANCE OF HER SONS WHO DIED IN THE WORLD WAR THIS CHAPEL IS ERECTED BY THE UNITED STATES OF AMERICA. A French translation of this text appears on the wall immediately to the right of the altar. The three remaining stained-glass windows are located above and to the left and right of the altar. The stained-glass window over the inscription on the wall to the left of the altar depicts St. Louis, one of the great Crusaders; the window over the altar depicts St. Michael triumphing over evil; and the window over the inscription on the wall to the right of the altar, St. Denis, patron saint of France.

GRAVES AREA

The graves area consists of two convex curved plots projecting from each side of the south end of the mall; Plot A is on the left (east) and Plot B is on the right (west). Each plot contains 13 rows of headstones and 1,144 graves. Stars of David mark the graves of those of the Jewish faith and latin crosses all others. Of the 2,288 burials in the cemetery, 249 are of Unknowns. Those interred in the cemetery came from all of the then forty-eight states and the District of Columbia.

Graves Area

Interior of Visitors' Room

VISITORS' BUILDING

On the right of the entrance avenue are the Visitors' building and parking area. Inside the building are the superintendent's office and a comfortably furnished room where visitors may rest and obtain information from the cemetery staff. The visitors' register is maintained there. Burial locations and sites of memorialization in each of the Commission's cemetery memorials, travel information, information on accommodations in the vicinity, local history and other information of interest are provided on request by the cemetery staff member on duty.

PLANTINGS

The long avenue leading from the entrance gate to the graves area is bordered by plane trees and polyantha and tree roses. Massifs of multicolored shrubs such as forsythia, laurel, boxwood, Japanese plum, deutzia, mock orange, Oregon grape and others screen the graves area from the north. Beds of polyantha and tree roses border the mall and extend to the chapel steps.

Visitors' Building and Office

View of Aisne-Marne Cemetery and Memorial Chapel

𝔅elleau 𝔚ood

Belleau Wood, 200 acres in extent, adjoins the Aisne-Marne American Cemetery behind the memorial chapel. It is maintained by the American Battle Monuments Commission as a memorial to the American fighting men who fought in the AEF during World War I. Vestiges of trenches, shell holes and relics of the war to include weapons found in the vicinity may be seen. A monument erected by the U.S. Marines and a flagpole are located on an island in the road passing through the clearing in the center of Belleau Wood. The monument is a black granite stele to which has been affixed a life-size bronze bas-relief by Felix de Weldon of a Marine attacking with rifle and bayonet. It commemorates

the 4th Marine Brigade of the U.S. 2d Division which was primarily responsible for capture of the Wood. Below the bas-relief at the base of the stele is a bronze plaque on which is engraved in English and French: BOIS DE BELLEAU OFFICIALLY RENAMED BOIS DE LA BRIGADE DE MARINE BY THE COMMANDING GENERAL FRENCH SIXTH ARMY ON 30 JUNE 1918 IN RECOGNITION OF THE COURAGEOUS ACTION OF THE 4TH UNITED STATES MARINE BRIGADE IN THE SEIZURE OF THIS WOOD IN THE FACE OF DETERMINED GERMAN RESISTANCE. ON 27 MAY 1918, THE GERMANS LAUNCHED A MAJOR SURPRISE OFFENSIVE WHICH CROSSED THE CHEMIN DES DAMES AND CAPTURED SOISSONS. BY 31 MAY, THEIR ARMIES WERE ADVANCING RAPIDLY DOWN THE MARNE VALLEY TOWARD PARIS. THE 2D UNITED STATES ARMY DIVI-

WW I Ruin in Belleau Wood

SION, OF WHICH THE 4TH MARINE BRIGADE FORMED A PART, WAS RUSHED INTO THE DEEPEST POINT OF THE PENETRATION TO ASSIST THE FRENCH FORCES IN STOPPING THE ADVANCE OF THE ENEMY. RAPIDLY OCCUPYING DEFENSIVE POSITIONS SOUTH AND WEST OF BELLEAU WOOD, THE 4TH MARINE BRIGADE, COMPOSED OF THE 5TH AND 6TH MARINE REGIMENTS AND THE 6TH MACHINE GUN BATTALION, STOOD FIRM UNDER UNREMITTING ENEMY ATTACKS FROM 1 TO 5 JUNE. ON 6 JUNE, THE MARINES BEGAN A SERIES OF ATTACKS WHICH CULMINATED ON 25 JUNE WITH THE CAPTURE OF THE ENTIRE BELLEAU WOOD AREA, AND THE DEFEAT OF THE GERMAN OFFENSIVE IN THIS SECTOR. MAY THE GALLANT MARINES WHO GAVE THEIR LIVES FOR CORPS AND COUNTRY REST IN PEACE.

Marine Monument at Belleau Wood

East Face

Chateau-Thierry Monument

The Chateau-Thierry Monument is situated on Hill 204, 2 miles/3 kilometers west of the town for which it is named. It is 54 miles/87 kilometers east of Paris and 4.5 miles/7 kilometers southeast of the Aisne-Marne Cemetery and Memorial. Two stone pylons inscribed AMERICAN AISNE-MARNE MEMORIAL mark the entrance to the monument from the Paris/Chateau-Thierry highway (N-3). The site, 25 acres in extent, commands a wide view of the Marne River valley.

Designed by Paul P. Cret of Philadelphia, the Chateau-Thierry Monument was constructed by the American Battle Monuments Commission to commemorate the sacrifices and achievements of American and French fighting men in the region, and the friendship and cooperation of French and American forces during World War I.

The monument is a large and impressive double colonnade set on a well landscaped terrace. It is ornamented on its west face by heroic size figures representative of France and the United States and the longstanding unity and friendship between the two nations. The figures were designed and executed by Alfred Bottiau of Paris, France. At either side of the figures on the base of the monument is engraved the dedicatory inscription: THIS MONUMENT HAS BEEN ERECTED BY THE UNITED STATES OF AMERICA TO COMMEMORATE THE SERVICES OF HER TROOPS AND THOSE OF FRANCE WHO FOUGHT IN THIS REGION DURING THE WORLD WAR. IT STANDS AS A LASTING SYMBOL OF THE FRIENDSHIP AND COOPERATION BETWEEN THE FRENCH AND AMERI-

Figures Depicting Unity of U. S. and France

CAN ARMIES. The text appears in English to the left (north) of the figures and in French to the right.

The east face of the monument is ornamented with an eagle and shield also of heroic proportions. Inscribed on the base of the sculpture are the words: TIME WILL NOT DIM THE GLORY OF THEIR DEEDS. Below the inscription is a large ornamental map of the region designed by Paul P. Cret showing the ground gained by U.S. Forces on 18 July 1918 and thereafter. In front of the map is an orientation table giving distances and directions to points of historical interest. From there and elsewhere on the terrace, an excellent view of the Marne River valley may be had. Along the base of the monument on either side of the map are carved the numerical designations and insignia of the U. S. corps and divisions commemorated there. These are from left (north) to right: the 1st, 2d and 3d Divisions, I and III Corps, and the 28th, 32d, 42d, 77th and 83d Divisions.

Inscribed above the columns on all fours sides of the monument are the names of places in the region where important battles were fought by American troops: GRIMPETTES WOOD VAUX FISMES MISSY-AUX-BOIS BELLEAU WOOD JUVIGNY MEZY NOROY-SUR-OURCQ — SERGY SERINGES-ET-NESLES VIERZY LE CHARMEL BAZOCHES FISMETTE BERZY-LE-SEC TRUGNY LA CROIX ROUGE FARM TORCY.

A brief resume of American fighting in the general vicinity is engraved on the north and south interior walls at the center of the colonnade: IN LATE MAY 1918 THE GERMAN ARMY MADE A SURPRISE ATTACK ALONG THE AISNE RIVER AND ADVANCED RAPIDLY TOWARD THE MARNE. ALLIED REINFORCEMENTS WERE HURRIEDLY BROUGHT UP, INCLUDING THE 2D AND 3D AMERICAN DIVISIONS WHICH WENT INTO POSITION DIRECTLY ACROSS THE GERMAN LINE OF ADVANCE TOWARD PARIS. AFTER SEVERE FIGHTING THESE DIVISIONS DEFINITELY STOPPED THE PROGRESS OF THE ATTACK ON THEIR FRONT AND THE LINES STABILIZED, THE GERMAN FORCES HAVING DRIVEN A DEEP SALIENT ROUGHLY DEFINED BY REIMS, CHATEAU-THIERRY AND SOISSONS INTO ALLIED TERRITORY.

THE LAST GERMAN OFFENSIVE OF THE WAR, ON 15 JULY, INCLUDED AN ATTACK IN THE EASTERN PART OF THIS SALIENT AND THERE THE 3D AMERICAN DIVISION AND ELEMENTS OF THE 28TH WERE IMPORTANT FACTORS IN THE SUCCESSFUL DEFENSE OF THE ALLIED POSITIONS.

ON JULY 18 THE ALLIED TROOPS BEGAN A GENERAL COUNTEROFFENSIVE AGAINST THE WHOLE SALIENT IN WHICH THE 1ST, 2D, 3D, 4TH, 26TH, 28TH, 32D AND 42D AMERICAN DIVISIONS, MOST OF WHICH SERVED UNDER THE I AND III CORPS, TOOK A BRILLIANT PART. THIS OFFENSIVE WAS A COMPLETE SUCCESS AND BY AUGUST 6 THE ENEMY HAD BEEN DRIVEN BEYOND THE VESLE RIVER. LATER THE 4TH, 28TH, 32D AND 77TH AMERICAN DIVISIONS AND ELEMENTS OF THE 3D AND 93D PLAYED A PROMINENT ROLE IN THE DESPERATE FIGHTING ON THE NORTH OF THE VESLE.

OF THE 310,000 AMERICAN SOLDIERS WHO FOUGHT IN THESE OPERATIONS, 67,000 WERE CASUALTIES. The resume is in French on the north interior wall and in English on the south interior wall.

Chateau-Thierry Monument

Bellicourt
Monument

Bellicourt Monument is 9 miles north of St. Quentin (Aisne), France, on the highway to Cambrai and 1 mile north of the village of Bellicourt; it is 97 miles northeast of Paris and 3 miles from the Somme American Cemetery. Erected above a canal tunnel built by Napoleon I, it commemorates the achievements and sacrifices of the 90,000 American troops who served in battle with the British Armies in France during 1917 and 1918.

The tunnel was one of the main defense features of the Hindenburg Line which was broken by American troops in a brilliant offensive in September 1918. Engraved on the rear facade of the memorial is a map illustrating the American operations; on the terrace is an orientation table.

Naval
Monument
at
Brest

Naval Monument at Brest, France stands on the ramparts of the city overlooking the harbor which was a major base of operations for American naval vessels during World War I. The original monument, built on this site to commemorate the achievements of the United States Navy during World War I, was destroyed by the enemy on July 4, 1941, prior to our entry into World War II. The present structure is a replica of the original and was completed in 1958.

The monument is a rectangular rose-granite shaft, rising 145 feet above the lower terrace and 100 feet above the Cours d'Ajot. All four sides are ornamented by sculpture of nautical interest. The surrounding area has been developed by the Commission into an attractive park.

Cantigny
Monument

Cantigny Monument is in the village of Cantigny (Somme), France, 4 miles northwest of Montdidier on route D-26 from Montdidier to Ailly-sur-Noye. From Paris, it is 66 miles north via Chantilly or Senlis.

This battlefield monument, commemorating the first offensive operation in May 1918 by a large American unit in World War I, stands in the center of the village which was captured in that attack and which was completely destroyed by artillery fire. It consists of a white stone shaft, on a platform, surrounded by an attractive park maintained by the Commission. The quiet surroundings now give no hint of the bitter hand-to-hand fighting that took place near the site of the monument.

𝕸𝖊𝖚𝖘𝖊-𝕬𝖗𝖌𝖔𝖓𝖓𝖊 𝕬𝖒𝖊𝖗𝖎𝖈𝖆𝖓 𝕮𝖊𝖒𝖊𝖙𝖊𝖗𝖞 𝖆𝖓𝖉 𝕸𝖊𝖒𝖔𝖗𝖎𝖆𝖑

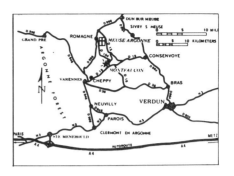

LOCATION

The Meuse-Argonne American Cemetery is the largest American military cemetery in Europe. It is located just east of the village of Romagne-Gesnes, Meuse, France, approximately 26 miles (42 kilometers) northwest of Verdun.

Verdun can be reached by train from the Gare de l'Est in Paris in approximately 3½ hours. Taxicab service is available at the station to complete the trip to the cemetery.

Romagne-Gesnes can be reached by automobile from Paris (152 miles/245 km) via Autoroute A-4 or highway N-3 to Ste-Menehould, continuing on N-3 to Clermont-en-Argonne which is 19 miles (31 km) south of the cemetery, and continuing via Varennes.

Hotel accommodations are available in Verdun and Dun-sur-Meuse.

The cemetery and the American monument at Montfaucon, Meuse, France, about seven miles (11 km) south of the cemetery, are included in most battlefield tours commencing in Verdun.

Cemetery Entrance

Chapel Interior

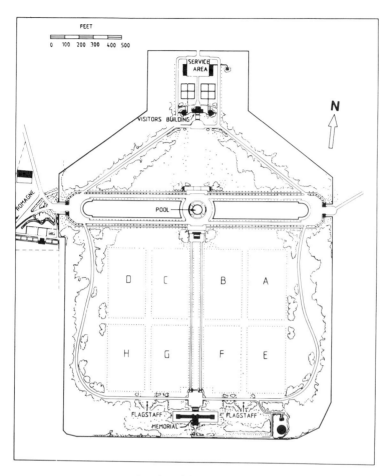

Location of Cemetery Features

Thirty-eight miles (61 km) to the west of the Meuse-Argonne American Cemetery is the Sommepy Monument located on Blanc Mont; this monument commemorates the actions of American and French troops in the Champagne region preceding and during the period of the Meuse-Argonne offensive.

HOURS

The cemetery is open to the public daily as shown below:

SUMMER (16 March–30 September)
   9:00 a.m.–6:00 p.m. — weekdays
10:00 a.m.–6:00 p.m. — Saturdays,
                        Sundays and holidays

WINTER (1 October–15 March)
   9:00 a.m.–5:00 p.m. — weekdays
10:00 a.m.–5:00 p.m. — Saturdays,
                        Sundays and holidays

When the cemetery is open to the public, a staff member is on duty in the Visitors' Building to answer questions and escort relatives to grave and memorial sites (except between noon and 3:00 p.m. on weekends and holidays).

HISTORY

The Meuse-Argonne Offensive was the climax toward which the efforts of American Expeditionary Forces were directed since arrival of

U.S. troops in France. It would be the largest battle ever fought by U.S. troops up to that time in U.S. history.

In 1918, the last year of the war, the armies of Germany launched a series of powerful attacks on the Western Front in an attempt to win a decisive victory before large numbers of American troops could be brought into action. The enemy assaults initially were highly successful and taxed Allied resources to the limit. Nevertheless, when the last great German offensive began on 15 July, Allied troops in heavy fighting quickly repulsed it. Three days later on 18 July, a U.S.–French counteroffensive was launched at Soissons. It was completely successful and marked the turning point of the war.

Determined to keep the Germans on the defensive and to maintain the initiative in battle, a series of strong offensive operations were planned by the Allies. The U.S. First Army was organized and given the mission of attacking in the St. Mihiel sector. The purpose of the St. Mihiel Offensive was to keep the enemy off balance, allowing him no opportunity to reorganize. Its plan required an assault on 12 September to reduce the German salient at St. Mihiel, followed two weeks later by a great offensive in a different area 40 miles away. Never before on the Western Front had a single army attempted such a colossal task. Four days after the St. Mihiel Offensive began, the German salient was eliminated.

The area between the Meuse River and the Argonne Forest was chosen for the U.S. First Army's greatest offensive of the war because it was the portion of the German front which the enemy could least afford to lose. The lateral communications between German forces east and west of the Meuse were in that area and they were heavily dependent upon two rail lines that converged in the vicinity of Sedan and lay within 35 miles of the battle line.

The nature of the Meuse–Argonne terrain made it ideal for defense. On the left, the heavily wooded and tangled Argonne Forest and the Aire River presented natural obstacles. On the right, the Meuse River and the Heights of the Meuse to the east formed not only natural barriers but also gave the enemy commanding ground from which it could observe the battlefield and cover it with artillery fire.

In between the Aire and the Meuse Rivers were a series of broken, wooded ridges that provided excellent observation. The first was the dominating hill of Montfaucon. Behind it were the Heights of Romagne and Cunel; beyond them was Barricourt Heights. To protect this vitally important area, the enemy had established almost continuous defensive positions for a depth of 10 to 12 miles to the rear of the front lines.

The movement of American troops and materiel into position for the Meuse–Argonne attack was made entirely under the cover of darkness. On most of the front, French soldiers remained in the outpost positions until the very last moment in order to keep the enemy from learning of the large American concentration. Altogether, about 220,000 Allied soldiers were withdrawn from the area and 600,000 American soldiers brought into position without the knowledge of the enemy, a striking tribute to the skill and abilities of the U.S. First Army.

Following a three-hour bombardment with 2,700 field pieces, the U.S. First Army jumped off on 26 September at 5:30 a.m. On the left, I Corps penetrated the Argonne Forest and advanced along the valley of the Aire River. In the center, V Corps advanced to the west of Montfaucon but was held up temporarily in front of the hill. On the

Aerial View of Cemetery

right, III Corps drove forward to the east of Montfaucon and a mile beyond. About noon the following day, Montfaucon was captured as the advance continued. Although complete surprise had been achieved, the enemy soon was contesting every foot of terrain stubbornly. Profiting from the temporary holdup in front of Montfaucon, the Germans poured reinforcements into the area. Even so, by 30 September, the U.S. First Army had driven the enemy back as far as six miles in some places.

The assault of the U.S. First Army was renewed on 4 October. Enemy forces continued to resist stubbornly, as additional German divisions arrived from other battle fronts. Though the U.S. First Army was subjected to furious counterattacks, its advance proceeded relentlessly. On 7 October, a strong flanking attack by I Corps on the left in the Aire Valley made capture of the Argonne Forest possible. The next day on the right, U.S. troops crossed the Meuse River, where severe fighting was encountered for possession of the heights beyond. On 9 October, V Corps began an attack in the center aided by III Corps on its right; both Corps then penetrated the Hindenburg Line.

It seemed on 14 October that the Allied assault would develop into another prolonged struggle, as the enemy continued to resist stubbornly. The III and V Corps, however, provided relief when they broke through the German main line of defense and seized the Heights of Cunel and Romagne. On the left, I Corps captured St. Juvin and Grand-Pre, enabling the French Fourth Army, which was positioned to the left of the U.S. First Army, to advance its attack.

The final chapter of the great offensive by the U.S. First Army began at daybreak on 1 November after a two-hour concentrated artillery preparation. Its progress exceeded all expectations. By early afternoon, the formidable position on Barricourt Heights had been captured, ensuring success of the whole operation. That night the enemy issued orders to withdraw west of the Meuse. By 4 November, after an additional crossing of the Meuse by the U.S. First Army, the enemy was in full retreat on both sides of the river. Three days later, when the heights overlooking the city of Sedan were taken, the U.S. First Army gained domination over the German railroad communications there, ensuring early termination of the war.

Meanwhile in mid-October, the U.S. Second Army was formed to take command of the St. Mihiel sector on the right of the U.S. First Army. In response to a directive that offensives be initiated and sustained all along the entire Allied front, the U.S. First and Second Armies both launched attacks on 10 November and made substantial gains. So perilous was the enemy position that it was compelled to seek an immediate armistice, which became effective on 11 November 1918.

To echo some of the words of General Pershing inscribed on the Montfaucon Monument: The Meuse–Argonne offensive (in which over 1,000,000 American soldiers fought) was suddenly conceived, hurried in plan and preparation, complicated by close association with a preceding major operation yet brilliantly executed and prosecuted with an unselfish and heroic spirit of courage and fortitude that demanded eventual victory. It stands out as one of the very great achievements in the history of American arms.

THE SITE

The cemetery, 130½ acres in extent, was established 14 October 1918 by the American Graves Regis-

Overall View of the Cemetery

tration Service on terrain captured by the 32d Infantry Division. The use of the land on which it rests has been granted by the French government free of charge or taxation in perpetuity, as an expression of its gratitude to the United States. In 1934, administration of the cemetery passed to the American Battle Monuments Commission.

The Commission landscaped the cemetery grounds and erected the memorial chapel and other structures.

ARCHITECTS

The architects for the cemetery and memorial were York and Sawyer of New York.

GENERAL LAYOUT

The cemetery is generally rectangular in shape with three-quarters of its area devoted to the grave plots and memorial chapel.

The memorial chapel is located on the high ground to the south. A grassy east–west entrance mall 600 yards long runs through the small valley across which the cemetery is located separating the graves and memorial area from the Visitors' Building and service area. There is an impressive entrance portal to the cemetery at each end of the east–west mall and a circular pool with a fountain at the center. This attractive pool with its goldfish and flowering lilies is a constant source of interest to visitors. A road bordered by a double avenue of beech trees runs from each portal and encircles the mall. A perimeter road encircles the graves area and the service area. Four rectangular grave plots are located on each side of the mall leading from the pool to the memorial chapel. The grave plots are framed by square-trimmed linden trees. These trees are especially beautiful

in the fall when their leaves are changing color. Over 65 varieties of evergreen shrubs and trees plus many varieties of flowers complete the tranquil beauty of this cemetery. A stone wall more than 1½ miles long encircles the cemetery in its entirety.

THE MEMORIAL

The memorial, a fine example of Romanesque architecture, faces north on the crest of a gently sloping hillside overlooking the graves area. It consists of a memorial chapel and two flanking loggias, on whose walls are engraved the names of those servicemen and women missing in the area and also those missing in northern Russia. The memorial's exterior walls and columns are of Euville Coquiller stone; its interior walls are of Salamandre travertine.

High above the main entrance to the chapel, on the exterior wall, is carved the following:

DEDICATED TO THE MEMORY OF THOSE WHO DIED FOR THEIR COUNTRY.

On the lintel directly over the chapel entrance is inscribed: IN SACRED SLEEP THEY REST. A sculpture bas-relief by L. Bottiau, Paris, France, with figures representing Grief and Remembrance appears above it in the tympanum. The beautiful bronze filigreed screen of the imposing entrance doors was cast by Henry Hope and Sons, Birmingham, England. Alongside the door, carved heads of American soldiers are included in the design of the column capitals. Across the ends and front of the loggias above the arches are names of places famous in the history of the American fighting in the region:

PONT-MAUGIS — BOIS-DE-CUNEL — MEUSE — CIERGES — BOIS-DES-RAPPES — CONSENVOYE — EXERMONT — GRAND-PRE — MEUSE HEIGHTS —

Memorial Chapel

Stained Glass Window in Chapel

BARRICOURT-HEIGHTS — GESNES — MONTFAUCON — CORNAY — BOIS-DE-FORET — STENAY — ARGONNE — CHEPPY — COTE-DE-CHATILLON.

Inside the chapel on the wall above the right entry-way is the inscription:

THIS CHAPEL IS ERECTED BY THE UNITED STATES OF AMERICA AS A SACRED RENDEZVOUS OF A GRATEFUL PEOPLE WITH ITS IMMORTAL DEAD.

The same text appears in French on the wall above the left entrance.

On entering the chapel, one's attention is immediately drawn to the apse, in the center of which is the altar backed by a semi-circle of flags of the United States and the principal Allied nations.

The insignia of many of the American divisions and larger units which served in the AEF are reproduced in its stained glass windows which were executed by Heinigke & Smith, New York, N.Y. Shown in the window of the west wall are:

I CORPS, GENERAL HEADQUARTERS, III CORPS, 1ST DIVISION, ADVANCE SECTION S.O.S., 30TH DIVISION, 3D DIVISION, 7TH DIVISION, 35TH DIVISION, 5TH DIVISION, 26TH DIVISION, 32D DIVISION, 4TH DIVISION, 28TH DIVISION, 36TH DIVISION, 6TH DIVISION, 29TH DIVISION, 37TH DIVISION, 2D DIVISION, 27TH DIVISION AND 33D DIVISION.

The window of the east wall includes:

IV CORPS, FIRST ARMY, V CORPS, 41ST DIVISION, 80TH DIVISION, 88TH DIVISION, 77TH DIVISION, 84TH DIVISION, 91ST DIVISION, 78TH DIVISION, 83D DIVISION, 90TH DIVISION, 89TH DIVISION, 85TH DIVISION, 92D DIVISION, 42D DIVISION, 81ST DIVISION, 76TH DIVISION, 79TH DIVISION, 82D DIVISION AND 93D DIVISION.

Through these windows a soft and subdued light is diffused throughout the chapel's interior and blends

with the deep colors of the marble floor.

On the arches over the door, apse and windows are the following inscriptions:

GOD HATH TAKEN THEM UNTO HIMSELF

THEIR NAMES WILL LIVE FOR EVERMORE

PEACEFUL IS THEIR SLEEP IN GOD

PERPETUAL LIGHT UPON THEM SHINES.

The memorial loggias flank the chapel. Engraved on a panel of the west loggia is an ornamental map, showing in color the operations of American divisions during the Meuse-Argonne offensive. A similar map appears in the Montfaucon Monument.

The names of 954 of the Missing who gave their lives in the service of their country, but whose remains were never recovered or identified are engraved on the remaining panels of the two loggias. Above the

Wall of the Missing

names high on the center panel of each loggia is inscribed:

THE NAMES HERE RECORDED ARE THOSE OF AMERICAN SOLDIERS WHO FOUGHT IN THIS REGION AND WHOSE EARTHLY RESTING PLACE IS KNOWN ONLY TO GOD.

Included among them, but inscribed on a separate panel in the east loggia are the names of the Missing of the Services of Supply. At the top of the panel is the inscription:

THE NAMES RECORDED ON THIS PANEL ARE THOSE OF AMERICAN SOLDIERS WHO DIED IN THE SERVICES OF SUPPLY DURING THE WORLD WAR AND HAVE NO KNOWN GRAVES.

Similarly, in the west loggia a sep-arate panel carries the names of the Missing from the American expedition to Northern Russia under the inscription:

THE NAMES RECORDED ON THIS PANEL ARE THOSE OF AMERICAN SOLDIERS WHO LOST THEIR LIVES IN NORTHERN RUSSIA DURING THE WORLD WAR AND HAVE NO KNOWN GRAVES.

On the floors of the pavilions at the ends of the loggias are directional arrows pointing to prominent terrain features relating to the operations which took place in the area. Also, from the ends of the loggias one can see, in the distance to the southeast, the dominating hill of Montfaucon with its imposing monument.

Section of the Tablets of the Missing

Chapel Altar

GRAVES AREA

The graves area lies on the southern slope of the valley and is divided into eight rectangular plots lettered from A to H. Each plot is surrounded by square-trimmed linden trees. Plots A, B, E and F are located on the east side of the grassy mall extending from the chapel to the circular pool and fountain below and C, D, G and H are on the west. The carefully clipped grass of the mall and graves area gives the impression of a vast green velvet carpet.

14,246 War Dead are interred within the cemetery, 486 of whom are Unknowns. The cemetery contains no multiple burials. Each of the Dead has his own headstone of white marble, a Star of David for those of the Jewish faith and a Latin cross for all others. The immense array of headstones is arranged in long parallel rows beginning at the east–west mall and extends row on row to the chapel crowning the ridge overlooking the graves area.

VISITORS' BUILDING

The Visitors' Building is located to the north of the cemetery. Here visitors may obtain information, sign the register and pause to refresh themselves. During visiting hours a member of the cemetery staff is available in the building to answer questions and provide information on burials and memorializations in the Commission's cemeteries, accommodations in the vicinity, travel, local history and other items of interest.

View of Interior of East Loggia of Memorial Chapel

Exterior of Visitors' Building

Interior of Visitors' Building

Graves Area

Meuse–Argonne American Cemetery, Romagne, France

𝕸𝖔𝖓𝖙𝖋𝖆𝖚𝖈𝖔𝖓 𝕸𝖔𝖓𝖚𝖒𝖊𝖓𝖙

The imposing shaft of the Montfaucon Monument rises 200 feet above the ruins of the former hilltop village of Montfaucon and dominates the surrounding countryside. Before its capture by the American 37th and 79th Divisions on 27 September 1918, the site provided the German forces with excellent observation.

The monument commemorates the victory of the U.S. First Army in the Meuse-Argonne offensive, 26 September–11 November 1918, and pays tribute to the heroic services of the French Armies before that time on that battlefront.

Construction of the monument was completed in 1933; it was dedicated in 1937 by the President of the French Republic, Mr. Albert Lebrun.

Architect for the memorial was John Russell Pope of New York. The 180 foot massive shaft is of Baveno granite in the form of a Doric column and is surmounted by a figure symbolic of Liberty. It faces the First Army's line of departure of 26 September 1918. From the observation platform at the top, one can see most of the Meuse-Argonne battlefield.

The names of the four most important areas captured by American troops, MEUSE HEIGHTS, BARRICOURT HEIGHTS, ROMAGNE HEIGHTS AND ARGONNE FOREST appear in large letters across the front of the monument.

On the wall surrounding the main terrace are listed the divisions which made up the U.S. First Army along with the names of three places now recorded in American military history, where each of the divisions encountered hard fighting:

1ST DIVISION, EXERMONT, COTE DE MALDAH, VILLEMONTRY; 2ND DIVISION, LANDRES-ST. GEORGES, BEAUMONT, BOIS DES FLAVIERS; 3RD DIVISION, BOIS DE CUNEL, CLAIRS CHENES, BOIS DE FORET; 4TH DIVISION, SEPT SARGES, BOIS DE FAYS, BOIS DE FORET; 5TH DIVISION, CUNEL, DUN-SUR-MEUSE, FORET DE WOEVRE; 26TH DIVISION, LE HOUPPY BOIS, LA WAVRILLE, BOIS DE VILLE; 28TH DIVISION, ARGONNE, VARENNES, APREMONT; 29TH

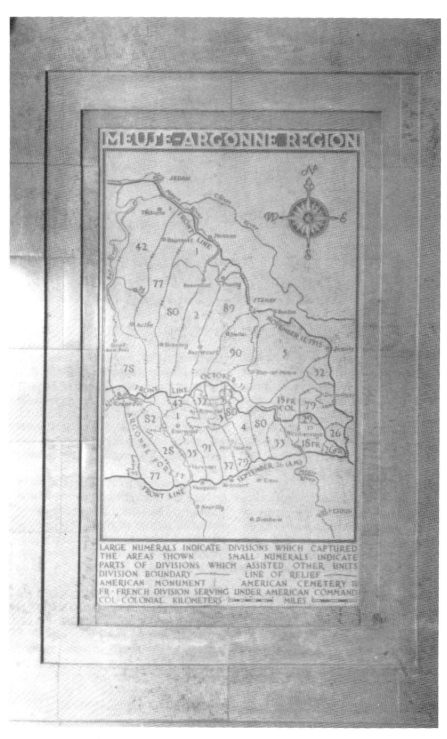

Map of the Meuse-Argonne Region on the Northeast Wall of the Vestibule

DIVISION, BOIS DE CONSENVOYE, MOLLEVILLE FARM, BOIS D'ETRAYE; 32ND DIVISION, COTE DAME MARIE, ROMAGNE, PEUVILLERS; 33RD DIVISION, BOIS DE FORGES, CONSENVOYE, BOIS PLAT-CHENE; 35TH DIVISION, VAUQUOIS, BAULNY, MONTREBEAU; 37TH DIVISION, BOIS DE MONTFAUCON, IVOIRY, BOIS BE BEUGE; 42ND DIVISION, COTE DE CHATILLON, BOIS DU MONT DIEU, SEDAN HEIGHTS; 77TH DIVISION, ARGONNE, ST. JUVIN, REMILLY-SUR-MEUSE; 78TH DIVISION, GRAND-PRE, BOIS DE LOGES, TANNAY; 79TH DIVISION, MONTFAUCON, NANTILLOIS, CHAUMONT; 80TH DIVISION, DANNE-VOUX, BOIS DES OGONS, BUZ ANCY; 81ST DIVISION, MANHEULLES, ABAUCOURT, GRIMAUCOURT; 82ND DIVISION, CORNAY, MARGO, ST. JUVIN; 89TH DIVISION, BOIS DE BARRICOURT, POUILLY, STENAY; 90TH DIVISION, BANTHEVILLE, HILL 343, STENAY; 91ST DIVISION, BOIS DE CHEPPY, EPINONVILLE, BOIS DE GESNES; AND THE 92ND DIVISION, BOIS DE LA GRURIE, VALLEE MOREAU, BINARVILLE. In addition, the five French units which fought with the First Army and the two American divisions which were in reserve are commemorated:

10E D.I.C. (FR) DAMLOUP, BOIS DE LA PLUME, NOBRAS; 15E D.I.C. (FR), SIVRY-SUR-MEUSE, HARAUMONT, DAMVILLERS; 18E D.I. (FR), HAUMONT, BOIS DES CHENES, BOIS D'ORMONT; 26E D.I. (FR), BOIS DE CAURES, ANGLEMONT FERME, BEAUMONT; IN RESERVE, 6TH DIVISION, 36TH DIVISION, 5E D.C. (FR).

On the paving of the main terrace in front of the entrance door, the following text is engraved in English and French:

ERECTED BY THE UNITED STATES OF AMERICA TO COMMEMORATE THE BRILLIANT VICTORY OF HER FIRST ARMY IN THE MEUSE-ARGONNE OFFENSIVE SEPTEMBER 26–NOVEMBER 11, 1918, AND TO HONOR THE HEROIC SERVICES OF THE ARMIES OF FRANCE ON THIS IMPORTANT BATTLEFRONT DURING THE WORLD WAR.

Inside the entranceway is a small vestibule decorated with the flags of the United States and France. On the northwest wall of the vestibule is a map of the Meuse-Argonne offensive, carved in polished marble and indicating in color the operations of the various divisions in the area. Inscribed on the southwest wall is a brief description in French and English of the American operations:

DURING SEPTEMBER 1918 THE ALLIED FORCES LAUNCHED A GENERAL OFFENSIVE AGAINST THE GERMAN ARMIES ON THE WESTERN FRONT. IN THIS OPERATION THE AMERICAN FIRST ARMY WAS ASSIGNED THE TASK OF BREAKING THROUGH THE EXTREMELY STRONG AND VITAL PORTION OF THE ENEMY DEFENSIVE SYSTEM LYING BETWEEN THE MEUSE RIVER AND THE ARGONNE FOREST.

THE AMERICAN ATTACK STARTED ON SEPTEMBER 26 AND AFTER TWO DAYS INTENSE FIGHTING MONTFAUCON UPON WHICH THIS MONUMENT STANDS WAS CAPTURED. BY SEPTEMBER 30 THE ENEMY HAD BEEN DRIVEN BACK SIX MILES. THE GERMAN TROOPS DEFENDED EACH POSITION TO THE UTMOST AND MANY DIVISIONS WERE RUSHED TO THEIR SUPPORT FROM OTHER BATTLEFRONTS.

THE BATTLE CONTINUED THROUGHOUT OCTOBER AGAINST DESPERATE RESISTANCE. A BRILLIANT ADVANCE DOWN THE AIRE VALLEY MADE IT POSSIBLE TO OUTFLANK AND CAPTURE THE ARGONNE FOREST. THE ATTACK THEN SPREAD EAST OF THE MEUSE WHERE SEVERE FIGHTING OCCURRED. THE PROLONGED STRUGGLES FOR THE STRONGLY FORTIFIED GERMAN MAIN LINE OF DEFENSE ON THE HEIGHTS NEAR BRIEULLES CUNEL AND ROMAGNE WERE UNSURPASSED IN FURY BUT BY OCTOBER 14 THIS LINE HAD BEEN BROKEN AND THE END OF THE MONTH FOUND IT AND THE VILLAGES OF ST. JUVIN AND GRAND-PRE

SECURELY IN THE GRASP OF THE AMERICAN ARMY.

ON NOVEMBER 1 THE ARMY LAUNCHED ITS LAST GREAT ATTACK. THE DOMINATING HEIGHTS NEAR BARRICOURT WERE CAPTURED AND THE ENEMY WAS DRIVEN BEYOND THE MEUSE RIVER. THESE SUCCESSES AND THOSE OF THE ALLIES ON OTHER BATTLEFIELDS COMPELLED THE GERMANS TO ASK FOR AN IMMEDIATE ARMISTICE WHICH BECAME EFFECTIVE ON NOVEMBER 11 1918.

DURING FORTY-SEVEN DAYS OF CONTINUAL BATTLE ON THIS FRONT THE FIRST ARMY ADVANCED 35 MILES CAPTURED 26,000 MEN 874 CANNON AND 3,000 MACHINE GUNS. AT ITS MAXIMUM STRENGTH THE ARMY COMPRISED MORE THAN 1,000,000 SOLDIERS. THE AMERICAN BATTLE CASUALTIES WERE 122,000.

A tribute by General Pershing, Commander-in-Chief of the American Expeditionary Forces, to his officers and men who served here appears on the southeast wall. The text of General Pershing's tribute reads:

THE MEUSE-ARGONNE BATTLE PRESENTED NUMEROUS DIFFICULTIES SEEMINGLY INSURMOUNTABLE. THE SUCCESS STANDS OUT AS ONE OF THE GREAT ACHIEVEMENTS IN THE HISTORY OF AMERICAN ARMS. SUDDENLY CONCEIVED AND HURRIED IN PLAN AND PREPARATION; COMPLICATED BY CLOSE ASSOCIATION WITH A PRECEDING MAJOR OPERATION; DIRECTED AGAINST STUBBORN DEFENSE OF THE VITAL POINT OF THE WESTERN FRONT; AND ATTENDED BY COLD AND INCLEMENT WEATHER; THIS BATTLE WAS PROSECUTED WITH AN UNSELFISH AND HEROIC SPIRIT OF COURAGE AND FORTITUDE WHICH DEMANDED EVENTUAL VICTORY. PHYSICALLY STRONG, VIRILE, AND AGGRESSIVE, THE MORALE OF THE AMERICAN SOLDIER DURING THIS MOST TRYING PERIOD WAS SUPERB. IN THEIR DEVOTION, THEIR VALOR, AND IN THE LOYAL FULFILLMENT OF THEIR OBLIGATIONS, THE OFFICERS AND MEN OF THE AMERICAN EXPEDITIONARY FORCES HAVE LEFT A HERITAGE OF WHICH THOSE WHO FOLLOW MAY EVER BE PROUD.

— John J. Pershing, General, Commander-in-Chief, American Expeditionary Forces.

A circular stairway of 234 steps leads from the base of the shaft to observation platforms from which large portions of the Meuse-Argonne battlefield may be seen. Eleven of the thirteen landings on the stairs are provided with benches where visitors may pause to rest.

Use of the monument site was given to the United States by the French Government in perpetuity, free of charge or taxation.

The area surrounding the monument is administered by the French Fine Arts Commission and is also of historical significance. The ruins upon which the monument is erected are believed to date back to the 6th century. Numerous battles have been fought in the vicinity. In one battle against the Normans about 888 A.D., 19,000 Dead are said to have been left on the battlefield. During the Hundred Years' War, the district was frequently ravaged by robbers; and during the 16th and 17th centuries, the town was twice destroyed. While making excavations for the foundations of the monument, an underground passage hollowed out of the soft rock was found running from the ruins behind the monument to the foot of the hill. To the left of the monument shaft, as seen from the parking plaza and about 12 feet underground, a cemetery was found which probably dates from the Middle Ages. Under the front of the wall on the right side of the terrace, three old cellars were found, one below the other, the lowest one showing evidence of having been used as a dungeon.

Sommepy Monument

The Sommepy Monument stands on the crest of Blanc Mont ridge, three miles (5 km) north of Sommepy in the Department of Marne, 38 miles (61 km) from the Meuse-Argonne American Cemetery. The site on which the monument stands was captured on 3 October 1918 after heavy fighting by the American 2d Division.

The nearest cities are Reims — 22 miles (35 km) to the west and Chalons-sur-Marne — 23 miles (37 km) to the south.

The monument commemorates the achievements of the 70,000 American soldiers who fought in the Champagne region of France during the summer and fall of 1918 and those of the French soldiers who fought with them.

The monument is in the form of a tower, its sturdy though graceful shape harmonizing with the surrounding landscape. The golden brown stones of different shades on its exterior give it a very attractive appearance.

Architect for the monument was Mr. Arthur Loomis Harmon of New York.

Carved on the exterior walls are the dedicatory inscription and the insignia and names of the American Divisions which the monument commemorates with the inclusive dates that they served in this region and the names of four locations where each of the divisions participated in difficult fighting:

93D DIVISION, SEPTEMBER 26–OCTOBER 6, 1918, RIPONT, SECHAULT, ARDEUIL, TRIERES FARM; 36TH DIVISION, OCTOBER 8–OCTOBER 27, 1918, MACHAULT, DRICOURT, ST. ETIENNE-A-ARNES, FOREST FARM; 2D DIVISION, OCTOBER 2–OCTOBER 9, 1918, BLANC MONT, MEDEAH FARM, ST. ETIENNE-A-ARNES, ESSEN TRENCH; 42D DIVISION, JULY 15–JULY 17, 1918, AUBERIVE-SUR-SUIPPES, ST. HILAIRE-LE-GRAND, SOUAIN, SPANDAU WOOD.

The dedicatory inscription is carved in both English and French below the eagle on the front face of the monument:

ERECTED BY THE UNITED STATES OF AMERICA TO COMMEMORATE THE ACHIEVEMENTS OF HER SOLDIERS AND THOSE OF FRANCE WHO FOUGHT IN THIS REGION DURING THE WORLD WAR.

Inside the tower, on a stone panel visible through the bronze grille of the door, is a brief description of the American operations in this vicinity:

IN EARLY JULY 1918 THE 42D AMERICAN DIVISION ENTERED THE BATTLE LINES WITH THE 13TH AND 170TH FRENCH DIVISIONS NEAR SOUAIN. THERE IT GALLANTLY ASSISTED IN REPELLING THE LAST GERMAN MAJOR OFFENSIVE OF THE WAR.

WHEN THE ALLIES BEGAN THEIR GREAT CONVERGENT OFFENSIVE IN LATE SEPTEMBER, THE 2D AND 36TH AMERICAN DIVISIONS WERE ASSIGNED TO THE FRENCH FOURTH ARMY. ON OCTOBER 3 THE 2D DIVISION, SUPPORTED ON THE LEFT BY THE 21ST FRENCH DIVISION AND ON THE RIGHT BY THE 167TH, IN A BRILLIANT OPERATION CAPTURED BLANC MONT RIDGE ON WHICH THIS MONUMENT STANDS. THE 36TH DIVISION RELIEVED THE 2D ON OCTOBER 10 AND CONTINUED THE ADVANCE NORTHWARD AS FAR AS THE AISNE RIVER.

THREE INFANTRY REGIMENTS OF THE 93D AMERICAN DIVISION, SERVING WITH THE 157TH AND 161ST FRENCH DIVISIONS, ENGAGED IN INTERMITTENT FIGHTING DURING SEPTEMBER AND OCTOBER TAKING PART IN THE CAPTURE OF RIPONT, SECHAULT AND TRIERES FARM.

A flight of steps leads to an observation platform at the top of the structure where a fine view of the surrounding countryside is available and where directional arrows point out prominent terrain features. The tower is open every Saturday, Sunday, Wednesday through Friday, it is closed on French holidays.

℮ise-Aisne American Cemetery and Memorial

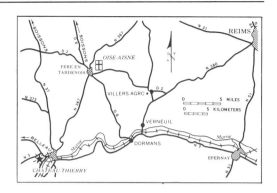

LOCATION

The Oise-Aisne American Cemetery and Memorial is located 1.5 miles (2.5 kilometers) east of Fere-en-Tardenois, along highway D-2, near the hamlet of Seringes-et-Nesles. It is approximately 70 miles (113 kilometers) northeast of Paris and can be reached by train from the Gare de l'Est in Paris via Chateau-Thierry and Fere-en-Tardenois in about two hours. Taxi service to the cemetery is available from each of these stations.

To travel by automobile to the Oise-Aisne American Cemetery from Paris, one should proceed east on Highway N-3 through Meaux and Forte-sous-Jouarre to Chateau-Thierry (54.5 miles/88 kilometers), turn left at Chateau-Thierry on Highway N-367, continue to Fere-en-Tardenois (14 miles/22.5 kilometers), and turn right on D-2 to the cemetery (1.5 miles/2.5 kilometers). Directional road signs to the cemetery may be found on the main highways in Chateau-Thierry, Soissons, Reims and Epernay. Road distances to Fere-en-Tardenois from nearby cities are: Soissons—16 miles/26 kilometers, Reims—28.5 miles/46 kilometers, Laon —33 miles/53 kilometers, and Senlis— 44.5 miles/72 kilometers.

Adequate hotel accommodations and restaurant facilities are available in Chateau-Thierry, Epernay, Fere-en-Tardenois, Reims, Senlis and Soissons.

Entrance to Graves Area

Chapel Interior

HOURS

The cemetery is open daily to the public during the following hours:
SUMMER (16 March - 30 September)
8 a.m. to 6 p.m.
WINTER (1 October - 15 March)
8 a.m. to 5 p.m.

During these hours, a staff member is on duty at the visitors' room to answer questions and to escort relatives to gravesites or the Tablets of the Missing.

HISTORY

Germany's strategic plan for 1918 entailed the destruction of the British Army in the spring followed by massive attacks against the French. During March and April, the Germans launched offensives against the British in Picardy and Flanders. The situation for the British was critical until several French divisions were dispatched to their aid. Although destruction of British forces was averted, heavy casualties were inflicted upon them and they lost considerable ground.

While these attacks were taking place, other German forces were preparing for a major offensive along the Aisne River. Unaware of this and anticipating that the assaults against the British Army in Picardy and Flanders would resume at any time, the French High Command shifted some of its forces from the Aisne River to reinforce the British sector.

On the morning of May 27, 1918, the Germans attacked in strength between Berry-au-Bac and Anizy-le-Chateau, surprising the French completely. By noon, German forces had crossed the Aisne River on captured bridges and by that evening were south of the Vesle River. Having met little resistance in their rapid advance toward the Marne River, the Germans decided to exploit their success by driving toward Paris.

Meanwhile, Allied reserves were rushed to the Aisne-Marne front from every quarter and the French government prepared to flee Paris for Bordeaux in the south. On May 31, four

days after the attack began, the U.S. 3d Division reached Chateau-Thierry where it fought stubbornly and successfully to prevent the Germans from crossing the Marne. The next day, the U.S. 2d Division arrived and deployed across the main route to Paris northwest of Chateau-Thierry, where it was able to halt the German offensive in that direction. With the aid of American divisions, the Allies were able to stop the Germans but not before a great salient had been driven into Allied lines roughly defined by the cities of Reims, Chateau-Thierry and Soissons. Despite the penetration of German forces west and southwest of Reims, the city itself and its vital rail facilities remained in Allied hands. This left the 40 German divisions in the salient dependent upon one railroad link through Soissons for resupply. To widen the salient and secure the railroad line between Compiegne and Soissons, two German armies attacked westward from the salient on June 9. They encountered such intense resistance, however, that their attack quickly ground to a halt.

Without delay, the Germans began preparing for a major offensive against Reims and the high ground to its south to provide them with the additional railroad link they so sorely needed for their forces in the salient. Luckily, Allied intelligence agents learned not only the line of the new German attack, but the exact day and hour it was scheduled to take place.

By mid-July, twelve of the twenty-six American divisions in France were ready for combat. (These statistics did not reveal the strength of American forces completely as American divisions were larger and had twice the fire power of French, British and German divisions). Capitalizing on availability of fresh American troops, Marshal Foch, the Allied commander, included in his counterattack plans an assault against the western face of the Aisne-Marne salient by two American divisions.

On July 15, 1918, the day of the German offensive, Allied forces reduced the manning of their front line units to weak detachments and gave them orders to retire under heavy bombardment. This tactic proved quite successful as much of the German preparatory fire was wasted on newly abandoned positions. Capitalizing further on their knowledge of the exact hour of the German attack, the Allies began bombarding likely German assembly areas shortly before their preparatory fire was expected to commence. The German assault forces suffered heavy casualties and were thrown into a state of complete confusion, causing them to terminate their offensive without attaining any of their objectives.

The following day, on July 18, the Allies launched a counterattack against the western face of the Aisne-Marne salient. Although the Germans resisted stubbornly, they soon realized their position was untenable and began withdrawing. Reduction of the salient was complete on August 4, when Allied troops reached the south bank of the Vesle River. The counterattack was terminated officially on August 6, 1918. Not only had a serious threat to Paris been removed, but important railways were freed once again for Allied use. Marshal Petain, who drew up the plans for meeting the German offensive, said that the counterattack could not have succeeded without use of American troops.

Quickly, Allied offensive operations were initiated elsewhere to maintain pressure on the Germans, who were now on the defensive, to make it difficult for them to regroup and reorganize. On August 8, the British began their highly successful Somme offensive. Ten days later, French forces with the support of American troops, began the very successful Oise-Aisne campaign in the Aisne-Marne region near Noyon, during which the German forces on the Vesle and the Aisne Rivers were outflanked, forcing them to withdraw. Many U.S. servicemen whose remains are interred in the Oise-Aisne American Cemetery lost their lives in the Oise-Aisne campaign. During the period August 28 to September 1, the U.S. 32d Division captured the town of Juvigny penetrating German positions to a depth of 2.5 miles (4 kilometers). The progress of the Allied offensive and the threat of being cut off caused the Germans to withdraw from the Vesle to the Aisne River during the night of September 3-4. The U.S. 28th and 77th Divisions pressed the Allied attack against the new German line. On September 8, the U.S. 28th Division was given a well-deserved rest. Following heavy fighting at the Ourcq and Vesle Rivers, the 77th Division was withdrawn from the lines on September 16 and also given a rest. During the latter part of September 1918, the 370th Infantry Regiment of the U.S. 93d Division and the French 59th Division advanced steadily north of the Vauxaillon. The 370th Infantry Regiment remained in the lines until the middle of October when it was given a rest. It reentered battle on November 5 and continued in the pursuit of the German Army until the signing of the Armistice six days later.

ARCHITECTS

Architects for the cemetery's memorial features were Cram and Ferguson of Boston, Massachusetts. The landscape architect was Mr. George Gibbs, Jr. The consulting architect for the American Battle Monuments Commission was Dr. Paul P. Cret of Philadelphia, Pennsylvania.

THE SITE

The Oise-Aisne American Cemetery, 36.5 acres in extent, is the second largest of eight permanent American World War I military cemeteries on foreign soil. Established initially as a temporary battlefield cemetery by the 42d Division on August 2, 1918, Congress authorized its retention as a permanent cemetery in 1921.

The majority of the 6,012 War Dead interred in the cemetery died fighting along the Ourcq River and in the area between the cemetery and the Oise

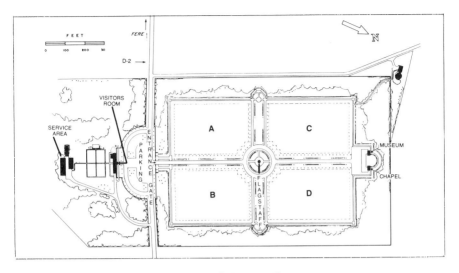

Location of Cemetery Features

River during the Aisne-Marne offensive and the Oise-Aisne offensive. An agreement with the French government grants use of the site as a military cemetery in perpetuity without charge or taxation.

In 1922, the remains of American servicemen buried in the general area west of Tours-Romorantin-Paris-Le-Harve, whose next of kin requested permanent interment overseas, were disinterred and permanently interred at the Oise-Aisne American Cemetery. All interments were made by the American Graves Registration Service. The memorial, the chapel, the visitors' room, the office, the Superintendent's quarters, and the service facilities were designed and constructed by the American Battle Monuments Commission as part of its program commemorating the achievements of the American Expeditionary Forces in the Great War.

GENERAL LAYOUT

The Oise-Aisne American Cemetery is generally rectangular in shape. Its memorial chapel, museum and grave plots, which encompass three-quarters of the cemetery, are located on the north side of highway D-2; and the parking area, service facilities and the superin-

tendent's quarters with the visitors' room and office are located on the south side.

Entrance to the graves area is through two iron pedestrian gates on highway D-2 which open onto the central mall leading to the memorial chapel and the museum at its northern end. A cross-axis mall intersects the central mall near the center of the graves area dividing it into four rectangular plots. At the intersection of the two malls is a circular island of grass and a flag staff from which the American flag flies daily. A small cul-de-sac with a stone bench and a planter backed by evergreen shrubbery lies at each end of the cross-axis mall. Bordering the malls are Oriental plane trees and beds of polyantha roses surrounded by dwarf boxwood hedges.

A path edged by privet hedge lies just inside the perimeter fence which encloses the graves area.

THE MEMORIAL

The Romanesque memorial consists of a semi-circular peristyle with a chapel on the right (east) end and a one-room museum on the left. Its columns of granite and multi-hued French and Italian marble encircle a

Cross-axis Mall

Cul-de-Sac at End of Cross Axis Mall

The Memorial

Altar on Terrace of Peristyle

raised stone terrace, in the center of which is a large rectangular altar of polished, golden, Rocheret Jaune marble. Entrance to the chapel and museum is from the terrace. The walls and piers of the peristyle are of pink Gres des Vosges sandstone with copings, bands, and openings of buff-grey Rippes Jaune sandstone.

An eagle rising, a palm wreath encircling a cross and a pelican feeding its young, early Christian symbols of redemption and resurrection, are carved on the front face of the outdoor stone altar in bas relief. Above the carving is inscribed in English and French: IN SACRED SLEEP THEY REST.

Engraved on the front and rear faces of the capitals of the ten double columns of the colonnade are the insignia of the 1st, 2d, 3d, 4th, 26th, 28th, 32d, 42d, 77th, and 93d Divisions which fought in this sector. Carved on the sides of the capitals are embellishments such as a rifle and bayonet, gas mask, one-pounder cannon, airplane propeller, field glasses, Stokes mortar, airplane bomb, entrenching tools, automatic pistol, field telephone set, hand grenade, mess kit, machine gun on a tripod,

Entrance to Chapel

cannon muzzle, mule's head, trench knife, canteen and cover, belt of machine gun ammunition, artillery shell and harness.

The columns of the peristyle are separated at regular intervals by one of four piers. Above each of the two outer piers is carved a soldier of World War I; above each of the two inner piers is carved St. George slaying the dragon on the left and St. Michael, the Archangel, on the right. Over them in the frieze of the peristyle in Rippes Jaune stone is the commemorative inscription: THESE ENDURED ALL AND GAVE THAT HONOR AND JUSTICE MIGHT PREVAIL AND THAT THE WORLD MIGHT ENJOY FREEDOM AND INHERIT PEACE. Engraved on the rear of the peristyle is the inscription: AMERICAN BATTLE MONUMENTS COMMISSION, CRAM AND FERGUSON ARCHITECTS.

In the frieze of the exterior walls of the chapel and museum are carved twenty-three shields depicting the branch and service insignia of U.S. Forces which served in the Oise-Aisne region: Infantry, Field Artillery, Engineers, Signal Corps, Air Service, Coast Artillery Corps, Quartermaster Corps, Ordnance Department, Medical Department, Chemical Warfare Service, Marine Corps, Tank Corps, Motor Transport Corps, Transportation Corps, Cavalry, Military Police, General Staff Corps, Adjutant General's Department, Inspector General's Department, Judge Advocate General's Department, Christian Chaplains, Jewish Chaplains and the American Field Service. Below the frieze on the front wall of both the chapel and museum is a stylized version of the Great Seal of the United States.

THE CHAPEL

The rectangular, stone chapel on the right (west) end of the peristyle, is entered from the raised terrace through a massive brass-studded oak door of dark panels trimmed in lighter-colored wood. Three stars within circles separated by laurel leaves are carved in the lintel above the door. At each end of the lintel is carved a fasces, symbol of authority of the magistrates of ancient Rome. Facing the entrance, inside the chapel, is a beautiful altar of black variegated Italian porter marble inset with two panels of Rocheret Jaune marble. A stylized oak tree, traditionally symbolizing strength, virtue and faith, is carved upon each of these panels. Between the two oak trees in a circle is the carved figure of a pelican feeding her young, symbolic of Christ feeding the masses.

The tall Rocheret Jaune marble back of the altar is embellished with decorative sculpture and panels, and carries the following inscription on a gilded background directly above the altar: WITH GOD IS THEIR REWARD. A gold cross between two candelabra sits upon the altar. Flanking the altar on each side is a large potted plant.

The names of 241 American soldiers missing in the area whose remains were never recovered or if recovered never identified, are inscribed upon the side walls. This inscription precedes the names on the south wall: THE NAMES RECORDED ON THESE WALLS ARE THOSE OF AMERICAN SOLDIERS WHO FOUGHT IN THIS REGION AND WHO SLEEP IN UNKNOWN GRAVES.

Two windows provide light for the chapel's interior, one high above the altar and one in the north wall. Each is made up of circles of thin, translucent Algerian onyx. A circular bronze filigreed chandelier suspended from the vaulted stone ceiling also provides light.

Completing the furnishings of this simple chapel are four hand-carved walnut prayer benches facing the altar.

MUSEUM

On the east end of the peristyle is the museum room. It is similar in construction and size to the chapel. Carved in the wall facing the entrance is a crusader's sword upon a gilded background flanked by vertical laurel leaves also upon a gilded background. The colors of the United States and France are dis-

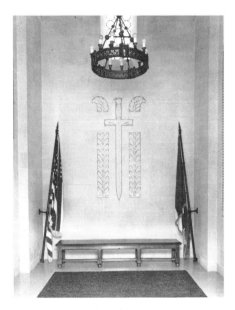

Interior of Museum

played from bronze standards at the corners of this wall. A carved walnut bench stands between them.

On the left (north) wall, also engraved on a gilded background is the dedicatory relief inscription: IN GRATEFUL REMEMBRANCE OF HER SONS WHO DIED IN THE WORLD WAR THIS CHAPEL IS ERECTED BY THE UNITED STATES OF AMERICA. The inscription appears in both English and French.

Opposite the inscription on the south wall is a carved battle map of the Oise-Aisne region. The map details the lines of advance and the areas where various American divisions fought during the Oise-Aisne Offensive and the Second Battle of the Marne. They are described briefly in the history section of this booklet.

The chandelier, oak door, and onyx windows match those of the chapel.

GRAVES AREA

The graves area contains four rectangular plots bordered by wide tree-lined paths and beds of polyantha roses. Grave plots A and C lie to the left (west) of the central mall and plots B and D to the right. Interred within them are the remains of 6,012 military and support personnel. They represent all of the then forty-eight States and the District of Columbia. Of these remains, 547 are Unknowns, i.e., those which could not be identified. Inscribed on the headstones of the Unknowns is: HERE RESTS IN HONORED GLORY AN AMERICAN SOLDIER KNOWN BUT TO GOD.

Stars of David mark the graves of those of the Jewish faith; Latin crosses mark the others. Each headstone was fabricated from white Carrara marble quarried in Italy. As one proceeds through the cemetery, their long rows rise gently from the main entrance of the graves area to the memorial on the north, presenting an ever changing array of geometric patterns.

Enclosing the graves area are a privet hedge, a low peripheral stone wall covered intermittently with ivy, and a screen of oak, birch, pine, fir, cedar, poplar, ash and maple. Between the stone wall and the privet hedge are groups of lilac, hibiscus and hydrangea.

VISITORS' ROOM

The visitors' room and the cemetery office are located in the superintendent's quarters, an ivy-covered building enframed by stately maple trees and flowering shrubs, on the south side of highway D-2 directly opposite the main entrance to the cemetery.

It is a comfortably furnished room, with toilet facilities, where visitors may obtain information, sign the register and pause to refresh themselves. During the day, a member of the cemetery staff is on duty in the building to answer questions and provide information on burials and memorializations in the Commission's cemeteries, accommodations in the vicinity, travel, local history and other things of interest.

Map of Aisne-Marne Region on Museum Wall

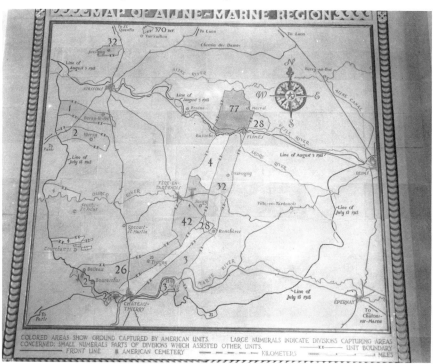

Flag Staff at Intersection of Malls

Central Mall of Graves Area

Somme American Cemetery and Memorial

Somme Cemetery is situated 1/2 mile southwest of the village of Bony (Aisne), France, which is 1 1/4 miles west of highway N-44, 13 miles north of St. Quentin and 14 miles southwest of Cambrai. The road leading to Bony leaves highway N-44 10 miles north of St. Quentin and a short distance north of the American monument near Bellicourt. The cemetery, 98 miles northeast of Paris, can be also reached by automobile via the Paris-Brussels autoroute (A-1) to Peronne, thence via Vermand and Belenglise. Hotel accomodations are available at Peronne, St. Quentin, and Cambrai which may be reached by train from Paris (Gare du Nord).

This 14-acre cemetery, sited on a gentle slope typical of the open, rolling Picardy countryside, contains the graves of 1,844 of our military Dead. Most of these lost their lives while serving in American units attatched to British Armies, or in operations near Cantigny. The headstones, set in regular rows, are separated into four plots by paths which intersect at the flagpole near the top of the slope. The longer axis leads to the chapel at the east end of the cemetery.

Sculptured on the outer walls of the chapel are pieces of military equipment. A massive bronze door surmounted by an American eagle forms its entrance. A cross-shaped window of crystal glass, above the marble altar, shines with luminous radiance in the subdued interior. On the walls are inscribed the names of 333 Missing in the area.

Somme American Cemetery and Memorial

St. Mihiel American Cemetery and Memorial

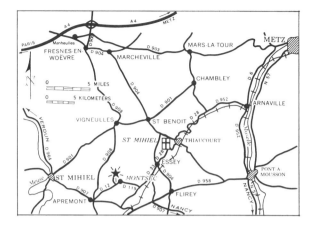

LOCATION

The St. Mihiel American Cemetery and Memorial is situated at the west edge of Thiaucourt, Meurthe-et-Moselle, France. The road from Verdun (29 miles/47 km), through Fresnes-en-Woevre, passes the entrance to the cemetery and continues on to Pont-à-Mousson and Nancy (29 miles/47 km). The cemetery may be reached from Paris by automobile (188 miles/300 km) via Autoroute A-3, from the Porte de Bercy, to the Fresnes-en-Woevre exit. From the village of Fresnes-en-Woevre, follow directions to Pont-à-Mousson (14 miles/22 km) to the cemetery. The cemetery may also be reached by train (Gare de l'Est) to Thiaucourt. Taxicab service is available at Thiaucourt. Hotels are available in Pont-à-Mousson, Metz, Nancy and Verdun. By calling the Superintendent or a member of his staff at 381-90-06, assistance will be provided to obtain hotel reservations or taxi service.

Entrance Gate

Chapel Interior

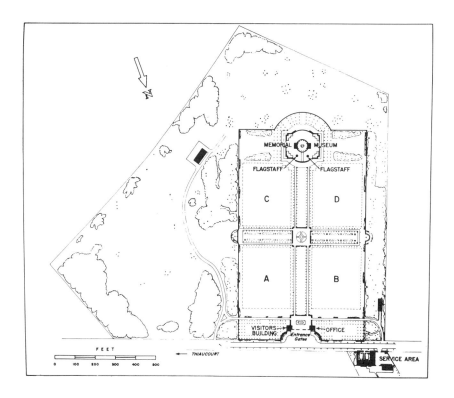

Location of Cemetery Features

HOURS

The cemetery is open to the public daily as shown below:

SUMMER (16 March–30 September)
9:00 a.m.–6:00 p.m. — weekdays
10:00 a.m.–6:00 p.m. — Saturdays, Sundays and holidays

WINTER (1 October–15 March)
9:00 a.m.–5:00 p.m. — weekdays
10:00 a.m.–5:00 p.m. — Saturdays, Sundays and holidays

When the cemetery is open to the public, a staff member is on duty in the Visitors' Building to answer questions and escort relatives to grave and memorial sites (except between noon and 3:00 p.m. on weekends and holidays).

HISTORY

Toward the end of 1916, French and British commanders on the western front were optimistic concerning a successful conclusion of the war in 1917. Except for the loss of Rumania, events during 1916 had appeared to be working in favor of the Allies, who had numerical superiority on all fronts.

As if to reinforce Allied optimism, the Germans on the western front began withdrawing some of their forces north of Paris to prepared positions approximately 20 miles to the rear that could be held by fewer divisions. These defensive positions were later to be known as the Hindenburg Line. The Russian Revolution broke out while the German withdrawal north of Paris was still in progress. The revolution delivered a serious blow to Allied plans, as the Russian Army had been counted upon heavily to keep German troops occupied on the eastern front. Although the Russian Army did not collapse immedi-

Aerial View of Cemetery

ately, it was apparent that it soon would do so.

On 6 April 1917, the United States entered World War I with no modern equipment and less than 200,000 men under arms scattered from the Mexican Border to China and the Philippines. It would take longer for the United States to mobilize, train, ship troops to France and equip and prepare them for combat than for the Russian Army to disintegrate. Despite this realization, the French and British Armies began the offensives that had been planned on the western front prior to the Russian Revolution in March. The initial British assault began on 9 April. It was followed by a French offensive on 16 April. Quickly, the French offensive turned into a disaster leaving the British Army to shoulder the main burden of the war on the western front, until French forces could reorganize and recuperate. On the eastern front, the Russians started to attack but were promptly driven back. Shortly thereafter, an assault by the Germans in the north caused the Russians to seek an armistice. Although the treaty

between Germany and Russia was not signed until March 1918, the Germans began moving divisions from Russia to France as early as November 1917, in an attempt to end the war before sufficient American troops could be brought into action to affect the outcome of the war.

As a consequence, the beginning of 1918 looked far worse for the Allies than the beginning of 1917. To take advantage of the troops that had been moved to France from the eastern front, the Germans launched a series of five powerful offensives on 21 March 1918. The first two offensives caused considerable concern among the Allies who vehemently contended that if American soldiers were not sent immediately as replacements to fill the depleted ranks of their units, the war would be lost. General Pershing, Commander-in-Chief of the American Expeditionary Forces, refused to allow his men to be used piecemeal and in a surprisingly short time organized, trained and equipped them into effective fighting units. When the French Army found itself in desperate need of assistance during

Ornamental Urn at Overlook

the third and fifth German drives, General Pershing quickly offered American troop units to halt the advancing enemy.

The outstanding achievements of these U.S. troop units are recorded at the Aisne-Marne American Cemetery and Memorial and at the Chateau-Thierry Monument. When the last great German offensive commenced on 15 July east of Chateau-Thierry, it was promptly repulsed in a severe struggle in which American troop units played a leading part. Quickly, a U.S.-French counteroffensive was launched on 18 July at Soissons. The highly successful three-week battle that followed, known officially as the "Aisne-Marne Offensive" but called the "Second Battle of the Marne" by Marshal Foch, marked the turning point of the war.

Determined to keep the enemy on the defensive, the Allied Commanders-in-Chief, at a conference on 24 July, planned a series of strong, offensive operations to maintain the initiative and give the enemy no respite or opportunity to reorganize. Following completion of the Aisne-Marne Offensive, the British, assisted by the French, were given the mission of conducting an offensive in the Amiens sector where the enemy had made such great gains in March and April.

At this conference, General Pershing chose the St. Mihiel sector for an American offensive. The objective of the offensive was a salient projecting 16 miles into the Allied line. Roughly shaped like a triangle, the salient ran from Verdun on the north, south to St. Mihiel and then east to Pont-à-Mousson on the Moselle River. It was bordered by a line of hills known as the Heights of the Meuse and a succession of marshes and lakes situated across deep ravines and dense forests. In addition to its natural defensive advantages, the salient protected the strategic rail center of Metz and the Briey iron basin so vital to the Germans as a source of raw material for

munitions. Offensively, it interrupted French rail communications and constituted a constant threat against Verdun and Nancy. Reduction of the salient was imperative before any large Allied offensive could be launched against Briey and Metz or northward between the Meuse River and Argonne Forest. At the conference, General Pershing insisted that the attack be a United States Army operation with its own sector, under the separate and independent control of the American Commander-in-Chief. When the decision was made, there were over 1,200,000 American soldiers in U.S. troop units widely scattered throughout France, either serving with French or British Armies or training in rear areas. In view of the splendid record that so many of the U.S. units had already achieved in combat, the Allies were forced to agree that a separate U.S. Army should be formed, although they requested that U.S. divisions continue to be permitted to fight with their armies.

The order creating the United States First Army became effective on 10 August 1918; on 30 August, the U.S. First Army took over the St. Mihiel sector. After a series of conferences, the Allies agreed that the St. Mihiel attack should be limited to a reduction of the salient, following which the U.S. First Army would undertake a larger scale offensive on the front between the Meuse River and the Argonne Forest. With the attack at St. Mihiel scheduled for 12 September, this would require winning an extraordinarily swift victory there, then concentrating an enormous force to launch a still greater operation 40 miles away, within just two weeks. Never before on the western front had a single army attempted such a colossal task.

At 0500 hours, 12 September 1918, following a four-hour bombardment by heavy artillery, the U.S. I and IV Corps composed of nine U.S. divi-

The Memorial Peristyle

The Sundial and Surrounding Gardens at the Center of the Cemetery

sions, began the main assault against the southern face of the salient, while the French II Colonial Corps made a holding attack to the south and around the tip of the salient. A secondary assault by the U.S. V Corps was made three hours later against the western face of the salient. Reports were soon received that the enemy was retreating. That evening, the order was issued for U.S. troops to press forward with all possible speed. By the dawn of 13 September, units of the U.S. IV and V Corps met in the center of the salient, cutting off the retreating enemy. By 16 September, the entire salient had been eliminated. Throughout these operations, the attacking forces were supported by the largest concentration of Allied aircraft ever assembled. The entire reduction of the salient was completed in just four days by which time some of the divisions involved had already been withdrawn to prepare for the Meuse-Argonne battle.

SITE

The cemetery, 40½ acres in extent, is located almost at the center of the salient where the majority of the 4,153 military Dead buried there gave their lives. The cemetery was first established as a temporary cemetery by the American Graves Registration Service following the offensive in 1918. After the war, the other temporary cemeteries in the area were discontinued and the military Dead of the region whose next-of-kin requested burial overseas were moved to the St. Mihiel cemetery for permanent interment. It is the third largest of the eight permanent World War I American military cemetery memorials in Europe. Postwar administration of the cemetery passed to the American Battle Monuments Commission in 1934.

Visitors' Building

View of Mall and Graves Area

ARCHITECT

Architect for the memorial chapel and other architectural features was Thomas Harlan Ellett of New York.

GENERAL LAYOUT

The formal entrance, with its ornamental grill gates and fencing and its gem-like buildings, is of striking beauty and offers an excellent view of the cemetery. To the right of the entrance is the Superintendent's Office; to the left is the Visitors' Building. Both are constructed of Euville limestone. Directly behind these buildings is the cemetery proper. Here, in a beautifully landscaped setting, are the graves area and the memorial. The pristine whiteness of the headstones is in striking contrast to the immaculately maintained emerald green lawn.

At the intersection of the central mall and transverse axis in the center of the cemetery is a large sundial of attractive design consisting of a carved stone eagle gnomon on a round base. The shadow cast by the eagle gnomon in relationship to the lead Roman numerals set in the flat surface of the base indicates the time of day. Around the circular base of the sundial is carved the inscription:

TIME WILL NOT DIM
THE GLORY OF THEIR DEEDS

From this point one can view the beautiful perspectives along the two axes of the cemetery. At the west end of the transverse axis is a sculptured stone figure of a youthful American officer, executed by Paul Manship of New York, standing in front of a stone cross in his field uniform, with trench helmet in hand and side arms and map case. Above his head is engraved:

IL DORT
LOIN DES SIENS
DANS LA DOUCE
TERRE DE FRANCE

(Translation: He sleeps far from his family in the gentle land of France.) and on the pedestal below him:

BLESSED ARE THEY THAT
HAVE THE HOME LONGING
FOR THEY SHALL GO HOME

At the opposite end of the transverse axis is an ornamental urn on a semi-circular platform flanked by two beautiful yews. From this platform, facing the east, an excellent view of the surrounding rural countryside may be seen.

THE MEMORIAL

At the north end of the cemetery stands the memorial, an open circular colonnade or peristyle flanked by a chapel room on the left and a museum room on the right. On the left front facade of the memorial is engraved a lamp representing an eternal flame and under it the inscription:

1914
1918
TO THOSE
WHO DIED
FOR THEIR
COUNTRY

Sculpture of a Young American Officer in Field Uniform

On the opposite facade appears the same lamp symbol and the same inscription in French.

The memorial rests on a slightly raised circular terrace and is enclosed by a stone faced wall. On the lawn in front of it are two large flagpoles with stone and bronze bases. Large chestnut trees frame it on the sides and rear and immediately behind the memorial are two large weeping willows.

The memorial is constructed of Rocheret limestone. On the inside surface of the lintel is carved in the stone:

THIS CHAPEL HAS BEEN
ERECTED BY THE UNITED
STATES OF AMERICA IN
GRATEFUL REMEMBRANCE OF
HER SONS WHO DIED IN
THE WORLD WAR

These words emphasize that the memorial and, indeed, the entire cemetery were erected not to commemorate the glory of battle won or the triumph of victory achieved, but to pay homage to those American servicemen who made the supreme sacrifice for their country.

The large rose-granite urn with its carved drapery at the center of the peristyle resembles an ancient funereal vase. One of its decorative features is a winged horse, Pegasus, symbolizing the flight of the immortal soul to its resting place in the life beyond.

To the left of the peristyle, bronze doors, decorated with stars and two miniature soldier heads, lead to the impressive interior of the chapel room. The carved white Italian marble altar holds a lighted bronze lamp symbolic of an eternal flame. Above the altar is a richly colored mosaic depicting the "Angel of Victory" sheathing a sword and "Doves of Peace" bearing olive branches. At the top of the wall, carved in white marble with gold letters, is the inscription:

*Sculpture at the Center of the
Peristyle Representing an
Ancient Funereal Vase*

I GIVE UNTO THEM
ETERNAL LIFE AND THEY
SHALL NEVER PERISH

The mosaics on the end walls have as their main features large shields displaying the national colors of the United States and of France.

The coffered ceiling is decorated in gold and blue, while the floor and lower wall-paneling are of inlaid marble with light and dark green markings. Dispersed about the chapel in appropriate places are graceful candelabra, cushioned seats and kneeling benches.

Crossing to the right side of the memorial one enters the museum through a similar set of bronze doors. On the wall directly opposite the doorway is a beautiful map of the St. Mihiel region inlaid with various colored marbles. This map shows the boundaries of the salient, the German lines before the offensive, the Allied lines after the battle and the progress of the campaign.

On the side walls of the museum are black marble panels, at the tops of which are engraved:

IN MEMORY OF THOSE AMERICAN SOL-
DIERS WHO FOUGHT IN THIS REGION
AND WHO SLEEP IN UNKNOWN GRAVES.

Listed below the inscription in gold letters are the names of the 284 American soldiers who gave their lives in this area, but whose remains were not recovered or identified.

THE GRAVES AREA

The graves area consists of four burial plots, lettered from A to D, separated by the central mall and the transverse axes. The 4,153 headstones are arranged in parallel rows across the green lawns which carpet the graves area. One hundred and seventeen of these headstones mark the graves of "Unknowns". The cemetery contains no multiple burials. Each of the Dead has his own headstone of white marble, a Star of David for those of the Jewish faith and a Latin

Wall of the Missing

cross for all others. The precise alignment of clean, polished marble headstones on clipped green grass assures the visitor that no feature of the cemetery receives more respectful care than does the graves area.

PLANTINGS

At the entrance gate to the cemetery is a large bed of flowering annuals. The main paths of the cemetery are bordered by square-trimmed European linden trees, their low overhanging boughs furnishing a canopy. Flower beds of polyantha roses are planted along the transverse axes. The base of the decorative sundial at the intersection of the center mall and transverse axes in the center of the cemtery is surrounded by beds of flowering annuals and bordered with dwarf boxwood hedge.

VISITORS' BUILDING

Located to the left of the entrance gate is the Visitors' Building. Here visitors may obtain information, sign the register and pause to refresh themselves. During visiting hours a member of the cemetery staff is available in the building to answer questions and provide information on burials and memorializations in the Commission's cemeteries, accommodations in the vicinity, travel, local history and other items of interest.

View of the Sculptured Eagle and Graves Area

Montsec Monument

On a high isolated hill, 12 miles/19 km. from the St. Mihiel American Cemetery, stands the Montsec Monument. It commemorates the capture of the St. Mihiel salient by the American First Army, the operations of the American Second Army on 9–11 November 1918, and other combat services of American divisions both in this region and in Alsace and Lorraine.

The monument consists of a large circular colonnade, at the center of which, on a raised platform, is a bronze relief map of the St. Mihiel salient. Its size, its commanding site, and the perfection of its proportions combine to make it one of the most impressive in Europe.

On the right side of a flight of steps leading to the monument is engraved:

THIS MONUMENT HAS BEEN
ERECTED BY THE UNITED
STATES OF AMERICA
TO COMMEMORATE THE
CAPTURE OF THE ST. MIHIEL

SALIENT BY THE TROOPS
OF HER FIRST ARMY AND
TO RECORD THE SERVICES
OF THE AMERICAN
EXPEDITIONARY FORCES ON
THE BATTLEFRONT IN THIS
REGION AND ELSEWHERE IN
LORRAINE AND IN ALSACE.
IT STANDS AS A LASTING
SYMBOL OF THE FRIENDSHIP
AND COOPERATION
BETWEEN THE FRENCH AND
AMERICAN ARMIES.

The same inscription is repeated in French on the left side of the flight of steps. Near the top of the monument on the outside lintel are engraved the names of villages and towns where battles were fought in this region:

THIAUCOURT — VIGNEULLES — FRESNES — VIEVILLE — ST. BENOIT — NORROY — BENEY — JAULNY — FRAPELLE — HAUMONT — ST. HILAIRE — XAMMES — NONSARD — VILCEY — ST. BAUSSANT — VANDIERES.

Suresnes American Cemetery and Memorial

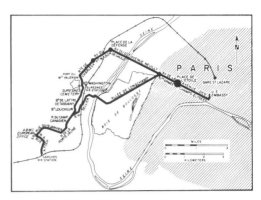

LOCATION

Suresnes American Cemetery Memorial is situated on the wooded east slope of Mont Valerien, 4 miles west of the center of Paris, in the city of Suresnes. The cemetery can be reached by taxi or automobile via the Bois de Boulogne and the Suresnes bridge over the Seine River. On leaving the bridge, visitors should bear right and follow the traffic signs indicating Mont Valerien. From Paris (Gare St. Lazare), suburban electric trains are available every 15 minutes to the Suresnes station. On arrival at the Suresnes station, visitors should take the exit toward the right passing in front of the Foch Hospital, go up the slope to Boulevard Washington, turn right on the boulevard and proceed approximately 200 yards to the cemetery entrance.

THE SITE

The cemetery site covers $7\frac{1}{2}$ acres. Perpetual use of this land free of charge or taxation was granted to the United States by the French Government.

The Memorial Chapel

"Memory"

The hill on which the cemetery is located is rich in history. Now called Mont Valerien, it was known as Mont Calvaire in earlier times and was the site of a hermitage which was itself the goal of many religious pilgrimages. The hermits maintained gardens and vineyards, as well as a guest house. Thomas Jefferson often visited the guest house while he was Ambassador to France, 1784–1789.

In 1811, Emperor Napoleon I confiscated Mont Valerien with the intention of building a home for the orphans of the Legion of Honor. During a subsequent visit to the site, he changed his mind and decided to build a fort. Napoleon's defeat at Waterloo in 1815 stopped the work and Mont Valerien again became a religious shrine. In 1840, however, the Fort of Mont Valerien was built and is presently in use by the French Signal Corps.

During World War II, German troops occupied the fort where they executed over 4,500 political prisoners and members of the Resistance Movement. The French people have erected an impressive monument along the south wall of the fort to commemorate this sacrifice. Thus, the hill in Suresnes has become a symbol to the French of democracy's struggle in the cause of freedom. Mont Valerien is a site of pilgrimage for both the French and the American peoples.

HISTORY OF THE CEMETERY

The American military cemetery at Suresnes was established in 1917 by the Graves Registration Service of the Army Quartermaster Corps. A majority of the World War I Dead buried there died of wounds or sickness in hospitals located in Paris or at other places in the Services of Supply. Many were victims of the influenza epidemic of 1918–1919.

The cemetery was dedicated by President Woodrow Wilson during Memorial Day ceremonies of 1919.

Administration of the cemetery passed to the American Battle Monuments Commission in 1934, the duties and functions of which are

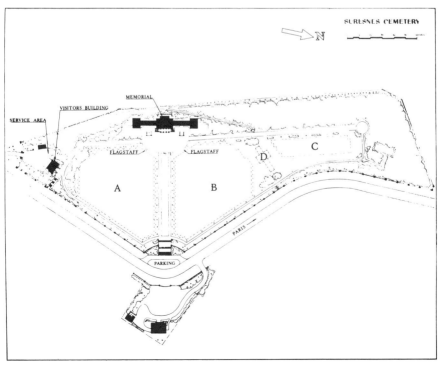

Location of Cemetery Features

The Commission was responsible for construction of the chapel and landscaping of the grounds, which were completed in 1932.

At the end of World War II, it was decided that this particular cemetery should serve to commemorate the Dead of both World Wars, and an additional grave plot was created as an eternal resting place for the unidentified remains of 24 World War II Unknowns. Commemorative loggias were also added to the original chapel.

The World War II section was dedicated in 1952 with an impressive ceremony presided over by General George C. Marshall, then Chairman of the Commission, and attended by distinguished representatives of the American and French Governments.

ARCHITECTS

The original chapel was designed by architect Charles A. Platt of New York. His sons, William and Geoffrey Platt, designed the loggias and memorial rooms which comprise the loggias added to the chapel after World War II.

GENERAL LAYOUT

From the gilded, wrought-iron entrance gates, an avenue of clipped lindens leads upward to the chapel, framing the classical facade. Groups of rhododendrons flank the chapel, while red polyantha roses form a border of color along its base.

The impeccable headstones and lawns of the graves area extend in gentle arcs on both sides of the central avenue.

The initial horticultural development has now matured and contributes greatly to the tranquil beauty of the grounds. Planted among the grave plots are beech, weeping willow, mountain ash, horse chestnut and paulownia. The latter is an exceptional sight in the spring, when it is covered with mauve flowers. The hillside, which rises steeply be-

The Chapel Interior

hind the graves area and chapel, is planted with pines, yews, acacia, and hornbeam to form a discreet background.

THE CHAPEL

The exterior walls of the chapel are of Val d'Arion, a creamy French limestone. The four columns supporting the peristyle are interesting monoliths. Above these columns is inscribed in large letters:

PEACEFUL IS THEIR SLEEP IN GLORY.

To the left of the bronze entrance doors, there is inscribed the text:

THIS MEMORIAL HAS BEEN ERECTED BY THE UNITED STATES OF AMERICA AS A SACRED RENDEZVOUS OF A GRATEFUL PEOPLE WITH ITS IMMORTAL DEAD.

The same text in French appears to the right of the entrance.

The interior walls and columns of the chapel are of Rocheret, a compact limestone quarried in central France. The ceiling is paneled in native oak. The principal decorative feature inside the chapel is the mosaic mural behind the altar, created by Barry Faulkner, which depicts the Angel of Victory bearing a palm branch to the graves of the Fallen. Four large bronze plaques, each one cast as a single unit, bear the names of 974 men who were buried or lost at sea during World War I. The altar is of Italian Levanto marble and is inscribed:

I GIVE UNTO THEM ETERNAL LIFE AND THEY SHALL NEVER PERISH.

WORLD WAR I LOGGIA

A portal in the left wall of the chapel leads to the World War I loggia, a covered passage with one side open to give a view of the graves area below and of Paris in the distance. The opposite or rear side is paneled in limestone. One panel of this wall bears the inscription:

TO THE ETERNAL MEMORY OF THOSE AMERICANS WHO GAVE THEIR LIVES IN THE SERVICE OF THEIR COUNTRY DURING WORLD WAR I ☆ ☆ ☆ INTO THY HANDS O LORD.

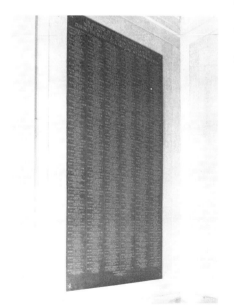

WW I Tablets of the Missing

Sculpture in Bas-relief WW I Loggia

Midway along the loggia, a relief portrays a group of soldiers carrying an empty bier. Beneath the frieze is the inscription:

SOME THERE BE WHICH HAVE NO SEPUL- CHRE. THEIR NAME LIVETH FOR EVER- MORE.

An engraved list of other World War I military cemeteries in Europe completes the texts appearing on the wall of this loggia.

WORLD WAR I MEMORIAL ROOM

At the end of the loggia, one enters the World War I memorial room and faces a pure white statue en- titled "Remembrance." This grace- ful figure was created in Carrara marble by the American sculptor John Gregory. The walls and floors of the memorial room are of Italian marbles of varying shades and give a rich, subdued effect to highlight the statue.

On one wall panel is inscribed the text:

THIS MEMORIAL HAS BEEN ERECTED BY THE UNITED STATES OF AMERICA IN PROUD AND GRATEFUL MEMORY OF HER SOLDIERS, SAILORS, AND MARINES WHO FAR FROM THEIR HOMES LAID DOWN THEIR LIVES THAT THE WORLD MIGHT LIVE IN FREEDOM AND INHERIT PEACE ☆ ☆ ☆ FROM THESE HONORED DEAD MAY WE TAKE INCREASED DEVOTION TO THAT CAUSE FOR WHICH THEY GAVE THE LAST FULL MEASURE.

WORLD WAR II LOGGIA

A portal in the right wall of the chapel leads to the World War II loggia, which is very similar in ap- pearance to the loggia previously de- scribed, except for the inscriptions on the wall. The dedicatory panel reads:

TO THE ETERNAL MEMORY OF THOSE AMERICANS WHO GAVE THEIR LIVES IN THE SERVICE OF THEIR COUNTRY DUR- ING WORLD WAR II ☆ ☆ ☆ INTO THY HANDS O LORD.

WW I Loggia

Beneath the frieze depicting a group of soldiers carrying the shrouded remains of an Unknown comrade, there is inscribed:

GRANT UNTO THEM O LORD ETERNAL REST WHO SLEEP IN UNKNOWN GRAVES.

GRANT UNTO THEM O LORD ETERNAL REST WHO SLEEP IN UNKNOWN GRAVES

Sculpture in Bas-relief WWII Loggia

Two other wall panels bear the following texts:

THE EAST COAST MEMORIAL
AT NEW YORK HARBOR
BEARS THE NAMES OF 4596 OF
OUR HEROIC DEAD WHO REST
BENEATH AMERICAN COASTAL WATERS
OF THE ATLANTIC OCEAN

☆ ☆ ☆

THE WEST COAST MEMORIAL
AT SAN FRANCISCO, CALIFORNIA
BEARS THE NAMES OF 412 OF OUR
HEROIC DEAD WHO REST BENEATH
THE AMERICAN COASTAL WATERS
OF THE PACIFIC OCEAN

The loggia inscriptions are completed with a tabulation of other overseas World War II military cemeteries. In addition to Puerto Rico, the list includes Hawaii and Alaska as these two territories had not attained statehood at the time.

WW II Loggia

World War II Grave Plot

WORLD WAR II MEMORIAL ROOM

The walls and floors in this room are finished in Italian marble corresponding to that in the World War I memorial room. A different statue is presented here, however, entitled "Memory." It is the work of another American sculptor, Lewis Iselin.

The wall panel bears the text:

THIS MEMORIAL HAS BEEN ERECTED BY THE UNITED STATES OF AMERICA IN PROUD AND GRATEFUL MEMORY OF HER SOLDIERS, SAILORS, MARINES, AND AIRMEN WHO LAID DOWN THEIR LIVES IN ALL QUARTERS OF THE EARTH THAT OTHER PEOPLES MIGHT BE FREED FROM OPPRESSION ☆ ☆ ☆ LET US HERE HIGHLY RESOLVE THAT THESE HONORED DEAD SHALL NOT HAVE DIED IN VAIN.

THE GRAVES AREA

The graves area consists of four burial plots; three of World War I, with a total of 1,541 graves, and one of World War II, containing the graves of 24 unknown soldiers, sailors or airmen. Each grave is marked with a headstone of white Italian marble, the Star of David for those of Jewish faith, a Latin Cross for all others.

The precise alignment of white marble headstones on well-kept lawns assures the visitor that no feature of the cemetery receives greater care than does the graves area.

The deceased are interred side by side without distinction as to rank, race or creed, so that all repose equally in everlasting dignity.

To view the graves area is poignant, and the presence of a pair of brothers, a pair of sisters and seven nurses is particularly touching.

Graves Area

Tours Monument

Tours Monument is located in the city of Tours, France, 146 miles southwest of Paris.

The monument commemorates the efforts of the 650,000 men who served during World War I in the Services of Supply of the American Expeditionary Forces and whose work behind the battle lines made possible the brilliant achievements of the American armies in the field. It is situated just east of the southern end of the Pont Wilson which crosses the Loire in prolongation of the main street (Rue Nationale) of Tours, and consists of a handsome fountain of white stone and bronze with appropriate sculpture. The surrounding area was developed by the Commission into a small park.

WORLD WAR I
CEMETERIES AND MEMORIALS:

UNITED KINGDOM

𝕭rookwood American Cemetery and Memorial

Brookwood Cemetery is located southwest of the town of Brookwood, Surrey, England, 6 miles north of Guildford, and 9 miles northeast of Aldershot. It may be reached by automobile from London, a distance of 28 miles, or by train from Waterloo station in less than an hour. The American cemetery is about 300 yards from the Brookwood railroad station. There are hotels and restaurants at Woking, Guildford, Aldershot and other nearby towns.

This small cemetery of 4 1/2 acres lies within the large civilian cemetery of the London Necropolis Co. and contains the graves of 468 of our military Dead. Close by are military cemeteries and monuments of the British Commonwealth and other Allied nations.

Automobiles may drive through the necropolis to the American Cemetery.

Within the American cemetery the headstones are arranged in four plots, grouped about the flagpole. The regular rows of white marble headstones on the smooth lawn are framed by masses of shrubs and evergreen trees which form a prefect setting for the chapel, a classic white stone building on the northwest side of the cemetery. The interior of the chapel is of tan-hued stone. Small stained glass windows light the altar and flags and the carved cross above them. On the walls within the chapel are inscribed the names of 563 of the Missing who gave their lives in the service of their Country and whose graves are in the sea.

Naval
Monument
at
Gibraltar

The Naval Monument at Gibraltar, the gateway to the Mediterranean, consists of a masonry archway bearing bronze seals of the United States and of the Navy Department. This monument, constructed from stone from the neighboring "Rock", commemorates the achievements and sacrifices of the United States Navy in nearby waters and its comradeship with the Royal Navy during World War I.

From this monument, located in the midst of historic surroundings, a flight of steps connects the extensive British naval establishments below with the picturesque town above.

Gibraltar is a port of call for many ships; a visit to the monument from the pier requires about half an hour.

WORLD WAR I
CEMETERIES AND MEMORIALS:

UNITED STATES

Statue of General Pershing

American Expeditionary
Forces
Memorial

The American Expeditionary Forces Memorial, located on Pennsylvania Ave. between 14th and 15th streets, NW in Washington, D.C., commemorates the two million American military personnel and their CinC, General John J. Pershing, who made up the AEF of WWI.

It consists of a stone plaza 52 ft. by 72 ft., an 8 ft. statue of General Pershing on a stone pedestal, a stone bench facing the statue and two 10 ft. high walls, one along the south side of the memorial area and one along the east. The south wall contains two battle maps with appropriate inscriptions. Inscribed upon the reverse face of the east wall is General Pershing's tribute to the officers and men of the AEF: "IN THEIR DEVOTION, THEIR VALOR, AND IN THE LOYAL FULFILLMENT OF THEIR OBLIGATIONS, THE OFFICERS AND MEN OF THE AMERICAN EXPEDITIONARY FORCES HAVE LEFT A HERITAGE OF WHICH THOSE WHO FOLLOW MAY EVER BE PROUD."

WORLD WAR II
CEMETERIES AND MEMORIALS:

BELGIUM

Ardennes American Cemetery and Memorial

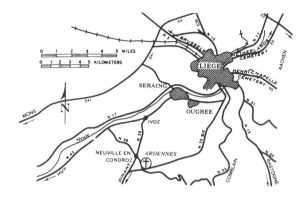

LOCATION

Ardennes Cemetery is situated near the southeast edge of the village of Neupre (formerly Neuville-en-Condroz), 12 miles southwest of Liège, Belgium. Highway N-35 bis from Liège to Marche or Dinant and Paris passes the main entrance. Excellent autoroutes lead to Liège from major cities in Belgium, the Netherlands and West Germany. Liège can be reached by train from Paris (Gare du Nord) in about 5½ hours, from Brussels in a little more than 1 hour, and from Germany via Aachen.

Taxicabs are available from Liège station. Hotel accommodations are available in Liège.

HOURS

The cemetery is open daily to the public during the following hours:

SUMMER (16 March-30 September)
8 a.m. to 6 p.m.

WINTER (1 October-15 March)
8 a.m. to 5 p.m.

Entrance Gate

Memorial Chapel

Aerial View of Cemetery and Memorial

During these hours, a staff member is always on duty at the Visitors' Building to answer questions, and to escort relatives to the gravesites and to the Tablets of the Missing.

THE SITE

The Ardennes American Cemetery, 90½ acres in extent, is one of fourteen permanent American World War II military cemeteries constructed on foreign soil by the American Battle Monuments Commission. The site was liberated on 8 September 1944 by the 1st Infantry Division. A temporary cemetery was established on the site on 8 February 1945. After the war, when the temporary cemeteries were disestablished by the Army, the remains of American military Dead whose next of kin requested permanent interment overseas were moved to one of the fourteen permanent cemetery sites on foreign soil, usually the one which was closest to the temporary cemetery. There they were interred by the Graves Registration Service in the distinctive grave patterns proposed by the cemetery's architect and approved by the Commission. The design and construction of all facilities at the permanent sites were the responsibility of the Commission, i.e., the chapel, museum, visitors' building, superintendent's quarters, service facilities, utilities and paths, roads and walls. The Commission was also responsible for the sculpture, landscaping and other improvements. Many of those interred here died during the enemy's final major counteroffensive in the Ardennes in December 1944 and January 1945; they include some service troops who were fighting as infantry. Others gave their lives in the advance to the Rhine and across Germany, and in the strategic bombardment of Europe.

ARCHITECTS

Architects for the cemetery and memorial were Reinhard, Hofmeister & Wal-

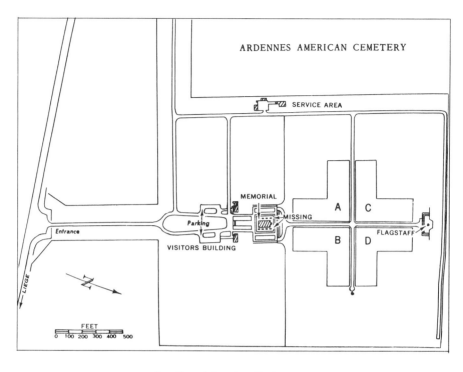

Location of Cemetery Features.

quist of New York City. The landscape architect was Richard K. Webel of Roslyn, Long Island.

GENERAL LAYOUT

The Ardennes American Cemetery is generally rectangular in shape. Its grave plots are arranged in the form of a Greek cross separated by two broad intersecting paths. The cemetery itself rests on a slope descending gently northward toward Neupre. To the south and east, it is enframed in woodland in which red and white oak, beech and ash predominate; its west side is lined by an avenue of stately lindens (Tilia platyphyllus) and its north boundary by informal tree groups. Entry is made into the cemetery through the main gate located on the north side of highway N-35 bis. It is set within plantings of black and white pine (Pinus Nigra Austriace and Pinus strobus); its wing walls are backed by an evergreen hedge.

Inside the main gate, a straight avenue bordered by horsechestnut (Aesculus hippocastanum) trees leads for 300 yards through woods to a broad green mall flanked on each side with parking spaces. At the far right (east) side is the Visitors' Building; on the left the Superintendent's house; the memorial is on the axis. From the parking area a flight of steps leads down to the memorial; this path divides to pass around the building and leads to the burial area beyond.

Beyond the woods to the west are the wells, reservoirs, and service building. Drinking water is treated in a purification system.

THE MEMORIAL

The memorial of English Portland Whitbed limestone is austerely rectangular in form. It projects on all sides beyond its base which, in turn, is set upon a Danube Gray granite podium reached by seven steps; these extend entirely around the building except where they are interrupted at the south end to permit access to the main door. The podium at the north end affords an impressive view of the burial area and of the countryside beyond.

Carved in high relief on the south facade of the memorial is an American eagle 17 feet high. Beside it are three figures symbolizing Justice, Liberty, and Truth; the composition is balanced by 13 stars representing the United States. This sculpture is from the design of C. Paul Jennewein of New York City; the work was executed by Jean Juge of Paris. The main doors to the memorial are of stainless steel and bear in relief the dates: 1941-1945.

The south, east, and west interior walls of the memorial are decorated with large maps composed of inlaid marbles embracing a range of colors from white through cream and gray to black. Much of the lettering is of bronze; other topographical and military details are rendered in mosaic, or enameled or plated bronze. The map above the door records both the last great enemy offensive ARDENNES, popularly known as "The Battle of the Bulge," which took place during the winter of 1944–45, and also the subsequent advance of the Allied forces across the RHINELAND to the Rhine River; it measures 19½ feet high by 22½ feet long. Elaborating this map is an inscription in English, French, and Flemish, of which this is the English text:

ON 16 DECEMBER 1944 THE ENEMY MADE HIS LAST CONCERTED EFFORT TO STAVE OFF DEFEAT, UNLEASHING THREE ARMIES ON A NARROW FRONT. PREPARED IN GREATEST SECRECY AND LAUNCHED UNDER COVER OF FOG AND RAIN, HIS ATTACK IN THE ARDENNES WAS INITIALLY SUCCESSFUL. BREAKING THROUGH ON A 45-MILE FRONT, HIS FORCES PENETRATED OVER 60 MILES, BUT AMERICAN SOLDIERS, FIGHTING VALIANTLY, HELD THE CRITICAL SHOULDERS OF THE SALIENT.

REACTING PROMPTLY AND DECISIVELY, THE ALLIES RUSHED ALL AVAILABLE RESERVES TO THE SCENE. A FURIOUS STRUGGLE DEVELOPED AT THE ROAD CENTER OF ST. VITH WHERE THE ENEMY ADVANCE WAS STUBBORNLY DELAYED. AT BASTOGNE, ALTHOUGH

Graves Area and North Facade of Chapel

Ardennes and Rhineland Operations Map, South End of Chapel

SURROUNDED FOR FIVE DAYS, AMERICAN TROOPS, WITH THE HELP OF SUPPLIES DROPPED BY IX TROOP CARRIER COMMAND AIRCRAFT, MAINTAINED THEIR DEFENSE. WHILE THE FIRST ARMY BLOCKED THE ENEMY'S EFFORTS TO BREAK THROUGH TOWARD LIEGE AND CROSS THE MEUSE, THE THIRD ARMY BY A MASTERFUL CHANGE OF FRONT TURNED NORTH AND ON 22 DECEMBER COUNTERATTACKED THE SOUTHERN FLANK OF THE PENETRATION. ON 23 DECEMBER THE SKIES CLEARED, ENABLING OUR EIGHTH AND NINTH AIR FORCES TO ENTER THE BATTLE AND STRIKE AT THE ENEMY ARMOR AND SUPPLY COLUMNS.

THE THIRD ARMY CONTINUED ITS ADVANCE, RELIEVING BASTOGNE ON 26 DECEMBER. THE FIRST ARMY'S COUNTERATTACK FROM THE NORTH CAME ON 3 JANUARY 1945. STRUGGLING FORWARD AGAINST DETERMINED OPPOSITION, ACROSS SNOW-COVERED MINE FIELDS IN BITTERLY COLD WEATHER, THE THIRD AND FIRST ARMIES MET AT HOUFFALIZE ON THE 16TH. THE SALIENT WAS COMPLETELY REDUCED BY 25 JANUARY.

WHILE MAINTAINING THEIR ADVANCE IN THE ARDENNES, AMERICAN TROOPS NOW PUSHED DOWN THE ROER VALLEY. ON 23 FEBRUARY, THE FIRST AND NINTH ARMIES LAUNCHED THEIR ASSAULT ACROSS THIS RIVER, WITH FIGHTERS AND MEDIUM BOMBERS OF THE NINTH AIR FORCE CLOSELY SUPPORTING THE FORWARD UNITS, AND SEIZED BRIDGEHEADS AT JULICH AND DUREN. AS THE OFFENSIVE GATHERED MOMENTUM, UNITS TO THE SOUTH JOINED THE ADVANCE. THE FIRST

ARMY REACHED COLOGNE BY 5 MARCH
AND WHEELED TO THE SOUTHEAST.
THE NEXT DAY THE THIRD ARMY AT-
TACKED NORTH OF THE MOSELLE. PRE-
CEDED BY AIRCRAFT STRIKES THAT DIS-
ORGANIZED THE RETREATING ENEMY,
OUR GROUND FORCES ADVANCED RAP-
IDLY. ON 7 MARCH THE FIRST ARMY
SEIZED THE UNDEMOLISHED BRIDGE
AT REMAGEN, THEN PROMPTLY ESTAB-
LISHED AND EXPANDED A BRIDGEHEAD
ACROSS THE RIVER. THE LINE OF THE
RHINE, THE LAST BARRIER IN THE
WEST, HAD BEEN BREACHED.

The map, 19½ by 26¼ feet, on the
west wall records the military operations in western Europe from the landings in Normandy and the French
Riviera up to the end of the war. On
this map also is depicted the great air
assault against the enemy's military and
industrial systems. Descriptive texts
in the three languages accompany the
map, this being the English version:

ON 6 JUNE 1944, PRECEDED BY AIR-
BORNE UNITS AND COVERED BY NAVAL
AND AIR BOMBARDMENT, UNITED
STATES AND BRITISH COMMONWEALTH
FORCES LANDED ON THE COAST OF
NORMANDY. PUSHING SOUTHWARD
THEY ESTABLISHED A BEACHHEAD SOME
20 MILES IN DEPTH. ON 25 JULY, IN
THE WAKE OF A PARALYZING AIR
BOMBARDMENT BY THE U.S. EIGHTH
AND NINTH AIR FORCES AND THE ROYAL
AIR FORCE, THE U.S. FIRST ARMY BROKE
OUT OF THE BEACHHEAD WEST OF ST.
LO. ON 1 AUGUST IT WAS JOINED BY
THE U.S. THIRD ARMY. TOGETHER THEY
REPULSED A POWERFUL COUNTERAT-
TACK TOWARDS AVRANCHES. CRUSHED
BETWEEN THE AMERICANS ON THE
SOUTH AND WEST AND THE BRITISH ON
THE NORTH, AND ATTACKED CONTIN-
UOUSLY BY THE U.S. AND BRITISH AIR
FORCES, THE ENEMY RETREATED ACROSS
THE SEINE.

SUSTAINED BY THE HERCULEAN
ACHIEVEMENTS OF ARMY AND NAVY
SUPPLY PERSONNEL, THE ALLIED
GROUND AND AIR FORCES PURSUED VIG-
OROUSLY. BY MID-SEPTEMBER THE U.S.

NINTH ARMY HAD LIBERATED BREST;
THE FIRST ARMY HAD SWEPT THROUGH
FRANCE, BELGIUM AND LUXEMBOURG
AND WAS STANDING ON THE THRESH-
OLD OF GERMANY; THE THIRD ARMY
HAD REACHED THE MOSELLE AND HAD
JOINED FORCES WITH THE U.S. SEV-
ENTH AND FRENCH FIRST ARMIES
ADVANCING NORTHWARD FROM THE
MEDITERRANEAN. ON THE LEFT FLANK,
BRITISH AND CANADIAN TROOPS HAD
ENTERED THE NETHERLANDS. ON 17
SEPTEMBER THE IX TROOP CARRIER
COMMAND AND THE ROYAL AIR FORCE
DROPPED THREE AIRBORNE DIVISIONS IN
THE NIJMEGEN-ARNHEM AREA IN A
BOLD BUT UNSUCCESSFUL ATTEMPT TO
SEIZE THE CROSSINGS OF THE LOWER
RHINE.

PROGRESS DURING THE NEXT THREE
MONTHS WAS SLOW, THE FIGHTING BIT-
TER AS OPPOSITION STIFFENED. THE
OPENING OF THE PORT OF ANTWERP ON
28 NOVEMBER MATERIALLY EASED THE
LOGISTICAL BURDEN. THE FIRST AND
NINTH ARMIES BROKE THROUGH THE
SIEGFRIED LINE AND CAPTURED
AACHEN. METZ FELL AS THE THIRD
ARMY PUSHED TO THE SAAR. ON ITS
RIGHT, THE SEVENTH ARMY AIDED BY
THE FIRST TACTICAL AIR FORCE DROVE
TO THE RHINE AT STRASBOURG, WHILE
FRENCH TROOPS FREED MULHOUSE.
THEN, IN THE ARDENNES, ON 16
DECEMBER, THE ENEMY LAUNCHED
HIS FINAL MAJOR COUNTEROFFEN-
SIVE. PROMPT TACTICAL COUNTER-
MEASURES AND THE SUPERB FIGHT-
ING QUALITIES OF AMERICAN SOLDIERS
AND AIRMEN FINALLY HALTED THIS
DRIVE. A CONCURRENT OFFENSIVE
LAUNCHED BETWEEN SAARBRUCKEN
AND COLMAR MET THE SAME FATE.

DURING FEBRUARY AND MARCH THE
WEST BANK OF THE RHINE WAS
CLEARED IN A SERIES OF HIGHLY SUC-
CESSFUL OPERATIONS. ON 7 MARCH
AMERICAN FORCES SEIZED THE ONE RE-
MAINING UNDEMOLISHED BRIDGE AT
REMAGEN. A SURPRISE CROSSING WAS
EFFECTED AT OPPENHEIM ON 22
MARCH, THEN, IN THE NEXT TWO
DAYS ALLIED TROOPS SPEARHEADED BY

Side Panels to Wall Maps.

Combat Arms.   *Combat Arms.*   *Supply Services.*   *Supply Services.*

Jennewein Statue of "Youth," East End of Transverse Pathway

A MASSIVE AIRBORNE ATTACK, MADE THEIR MAJOR ASSAULT CROSSING NEAR WESEL. PUSHING RAPIDLY EASTWARD OUR ARMIES ENCIRCLED THE ENTIRE RUHR VALLEY IN A GIGANTIC DOUBLE ENVELOPMENT. WITH AIR AND GROUND FORCES OPERATING AS A TEAM, THE ALLIES SWEPT ACROSS GERMANY TO MEET THE ADVANCING TROOPS OF THE U.S.S.R. AT THE ELBE AND FORCE THE COMPLETE SURRENDER OF THE ENEMY ON 8 MAY 1945, 337 DAYS AFTER THE INITIAL LANDINGS IN FRANCE.

Ranged along each side of the map are six panels illustrating the combat arms; they are painted in black upon white Carrara marble, the background of each picture being cut back and gilded, recalling the golden finish of the ceiling. The subjects of these panels are (as one faces them) see page 9:

1. Heavy Bombers
1. Battlefield Communications
2. Naval Fire Support
3. Paratroopers
4. Battlefield First Aid
5. Armor in Action
6. Infantry Support Weapons
2. Antiaircraft Artillery
3. Medium Bombers
4. Field Artillery
5. Infantry in Action
6. Combat Engineer Bridging

The map on the opposite (east) wall portrays the Services of Supply of the European Theater of Operations. The English version of its descriptive text reads:

THE FIRST CONTINGENT OF AMERICAN TROOPS REACHED THE BRITISH ISLES ON 26 JANUARY 1942. THE SERVICES OF SUPPLY WAS PROMPTLY ORGANIZED TO PROVIDE FOR THE TRANSPORTATION, SHELTER, SUPPLY AND HOSPITALIZATION OF THEIR CONSTANTLY INCREASING NUMBERS. BY JUNE 1942 IT WAS

ACTIVELY FUNCTIONING — PREPARING AIRFIELDS, TRAINING CAMPS, PORTS AND DEPOTS, AS WELL AS RECEIVING, STORING AND DISTRIBUTING THE 16,-000,000 TONS OF CARGO WHICH REACHED THE UNITED KINGDOM FROM THE UNITED STATES PRIOR TO THE CROSS-CHANNEL ATTACK. IN NOVEMBER 1942 THE INVASION OF NORTH AFRICA DEFERRED FOR MANY MONTHS THE BUILD-UP FOR THE EUROPEAN ASSAULT. NEVERTHELESS, ON 6 JUNE 1944 WHEN THE ALLIES LANDED IN NORMANDY, THE SERVICES WERE READY FOR THIS SUPREME TEST.

INITIALLY SUPPLIES WERE LANDED OVER THE OPEN BEACHES, BUT NAVAL PERSONNEL PROMPTLY ESTABLISHED TEMPORARY ANCHORAGES AND TWO ARTIFICIAL HARBORS (KNOWN AS "MULBERRIES") BY SINKING SHIPS AND PRE-FABRICATED CONCRETE CAISSONS. THESE WERE OF PRICELESS AID IN THE UNLOADING OF TROOPS AND CARGO. IN SPITE OF THE LACK OF A MAJOR PORT, WHEN THE ADVANCE WAS RESUMED IN JULY ADEQUATE SUPPLIES HAD BEEN ASSEMBLED IN THE BEACHHEAD.

WHILE THE ALLIED ARMIES SWEPT FORWARD FROM NORMANDY, U.S. AND FRENCH TROOPS LANDED IN SOUTHERN FRANCE. AS THE DISTANCES FROM THE PORTS LENGTHENED, THE TRANSPORTATION PROBLEM BECAME ACUTE. NEVERTHELESS, THE SUPPLY ORGANIZATION FUNCTIONED MOST EFFECTIVELY, REPAIRING AND BUILDING ROADS AND RAILROADS, OPERATING HIGH-SPEED TRUCK CONVOYS SUCH AS THE "RED BALL EXPRESS," EXTENDING FUEL PIPELINES AND PROVIDING AIR LIFT.

THE ALLIED NAVIES PLAYED A VITAL ROLE BY SAFEGUARDING A CONTINUOUS FLOW OF TROOPS AND SUPPLIES ACROSS THE SEAS. THE LINE OF SUPPLY WAS DEVELOPED FIRST FROM THE ASSAULT BEACHES, THEN THROUGH CHERBOURG AND LE HAVRE. WHEN ANTWERP WAS OPENED IN LATE NOVEMBER THE MAIN LINES OF COMMUNICATION FOR THE 12TH AND 21ST ARMY GROUPS WERE SHIFTED TO THAT PORT. FROM THE SOUTH THE SUPPLY LINE FOR THE 6TH ARMY GROUP CAME UP THE RHONE VALLEY FROM MARSEILLE.

ON 21 MARCH 1945 ON THE EVE OF THE MAIN CROSSING OF THE RHINE THE U.S. COMMUNICATIONS ZONE, WHICH NOW CONTROLLED THE SUPPLY OF U.S. TROOPS, COMPRISED FIVE BASE SECTIONS, ONE INTERMEDIATE SECTION AND TWO ADVANCE SECTIONS. THESE PREPARED AND OPERATED THE FACILITIES AND INSTALLATIONS REQUIRED TO MAINTAIN AND REINFORCE OUR TROOPS ON THE CONTINENT AND IN THE UNITED KINGDOM. AFTER THE LANDINGS IN NORMANDY, THE BEACHES AND PORTS OPERATED BY AMERICAN FORCES IN FRANCE AND BELGIUM DISCHARGED OVER 15,300,000 TONS OF CARGO ORIGINATING IN THE UNITED STATES, THE UNITED KINGDOM AND THE MEDITERRANEAN AREA.

THE ADVANCE SECTIONS OPERATED IN DIRECT SUPPORT OF THE ARMIES, DRAWING SUPPLIES FROM THE BASE AND INTERMEDIATE SECTIONS. THESE SUPPLIES WERE FORWARDED TO THE COMBAT UNITS. AN EFFICIENT SYSTEM FOR THE HOSPITALIZATION AND EVACUATION OF THE SICK AND WOUNDED OPERATED CONTINUOUSLY. IN WORLD WAR II THE DECISIVE IMPORTANCE OF THE SUPPLY AND TECHNICAL SERVICES IN MODERN WARFARE WAS CLEARLY MANIFESTED.

This map also is embellished by 12 panels (see page 9) representing functions of the Services of Supply, viz:

1. Atlantic Supply Convoy	1. Ordnance Repair
2. Military Railroad Operations	2. Supply Depots
3. Rear Area Communications	3. Supply By Air
4. Port Operation	4. Military Chaplain
5. Military Police-Traffic Control	5. Airfield Construction
6. Engineer Heavy Bridge	6. Medical Corps

The maps were designed by Dean Cornwell of New York City from data

Ardennes American Cemetery and Memorial

prepared by The American Battle Monuments Commission. They were fabricated by the Pandolfini Company of Pietrasanta, Italy. The panels were both designed and executed by Dean Cornwell.

At the far (north) end of the building is the chapel. The west wall bears the dedication:

1941–1945 IN PROUD REMEMBRANCE OF THE ACHIEVEMENTS OF HER SONS AND IN HUMBLE TRIBUTE TO THEIR SACRIFICES THIS MEMORIAL HAS BEEN ERECTED BY THE UNITED STATES OF AMERICA.

Engraved on the opposite wall is this prayer abridged from that ascribed to Cardinal Newman:

O LORD SUPPORT US ALL THE DAY LONG UNTIL THE SHADOWS LENGTHEN AND OUR WORK IS DONE ☆ THEN IN THY MERCY GRANT US A SAFE LODGING AND A HOLY REST AND PEACE AT THE LAST.

Outlined in gilt metal against the white Carrara marble wall above the altar, and illuminated through the oculus in the ceiling is an angel, designed by Dean Cornwell and executed by Kersten-Leroy of Maastricht.

The altar also is of Carrara marble. On each side of the chapel is a United States flag and a bronze screen into which have been cast the insignia of the principal major units which operated in Northwest Europe; viz, Supreme Headquarters, Allied Expeditionary Force; U.S. Strategic Air Forces in Europe; European Theater of Operations; 12th Army Group; 6th Army Group; Eighth Air Force; First Army; Ninth Air Force; Third Army; Seventh Army; Ninth Army. The chapel chairs and prie-dieu are of ebonized birchwood, fabricated in Rome, Italy by A. Patriarca.

To the right and left of the chapel are stainless steel doors leading outside to the north end of the memorial podium.

On the north facade of the memorial the shoulder insignia of the major mil-itary units again appear; here they are of colored mosaic set in the Portland Whitbed stone and grouped around a classic helmet. Beneath them is the inscription:

TO THE SILENT HOST WHO ENDURED ALL AND GAVE ALL THAT MANKIND MIGHT LIVE IN FREEDOM AND IN PEACE.

THE NAMES OF THE MISSING

The names and particulars of 462 of our Missing are engraved in 12 large slabs of dark gray granite set slightly above the podium, 6 on each of the east and west sides of the memorial:

United States Army & Army Air Forces*	447
United States Navy	15

These men gave their lives in the service of their country, but their remains have not been recovered and identified. Their names include men from 45 different States as well as the District of Columbia. Above these names this in-inscription is engraved upon the sides of the memorial:

HERE ARE RECORDED THE NAMES OF AMERICANS WHO GAVE THEIR LIVES IN THE SERVICE OF THEIR COUNTRY AND WHO SLEEP IN UNKNOWN GRAVES ☆ 1941–1945

On the east side, this is added:

IN PROUD REMEMBRANCE OF THEIR VALOR

On the west side, this is added:

IN HUMBLE TRIBUTE TO THEIR SACRIFICE

The memorial podium is flanked by masses of rhododendrons bordered by dwarf roses and boxwood edging, and backed by clipped purple beech (*Fagus sylvatica purpurea*) hedges.

THE GRAVES AREA

From the base of the memorial podium

---

*It will be recalled that during World War II the Air Forces still formed part of the United States Army.

Visitors' Building

a flight of broad steps leads down to the graves area. Here are buried 5,319 of our military Dead; three-fifths of whom were airmen.

These Dead, who gave their lives in our country's service, came from almost every State in the Union as well as from the District of Columbia, Canada, Denmark, England, France, Germany, Ireland, Philippine Islands, and the British West Indies. Seven hundred seventy-one of the headstones mark the graves of 786 "Unknowns." Among the headstones also are those of 11 instances in which 2 brothers are buried side by side. There are also three cases in which two identified airmen are buried in single graves; the headstones in these cases are inscribed: HERE REST IN HONORED GLORY TWO COMRADES IN ARMS. Bronze plaques bearing their names and particulars are set in the ground before the headstones.

The reentrants of the huge cross formed by the headstone pattern are planted with groups of oak, beech, hornbeam and tulip trees, intended to extend the natural woodland enframement, and the entire burial area is surrounded on four sides by wide borders of shrub roses (Rosa rugosa).

At the east end of the central transverse path is a bronze figure symbolizing American youth, designed by C. Paul Jennewein and cast by Bruno Bearzi of Florence, Italy.

The burial area and its axial path gently slope down to the flagstaff and its platform at the north end of the cemetery. Groups of spruce (Ticea excelia) and caucasian fir (Abies Nordmanniana) form the background for this feature. A transverse path leads westward to the linden avenue which intersects the path at the head of the burial area.

Construction of the cemetery and memorial was completed in 1962.

Interior of Visitors' Room

Henri-Chapelle American Cemetery and Memorial

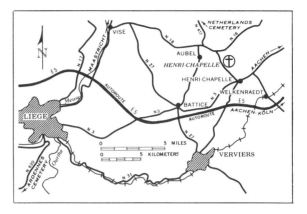

LOCATION

The Henri-Chapelle Cemetery and Memorial lies 2 miles northwest of the village of Henri-Chapelle which is on the main highway from Liege, Belgium to Aachen, Germany (18 miles/29 km from Liege or 10 miles/16 km from Aachen). It can be reached by train from Paris (Gare du Nord — 5½ hours), from Brussels (2 hours) and Liege, Belgium, or from Germany via Aachen, to Welkenraedt, Belgium, where taxicab service to the cemetery, 4½ miles distant, is available. To reach the cemetery by automobile, follow N-3 from Liege or Aachen to the road fork in Henri-Chapelle, thence northwest on N-18 to the cemetery; or, from Margraten follow Aachen highway east approximately 1 mile/1.6 km, then turn right on Aubel Road 7.5 miles/12 km to Hagelstein, thence left on N-18 to the cemetery or by Autoroute E-5, Liege or Aachen to the Battice exit and then turn right on N-3 to Henri-Chapelle.

HOURS

The cemetery is open daily to the public as shown below:

SUMMER (16 March–30 September)
9:00 a.m.–6:00 p.m. — weekdays
10:00 a.m.–6:00 p.m. — Saturdays, Sundays and holidays

WINTER (1 October–15 March)
9:00 a.m.–5:00 p.m. — weekdays
10:00 a.m.–5:00 p.m. — Saturdays, Sundays and holidays

Entrance Pylons

The Guardian Angel

View of memorial with cemetery in the distance

Aerial View of Cemetery

When the cemetery is open to the public, a staff member is on duty in the Visitors' Room to answer questions and escort relatives to grave and memorial sites (except between noon and 3:00 p.m. on weekends and holidays).

HISTORY

Following the successful landings on the beaches of Normandy on 6 June 1944, the Allies slowly but relentlessly fought their way inland to expand the beachhead. Then on 25 July, after a paralyzing air bombardment, the U.S. First Army launched the attack southward to break out. Joining the assault a few days later, the U.S. Third Army on the right flank thrust southward along the coast while the British and Canadians advanced on the left flank.

When the breakout occurred, Allied planners had expected the enemy to withdraw and re-establish a defense at the line of the Seine River to the northeast. Instead, the enemy

launched a powerful counterattack in an attempt to split the Allied forces and isolate the U.S. Third Army. Resisting vigorously, Allied ground and air forces not only stopped the attacking enemy but threatened him with complete encirclement. Thoroughly defeated after suffering great losses, the enemy beat a hasty retreat across the Seine River.

Rapid exploitation of this victory resulted in swift Allied advances far exceeding expectations. On the left flank, the Canadian First Army drove along the coast reaching the Netherlands frontier and liberating Ostend and Bruges early in September, while the British Second Army advanced rapidly through central Belgium liberating Brussels on 3 September and Antwerp the following day. The British Second Army then moved to join with the Canadian First Army astride the Netherlands frontier.

In the center of the advance, the U.S. First Army freed Liege in eastern Belgium on 8 September and continued northeastward toward the Ger-

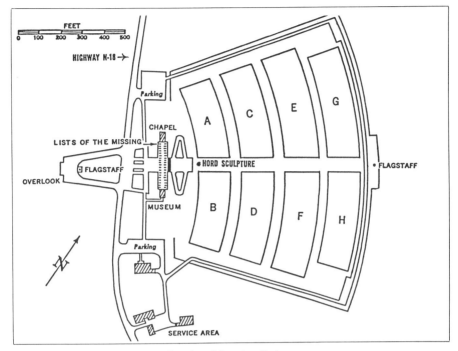

Location of Cemetery Features

man city of Aachen, while at the same time liberating Luxembourg. On the right, the U.S. Third Army swept across France to reach the Moselle River and make contact with the troops of the U.S. Seventh Army advancing from the beaches of southern France, where they had landed on 15 August.

Patrols of the U.S. First Army crossed the German frontier in the Ardennes area on 11 September. The next day, elements of the U.S. First Army crossed the frontier near Aachen and moved eastward toward the Siegfried Line, where strong resistance was encountered immediately. Almost simultaneously, progress slowed all along the advancing Allied line as opposition stiffened. The retreating enemy had at last stabilized its line of defense.

The Siegfried Line formed the core of resistance at the center of the enemy defenses. To the south in front of the U.S. Third and Seventh Armies,

and the French First Army which extended Allied lines to the Swiss border, resistance was organized around heavily fortified cities forming strongpoints in front of the Siegfried Line. In the north, the defenders utilized to advantage against the British and Canadians the barriers formed by the extensive canal and river systems. On 17 September, a valiant combined airborne–ground assault in the Netherlands intended to outflank the north end of the enemy line, achieved only partial success as it failed to seize crossings of the lower Rhine.

For the next three months, intensive fighting produced only limited gains against fierce opposition. During this period, the principal Allied offensive effort was concentrated in the center of the enemy line where some of the most bitter fighting of the war occurred in the battle to capture the city of Aachen, the first large German city to be captured by the Allies, and penetrate the Siegfried Line. Finally, encircled in mid-October after savage house-to-house fighting, Aachen fell on 31 October. Meanwhile, the U.S. Ninth Army organized at Brest in Brittany, moved into the lines on the right flank of the U.S. First Army. To the south, the U.S. Third and Seventh Armies continued to advance slowly, as the U.S. Seventh Army forced the enemy back into the Vosges Mountains.

On 4 November, the U.S. First Army began the difficult struggle through the dense woods of the Hurtgen Forest. Shortly thereafter, the U.S. Ninth Army was shifted to the U.S. First Army's left flank. Then, on 16 November preceded by a massive air bombardment, the two armies attacked together opening a wide gap in the Siegfried Line. By 1 December, the Roer River line was reached. On the right, the city of Metz was captured by the U.S. Third Army on 22 November, although the last fort defending that city did not surrender until 13 December. The greatest territorial gains, however, came in the south where the U.S. Seventh Army penetrated the Vosges Mountains to liberate the city of Strasbourg on 23 November as French troops on the extreme right flank liberated Mulhouse.

The Schelde estuary was finally cleared of the enemy by the Canadian First Army and the great port city of Antwerp became available on 28 November to supply the Allied armies.

Suddenly on 16 December 1944, the Allied advance was interrupted when the enemy launched in the Ardennes its final major counteroffensive of the war, with a second major assault on New Year's Eve in Alsace to the south. After furious fighting in bitterly cold weather these last enemy onslaughts were halted and the lost ground regained. The Allies then developed their plan for final victory.

The first step of the plan was to clear all enemy from west of the Rhine; the subsequent step was to invade Germany itself. During February and March, with the aid and assistance of fighters and medium bombers, the first step was successfully completed and heavy losses were inflicted on the enemy. Because of those losses, the subsequent crossing of the Rhine did not meet with the violent opposition that had been anticipated. Working together, Allied ground and air forces swept victoriously across Germany, bringing the war in Europe to a conclusion on 8 May 1945.

SITE

The cemetery, 57 acres in area, lies on the crest of a ridge affording an excellent view to the east and west. The memorial is visible from Highway N-3 several miles away. Highway N-18 separates the overlook to the northwest from the rest of the cemetery.

The site was liberated on 12 September 1944 by troops of the U.S. 1st Infantry Division. A temporary cemetery was established on 28 September 1944 two or three hundred yards to the north of the present site which was selected because of its more attractive setting. Here rest 7,989 of our military Dead, most of whom gave their lives in the repulse of the German counteroffensive in the Ardennes or during the advance into, and across, Germany during the fall and winter of 1944 and the spring of 1945. Others were lost in air operations over the region. The cemetery and memorial were completed in 1960.

ARCHITECTS

Architects for the cemetery and memorial were Holabird, Root and Burgee of Chicago, Illinois. The landscape architect was Franz Lipp of Chicago.

GENERAL LAYOUT

To the west of Highway N-18 where it crosses the reservation is the overlook

The Colonnade — Names of the Missing

The Colonnade Inscription

area with its flagstaff. From the west end of this area a wide view is afforded over the broad valley of the Berwinne streamlet (which lies in the sector of advance of the U.S. 1st Infantry Division) and the ridges beyond. The roadway on the overlook is lined with linden trees.

East of the highway is the memorial; there are parking areas at both the north and south ends. Beyond the memorial is the graves area. Located in the south end of the memorial is the Visitors' Room and Museum.

THE MEMORIAL

The memorial consists of the chapel (north end) and the combined Visitors' and Museum building (south end) connected by a colonnade of 12 pairs of rectangular pylons. East of the colonnade is a wide terrace with ramps leading down to the graves area. The exterior of the memorial is of Massangis limestone from the Cote d'Or region of France. The colonnade, chapel and museum room are paved with gray St. Gothard granite from Switzerland.

THE COLONNADE

On the 48 faces of the 24 pylons and the 4 faces of the engaged pylons at the ends of the colonnade are engraved the seals of the wartime 48 States, 3 territories and the District of Columbia. The obverse of the Great Seal of the United States, in bronze, is set into the floor at the intersection of the axes. The names and particulars of 450 of the Missing of the United States Army and Army Air Forces* are engraved on the 48 faces of the columns. The engaged end pylons bear this inscription in English, French and Flemish:

HERE ARE RECORDED THE NAMES OF AMERICANS WHO GAVE THEIR LIVES IN THE SERVICE OF THEIR COUNTRY AND WHO SLEEP IN UNKNOWN GRAVES.

---

*It will be recalled that during World War II the Air Forces still formed part of the United States Army.

Interior of Chapel

Map of Military Operations in Northwestern Europe

These Dead, who gave their lives in our country's service, came from 42 States, the District of Columbia and England.

In the soffit of the colonnade are 13 stars of golden glass mosaic.

THE CHAPEL

At the entrance to the chapel, on the east side, is the dedicatory inscription:

1941–1945 ☆ ☆ IN PROUD REMEMBRANCE OF THE ACHIEVEMENTS OF HER SONS AND IN HUMBLE TRIBUTE TO THEIR SACRIFICES THIS MEMORIAL HAS BEEN ERECTED BY THE UNITED STATES OF AMERICA.

The doors of the chapel are bronze with polished panels.

The interior is rectangular in shape and of somewhat austere design. The altar of Belgian blue and French vert d'Issorie marble bears the inscription (from St. John X, 28):

I GIVE UNTO THEM ETERNAL LIFE AND THEY SHALL NEVER PERISH.

The wall behind the altar is of Belgian blue marble with white veinings. The south wall is of French green d'Issorie marble. Hung along the west wall are flags of the Air Force, Armor, Christian Chapel, Jewish Chapel, Engineers, Field Artillery, Infantry and Navy Infantry Battalion. Engraved on the same wall beneath the flags is this inscription from Cardinal Newman's prayer:

O LORD SUPPORT US ALL THE DAY LONG UNTIL THE SHADOWS LENGTHEN AND OUR WORK IS DONE. THEN IN THY MERCY GRANT US A SAFE LODGING AND A HOLY REST AND PEACE AT THE LAST.

The pews are of walnut and were fabricated in Holland. The cross and the pews were intentionally designed to be off-center (with off-center lighting) thus balancing each other.

THE MUSEUM ROOM

At the opposite (south) end of the colonnade is the combined Museum and Visitors' Room; the doors, similar to those of the chapel, are of dark bronze with polished panels inset. Built into the west interior wall, of English Portland Whitbed stone, is a map portraying the military operations in northwestern Europe from the landings in Normandy until the end of the war. This map is of Swedish black granite; the geographical and military data are indicated by means of inlaid mosaic, engraved and colored chases, anodyzed aluminum, bronze, etc. Amplifying the map are inscriptions in English, French and Flemish, of which this is the English version:

ON 6 JUNE 1944, PRECEDED BY AIRBORNE UNITS AND COVERED BY NAVAL AND AIR BOMBARDMENT, UNITED STATES AND BRITISH COMMONWEALTH FORCES LANDED ON THE COAST OF NORMANDY. PUSHING SOUTHWARD THEY ESTABLISHED A BEACHHEAD SOME 20 MILES IN DEPTH. ON 25 JULY, IN THE WAKE OF A PARALYZING AIR BOMBARDMENT BY THE U.S. EIGHTH AND NINTH AIR FORCES AND THE ROYAL AIR FORCE, THE U.S. FIRST ARMY BROKE OUT OF THE BEACHHEAD WEST OF ST. LO. ON 1 AUGUST IT WAS JOINED BY THE U.S. THIRD ARMY. TOGETHER THEY REPULSED A POWERFUL COUNTERATTACK TOWARDS AVRANCHES. CRUSHED BETWEEN THE AMERICANS ON THE SOUTH AND WEST AND THE BRITISH ON THE NORTH, AND ATTACKED CONTINUOUSLY BY THE U.S. AND BRITISH AIR FORCES THE ENEMY RETREATED ACROSS THE SEINE.

SUSTAINED BY THE HERCULEAN ACHIEVEMENTS OF ARMY AND NAVY SUPPLY PERSONNEL, THE ALLIED GROUND AND AIR FORCES PURSUED VIGOROUSLY. BY MID-SEPTEMBER THE U.S. NINTH ARMY HAD LIBERATED BREST. THE FIRST ARMY HAD SWEPT THROUGH FRANCE, BELGIUM, AND LUXEMBOURG AND WAS STANDING ON THE THRESHOLD OF GERMANY; THE

Combined Museum and Visitors' Area

THIRD ARMY HAD REACHED THE MO-
SELLE AND HAD JOINED FORCES WITH
THE U.S. SEVENTH AND FRENCH FIRST
ARMIES ADVANCING NORTHWARD
FROM THE MEDITERRANEAN. ON THE
LEFT FLANK, BRITISH AND CANADIAN
TROOPS HAD ENTERED THE NETHER-
LANDS. ON 17 SEPTEMBER THE IX TROOP
CARRIER COMMAND AND THE ROYAL
AIR FORCE DROPPED THREE AIRBORNE
DIVISIONS IN THE EINDHOVEN-ARNHEM
AREA IN A BOLD BUT UNSUCCESSFUL AT-
TEMPT TO SEIZE THE CROSSINGS OF THE
LOWER RHINE.

PROGRESS DURING THE NEXT THREE
MONTHS WAS SLOW, THE FIGHTING
BITTER AS OPPOSITION STIFFENED. THE
OPENING OF THE PORT OF ANTWERP ON
28 NOVEMBER MATERIALLY EASED THE
LOGISTICAL BURDEN. THE FIRST AND
NINTH ARMIES BROKE THROUGH THE
SIEGFRIED LINE AND CAPTURED
AACHEN. METZ FELL AS THE THIRD
ARMY PUSHED TO THE SAAR. ON ITS
RIGHT, THE SEVENTH ARMY AIDED BY
THE FIRST TACTICAL AIR FORCE DROVE
TO THE RHINE AT STRASBOURG, WHILE
FRENCH TROOPS FREED MULHOUSE.

THEN, IN THE ARDENNES, ON 16 DECEM-
BER, THE ENEMY LAUNCHED HIS FINAL
MAJOR COUNTEROFFENSIVE. PROMPT
TACTICAL COUNTERMEASURES AND
THE SUPERB FIGHTING QUALITIES OF
AMERICAN SOLDIERS AND AIRMEN FI-
NALLY HALTED THIS DRIVE. A CON-
CURRENT OFFENSIVE LAUNCHED BE-
TWEEN SAARBRUCKEN AND COLMAR
MET THE SAME FATE.

DURING FEBRUARY AND MARCH THE
WEST BANK OF THE RHINE WAS
CLEARED IN A SERIES OF HIGHLY SUC-
CESSFUL OPERATIONS. ON 7 MARCH
AMERICAN FORCES SEIZED THE ONE RE-
MAINING UNDEMOLISHED BRIDGE AT
REMAGEN. A SURPRISE CROSSING WAS
EFFECTED AT OPPENHEIM ON 22 MARCH.
THEN, IN THE NEXT TWO DAYS ALLIED
TROOPS SPEARHEADED BY A MASSIVE
AIRBORNE ATTACK MADE THEIR MAJOR
ASSAULT CROSSING NEAR WESEL. PUSH-
ING RAPIDLY EASTWARD U.S. FORCES
ENCIRCLED THE ENTIRE RUHR VALLEY IN
A GIGANTIC DOUBLE ENVELOPMENT.
WITH AIR AND GROUND FORCES OPER-
ATING AS A TEAM, THE ALLIES SWEPT
ACROSS GERMANY TO MEET THE

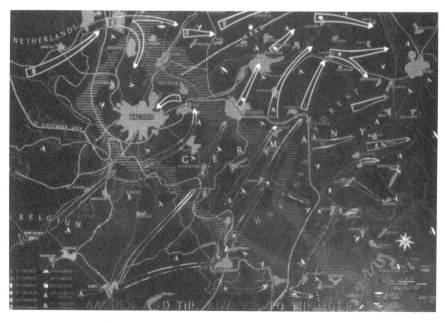

Operations Map "Aachen and the Advance to the Roer"

ADVANCING TROOPS OF THE U.S.S.R. AT THE ELBE AND FORCE THE COMPLETE SURRENDER OF THE ENEMY ON 8 MAY 1945, 337 DAYS AFTER THE INITIAL LANDINGS IN FRANCE.

On the south wall is a somewhat smaller map, of materials similar to the other, entitled "Aachen and the Advance to the Roer"; it illustrates the military operations in this region. Accompanying this map is an inscribed text, also in three languages, the English version reading as follows:

ON 12 SEPTEMBER 1944 THE U.S. FIRST ARMY CROSSED THE GERMAN FRONTIER NEAR AACHEN. HERE THE BROAD, SWEEPING ADVANCE ACROSS FRANCE AND BELGIUM WAS SLOWED BY THE STRONGLY FORTIFIED SIEGFRIED LINE. STRUGGLING FORWARD AGAINST INCREASING RESISTANCE, INFANTRY AND ARMORED FORCES BROKE THROUGH TO STOLBERG, EAST OF AACHEN. PROGRESS WAS SLOW, THE FIGHTING OBSTINATE, AS OUR TROOPS FORCED THEIR WAY INTO HURTGEN FOREST TO SCHEVENHUTTE AND BEYOND LAMMERSDORF, THREATENING THE ROER RIVER DAMS.

ON 2 OCTOBER THE FIRST ARMY LAUNCHED AN ATTACK NORTH OF AACHEN. AFTER SIX DAYS OF HEAVY FIGHTING, AIDED BY FIGHTERS AND MEDIUM BOMBERS OF THE NINTH AIR FORCE, OUR GROUND FORCES HAD PUSHED THROUGH THE SIEGFRIED LINE AND TURNED SOUTHWARD TOWARDS WURSELEN. UNITS TO THE EAST THEN JOINED THE ASSAULT. WHEN THE GARRISON IN AACHEN REFUSED A SURRENDER ULTIMATUM, U.S. FORCES LAUNCHED A MASSIVE AIR AND ARTILLERY BOMBARDMENT AGAINST THEM; FURIOUS FIGHTING MARKED THE ENEMY'S DETERMINED EFFORT TO REINFORCE THE AREA. BY 16 OCTOBER THE CITY HAD BEEN ENCIRCLED; SUCCESSIVE ATTEMPTS TO RELIEVE THE GARRISON WERE FIRMLY REPULSED. ON 21 OCTOBER AACHEN SURRENDERED, THE FIRST LARGE GERMAN CITY TO FALL INTO ALLIED HANDS.

THE U.S. NINTH ARMY THEN MOVED INTO POSITION ON THE LEFT OF THE FIRST ARMY. ON 16 NOVEMBER, FOLLOWING A DEVASTATING BOMBING BY THE EIGHTH AND NINTH AIR FORCES, OUR ARMIES LAUNCHED AN OFFENSIVE TOWARDS THE ROER. THE ATTACK ADVANCED SLOWLY EASTWARD AGAINST DETERMINED RESISTANCE AND FURIOUS COUNTERATTACKS. THE NATURAL BARRIER OF THE HURTGEN FOREST, NOW GREATLY STRENGTHENED BY INGENIOUS FORTIFICATIONS, PRESENTED A SERIOUS DELAYING OBSTACLE.

NOT IN YEARS HAD EUROPEAN WEATHER BEEN SO UNFAVORABLE FOR MILITARY OPERATIONS BUT BY 15 DECEMBER FIRST ARMY UNITS HAD REACHED THE ROER FROM DUREN NORTHWARD. ATTACKS THROUGH THE HURTGEN FOREST WERE STILL IN PROGRESS WHEN, IN THE ARDENNES, ON 16 DECEMBER, THE ENEMY LOOSED HIS LAST GREAT COUNTEROFFENSIVE OF THE WAR. THE FIRST ARMY MOVED INSTANTLY TO MEET THE THREAT, SUSPENDING OFFENSIVE ACTION IN THE HURTGEN FOREST AREA UNTIL AFTER THE VICTORIOUS CONCLUSION OF THE ARDENNES CAMPAIGN ON 25 JANUARY 1945.

The maps were designed by Sante Graziani of Worcester, Massachusetts, from information furnished by the American Battle Monuments Commission. They were fabricated by Enrico Pandolfini of Pietrasanta, Italy. Under the map of military operations in Northwestern Europe is a stand of white Carrara marble bearing the two sets of key maps, "The War Against Germany" and "The War Against Japan."

THE GRAVES AREA

East of the colonnade a terrace affords a prospect over the burial area. Immediately in front is the bronze statue of the Archangel bestowing the laurel branch upon the heroic Dead for whom he makes special commendation to the Almighty. This was designed by Donal Hord of San Diego, California, and cast by Battaglia of Milan, Italy.

The graves area is divided into 8 plots, lettered "A" to "H"; these are separated by the broad axial mall and by longitudinal grass paths. The 7,989 headstones are arranged in broad sweeping curves upon the gently sloping lawn. These Dead came from 49 States, and from the District of Columbia, Panama and England. Among the graves are 33 instances in which 2 brothers rest side by side, and one instance of 3 brothers; also there are headstones marking the tombs of 94 Unknowns.

The central mall terminates in a wall-enclosed flagpole plaza, backed by a copse of oak and spruce trees. On the wall is the inscription: IN HONORED MEMORY OF THOSE WHO GAVE THEIR LIVES FOR THEIR COUNTRY.

PLANTINGS

The memorial is set within a framework of Box hedges *(Buxus sempervirens)*, which has been extended to form a border to the paths which lead to the graves area.

In the lawns at each end of the memorial are groups of weeping willows *(Salix babylonia)*; flanking the memorial north and south of the grass terrace on which it stands, are groups of Serbian Spruce *(Picea Omorika)* and Norway Spruce *(Picea excelsa)* mixed with Hawthorns *(Crataegus oxyacantha)*.

Along the paved approach to the memorial are large beds of pink Polyantha roses and adjoining the colonnade itself are to be found other massifs of white roses.

View of the Graves Area

Within the graves areas Birch *(Betula alba and B. nigra)*, Hornbeam *(Carpinus betulus)*, and Yew *(Taxus baccata)* have been planted and free growing Box has been massed in groups against the surrounding walls. Beyond the wall also are groups of Rhododendron ponticum and shrubby Chestnut *(Aesculus parviflora)* and a number of Norway Spruce.

VISITORS' ROOM

The Visitors' Room is in the south end of the memorial and can be reached either from the colonnade or from the south parking area and a door at the south end of the memorial. It contains the superintendent's office, restroom facilities and a comfortably furnished area where visitors may rest, obtain information, sign the register and pause to refresh themselves. Whenever the cemetery is open to the public, a staff member is available to provide information on specific burial and memorialization locations in any of the Commission's cemeteries, accommodations in the vicinity, best means and routes of travel, local history and other items that may be of interest.

WORLD WAR II
CEMETERIES AND MEMORIALS:

FRANCE

Brittany American Cemetery and Memorial

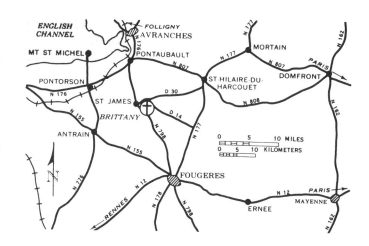

LOCATION

The Brittany American Cemetery and Memorial is situated about one mile southeast of the village of St. James, Manche, France on highway N-798. St. James lies 12 miles/19 kilometers south of Avranches, 9 miles/15 kilometers southeast of Pontorson, 15 miles/25 kilometers southeast of Mont St. Michel and 14 miles/22 kilometers north of Fougeres. It may be reached by automobile from Paris (201 miles/324 kilometers) in about 5½ hours via highway N-12 to Fougeres and thence north on N-798 to St. James.

Rail service to St. James is available from Gare Montparnasse (Gare du Maine) in Paris via Avranches or Pontorson with a change of trains at Folligny. The trip by rail also takes approximately 5½ hours. Taxi service to the cemetery is available from the railroad stations in Avranches, Pontorson, and St. James. Bus ser-

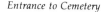

Entrance to Cemetery

Chancel in West End of Chapel

Aerial View of Cemetery

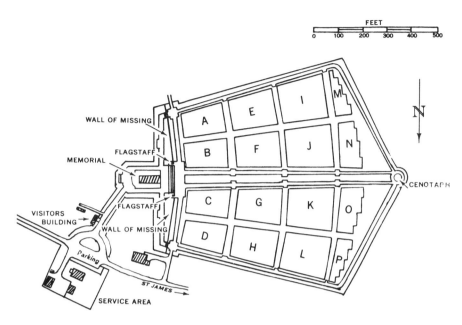

Location of Cemetery Features

vice is available from Pontorson to St. James.

Avranches, Pontorson, Mont St. Michel, and Fourgeres have adequate hotel accommodations; those in the village of St. James are somewhat austere.

HOURS

The cemetery is open daily to the public as follows:

SUMMER (16 March –30 September)
9:00 a.m.–6:00 p.m. — weekdays
10:00 a.m.–6:00 p.m. — Saturdays, Sundays, and Holidays
WINTER (1 October –15 March)
9:00 a.m.–5:00 p.m. — weekdays
10:00 a.m.–5:00 p.m. — Saturdays, Sundays, and Holidays

During weekdays, a staff member is on duty in the Visitors' Building to answer questions, and to escort relatives to grave or memorial sites. On weekends and holidays, the Visitors' Building is open and staffed except from noon to 3:00 p.m.

HISTORY

Ground combat in northwestern France commenced with the Allied landings on the beaches of Normandy, 6 June 1944. During the early morning hours of darkness, three airborne divisions (the British 6th and the U.S. 82nd and 101st) were dropped in the rear of the beach areas to cover deployment of the seaborne assault forces. Simultaneously, Allied naval forces swept the English Channel of mines and preceded the assault vessels to the landing areas. At 6:30 a.m., under the cover of intense naval and air bombardment, six U.S., British and Canadian divisions began landing on Utah, Omaha, Gold, Juno and Sword beaches in the greatest amphibious assault of recorded history.

The U.S. 4th Division pushed rapidly inland from Utah Beach to join the previously dropped airborne divisions. Its early success and light casualties contrasted sharply with those of the U.S. 1st and 29th

Divisions on Omaha Beach to the east, where the enemy resisted with every device and weapon at his disposal. The configuration of Omaha Beach alone presented a major obstacle. Instead of sloping gently from the high ground to its rear, the beach area terminated in precipitous steep sandy bluffs. U.S. Troops had to cross an open area varying in width from a few yards at each end to about 200 yards in the center, and then attack up the steep bluffs to the plateau on which the Normandy American Cemetery now stands. The only concealment available was patches of tall marsh grass. Fighting was bitter and casualties heavy. Nevertheless, before D-Day was over, the U.S. 1st Division had taken the high ground to its front. To the east on Gold, Juno and Sword landing beaches, the British and Canadian divisions forged steadily ahead. Under the cover of continuous naval gunfire and air support, the landings' first objective, to link together the individual beachheads, was accomplished within a week. During the same period, temporary anchorages and artificial harbors were created off the beachhead area by sinking ships and prefabricated concrete caissons to the channel floor, to facilitate the unloading of troops and supplies. As a result, the Allies were able to reinforce and increase the size and strength of their Armies rapidly. The second objective of the landings was to clear the Cotentin Peninsula with its port of Cherbourg and capture Caen and St. Lô. On 26 June, American troops freed Cherbourg; 13 days later on 9 July British and Canadian troops fought their way into Caen; and on 18 July 1944 Americans took St. Lô, accomplishing the second objective. The final objective was to break through the ring of defenses that the enemy had established around the beaches. The stage was set for the breakout with a paralyzing air bombardment on 25 July by the U.S. Eighth and Ninth Air Forces and the Royal Air Force along a five mile front west of St. Lô. Aided by British forces pinning down the enemy in the eastern portion of the beach area toward Caen, the U.S. First Army stormed out of the beachhead liberating Coutances three days later. Within a week, the newly activated U.S. Third Army had cleared Avranches and was advancing toward Paris on a broad front with the First Army. The two armies fanned out westward toward Brest, southward toward the Loire, and eastward toward the Seine. On 7 August 1944, one week after the opening of the Avranches gap, a powerful counterattack was launched by the enemy, in an attempt to cut the columns of the advancing U.S. First and Third Armies. After initial success in the region of Mortain, the U.S. First Army was able to stem the counterattack and push back enemy forces.

In mid-August, enemy forces were threatened with encirclement by the U.S. Third Army which had turned northward from Le Mans, to meet the Canadian Army advancing southward from its beachhead. Despite desperate resistance by the enemy to prevent encirclement, the two Allied armies met at Chambois on 21 August. Enemy forces had the choice of remaining in the Falaise pocket or fleeing toward the Seine River in disorder. In a matter of days, U.S. Third Army troops were in the outskirts of Paris and it was liberated on 25 August 1944.

While these actions were taking place, the newly-formed Ninth U.S. Army relieved the Third Army units that had remained in Brittany and took over their mission of containing the strong enemy garrisons which still held out there. Although stubbornly contested, St. Malo fell to U.S. forces on 1 September and Brest on 18 September 1944. At this

Central Mall and Graves Area

time, most of the U.S. Ninth Army was ordered to the German border where enemy resistance was stiffening. Some Ninth Army units remained to contain the enemy garrisons at Lorient and St. Nazaire which did not surrender until 10 and 11 May 1945, respectively.

SITE

The Brittany American Cemetery, 28 acres in extent, lies among the hedgerows in rolling farm country near the border between the Brittany and Normandy regions of France. It is one of fourteen permanent American World War II military cemetery memorials erected by the American Battle Monuments Commission on foreign soil. The site was liberated on 2 August 1944 by the 8th Infantry Division; a temporary military cemetery was established on it three days later. Subsequently, the site

was selected to be one of fourteen permanent American World War II military cemeteries on foreign soil. After the war, when the temporary cemeteries were being disestablished by the American Graves Registration Service, the remains of American military Dead whose next of kin had requested interment on foreign soil were moved from the temporary cemeteries to one of the permanent cemetery sites, usually the one closest to the temporary location. The 4,410 American military Dead buried in the Brittany American Cemetery lost their lives in the area of northwestern France extending from the beachhead westward to Brest and eastward to the Seine and represent 43 percent of the burials originally made in the region. They were interred there by the American Graves Registration Service in the distinctive grave patterns proposed by the cemetery's architect and ap-

Cenotaph at East End of Mall

proved by this Commission. Most of them died in the fighting in and around St. Lô.

The design and construction of all cemetery facilities in the permanent World War I and II cemeteries, were the responsibility of the American Battle Monuments Commission, i.e., the memorial, chapel, visitors' building, superintendent's quarters, service facilities and paths, roads and walls. The Commission was also responsible for the sculpture, landscaping and other improvements. Construction of the permanent cemetery memorial at Brittany was completed in 1956.

ARCHITECTS

Architect for the cemetery and its memorial was William T. Aldrich of Boston, Massachusetts. The landscape architects were Shurcliff and Shurcliff, also of Boston.

GENERAL LAYOUT

The main entrance of the cemetery is located on the south side of Highway N-798 across from the service area and the superintendent's quarters. A short semi-circular driveway flanked by a low granite wall leads from the highway to the wrought iron main entrance gate with its piers of gray granite. The driveway contains space for limited visitor parking and there is a small parking area across the highway.

Immediately inside the entrance gate, on the left, is the Visitors' Building. A surfaced path, gently curving to the right, leads past the Visitors' Building to the rear of the memorial chapel. In front of it is a terrace flanked by two flag poles. Emanating from each side of the terrace, inset from the base of the flag poles and facing the graves area, is a low stone wall with tablets in which are engraved the names of the servicemen Missing in Action in the region.

Steps lead down from the terrace in front of the chapel to the central mall lined with bottom boxwoods and European chestnut trees, which bisects the graves area into two groups of eight fanshaped plots. At the far (east) end of the mall is a rectangular stone cenotaph.

Inside the main entrance along the perimeter wall to the right is the assistant superintendent's quarters.

THE MEMORIAL

The Memorial Chapel consists of an antechamber and tower, museum room and chancel. Typical of the ecclesiastical architecture of the region, it is Romanesque in design.

THE EXTERIOR

The exterior of the memorial is constructed of local La Pyrie granite. At its east end is a sculpture group, "Youth Triumphing Over Evil," designed by Lee Lawrie of Easton, MD and executed in Chauvigny limestone from the Poitiers region by Jean Juge of Paris. Carved in its granite base is the inscription: I HAVE FOUGHT A GOOD FIGHT ☆ I HAVE FINISHED MY COURSE ☆ I HAVE KEPT THE FAITH (2 Timothy IV, 7).

Over the entrance door is a sculpture group, also designed by Lee Lawrie and executed by Jean Juge, consisting of an eagle, shield, stars, laurel and arrows representing the Great Seal of the United States; the shield is flanked by two floating angels representing victory. The one to the left of the observer, wearing the Columbian cap, is in mourning. She holds in her right hand the laurel of the brave, and in her left hand the palm of sacrifice. The figure to the right is a triumphant Victory, clothed in mail and wearing a helmet. Her right hand holds a sword, her left hand a trumpet. Below the sculpture over the tympanum is the inscription: IN MEMORY OF THE VALOR AND THE SACRIFICES WHICH CONSECRATE THIS SOIL.

ANTECHAMBER

Inside the main entrance door to the right of the antechamber is a small room with a stained-glass window in the north wall containing the figure of St. James of Compostello. On the east wall is engraved the dedicatory inscription in French and English, of which this is the English version:

1941—1945 ☆ IN PROUD REMEMBRANCE OF THE ACHIEVEMENTS OF HER SONS AND IN HUMBLE TRIBUTE TO THEIR SACRIFICES THIS MEMORIAL HAS BEEN ERECTED BY THE UNITED STATES OF AMERICA.

On the opposite wall is this prayer:

O GOD WHO ART THE AUTHOR OF PEACE AND LOVER OF CONCORD, DEFEND US THY HUMBLE SERVANTS IN ALL ASSAULTS OF OUR ENEMIES, THAT WE SURELY TRUSTING IN THY DEFENSE MAY NOT FEAR THE POWER OF ANY ADVERSARIES.

In the tympanum above the main entrance door is a stained-glass window containing the emblem of SHAEF — the Supreme Headquarters Allied Expeditionary Force.

To the left of the antechamber is the stairway leading to the tower. The tower has an overall height of 99 feet/30.2 meters. The lookout platform, 63 feet/19.2 meters above the ground, is reached from the antechamber by a stairway of 98 steps and landings. From the platform Mont St. Michel, 15 miles/24 kilometers to the northwest, is visible on clear days. The tower also affords an impressive view of the stately pattern of the headstones extending before the memorial, as well as of the peaceful surrounding countryside.

MUSEUM ROOM

Beyond the antechamber is the museum room. Projecting from high on its north and south walls are the flags of the following components of our military services during World War II: Air Corps; Armor; Cavalry; Chemical Warfare Service; Coast Artillery Corps; Corps of Engineers; Field Artillery; Chaplains, Christian;

Museum Room

Memorial Chapel – Rear View

Youth Triumphing over Evil

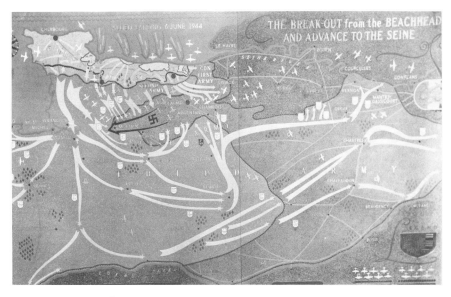

Breakout from the Beachhead and Advance to the Seine

Chaplains, Jewish; Infantry; Medical Department; Navy Artillery Battalion; Navy Infantry Battalion; Ordnance Department; Quartermaster Corps; Signal Corps.

Immediately above the entrance door in the museum room are the American, British, and French national flags, and the engraved inscription: DUTY ✫ HONOR ✫ COUNTRY.

Within the museum room, on the interior wall flanking the doorway to the south, is engraved this extract from President Franklin D. Roosevelt's D-Day prayer on the occasion of the invasion of Normandy:

ALMIGHTY GOD: OUR SONS, PRIDE OF OUR NATION, THIS DAY HAVE SET UPON A MIGHTY ENDEAVOR, A STRUGGLE TO PRESERVE OUR REPUBLIC, OUR RELIGION, AND OUR CIVILIZATION.

THEY WILL BE SORE TRIED, BY NIGHT AND BY DAY, WITHOUT REST — UNTIL THE VICTORY IS WON. SOME WILL NEVER RETURN. EMBRACE THESE, FATHER, AND RECEIVE THEM, THY HEROIC SERVANTS, INTO THY KINGDOM.

On the interior wall north of the doorway is engraved this extract from General Eisenhower's final report to the Combined Chiefs of Staff:

MORE IMPORTANT THAN WEAPONS WAS THE INDOMITABLE FIGHTING SPIRIT OF THE MEN WHO WIELDED THEM. THE COURAGE AND DEVOTION TO DUTY WHICH THEY EXHIBITED THROUGHOUT THE CAMPAIGN WERE UNSURPASSABLE.

TO THOSE WHO GAVE THEIR LIVES, AND TO THOSE WHO BEAR THE WOUNDS OF BATTLE, WE, THEIR COMRADES IN ARMS, RENDER MOST GRATEFUL AND HUMBLE TRIBUTE.

Windows of stained glass, four on each side, portray the coats of arms of eight towns or cities liberated during these operations; viz, Carentan, Cherbourg, St. Lô, Mont St. Michel, Mortain, Paris, Chartres, and Brest. Each window also illustrates a characteristic feature of the respective towns. The stained glass windows throughout the memorial were designed and fabricated by Francois Lorin of Chartres, France.

On the north wall of the museum is the map, "The Breakout from the

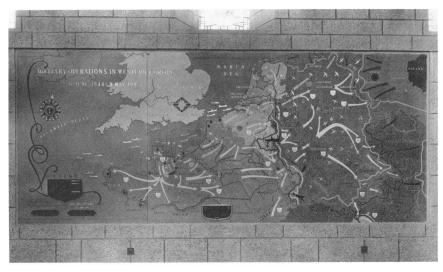

Military Operation in Western Europe

Beachhead and Advance to the Seine." Both this map and the operations map on the south wall were designed by Edward Shenton of West Chester, PA, and fabricated by the Earley Studios of Rosslyn, VA. The backgrounds are colored concretes with various brilliantly colored glass aggregates into which have been set bronze lettering, other metal features, enameled panels, etc. The map, "The Breakout from the Beachhead and Advance to the Seine," is designed in perspective as seen from the south. It is flanked on its west end by the following explanatory inscription in English, on its east end by a similar explanatory inscription in French:

ON 6 JUNE 1944, UNITED STATES AND BRITISH COMMONWEALTH FORCES CROSSED THE ENGLISH CHANNEL TO ENTER OCCUPIED FRANCE. THIS WAS THE CULMINATION OF MONTHS OF PREPARATION AND NATION-WIDE EFFORT. AS THE VAST ARMADA MOVED TOWARD THE NORMANDY BEACHES, ONE BRITISH AND TWO AMERICAN AIRBORNE DIVISIONS DROPPED IN THE DARKNESS TO COVER THE DEPLOYMENT FROM THE

BEACHES. AT 0630 HOURS, UNDER COVER OF CONCENTRATED AERIAL AND NAVAL BOMBARDMENT, THREE AMERICAN, ONE CANADIAN, AND TWO BRITISH DIVISIONS STORMED ASHORE.

THE ASSAULTING FORCES, DESPITE DESPERATE RESISTANCE, DROVE VALIANTLY INLAND AND WITHIN A WEEK LINKED UP THE INDIVIDUAL BEACHES. TURNING NORTH, AMERICAN UNITS, AIDED BY NAVAL AND AIR BOMBARDMENT, CAPTURED CHERBOURG WHILE OTHER ALLIED FORCES HACKED OUT THE BEACHHEAD TO A DEPTH OF 20 MILES AGAINST TENACIOUS OPPOSITION IN THE AGGRESSIVELY DEFENDED HEDGEROWS. THE ENEMY'S EFFORTS TO RUSH REINFORCEMENTS TO HIS MENACED ARMIES WERE PERSISTENTLY DISRUPTED BY ATTACKS BY THE U.S. EIGHTH AND NINTH AIR FORCES AND THE ROYAL AIR FORCE, EXTENDING FAR TO HIS REAR, ON BRIDGES, HIGHWAYS, AND RAILROADS.

ON 25 JULY THE U.S. FIRST ARMY LAUNCHED THE ATTACK TO BREAK OUT OF THE BEACHHEAD. BLASTED ALONG A FIVE-MILE FRONT WEST OF ST. LO BY A PARALYZING AIR BOMBARDMENT, THE ENEMY GAVE WAY BEFORE THE FURIOUS GROUND ASSAULT WHICH FOLLOWED. JOINING IN THE ATTACK, THE U.S. THIRD ARMY THRUST RAPIDLY

SOUTHWARD TOWARD THE LOIRE. NEAR MORTAIN A POWERFUL COUNTERATTACK, INTENDED BY THE GERMANS TO CUT OFF OUR ADVANCING COLUMNS, WAS REPULSED WITH HEAVY LOSSES. THEN, WHILE THE ARMIES IN THE BEACHHEAD CONTINUED TO PRESS FORWARD, AMERICAN FORCES SWUNG UP FROM THE SOUTH TOWARD ARGENTAN. THREATENED WITH ENCIRCLEMENT, POUNDED INCESSANTLY BY WAVES OF AIRCRAFT, THE ENEMY STROVE DESPERATELY TO ESCAPE TO THE EAST BUT BY 21 AUGUST HIS TROOPS IN THE FALAISE POCKET HAD BEEN ANNIHILATED AS A FIGHTING FORCE.

AS THE ALLIED FORCES STEADILY GREW IN STRENGTH THEIR SWEEP ACROSS FRANCE GAINED MOMENTUM. BY 25 AUGUST THEY HAD CROSSED THE SEINE, HAD LIBERATED PARIS, AND WERE IN FULL PURSUIT TOWARD THE GERMAN BORDER.

ALREADY THE UNITED STATES AND ALLIED NAVIES HAD TRANSPORTED OR ESCORTED TO NORMANDY MORE THAN 3,000,000 TONS OF SUPPLIES AND 2,000,000 TROOPS TOGETHER WITH THEIR ARTILLERY, TANKS, AND VEHICLES.

Beneath each of these inscriptions is a set of three key maps, "The War Against Germany" on the west and "The War Against Japan" on the east.

On the south wall is the map, "Military Operations in Western Europe" showing the progress of the military operations in northern France and northwest Europe from the landings in Normandy to the end of the war, together with a flanking descriptive text in English and French, of which the following is the English version at the east end:

IN THE WAKE OF THE SWIFT ALLIED ADVANCE ACROSS NORTHERN FRANCE STRONG ENEMY GARRISONS STUBBORNLY CLUNG TO MANY LARGE SEAPORTS. THUS DENIED ADEQUATE HARBORS THE ALLIES HAD NO ALTERNATIVE BUT TO UNLOAD THEIR SUPPLIES AND REINFORCEMENTS OVER THE NORMANDY BEACHES OR THROUGH THE SINGLE CRIPPLED PORT OF CHERBOURG. THE EFFICIENT PERFORMANCE OF THE TREMENDOUS TASKS PLACED UPON SUPPLY PERSONNEL OF THE ARMY AND NAVY WAS A VITAL CONTRIBUTION TO THE SWEEPING VICTORY WHICH LIBERATED FRANCE.

ALTHOUGH HANDICAPPED BY RAPIDLY LENGTHENING SUPPLY LINES, THE ALLIED FORCES, AIDED BY AIR LIFT, MAINTAINED THEIR VIGOROUS PURSUIT OF THE FLEEING ENEMY. BY MID-SEPTEMBER 1944 THE BRITISH AND CANADIANS HAD CLEARED THE CHANNEL COAST, EXCEPT FOR A FEW ISOLATED PORTS, HAD CAPTURED THE CITY OF ANTWERP, AND HAD ENTERED HOLLAND. THE U.S. FIRST ARMY OF THE 12TH ARMY GROUP HAD SWEPT THROUGH FRANCE, BELGIUM, AND LUXEMBOURG, AND WAS STANDING ON THE THRESHOLD OF GERMANY, WHILE THE U.S. THIRD ARMY IN A SWIFT ADVANCE HAD REACHED THE MOSELLE. ON THE RIGHT FLANK, THE 6TH ARMY GROUP (U.S. SEVENTH AND FRENCH FIRST ARMIES), ROLLING NORTHWARD FROM THE BEACHES OF SOUTHERN FRANCE, HAD JOINED FORCES WITH THE U.S. THIRD ARMY AT SOMBERNON. IN BRITTANY THE RECENTLY ACTIVATED U.S. NINTH ARMY, ASSISTED BY AIR AND NAVAL BOMBARDMENT, WAS BESIEGING BREST WHOSE GARRISON SURRENDERED ON 18 SEPTEMBER.

THE NEXT THREE MONTHS SAW BITTER FIGHTING IN THE EFFORT TO BREAK THROUGH THE GERMAN FRONTIER DEFENSES. ON 11 SEPTEMBER THE ALLIED ARMIES SET FOOT ON GERMAN SOIL. ON 17 SEPTEMBER THE ALLIED FIRST AIRBORNE ARMY DROPPED IN THE EINDHOVEN-ARNHEM AREA IN A GALLANT BUT UNSUCCESSFUL ATTEMPT TO OUTFLANK THE FORTIFIED SIEGFRIED LINE. BY DOGGED EFFORT THE BRITISH SECOND ARMY, THE CANADIAN FIRST ARMY, AND THE NEWLY ARRIVED U.S. NINTH ARMY REACHED THE MEUSE AND ROER RIVERS. THE U.S. FIRST ARMY FOUGHT ITS WAY THROUGH THE SIEGFRIED LINE TO REACH AACHEN AND THE HURTGEN FOREST. THE FORTRESS OF METZ FELL AS THE U.S. THIRD ARMY PUSHED TO THE SAAR. FARTHER SOUTH THE 6TH ARMY GROUP CAPTURED STRASBOURG AND MULHOUSE.

Tablets of the Missing on Wall in front of Chapel

ON 16 DECEMBER THE ENEMY MADE HIS LAST DESPERATE EFFORT TO STAVE OFF DISASTER. PREPARED IN GREATEST SECRECY AND LAUNCHED UNDER COVER OF FOG AND RAIN, HIS ATTACK IN THE ARDENNES WAS INITIALLY SUCCESSFUL. PROMPT DECISIVE MEASURES AND THE SUPERB FIGHTING QUALITIES OF AMERICAN SOLDIERS AND AIRMEN TURNED THE GERMAN ADVANCE INTO RETREAT. THE CONCURRENT GERMAN OFFENSIVE BETWEEN SAARBRUCKEN AND COLMAR MET THE SAME FATE.

DURING FEBRUARY AND EARLY MARCH THE WEST BANK OF THE RHINE WAS CLEARED IN A SERIES OF BRILLIANTLY SUCCESSFUL TACTICAL OPERATIONS. ON 7 MARCH AMERICAN FORCES SEIZED A BRIDGE AT REMAGEN. A SURPRISE CROSSING WAS EFFECTED AT OPPENHEIM ON 22 MARCH. IN THE NEXT TWO DAYS ALLIED TROOPS ASSISTED BY NAVAL LANDING CRAFT STAGED ASSAULT CROSSINGS FARTHER DOWNSTREAM AND THEN SURGED FORWARD TO ISOLATE THE ENTIRE RUHR VALLEY REGION AND ITS DEFENDING FORCES BY A DOUBLE ENVELOPMENT. WITH AIR AND GROUND FORCES OPERATING AS A TEAM THE ALLIED FORCES SWEPT ACROSS GERMANY TO MEET THE ADVANCING TROOPS OF THE U.S.S.R. AT THE ELBE, ENTER CZECHOSLOVAKIA AND AUSTRIA, AND FORCE THE COMPLETE SURRENDER OF ALL GERMAN FORCES CONFRONTING THEM ON 8 MAY, 337 DAYS AFTER THE INITIAL LANDINGS IN NORMANDY.

The map also bears this significant reminder of the part played by the Strategic Air Forces:

FROM 1942 TO 1945 THE UNITED STATES ARMY AIR FORCES AND THE ROYAL AIR FORCE INCESSANTLY ATTACKED DEEP INTO ENEMY TERRITORY TO DISLOCATE AND DESTROY HIS MILITARY AND INDUSTRIAL SYSTEMS.

CHAPEL

At the east end of the museum, separated from it by a low granite divider and wrought iron gates, is the chancel. The face of the granite divider bears this inscription:

O LORD SUPPORT US ALL THE DAY LONG UNTIL THE SHADOWS LENGTHEN AND OUR WORK IS DONE ☆ THEN IN THY MERCY GRANT US A SAFE LODGING AND PEACE AT THE LAST.

The altar in the chancel is of French Harteville Perle limestone from the Juras. High above it is a large stained glass window in the shape of a sexfoil. Centered in the window is the seal of the United States. Each of the six circular stained glass areas on the perimeter of the sexfoil contain three stars. Above the window is engraved the inscription from Exodus XVI, 7: IN THE

Office and Visitors' Building

Visitors' Room

MORNING YE SHALL SEE THE GLORY OF THE LORD.

On the wall below the window and above the altar is a blue and gold damask hanging. Centered on the altar is a latin cross flanked by two candlesticks.

TABLETS OF THE MISSING

Along the gently curving walls emanating from the memorial terrace are inscribed the name, rank, organization, and State of 498 of our Missing:

United States Army and Army Air Forces, 449
United States Navy, 48
United States Coast Guard, 1

These men have given their lives in the service of their Country but their remains have not been recovered or if recovered not identified. They came from the District of Columbia, Canada, and every State of the Union except Alaska, Hawaii, Nevada, and New Hampshire.

On the walls below the flagstaffs is this inscription together with the French translation:

HERE ARE RECORDED THE NAMES OF AMERICANS WHO GAVE THEIR LIVES IN THE SERVICE OF THEIR COUNTRY AND WHO SLEEP IN UNKNOWN GRAVES 1941—1945.

These inscription panels are of Beaumont stone from southwestern France.

GRAVES AREA

There are 4,410 American military personnel buried in the cemetery. Their 4,408 headstones are set in 16 fan shaped plots, curving from the central mall. These Dead, who gave their lives in our Country's service, came from every State in the Union and the District of Columbia.

Ninety-five of the headstones mark graves of "unknowns;" two of these graves contain the remains of two Unknowns that could not be separated.

Here also, in twenty instances, two brothers rest side by side.

At the far (east) end of the mall is a rectangular stone cenotaph of La Pyrie granite designed by Lee Lawrie and executed by the French sculptor, Augustine Beggi. Carved upon it are a torch and laurel wreath in bas relief and the words PRO PATRIA 1941–1945.

PLANTINGS

The cemetery is surrounded by a Hawthorn (Crataegus oxyacantha) hedge with an interior hedge of Boxwood (Buxus sempervirens) enclosing the grave plots. The space of varying width between the two hedges is planted with shade trees, both evergreen and deciduous, including Giant Sequoia (Sequoia gigantea), White Fir (Abies concolor), Norway Spruce (Picea abies), Scotch Pine (Pinus sylvestris), Holly Oak (Quercus ilex), Tulip Tree (Liriodendron tulipifera), Purple Beech (Fagus sylvatica purpurea), European Chestnut (Castanea sativa), European Hornbeam (Carpinus betulus), European Oak (Quercus robur) and European Elm (Ulmus procera). In the broad grass walks dividing the grave plots are flowering trees which bloom from late spring far into the summer. These include Crabapple (Malus floribunda), Double Hawthorn (Crataegus oxyacantha flora plena), Pagoda Tree (Sophora japonica), Golden Rain Tree (Koelreuteria paniculata), and Yellow Wood Tree (Cladrastis lutea). The central mall of the cemetery and the perimeter of the grave plots are lined with rows of European Chestnut (Castanea sativa). A number of rose beds and blooming shrubs such as rhododendron are grown in various locations and provide a colorful aspect.

Epinal American Cemetery and Memorial

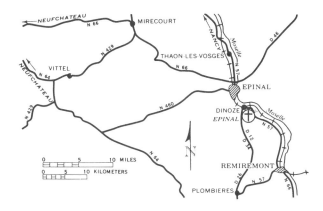

LOCATION

The Epinal American Cemetery and Memorial is situated 4 miles/6.5 kilometers south of Epinal, Vosges, France on Highway N-57, the main route between Nancy and Belfort. It can be reached by automobile from Paris (231 miles/372 kilometers) in about five hours via Porte Pantin to Autoroute A-4, eastward to the Nancy exit, then southward on N-57, to the entrance road leading to the cemetery.

Rail service to Epinal is available from the Gare de l'Est in Paris via Nancy, where it may be necessary to change trains. The journey by train also takes about 5 hours. Adequate hotel accommodations and taxi service to the cemetery may be found in Vittel (30 miles/48 kilometers), Plombieres (22 miles/35 kilometers) and Epinal (4 miles/6.5 kilometers).

HOURS

The cemetery is open daily to the public as follows:
SUMMER (16 March – 30 September)
    9:00 a.m. – 6:00 p.m. — weekdays
    10:00 a.m. – 6:00 p.m. — Saturdays, Sundays, and Holidays
WINTER (1 October – 15 March)
    9:00 a.m. – 5:00 p.m. — weekdays
    10:00 a.m. – 5:00 p.m. — Saturdays, Sundays, and Holidays

Entry Road to Cemetery

Aerial View of Cemetery

When the cemetery is open to the public, a staff member is on duty in the Visitors' Building to answer questions and to escort relatives to grave and memorial sites, except between noon and 3:00 p.m. on weekends and holidays.

HISTORY

On 15 August 1944, just a little over two months after the landings in Normandy, Allied Forces launched an amphibious assault to free southern France. Air bombardment in preparation for the landings began in July and grew steadily in intensity. Preceded by Allied assault groups and U. S. airborne and glider troops, under cover of heavy Naval and aerial bombardment, the 3d, 36th and 45th Divisions of the U.S. VI Corps landed on beaches in southern France from Cape Cavalaire to Agay and thrust rapidly inland. As advancing VI Corps troops of the U.S. Seventh Army pursued the enemy, French units landed and moved westward toward Toulon and Marseilles. Within two weeks both ports had been liberated and U.S. forces had advanced northward up the Rhone Valley to seize Montelimar, cutting off large numbers of the retreating enemy.

In less than one month, U.S. troops from southern France had advanced 400 miles and made contact with those from Normandy on 11 September 1944 at Sombernon, west of Dijon. Ten days later, when these forces had joined in strength near Epinal, a solid line was established extending to the Swiss frontier. Progress in the next three months was slow and fighting bitter, as opposition stiffened. Neverthe-

Interior of Chapel – East End of the Memorial

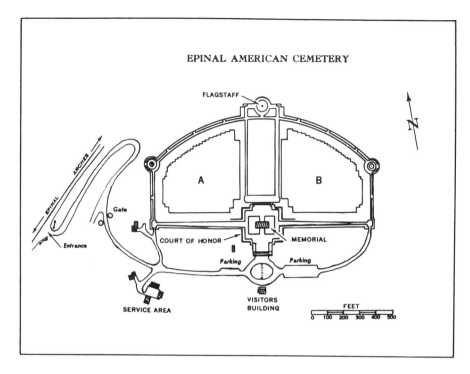

Location of Cemetery Features

less, Allied Forces continued their advance to the Siegfried Line and westward to the Rhine River where our troops held the west bank except for an area between Strasbourg and Mulhouse known as the "Colmar Pocket."

The enemy launched his final major counteroffensive of the war on 16 December 1944. Officially designated the Ardennes-Alsace Campaign, it was popularly known as the "Battle of the Bulge." The U.S. Third Army to the north moved quickly to counter the threat. This required the 6th Army group in the south, consisting of the U. S. Seventh and the French First Armies, to extend its lines northward to cover a much longer front. Against this line, the enemy launched the second half of his planned counteroffensive on New Year's eve by driving for the Saverne Gap in the Vosges Mountains and following with an attack

across the Rhine and an offensive from the Colmar Pocket toward Strasbourg. After furious struggles in bitterly cold weather, all of these attacks were halted. Quickly, the American and French troops joined forces to eliminate the enemy army in the Colmar Pocket; their mission was successfully completed by 9 February 1945. The U.S. Seventh Army thereupon undertook a progressive assault against the Siegfried Line to the north, while the U.S. Third Army continued to assault the Line and the enemy's flanks and rear. Soon, the Siegfried Line was broken and the remaining enemy units cleared from the west bank of the Rhine.

The final offensive of the U.S. Seventh Army began in late March when it crossed the Rhine near Worms and seized Mannheim. Promptly, the French First Army crossed behind it and took

South Facade of Memorial

Karlsruhe. Preceded by aircraft that constantly harassed and demoralized the enemy, Allied Forces swept throughout Germany. As the French captured Stuttgart and cut off escape into Switzerland, the U.S. Seventh Army fought through Nurnberg, took Munich, then drove through the Brenner Pass for its historic meeting with the U.S. Fifth Army on 4 May 1945 at Vipiteno, Italy.

SITE

The Epinal American Cemetery and Memorial, 48 acres in extent, is situated on a plateau in the foothills of the Vosges Mountains, 100 feet above and overlooking the Moselle River. It is one of fourteen permanent World War II American military cemeteries erected on foreign soil by the American Battle Monuments Commission. The site was liberated on 21 September 1944 by the U.S. 45th Infantry Division and a temporary military burial ground was established there fifteen days later. Subsequently, the burial ground was selected to be a permanent cemetery site. After the war, when the temporary burial grounds were being disestablished by the American Graves Registration Service (AGRS), the remains of American military Dead whose next of kin directed permanent interment on foreign soil were moved by the AGRS to a permanent site, usually the one closest to the temporary burial location. They were then interred by the AGRS in the distinctive grave patterns proposed by the cemetery's architect and approved by the Commission. Free use of the Epinal site as a permanent American military cemetery was granted by the French government in perpetuity without charge or taxation. Included in the site is a right of way approximately 500 meters in length leading from Highway N-57 to the main gate of the cemetery. The 5,255 American military Dead buried in the Epinal American Cemetery lost their lives in the fighting across central France, the Rhone Valley, the Vosges Mountains, the Rhine Valley and Germany; they represent 42% of the original burials in the region.

Design and construction of all facilities at the permanent American military cemeteries on foreign soil were the responsibility of the American Battle Monuments Commission, i.e., the memorial, the chapel, the visitors' building, superintendent's quarters, paths, roads, walls and service facilities. It was also responsible for the sculpture, landscaping and other improvements on the site. Construction of the permanent cemetery at Epinal was completed in the spring of 1956 and the cemetery and its memorial were dedicated on 23 July 1956.

On the morning of 12 May 1958, 13 caskets draped with American flags were placed side by side under a canopy at the north end of the memorial in the cemetery. Each casket contained one Unknown serviceman from each of the thirteen permanent American military cemeteries established in the Atlantic theaters of World War II. As soon as the caskets were in place, an honor guard took a position at attention about the canopy. When the invited dignitaries had arrived, General Edward J. O'Neill, Commanding General of the United States Army Communications Zone, Europe, walked slowly past the thirteen caskets, returned to the front of the canopy, picked up a wreath and proceeded to the fifth casket from the east and placed the wreath upon it. He then drew himself to attention and saluted as taps were played. The simple ceremony of selection terminated with the band playing "Miserere," as the pall bearers carried the Unknown selected by General O'Neill behind an honor guard to a waiting hearse. The hearse, under escort, proceeded to Toul-Rosiers Air Base in France where the Unknown was flown to Naples, Italy and loaded aboard the destroyer *USS Blandy*. As soon as loading was completed, the *USS Blandy* departed Naples to rendezvous in the Atlantic with a U.S. Naval Task Force carrying two other Unknowns, one from the Pacific Theater of World War II and one from the Korean War. A similar ceremony to the one held at the Epinal American Cemetery was conducted by the Commander of the Naval Task Force to determine which of the World War II Unknowns would represent both the Atlantic and Pacific theaters of that war. After the selection was made, the Task Force proceeded to Washington, D.C. where, on Memorial Day 1958, the World War II and the Korean War Unknowns joined the Unknown soldier of World War I in Arlington National Cemetery at the Tomb of the Unknown Soldier.

ARCHITECTS

Architects for the cemetery memorial were Delano and Aldrich of New York City. The landscape architect was Homer L. Fry of Austin, Texas.

GENERAL LAYOUT

Six kilometers south of Epinal, a winding road 0.5 of a kilometer in length leads from the east side of Highway N-57 to the main gate of the cemetery. Marking entry to the road on the right is a rectangular stone on which is carved the U.S. Great Seal above the words "Epinal American Cemetery and Memorial." Marking entry to the road on the left is a low curved wall on which the name of the cemetery also is carved.

About 90 meters inside the main gate, a crossing road leads north (left) to the superintendent's quarters and south (right) to the assistant superintendent's quarters and the service area. The Visitors' Building is about 300 meters inside the main gate on the south (right) side of the entry road where the road forms an elliptical drive. Visitor parking is available just before and beyond the elliptical drive. A stone pathway leads northward from the Visitors' Building across the drive to the

Crusade in Europe – South Facade of Memorial

Court of Honor. In the center of the court under a single roof are the museum and chapel. Enclosing the court are low walls engraved with the names of the Missing in Action in the region. The Court of Honor sits at the south end of a wide grassy mall flanked by trees separating the graves area into two plots. A 75′ flagpole stands at the opposite (north) end of the grassy mall. Located in the northeast and northwest portions of the graves area are small circular cul-de-sacs with benches and fountains. Like the Court of Honor, the graves area is enclosed by a stone wall.

COURT OF HONOR

The Court of Honor is rectangular in shape. It is enclosed by low walls of Rocheret, a hard limestone from the Jura Mountains of eastern France.

Engraved on the walls enclosing the court are the names of 424 Missing in Action in the region:

United States Army
   and Army Air Force 419
United States Navy 5

These Missing lost their lives in the service of their country, but their remains were not recovered, or if recovered, not identified. They represent every State of the Union (and the District of Columbia) except Alaska, Delaware, Hawaii, Neveda, North Dakota, Rhode Island, Vermont and Wyoming. The following inscriptions appear in English and French on the walls above their names:

HERE ARE RECORDED THE NAMES OF AMERICANS WHO GAVE THEIR LIVES IN THE SERVICE OF THEIR COUNTRY AND WHO SLEEP IN UNKNOWN GRAVES.

IN GRATEFUL REMEMBRANCE OF THOSE WHO DIED IN WORLD WAR II ** 1941 – 1945.

Resurrection – South Facade of Memorial

THIS IS THEIR MEMORIAL — THE WHOLE EARTH THEIR SEPULCHRE.

MEMORIAL STRUCTURE

A rectangular memorial, consisting of a chapel on the east end and a museum room on the west end separated by an open but covered portico, stands in the center of the court. The overall structure is 81 feet long, 35 feet wide and 36 feet high. The walls of the structure like those enclosing the court are of Rocheret limestone. The floor of the portico is patterned with Rocheret and Roc Argente' another French limestone from the Jura region.

EXTERIOR

The south face of the memorial contains two large bas-relief carvings designed and sculpted by Malvina Hoffman of New York. The carving on the western end of the south face depicts the Crusade in Europe. It is a composition of United States military forces advancing on the enemy and consists of infantry, tanks, artillery, antiaircraft guns, paratroopers, grenade throwers, signalmen and search lights with a large eagle overhead to symbolize U.S. Army Air Forces. The carving on the eastern end of the south face depicts Survival of the Spirit. In it, a kneeling figure of a sorrowing woman — humanity — in the center of the carving comforts a dying soldier, while the souls of two brave young men who have preceded him in death are raised upward by an angel on rays of light, as their earthly bodies remain behind under a Latin Cross or Star of David headstone. In the upper left portion of the carving, an angel precedes them with a torch to light their way and two angels in the upper

Teakwood Pew, South End of Chapel

right portion herald their approach with trumpets. Carved on the attic above the south face of the memorial are an eagle, also the work of Miss Hoffman, and the following inscription from Exodus XIX 4: I BARE YOU ON EAGLE WINGS AND BROUGHT YOU UNTO MYSELF.

The frieze of the memorial bears the following inscriptions: (south face) CITIZENS OF EVERY CALLING BRED IN THE PRINCIPLES OF THE AMERICAN DEMOCRACY ☆ ☆ (east face) DEFENDERS OF CHALLENGED FREEDOMS ☆ ☆ (north face) FROM NORMANDY AND PROVENCE — TO ARDENNES LORRAINE AND ALSACE — BEYOND THE RHINE ☆ ☆ and (west face) CHAMPIONS OF THE RIGHTS OF MAN.

On the north face of the memorial appears the following dedicatory inscription in English and French:

1941–1945 ☆ ☆ IN PROUD REMEMBRANCE OF THE ACHIEVEMENTS OF HER SONS AND IN HUMBLE TRIBUTE TO THEIR SACRIFICES THIS MEMORIAL HAS BEEN ERECTED BY THE UNITED STATES OF AMERICA.

The eagle by Miss Hoffman that appears on the exterior attic wall above the south face also appears on the exterior attic wall above the

north face, but without the inscription from Exodus.

INTERIOR

Within the portico and over the entrance to the chapel in the eastern portion of the memorial is a roundel in the center of which is the Lamb of God encircled by a Latin Cross, Tablets of Moses and a Star of David. Opposite it over the entrance to the museum to the west is a roundel on which appears the Great Seal of the United States. Both roundels were designed by Miss Hoffman. All carvings on the exterior and interior of the memorial were executed by Jean Juge of Paris.

INTERIOR—CHAPEL

The chapel at the east end of the memorial is entered from the portico through bronze doors inset with rectangular panes of glass. Directly in front of the entrance doors against the east wall of the chapel is a long teakwood planter. Above the planter are three tall narrow windows. The altar, flanked by circular planters of teak, is in an apse in the

Museum Wall Map (left section)

north wall of the chapel to the left of the entrance door. The altar and the two plinths on which it rests are Rouge Antique marble from southern France. On the wall above the altar is a large sculpture of the Angel of Peace designed by Miss Hoffman. Inscribed on the wall to the left of the Angel of Peace is: GIVE LIGHT TO THEM THAT SIT IN DARKNESS; inscribed on the wall to the right of the Angel of Peace is: AND GUIDE OUR FEET INTO THE WAY OF PEACE. These inscriptions are from St. Luke I 79.

Flanking the apse are two groups of flags. The group on the left consists of the U.S. Army flag of 1775, the U.S. flag and the U.S. Marine Corps flag. The group on the right consists of the U.S. Navy flag, the U.S. flag and the U.S. Air Force flag. A teakwood pew rests against the south wall of the chapel to the right of the entrance door. Carved in the front of the pew, from St. John X 28, is: I GIVE THEM ETERNAL LIFE AND THEY

SHALL NEVER PERISH. Inscribed in the wall above the pew is: TAKE UNTO THY-SELF O LORD THE SOULS OF THE VALOROUS THAT THEY MAY DWELL IN GLORY. Two roundels flank the inscription. The one on the left or to the east is of a Latin Cross; the one on the right is of the Tablets of Moses surmounted by a Star of David. The walls of the chapel are of Savonniere French limestone and the floor is of Comblanchien, another durable French limestone from the Jura region. The ceiling is of teakwood. Suspended from the ceiling is a large hexagonal lamp of antique design with frosted glass panels.

INTERIOR—MUSEUM

The primary feature of the museum room in the western portion of the memorial is the large colored glass mosaic map depicting American and allied military operations from the landings in southern France on 15

Museum Wall Map (center section)

August 1944 to the junction with Allied Forces advancing from Normandy on 11 September at Sombernon, near Dijon; and their subsequent advances after turning eastward, crossing the Rhine and sweeping across Germany to meet with the spearhead of the U.S. Fifth Army south of the Brenner Pass. The mosaic, 54 feet long and 14 feet high, was designed and fabricated by Eugene Savage of Branford, Connecticut, utilizing data provided by the American Battle Monuments Commission. The map is laid out in perspective as seen from the south; consequently, the lines of longitude and latitude are tilted to accommodate the map to the proportions of the room. Thus, north is toward the upper right instead of vertically upward. Symbolically, the figures on the semi-circular wall depict the Spirit of Columbia leading the Army, Navy, and Air Forces to the landings on the south coast of France. The final victory is symbolized by the Angel of Victory with laurel branch above the central altar group composed of trumpets, the American and French flags emerging from the clouds of war, and the outstretched hands of women who offer flowers as tribute to the victors.

In the border of the map are the insignia of the following military units of division size or larger that participated in ground operations in the region: 6th Army Group and 12th Army Group; Third Army and Seventh Army; VI Corps, XV Corps, and XXI Corps; 3d, 4th, 28th, 35th, 36th, 42d, 44th, 45th, 63d, 65th, 70th, 71st, 75th, 79th, 80th, 86th, 87th, 90th, 94th, 99th, 100th and 103d Infantry Divisions; 6th, 10th, 11th, 12th, 13th, 14th and 20th Armored Divisions; and the 101st Airborne Division.

The principal allied ground, naval and air forces that were engaged in these operations are listed in panels

Museum Wall Map (right section)

at the ends of the mosaic. On the straight wall adjacent to the south end of the map is a description in English, beneath the torch of Liberty, of these operations:

ON 15 AUGUST 1944 THE ALLIED FORCES LAUNCHED THEIR CAMPAIGN TO ASSIST THE NORMANDY OPERATION AND TO LIBERATE SOUTHERN FRANCE. AN OVERWHELMING AIR EFFORT FORMED THE PRELUDE. PRECEDED BY ALLIED ASSAULT GROUPS AND AIRBORNE TROOPS, THE VI CORPS OF THE U.S. SEVENTH ARMY STORMED ASHORE UNDER COVER OF INTENSE BOMBARDMENT BY THE WESTERN NAVAL TASK FORCE. THE U.S. 3D, 36TH, AND 45TH INFANTRY DIVISIONS PROMPTLY BROKE THROUGH THE STEEL AND CONCRETE BEACH FORTIFICATIONS, SUBDUED THE DEFENDERS, AND SURGED INLAND.

SWIFTLY PURSUING THE DISINTEGRATING ENEMY UNITS UP THE RHONE VALLEY THE U.S. SEVENTH ARMY FREED LYON WHILE THE FRENCH FIRST ARMY REOCCUPIED MARSEILLE AND TOULON. IN LESS THAN ONE MONTH THE ALLIES PUSHED 400 MILES TO JOIN HANDS AT SOMBERNON WITH THE FORCES

ADVANCING FROM NORMANDY. BY 21 SEPTEMBER, NEAR EPINAL, THE TROOPS FROM THE MEDITERRANEAN, NOW ORGANIZED AS THE 6TH ARMY GROUP, HAD FORGED WITH THE U.S. THIRD ARMY OF THE 12TH ARMY GROUP A SOLID FRONT WHICH ISOLATED ALL GERMAN UNITS REMAINING IN THE SOUTH OF FRANCE.

DURING OCTOBER AND NOVEMBER THE ADVANCE CONTINUED AGAINST PERSISTENT AND DESPERATE OPPOSITION REACHING THE RHINE AT STRASBOURG AND MULHOUSE; BETWEEN THESE CITIES THE ENEMY CLUNG TO AN AREA ABOUT COLMAR. ON 16 DECEMBER, IN THE ARDENNES, FARTHER TO THE NORTH, THE ENEMY LOOSED HIS LAST GREAT COUNTEROFFENSIVE OF THE WAR. THE U.S. THIRD ARMY MOVED INSTANTLY TO MEET THE THREAT, LEAVING THE 6TH ARMY GROUP TO DEFEND THE ENTIRE FRONT FROM SAARBRUCKEN SOUTHWARD. ON NEW YEAR'S EVE THE GERMANS ATTACKED FROM BITCHE TOWARD SAVERNE, THEN FOLLOWED WITH ONE THRUST ACROSS THE RHINE NORTH OF STRASBOURG AND ANOTHER FROM THE COLMAR POCKET. AFTER A FURIOUS STRUG-

GLE IN BITTERLY COLD WEATHER THE AT-
TACKERS WERE REPULSED. RESUMING ITS IN-
ITIATIVE THE 6TH ARMY GROUP OVERRAN
THE COLMAR POCKET EARLY IN FEBRUARY
AFTER THREE WEEKS OF SUSTAINED COMBAT
IN WHICH THE GERMAN NINETEENTH ARMY
WAS ANNIHILATED AS A FIGHTING FORCE.

U.S. NAVAL FORCES TOGETHER WITH THE
ALLIED NAVIES IN THE MEDITERRANEAN
PLAYED A VITAL ROLE BY SAFEGUARDING A
CONTINUOUS FLOW OF TROOPS AND
SUPPLIES AGAINST PERSISTENT SUBMARINE
AND AIR ATTACKS. ALLIED AIR FORCES GAVE
THE GROUND ARMIES INDISPENSABLE
ASSISTANCE PRIOR TO AND THROUGHOUT
THE OPERATIONS. THE U.S. FIRST TACTICAL
AIR FORCE PERFORMED MAGNIFICENTLY
DURING CONSISTENTLY BAD WINTER
WEATHER. WHEN THE ALLIED ARMIES
LAUNCHED THEIR FINAL ATTACK THE EFFECT
OF THE STRATEGIC AIR BOMBARDMENT OF
GERMANY WAS TO BE REFLECTED IN THE
RAPID DESTRUCTION OF HER FIGHTING
FORCES.

THE FINAL OFFENSIVE BEGAN IN MARCH.
PACED BY THE U.S. NINTH AIR FORCE AND
THE FIRST TACTICAL AIR FORCE, WHOSE AT-
TACKS DISRUPTED COMMUNICATIONS AND
DESTROYED GERMAN TROOPS AND SUPPLIES,
THE U.S. THIRD AND SEVENTH ARMIES
CROSSED THE RHINE AND SWEPT ACROSS
GERMANY. WHILE THE FRENCH FIRST ARMY
CUT OFF THE ENEMY'S AVENUES OF ESCAPE
INTO SWITZERLAND, THE U.S. SEVENTH
ARMY CAPTURED NURNBERG, SWUNG
SOUTHWARD TO MUNICH AND SEIZED THE
BRENNER PASS. ITS JUNCTION ON 4 MAY WITH
THE U.S. FIFTH ARMY AT VIPITENO IN ITALY
MARKED THE COMPLETE DEFEAT OF THE NAZI
FORCES IN THIS MOUNTAIN REGION.

THE UNITY OF PURPOSE WHICH INSPIRED
ALL WHO SHARED IN THESE CAMPAIGNS
WAS A DECISIVE FACTOR IN THEIR SUCCESS.
THEIR COURAGE AND THEIR DEVOTION TO
DUTY WERE UNSURPASSABLE.

At the opposite end of the room is
the French version of this inscription. Beneath these inscriptions are
two sets of key maps: The War
Against Germany and The War
Against Japan.

The plinth below the map is of
Verte des Alpes and Italian green

veined marble. The floor is paved
with Comblanchien limestone.

GRAVES AREA

Interred in the cemetery are 5,255
American military Dead of World
War II. Their 5,252 graves are set in
two fanshaped plots separated by a
wide north/south mall lined with
sycamore (Platenus orientalis) trees.
Plot A lies west of the mall, plot B to
the east. The servicemen and
women interred here died in the service of their country. They came
from every state of the Union except
Alaska, Hawaii, and the District of
Columbia. Two graves hold the
commingled remains of two identified Dead that could not be separately identified. In 14 instances, two
brothers lie side by side. Sixty-nine
graves hold the remains of American
Dead that could not be identified
(Unknowns). One of these graves
contains the remains of two comrades in arms.

Each grave is marked by a white
marble headstone, a Star of David
for those of the Jewish faith, a Latin
Cross for all others. The lines of
white headstones against the background of green grass harmonize
well with the memorial and the
Court of Honor at the south end of
the mall. A 75 foot flagpole overlooks the graves area from the north
end of the mall. Its circular bronze
base sits on a pedestal of Rocheret
limestone which in turn rests on two
circular plinths of Ampilly limestone
from the Cote d'Or region. The base
plinth contains a thirteen-point star
of Noir d'Izeste from the Pyrenees.
Two small cul-de-sacs with fountains are located in the graves area,
one in the northeast corner and one
in the northwest corner. The graves
area itself is enclosed by a wall of
granite from the local region with a
coping of Euville limestone from the
Verdun region.

Wall of Court of Honor with Tablets of the Missing

Memorial from Plot B

Epinal American Cemetery and Memorial

Plot A of Graves Area

PLANTINGS

The paths near the perimeter wall of the graves area afford magnificent views of the Moselle Valley and its wooded slopes. Immediately to the south of the cemetery is a beautiful natural woodland of oak, spruce and beech on the hillside. Within the cemetery itself are several groups of English beech (Fagus sylvatica); sycamores (planetrees — Platenus orientalis) line the paths of the cemetery. Oriental cherry (Cerasus serulata), red bud (Cercis canadensia) and English hawthorne (Crataegus oxycantha) were planted in the edges of the woods adjacent to the memorial to add color and density. Flanking the Memorial on the north side are two Cedars of Lebanon as well as a large massif of shrubbery. In the entrance court of the cemetery are holly hedges (Ilex aquifolium) and in the Court of Honor are box hedges (Buxus sempervirens) and Polyantha and Red Globe roses. Informal massifs of other plantings in the vicinity of the Court of Honor contain barberry (Berberis thunbergii), flowering quince (Cydonis japonica), rhododendrons, azaleas, forsythia, scotch broom (Cytisus scoparius), cotoneaster and dwarf yew.

Lorraine American Cemetery and Memorial

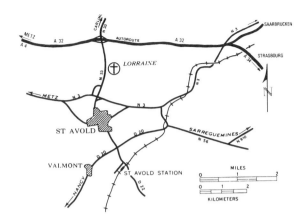

LOCATION

The Lorraine American Cemetery is situated three-quarters of a mile north of the town of St. Avold (Moselle), France on Highway N-33. St. Avold, which lies 28 miles east of Metz and 17 miles southwest of Saarbrucken, can be reached by automobile from Paris (220 miles) via autoroutes A-4 and A-32 in 4 hours. From the St. Avold exit of A-32, Highway N-33, cemetery signs will lead the visitor to the cemetery. The St. Avold train station, located 3 miles from the town, can be reached by rail from Paris (Gare de L'Est) in approximately 5 hours; taxicabs are available in the vicinity of the sta-

tion. There are hotels at Metz and at Saarbrucken and smaller ones at St. Avold.

HOURS

The cemetery is open daily to the public as shown below:

SUMMER (16 March–30 September)
9:00 a.m.–6:00 p.m. — weekdays
10:00 a.m.–6:00 p.m. — Saturdays, Sundays and holidays

WINTER (1 October–15 March)
9:00 a.m.–5:00 p.m. — weekdays
10:00 a.m.–5:00 p.m. — Saturdays, Sundays and holidays

Whenever the cemetery is open to the public, a staff member is on duty

Cemetery Entrance

Chapel Interior facing Altar

Aerial View of Cemetery

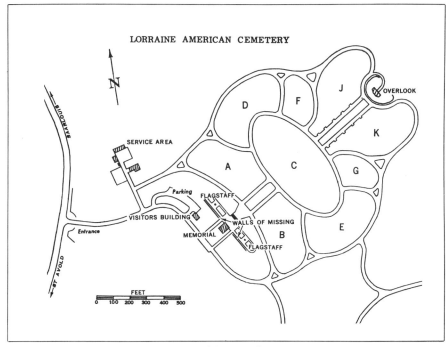

Location of Cemetery Features

in the building to answer questions and to escort relatives to grave and memorialization sites (except between the hours of noon and 3:00 p.m. on weekends and holidays).

HISTORY

The U.S. Third Army resumed its pursuit of the enemy across France early in September 1944, after a brief halt because of a shortage of fuel. Except at Metz, where extremely heavy fortifications and resistance were encountered, the U.S. Third Army advanced rapidly and crossed the Moselle River. By late September, Nancy was liberated and a juncture with the U.S. Seventh Army, which was advancing northward from the beaches of southern France, was made near Epinal. Upon the joining of these two Armies, a solid Allied front was established extending to the Swiss border.

Throughout October, the two Armies pushed aggressively eastward against increasingly strong resistance. The U.S. Third Army drove toward the Saar River and the U.S. Seventh Army into the Vosges Mountains, as the enemy fortress at Metz continued to resist. On 8 November 1944, the U.S. Third Army launched a major offensive toward the Saar River. During this offensive, the main fortress at Metz was encircled and it capitulated on 22 November. Its outer forts, however, did not surrender until 13 December. Bypassing this resistance, the U.S. Third Army continued to advance, capturing Saarguemines on 6 December 1944. By mid-December, several bridgeheads had been established across the Saar River and the U.S. Third Army had begun preparations for breaching the Siegfried Line. Meanwhile on 11 November, the U.S. Seventh Army to the south launched an attack eastward capturing Saarebourg on 20 November 1944. Moving rapidly, it outflanked, then penetrated the

Overall View of Graves Area

East Facade of Memorial

vital Saverne Gap in the Vosges Mountains. Sending the French 2d Armored Division to liberate Strasbourg on the Rhine River, the U.S. Seventh Army turned northward advancing along the west bank of the Rhine against the defenses of the Siegfried Line, simultaneously aiding the U.S. Third Army's operations to the north.

Throughout these operations, the U.S. Ninth Air Force and the U.S. First Tactical Air Force rendered vital air support to the U.S. Third and

Seventh Armies, respectively, despite severe rainstorms and cold weather.

The progress of the two U.S. armies was halted temporarily by the enemy's final major counteroffensive of the war, which began in the Ardennes Forest on 16 December 1944. Officially designated the Ardennes–Alsace Campaign, it became known as the "Battle of the Bulge." The U.S. Third Army moved quickly northward to counter this threat, as the U.S. Seventh Army and the French First Army to its south extended their lines northward to cover more front. The second phase of the enemy's final counteroffensive was launched on New Year's eve against the U.S. Seventh Army and the French First Army. The assault began as a drive for the Saverne Gap followed by an attack across the Rhine toward Strasbourg. After furious fighting on all fronts in bitterly cold weather, the last major enemy offensive was halted and the U.S. Third and Seventh Armies resumed their assault on the Siegfried Line. The line was soon broken and all enemy units were cleared from the west bank of the Rhine. In March 1945, the two U.S. armies crossed the Rhine River and began their drive into Germany.

SITE

The cemetery site covers 113½ acres of rolling landscape on the west edge of the Saar mining region. Immediately to the north and east are natural stands of oak, pine and other trees; these have been extended by a planted enframement around the northeast and south sides.

A temporary American military cemetery was established on 16 March 1945 about one-half mile to the south of the present cemetery. The surrounding area was liberated by troops of the 80th Infantry Divi-

sion on 27 November 1944. When the permanent cemetery was built, the present site was chosen because of its superior location, prospects and aspect. It is the largest American military cemetery of World War II in Europe. Buried here are 10,489 of our military Dead, representing 41 percent of the burials which were originally made in this region. Most of those interred here gave their lives during the advance to the Rhine and the advance across Germany in the spring of 1945. Construction of the cemetery and memorial was completed in 1960.

ARCHITECTS

The architects for the cemetery and memorial were Murphy and Locraft of Washington, D.C.; the landscape architect was Allyn R. Jennings of Oley, Pennsylvania.

GENERAL LAYOUT

The Lorraine American Cemetery is entered from Highway N-33 at the west end of the cemetery. From the main entrance, a linden-lined avenue leads past the service and utilities area on the left and rises gently to the right toward the Visitors' Building and parking area. A short distance southeast of the Visitors' Building, at the crest of the hill, is the memorial flanked by Walls of the Missing on either side. A flagstaff from which the American flag flies daily, stands in front of each wall. A broad flight of steps lined with yew hedges descends from the east front of the memorial to the graves area. A dual path enclosing a grassy mall leads one-third of the way through the graves area where it separates to encircle a wide oval grave plot. Beyond the oval plot, the paths continue and the ground rises to a knoll on which an overlook affords a prospect of the entire cemetery as well as of the countryside for miles to the west.

THE MEMORIAL

The memorial, which consists of a tall rectangular tower and the Walls of the Missing extending to the north and south thereof, is normally approached from the rear (west) side. This tower, 67 feet high, is of Euville limestone from the region of Commercy near the Meuse River some 70 miles to the southwest; its walls are carved with bold vertical flutings. The dark stone of its base is Belgian "petit granit." On the west facade is a sculptured roundel bearing the obverse of the Great Seal of the United States; high on the tower are three superimposed angels of Victory each bearing a laurel wreath, designed by Walker Hancock of Gloucester, Massachusetts.

The entrance to the memorial building is at its east side through tall bronze doors. Above these doors, carved in Euville stone, is a tall (26 feet) figure of St. Avold extending his blessing upon those who rest here or who are commemorated on the Walls of the Missing. "St. Avold" is another spelling of "St. Nabor," a Roman Christian soldier who was martyred about A.D. 303 in the reign of the Emperor Maximian; above his head is an Archangel with trumpet.

INTERIOR

On the far (west) wall opposite the door are five sculptured figures lighted from the north by a tall window. This group represents the eternal struggle for freedom, typified by the youthful figure in the center; flanking him are typical religious and military heros who, throughout history, have taken part in this struggle — King David, Emperor Constantine, King Arthur, George Washington. The sculptor of these figures and of the exterior figure of St. Avold was Michael Lantz of New Rochelle, New York;

all of the sculpture was carved by Jean Juge of Paris.

Beneath the five figures is inscribed:

OUR FELLOW COUNTRYMEN — ENDURING ALL AND GIVING ALL THAT MANKIND MIGHT LIVE IN FREEDOM AND IN PEACE. THEY JOIN THAT GLORIOUS BAND OF HEROES WHO HAVE GONE BEFORE.

The wall bearing the sculptured figures which form the background of the chapel is of Massangis limestone from the Cote d'Or region of France; beneath the figures is the altar of French green Antique Patricia marble upon which is inscribed this text from St. John X, 28:

I GIVE UNTO THEM ETERNAL LIFE AND THEY SHALL NEVER PERISH.

The stone pews are of Euville limestone.

The east, west and north interior walls are of French yellow Salamandre travertine limestone from west-central France; the base course is of Ruoms, a compact limestone from south-central France. The memorial floor is of Buxy, a French compact limestone from Burgundy, with green Antique Patricia marble inlays.

On the left (south) wall is a large map in colored glazed ceramic portraying military operations in western Europe from the landings in Normandy until the end of hostilities. A smaller map inserted in its lower right-hand corner: "FROM THE MOSELLE TO THE RHINE" records the fighting in the region of St. Avold.

The maps were designed by Pierre Bourdelle of Oyster Bay, New York and Georgette Pierre of Paris from data furnished by the American Battle Monuments Commission; they were fabricated by Miss Pierre. Accompanying these maps are inscriptions in both French and English, of which this is the English text:

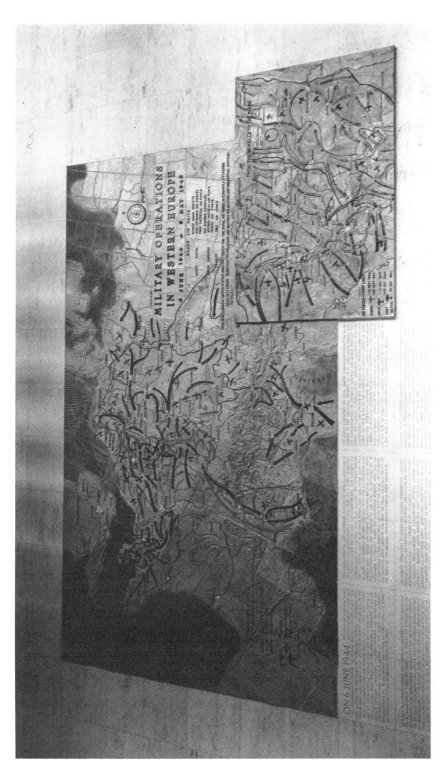

Military Operations in Western Europe

Sculptured Hedges

ON 6 JUNE 1944, PRECEDED BY AIRBORNE UNITS AND COVERED BY NAVAL AND AIR BOMBARDMENT, UNITED STATES AND BRITISH COMMONWEALTH FORCES LANDED ON THE COAST OF NORMANDY. PUSHING SOUTHWARD THEY ESTABLISHED A BEACHHEAD SOME 20 MILES IN DEPTH. ON 25 JULY, IN THE WAKE OF A PARALYZING AIR BOMBARDMENT, THE U.S. FIRST ARMY BROKE OUT OF THE BEACHHEAD WEST OF ST LO AND WAS JOINED ON 1 AUGUST BY THE U.S. THIRD ARMY. TOGETHER THEY REPULSED A POWERFUL COUNTERATTACK TOWARDS AVRANCHES. CRUSHED BETWEEN THE AMERICANS ON THE SOUTH AND WEST AND THE BRITISH ON THE NORTH, AND ATTACKED CONTINUOUSLY BY THE U.S. EIGHTH AND NINTH AIR FORCES AND THE ROYAL AIR FORCE, THE ENEMY RETREATED ACROSS THE SEINE.

THE ALLIED GROUND AND AIR FORCES PURSUED VIGOROUSLY, SUSTAINED BY THE HERCULEAN ACHIEVEMENTS OF ARMY AND NAVY SUPPLY PERSONNEL. BY MID-SEPTEMBER BRITISH AND CANADIAN TROOPS HAD ENTERED THE NETHERLANDS; THE U.S. FIRST ARMY HAD REACHED THE GERMAN BORDER; THE U.S. NINTH ARMY HAD FREED BREST; AND THE THIRD ARMY HAD REACHED THE MOSELLE IN FIRM CONTACT WITH THE U.S. SEVENTH AND FRENCH FIRST ARMIES ADVANCING NORTHWARD SINCE 15 AUGUST FROM THE MEDITERRANEAN. THE OPENING OF THE PORT OF ANTWERP ON 28 NOVEMBER MATERIALLY EASED THE LOGISTICAL BURDEN. METZ FELL ON 22 NOVEMBER AS THE THIRD ARMY MOVED INTO THE SAAR. ON ITS RIGHT, THE SEVENTH ARMY, AIDED BY THE FIRST TACTICAL AIR FORCE, DROVE TO THE RHINE AT STRASBOURG, WHILE FRENCH FORCES FREED MULHOUSE.

THE ENEMY LAUNCHED HIS FINAL MAJOR COUNTEROFFENSIVE ON 16 DECEMBER IN THE ARDENNES. PROMPT TACTICAL COUNTERMEASURES AND THE SUPERB FIGHTING OF AMERICAN SOLDIERS AND AIRMEN BROUGHT THIS EFFORT TO NAUGHT. A CONCURRENT OFFENSIVE LAUNCHED BETWEEN

View of the Overlook

East Facade of Memorial and Wall of the Missing

SAARBRUCKEN AND COLMAR MET THE SAME FATE. DURING FEBRUARY AND MARCH THE WEST BANK OF THE RHINE WAS CLEARED IN A SERIES OF SWIFT MANEUVERS. THEREUPON, IN RAPID SUCCESSION, AMERICAN FORCES SEIZED A BRIDGE AT REMAGEN, CROSSED THE RHINE AT OPPENHEIM, THEN STAGED WITH THE BRITISH, NORTH OF THE RUHR, THEIR MAJOR ASSAULT. SWEEPING ACROSS GERMANY, THE ALLIES MET THE ADVANCING TROOPS OF THE U.S.S.R ON THE ELBE TO FORCE THE COMPLETE SURRENDER OF THE ENEMY ON 8 MAY 1945, 337 DAYS AFTER THE INITIAL LANDINGS IN FRANCE.

High on the wall above the maps, as well as on the opposite (north) wall, are the flags of these components of our military services: Air Corps, Armor, Cavalry, Christian Chaplain, Jewish Chaplain, Chemical Warfare Service, Coast Artillery Corps, Corps of Engineers, Field Artillery, Infantry, Medical Department, Military Police Corps, Navy Infantry Battalion, Ordnance Department, Quartermaster Corps, Signal Corps and Transportation Corps.

Above the doorway is a stand of two United States and two French national flags flanking a 13-star Betsy Ross flag.

On the north wall are six color photographs of the American military cemeteries located in Europe.

Above these photographs is this inscription taken from General Eisenhower's dedication of the Golden Book in St. Paul's Cathedral in London:

HERE WE AND ALL WHO SHALL HEREAFTER LIVE IN FREEDOM WILL BE REMINDED THAT TO THESE MEN AND THEIR COMRADES WE OWE A DEBT TO BE PAID, WITH GRATEFUL REMEMBRANCE OF THEIR SACRIFICE AND WITH THE HIGH RESOLVE THAT THE CAUSE FOR WHICH THEY DIED SHALL LIVE.

Graves Area with Memorial and Walls of the Missing

Flanking the door, to the right, is the dedicatory inscription:

IN PROUD REMEMBRANCE OF THE ACHIEVEMENTS OF HER SONS AND IN HUMBLE TRIBUTE TO THEIR SACRIFICES THIS MEMORIAL HAS BEEN ERECTED BY THE UNITED STATES OF AMERICA.

A French translation thereof appears to the left of the door.

THE WALLS OF THE MISSING

Extending to the north and south of the tower and facing the graves area are the Walls of the Missing upon which are inscribed the name, rank, organization and State of 444 men of the United States Army and Army Air Forces.* These gave their lives in the service of their country, but their remains have not been recovered or identified. Their names include men from 43 different States. At the end of the walls is this inscription as well as a French translation:

HERE ARE RECORDED THE NAMES OF AMERICANS WHO GAVE THEIR LIVES IN THE SERVICE OF THEIR COUNTRY AND WHO SLEEP IN UNKNOWN GRAVES.

THE GRAVES AREA

The graves area is reached by a broad flight of steps from the front of the Memorial. It consists of nine plots laid out about the axis in a symmetrical pattern, divided by gracefully curved paths. The headstones are set in straight lines in each of the plots.

These 10,489 Dead who gave their lives in our country's service came from every State in the Union, and the District of Columbia, as well as from Puerto Rico, Panama, Canada, the United Kingdom and Mexico.

One hundred and fifty-one of the headstones mark the graves of

---

*It will be recalled that during World War II the Air Forces still formed part of the United States Army.

"Unknowns." Among the headstones are 26 instances in which two brothers lie side by side. Among the headstones, also, is one which marks the burial of three men whose names are known and who were buried together; a bronze tablet covers the grave and records their names. There are three Medal of Honor winners whose headstones are inscribed in goldleaf.

These inscriptions are engraved upon the Euville stone pylons at the overlook:

NORTH PYLON:

TO THESE WE OWE THE HIGH RESOLVE THAT THE CAUSE FOR WHICH THEY DIED SHALL LIVE.

SOUTH PYLON:

THROUGH THE GRAVE AND GATE OF DEATH MAY THEY PASS TO THEIR JOYFUL RESURRECTION.

PLANTINGS

The whole cemetery is enclosed within a plantation of Scotch pine interspersed with groups of beech, oak and maple. Color has been introduced not only by the flowering shrubs already mentioned but also by means of long borders of pink polyantha roses, both on the memorial terrace and flanking the central mall. North and south of the Memorial, large masses of *Rosa rugosa* and *Cotoneaster horizontalis* link the terrace with the burial area, while further groups of *Rosa rugosa* in association with scarlet roses provide additional color at the intersection of the paths, north and south of the burial area.

Flanking the Memorial Tower on each side are massive hedges of European beech *(Fagus sylvatica)* backed by lindens *(Tilia vulgaris)*.

In the graves area are informal groups of trees consisting principally of English oak *(Quercus robur)*,

View of Graves Area through Morning Mist

Sculpture of St. Avold

Visitors' and Office Building

Inscribed Pylon at Overlook

honey locust *(Gleditschia triacanthos)*, white and red flowering hawthorns *(Crataegus oxyacantha)* and the pagoda tree *(Sophora japonica)*. Flowering shrubs have been grouped in the open grass areas and include hibiscus, philadelphus, hydrangea, lilac and buddleia.

At the far (east) end of the central mall is the knoll and overlook, backed by a group of trees with shrub underplantings in which predominate the dwarf horse-chestnut *(Aesculus parviflora)*, snowball hydrangea *(Hydrangea arborea)*, *Cotoneaster horizontalis* and St.-Johnswort *(Hypericum prolificum)*.

VISITORS' BUILDING

The Visitors' Building and parking area are situated at the end of the entrance drive, just southwest of the Memorial. It contains the superintendent's office and a comfortably furnished room where visitors may rest, obtain information, sign the register and pause to refresh themselves. A staff member is on duty to provide information on specific locations in any of the Commission's cemeteries, accommodations in the vicinity, best means and routes of travel, local history and other items that may be of interest.

Visitors' Room

Lorraine American Cemetery and Memorial

Normandy American Cemetery and Memorial

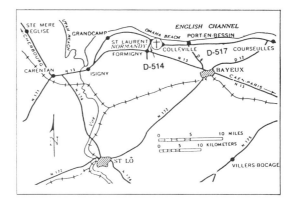

LOCATION

The Normandy American Cemetery is situated on a cliff overlooking Omaha Beach and the English Channel just east of St-Laurent-sur-Mer and northwest of Bayeux in Colleville-sur-Mer. Travel time by train from the Gare St-Lazare (St. Lazare railway station) in Paris to Bayeux is three to four hours. The rail service between Paris and Bayeux is frequent, with at least four daily express trains each way. Taxi service is available from Bayeux Station to the cemetery. To travel to the cemetery from Paris by automobile, it is suggested that one take the Au-toroute de l'Ouest (A-13, toll high-way) from Paris to Caen, then high-way N-13 to Bayeux and Formigny. At Formigny turn right on D-517 to-wards St-Laurent-sur-Mer; then right on D-514 to Colleville-sur-Mer, where directional signs mark the ac-cess to the American Cemetery.

The road distances to the Ceme-tery from some of the other cities in France are: Le Havre, 94 miles/152 kms.; Caen, 29 miles/46 kms.; Rouen, 110 miles/177 kms.; and Cherbourg, 50 miles/81 kms. Ade-quate hotel accommodations are available in Caen and Bayeux as well as in surrounding villages.

Graves Area with English Channel in Background

Aerial View of the Cemetery and its Memorial

HOURS

The cemetery is open daily to the public as shown below:

SUMMER (16 March – 30 September)
   9:00 a.m. – 6:00 p.m. — weekdays
   10:00 a.m. – 6:00 p.m. — Saturdays, Sundays and holidays
WINTER (1 October – 15 March)
   9:00 a.m. – 5:00 p.m. — weekdays
   10:00 a.m. – 5:00 p.m. — Saturdays, Sundays and holidays

When the cemetery is open to the public, a staff member is on duty in the Visitors' building to answer questions and escort relatives to grave and memorial sites (except between noon and 3:00 p.m. on weekends and holidays).

HISTORY

Many months of planning and preparation preceded the 6 June 1944 D-Day landings in Normandy. Beginning in March 1944, Allied air forces disrupted transportation between the Seine and Loire Rivers and conducted strategic air bombardment deep into enemy territory in an attempt to keep the German air force occupied and on the defensive and to isolate the landing areas.

On 6 June 1944 during the early morning hours of darkness, three airborne divisions (the British 6th and the U.S. 82d and 101st) were dropped to the rear of the beach areas to cover deployment of the seaborne assault forces. Simultaneously, Allied naval forces swept the English Channel of mines and preceded the assault vessels to the landing areas. At 6:30 a.m., under cover of intense naval and air bombardment, six U.S., British and Canadian divisions began landing on Utah, Omaha, Gold, Juno and Sword beaches in what was to be the greatest amphibious assault of recorded history.

The U.S. 4th Division landed at Utah Beach and pushed rapidly inland to join the airborne division. The early success and extraordinarily light casualties on Utah Beach

Orientation Table at the Overlook
"The Landing Beaches 6–8 June 1944"

contrasted sharply with the difficulties of the US 1st and 29th Divisions on Omaha Beach to the east, where the enemy was resisting with every device and weapon at his disposal. Its terrain alone was a major obstacle. Instead of sloping gently from the high ground to the rear, the beach area terminated in steep sandy bluffs. Troops had to cross an open area varying in width from a few yards at each end to about 200 yards in the center, and then attack up the steep bluffs to the plateau where the Normandy American Cemetery now stands. The only concealment available was patches of tall marsh grass. Fighting was bitter and casualties heavy. Nevertheless, the US 1st Division took the high ground on which the cemetery stands before D-Day was over.

Further to the east on Gold, Juno and Sword landing beaches, the British and Canadian divisions forged steadily ahead. Within a week, under the cover of continuous naval gunfire and air support, the individual beachheads were linked together. Temporary anchorages and artificial harbors were constructed off the beachhead area during this period by sinking ships and prefabricated concrete caissons to the channel floor, facilitating the unloading of troops and supplies.

Rapidly, the Allied armies increased in size and strength. On 26 June, Americans freed Cherbourg; on 9 July, British and Canadians fought their way into Caen; and on 18 July Americans took St. Lo. Preceded by a paralyzing air bombardment on 25 July, the US First Army stormed out of the beachhead area. Coutances was liberated three days later and, within a week, the recently activated US Third Army cleared Avranches and was advancing toward Paris on a broad front.

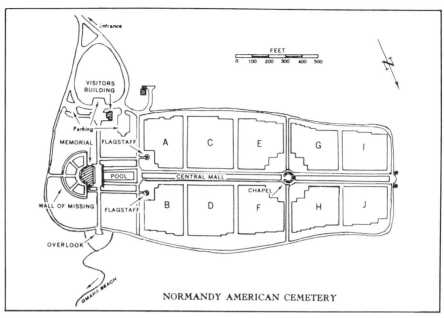

Location of Cemetery Features

THE SITE

The Normandy American Cemetery, 172.5 acres in extent, is one of fourteen permanent American World War II military cemeteries constructed on foreign soil by the American Battle Monuments Commission. Nearby, on D + 1 (7 June 1944), the first temporary American World War II cemetery in France was established by the Army's Graves Registration Service. After the war, when the temporary cemeteries were disestablished by the Army, the remains of American military Dead whose next-of-kin requested permanent interment overseas were moved to one of the fourteen permanent cemetery sites on foreign soil, usually the one which was closest to the temporary cemetery. There they were interred by the Graves Registration Service in the distinctive grave patterns proposed by the cemetery's architect and approved by the Commission. The design and construction of all facilities at the permanent sites were the responsibility of the Commission; i.e., the memorial, chapel, visitors' building, superintendent's quarters, service facilities and paths and roads. The Commission was also responsible for sculpture, landscaping and other improvements.

ARCHITECTS

Architects for the cemetery's memorial features were Harbeson, Hough, Livingston & Larson of Philadelphia, Pa. The landscape architect was Markley Stevenson, also of Philadelphia.

GENERAL LAYOUT

The Normandy American Cemetery is generally rectangular in shape. Its main paths are laid out in the form of a Latin cross.

An avenue bordered by hedgerows, about one-half mile in length, leads from highway D-517 to the main entrance at the southeast corner of the cemetery. Inside the main gate are the parking areas, the

Graves Area with Chapel and Memorial in Background

visitors' building, and the superintendent's quarters. Beyond them, filling most of the eastern end of the cemetery is a beautiful, semi-circular memorial with a memorial garden and Tablets of the Missing to its rear. Facing west, the memorial overlooks a large reflecting pool, two flagpoles from which the American flag flies daily, the graves area and the chapel.

A wide, grassy mall extends westward from the reflecting pool bisecting the graves area. The memorial chapel is located on the mall about one-third of the way from its western end. A narrower north-south mall intersects the central mall at the chapel. Two Italian granite (Baveno) figures representing the United States and France rise above the graves area at the western end of the central mall. Encircling the cemetery proper is a service road.

An overlook, on a small jut of land just north of the memorial affords an excellent view of Omaha Beach directly below and the English Channel. Located at the overlook is an orientation table showing the vari-

ous beaches and forces involved in the Normandy landings. A low railing forms a parapet to the front at the edge of the cliff. From here, the whole action of the landings and the scaling of the escarpment may be visualized. Steps and a path descend to the beach below from the overlook. Along the path is a second orientation table showing the artificial harbour or "Mulberry" in some detail. Prior to the 1944 landings, the enemy had installed artillery and machine-guns along the cliffs so that he could fire lengthwise along the beaches. The cemetery is surrounded on the east, south and west by heavy masses of plantings.

THE MEMORIAL

The memorial structure consists of a semicircular colonnade with a loggia housing battle maps at each end and a large bronze sculpture in the open area formed by its arc. The loggias and colonnade are of Vaurion, a French limestone from the Cote d'Or region; the plinths and steps are of Ploumanach granite from Brittany.

Memorial from the Reflecting Pool

The ceilings of the loggias are of blue ceramic tile by Gentil et Bourdet of Paris. The floor of the open area within the arc is surfaced with pebbles taken from the invasion beach below the cliff and imbedded in mortar.

Centered in the open arc of the memorial facing toward the graves area is a 22-foot bronze statue, "The Spirit of American Youth Rising from the Waves," on a rectangular pedestal of Ploumanach granite. The sculptor of this was Donald De Lue of Leonardo, New Jersey. It was cast in Milan, Italy by the Battaglia Foundry. Encircling the pedestal of the statue on the floor in bronze letters is the inscription, MINE EYES HAVE SEEN THE GLORY OF THE COMING OF THE LORD.

Inset in the floor directly behind the statue are two small curved garden plots. Additionally, four small rectangular plots edged with boxwood are inset in the floor, two on each side of the statue. Adjacent to each rectangular plot on the side closest to the statue is a stone bench.

Carved on the inner face of the colonnade's lintel is the inscription:

THIS EMBATTLED SHORE, PORTAL OF FREEDOM, IS FOREVER HALLOWED BY THE IDEALS, THE VALOR AND THE SACRIFICES OF OUR FELLOW COUNTRYMEN.

On the interior walls of the south loggia are three maps engraved in the stone and embellished with colored enamels. The largest map is on the south wall and is oriented with south at the top. It is entitled THE LANDINGS ON THE NORMANDY BEACHES AND THE DEVELOPMENT OF THE BEACHHEAD and portrays the landings of 6 June 1944, the establishment of the firm beachhead, the liberation of Cherbourg and St. Lo, and the subsequent attack by which the allied forces broke out of the beachhead.

The map on the west wall of the south loggia is entitled AIR OPERATIONS OVER NORMANDY MARCH–AUGUST 1944 and depicts air operations prior to the landings to include isolation of the

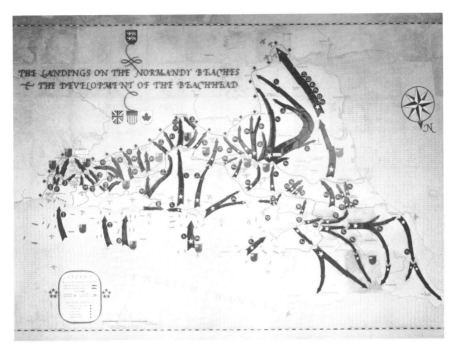

Operations Map in South Loggia

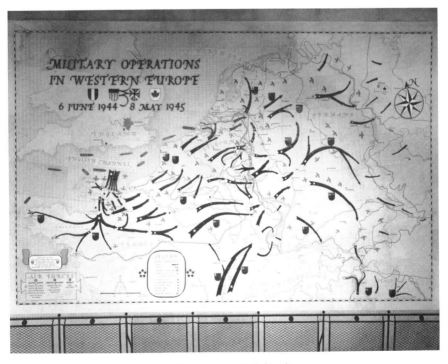

Operations Map in North Loggia

View of the Cemetery from the Memorial

beachhead area from the interior of France.

The following text is inscribed in English on the west wall above the map (a French version is inscribed on the east wall above the map):

THE ASSAULT AND THE BEACHHEAD

MANY MONTHS OF PLANNING AND DETAILED PREPARATION PRECEDED THE ALLIED LANDINGS IN NORMANDY. THE AIR BOMBARDMENT TO ISOLATE THE BATTLEFIELD BEGAN IN MARCH 1944. DURING THE NEXT THREE MONTHS THE ALLIED AIR FORCES, BY SYSTEMATICALLY BOMBING BRIDGES AND RAIL CENTERS, DISRUPTED ALL FORMS OF TRANSPORTATION BETWEEN THE SEINE AND THE LOIRE; MEANWHILE STRATEGIC AIR OPERATIONS WERE CONTINUED DEEP INTO ENEMY TERRITORY TO COMPEL THE GERMAN AIR FORCE TO REMAIN ON THE DEFENSIVE.

IN THE DARKNESS OF THE EARLY MORNING HOURS OF 6 JUNE THREE AIRBORNE DIVISIONS (THE BRITISH 6, THE U.S. 82D AND 101ST) DROPPED BEYOND THE BEACHES TO DESTROY ENEMY FORCES AND TO COVER THE DEPLOYMENT OF THE SEABORNE ASSAULT TROOPS. SIMULTANEOUSLY THE ALLIED NAVAL FORCES SWEPT THE ENGLISH CHANNEL OF MINES AND PRECEDED THE ASSAULT VESSELS TO THE LANDING AREAS. AT 0630 HOURS, UNDER COVER OF NAVAL GUNFIRE AND AIR BOMBARDMENT, SIX U.S., BRITISH AND CANADIAN DIVISIONS LANDED IN THE GREATEST AMPHIBIOUS ASSAULT RECORDED IN HISTORY.

AT UTAH BEACH, THE U.S. 4TH DIVISION PUSHED RAPIDLY INLAND TO JOIN THE U.S. AIRBORNE DIVISIONS. AT OMAHA BEACH, PROGRESS OF THE U.S. 1ST AND 29TH DIVISIONS WAS SLOWER, CASUALTIES WERE HEAVIER, THE FIGHTING BITTER. ON GOLD, JUNO AND SWORD BEACHES, THE BRITISH AND CANADIANS FORGED STEADILY AHEAD. WITHIN A WEEK, UNDER COVER OF CONTINUOUS NAVAL GUNFIRE AND AIR SUPPORT, THE INDIVIDUAL BEACHHEADS HAD BEEN LINKED TOGETHER.

MEANWHILE, NAVAL PERSONNEL WERE ESTABLISHING TEMPORARY ANCHORAGES AND ARTIFICIAL HARBORS BY SINKING SHIPS AND PREFABRICATED CONCRETE CAISSONS. THESE EXPEDIENTS WERE OF PRICELESS AID IN THE UNLOADING OF TROOPS AND CARGO OVER THE UNSHELTERED BEACHES.

THE ALLIED ARMIES GREW RAPIDLY IN STRENGTH. DRIVING NORTHWARD, AMERICAN FORCES, AIDED BY STRONG NAVAL AND AIR BOMBARDMENT, FREED CHERBOURG ON 26 JUNE. ON 9 JULY, THE BRITISH AND CANADIANS FOUGHT THEIR WAY INTO CAEN: NINE DAYS LATER U.S. UNITS TOOK ST. LO. THE ALLIES COULD NOW UNLEASH THEIR PLANNED ATTACK TO BREAK OUT OF THE BEACHHEAD. WHILE BRITISH FORCES HEAVILY ENGAGED THE ENEMY ON THE ALLIED LEFT FLANK, AMERICAN TROOPS WEST OF ST. LO UNDERTOOK THE MAJOR EFFORT TO DRIVE THROUGH THE ENEMY DEFENSES. ON 25 JULY, FOLLOWING A PARALYZING BOMBARDMENT BY THE U.S. EIGHTH AND NINTH AIR FORCES AND THE ROYAL AIR FORCE, THE U.S. 4TH, 9TH AND 30TH DIVISIONS OPENED A GAP IN THE ENEMY LINE WHICH WAS PROMPTLY EXPLOITED BY THE 1ST INFANTRY AND 2D AND 3D ARMORED DIVISIONS. OTHER AMERICAN FORCES PROGRESSIVELY ADDED THEIR EFFORTS, LIBERATING COUTANCES ON 28 JULY. IN A WEEK THE DRIVE HAD CLEARED AVRANCHES.

AFTER NEARLY TWO MONTHS CONFINEMENT TO THE BEACHHEAD AREA, THE ALLIED ARMIES HAD FINALLY BROKEN INTO THE OPEN AND WERE MOVING FORWARD ON A BROAD FRONT.

The map on the east wall is entitled 6 JUNE 1944 THE AMPHIBIOUS ASSAULT LANDINGS and shows the naval plan for the landings and the manner in which it was executed.

Carved in the north wall of the north loggia of the memorial is a large map executed in a technique similar to that of the south loggia maps, entitled MILITARY OPERATIONS IN WESTERN EUROPE, 6 JUNE 1944-8 MAY 1945. It records the progress of the military operations in northwest Europe from the landings in Normandy to the end of the war. On the east and west walls are descriptive texts in English and French and six key maps. The English text is as follows:

FROM NORMANDY TO THE ELBE

REACTING TO THE BREAK-OUT BY THE ALLIED FORCES FROM THE NORMANDY BEACHHEAD, THE ENEMY LAUNCHED A COUNTERATTACK TOWARD AVRANCHES WITH THE DESPERATE HOPE OF CUTTING OFF OUR ADVANCING COLUMNS, BUT WAS REPULSED WITH HEAVY LOSSES. THEREUPON, AMERICAN FORCES SWUNG NORTHWARD TOWARD ARGENTAN WHILE AT THE SAME TIME THE BRITISH AND CANADIANS ADVANCED SOUTHWARD ON FALAISE. THREATENED WITH ENCIRCLEMENT, THE ENEMY TURNED BACK. HARASSED BY AIRCRAFT, HAMMERED INCESSANTLY BY ARTILLERY, HIS RETREAT BECAME A ROUT. BY 22 AUGUST, THE POCKET WAS ELIMINATED.

PRECEDED BY AIRCRAFT OF THE U.S. EIGHTH AND NINTH AIR FORCES AND THE BRITISH SECOND TACTICAL AIR FORCE, WHOSE CONSTANT ATTACKS HASTENED THE DISORGANIZATION OF THE RETREATING ENEMY, THE ALLIED ARMIES CROSSED THE SEINE, LIBERATED PARIS, AND SWEPT ONWARD. AS THE DISTANCE FROM NORMANDY INCREASED THE SUPPLY PROBLEM BECAME ACUTE. STRONG ENEMY GARRISONS STILL HELD MOST OF THE CHANNEL PORTS, THUS PLACING A TREMENDOUS BURDEN UPON OUR LIMITED HARBOR FACILITIES. THE ACHIEVEMENT OF ARMY AND NAVY SUPPLY SERVICES IN SUSTAINING THE ADVANCING ARMIES CONTRIBUTED VITALLY TO THE LIBERATION OF NORTHERN FRANCE.

BY MID-SEPTEMBER, BRITISH AND CANADIAN TROOPS HAD FREED BRUSSELS AND ANTWERP AND ENTERED THE

NETHERLANDS. THE U.S. FIRST ARMY HAD SWEPT ACROSS BELGIUM AND LUXEMBOURG TO THE GERMAN BORDER, WHILE THE THIRD ARMY, AIDED BY AIRBORNE SUPPLY, REACHED THE MOSELLE IN A RAPID ADVANCE. IN BRITTANY THE GARRISON OF BREST SURRENDERED TO THE NEWLY ACTIVATED NINTH ARMY ON 18 SEPTEMBER. ON THE RIGHT FLANK THE U.S. SEVENTH AND FRENCH FIRST ARMIES, SUPPORTED BY THE U.S. FIRST TACTICAL AIR FORCE, ADVANCED FROM THE BEACHES OF SOUTHERN FRANCE TO EXTEND THE ALLIED FRONT SOLIDLY TO THE SWISS FRONTIER.

PROGRESS IN THE NEXT THREE MONTHS WAS SLOW, THE FIGHTING BITTER, AS OPPOSITION STIFFENED. A MINOR ADVANCE WAS EFFECTED IN THE NETHERLANDS WHEN THE ALLIED FIRST AIRBORNE ARMY LANDED IN THE ARNHEM-EINDHOVEN AREA IN A VALIANT BUT UNSUCCESSFUL EFFORT TO SEIZE THE CROSSINGS OF THE LOWER RHINE; THERE FOLLOWED A SERIES OF GALLANT AMPHIBIOUS OPERATIONS TO CLEAR THE WATER APPROACHES TO THE PORT OF ANTWERP. IN THE CENTER, AMERICAN TROOPS BROKE THROUGH THE SIEGFRIED LINE, SEIZED AACHEN,

AND FOUGHT THEIR WAY TO THE ROER RIVER. FARTHER SOUTH THE FORTRESS OF METZ CAPITULATED AFTER A BITTER STRUGGLE, WHILE ON THE RIGHT FLANK THE AMERICANS AND FRENCH REACHED THE RHINE AT STRASBOURG AND MULHOUSE.

IN THE ARDENNES ON 16 DECEMBER THE ENEMY LAUNCHED HIS FINAL MAJOR COUNTER-OFFENSIVE, UNLEASHING THREE ARMIES ON A NARROW FRONT. THE STALWART DEFENSE AND SUPERB FIGHTING SKILL OF THE AMERICAN SOLDIER FINALLY HALTED THIS DRIVE. PROMPT AND CONTINUOUS COUNTERMEASURES BY GROUND AND AIR FORCES SUCCEEDED IN ELIMINATING THE GERMAN SALIENT BY MID-JANUARY. ON NEW YEAR'S EVE AN ENEMY ATTACK NEAR COLMAR WAS ALSO REPULSED AFTER A FURIOUS STRUGGLE.

ALLIED OPERATIONS TO CLEAR THE WEST BANK OF THE RHINE IN FEBRUARY AND EARLY MARCH WERE BRILLIANTLY SUCCESSFUL; THE ARMIES INTENDED FOR THE DEFENSE OF GERMANY WERE SHATTERED BEYOND REPAIR. IN RAPID SUCCESSION, OUR FORCES THEN SEIZED A BRIDGE AT REMAGEN, FORCED A CROSSING AT OPPENHEIM, AND STAGED THEIR MAJOR AMPHIBIOUS

AND AIRBORNE ASSAULT NORTH OF THE RUHR VALLEY. AS OUR GROUND FORCES RUSHED EASTWARD, PRECEDED BY AIRCRAFT WHICH HARASSED AND DEMORALIZED THE RETREATING ENEMY, THE RUHR WAS ENCIRCLED IN A GIGANTIC DOUBLE ENVELOPMENT. SWEEPING THROUGH GERMANY THE ALLIED ARMIES MET THE ADVANCING TROOPS OF THE U.S.S.R. AT THE ELBE. HIS FORCES HAVING COMPLETELY DISINTEGRATED, THE ENEMY CAPITULATED ON 8 MAY 1945, THUS BRINGING TO AN END THE CAMPAIGN BEGUN ELEVEN MONTHS BEFORE ON THE BEACHES OF NORMANDY.

Three engraved stars separate the narrative and this inscription:

THE DEVELOPMENT OF THE GLOBAL WAR 1941-1945. THESE SMALLER MAPS PORTRAY THE VAST AND DECISIVE EFFORT EXERTED BY THE UNITED STATES OF AMERICA AND HER ALLIES IN THE MANY INTERDEPENDENT THEATERS OF GLOBAL WAR. THEY RELATE THE MAJOR EVENTS TO EACH OTHER IN TERMS OF TIME AND SPACE

The maps in each loggia were designed by Robert Foster of New York City from data furnished by the American Battle Monuments Commission and were executed by Maurice Schmit of Paris

The following dedicatory inscription appears in French on the west face of the south loggia and in English on the west face of the north loggia: 1941-1945 IN PROUD REMEMBRANCE OF THE ACHIEVEMENTS OF HER SONS AND IN HUMBLE TRIBUTE TO THEIR SACRIFICES THIS MEMORIAL HAS BEEN ERECTED BY THE UNITED STATES OF AMERICA.

Inset in a tall rectangular aperture in the east and west walls of each loggia is a large bronze urn on which are sculptured two different scenes in high relief. The urns were designed by Donald De Lue and cast by the Marinelli Foundry of Florence, Italy. The scene on one urn in each loggia is that of a dying warrior astride a charging horse, symbolic of war, as an Angel of God supports him and receives his spirit. On the opposite side of the urn, a woman kneels holding her child beside the wreath-decorated grave of a soldier as the Star of Eternal Life shines above, symbolic of the immense sacrifice by women and children bereaved in war. The laurel leaf design around the top of the urn signifies victory and honor.

Memorial Chapel

On the other urn in each loggia is a figure representative of God in Genesis, Chapter 1: "The spirit of the Lord moved on the face of the waters." On the water below the figure is a spray of laurel recalling to memory those who lost their lives at sea; a rainbow emanates from each hand of the figure symbolizing hope and peace. The opposite side of the urn shows an angel pushing away a stone, symbolic of the Resurrection and Eternal Life.

The four scenes on the urns in the north loggia are the same as the four scenes on the urns in the south loggia. The urns, however, have been emplaced on their pedestals so that the scenes facing into the loggias are different.

The Great Seal of the United States is inscribed on the south face of the south loggia. Beneath the seal is engraved: A.D. 1954, AMERICAN BATTLE MONUMENTS COMMISSION HARBESON HOUGH LIVINGSTON AND LARSON ARCHITECTS PAUL BRANCHE ARCHITECTE REPRESENTANT LOCAL.

The reverse of the Great Seal is inscribed on the north face of the north loggia.

THE CHAPEL

The circular chapel in the graves area is constructed of Vaurion limestone except for its steps which are of granite. Surmounting the chapel is a bronze finial with armillary sphere which serves as a lightning arrester.

Chapel Interior

Inscription and Relief Carving on North Chapel Wall

On the outside wall of the chapel to the north of its entrance are the inscriptions:

THIS CHAPEL HAS BEEN ERECTED BY THE UNITED STATES OF AMERICA IN GRATEFUL MEMORY OF HER SONS WHO GAVE THEIR LIVES IN THE LANDINGS ON THE NORMANDY BEACHES AND IN THE LIBERATION OF NORTHERN FRANCE.

THEIR GRAVES ARE THE PERMANENT AND VISIBLE SYMBOL OF THEIR HEROIC DEVOTION AND THEIR SACRIFICE IN THE COMMON CAUSE OF HUMANITY.

An engraved star separates the two inscriptions. A French translation of the texts is inscribed on the outside wall of the chapel to the south. On the exterior of the lintel of the chapel is inscribed:

THESE ENDURED ALL AND GAVE ALL THAT JUSTICE AMONG NATIONS MIGHT PREVAIL AND THAT MANKIND MIGHT ENJOY FREEDOM AND INHERIT PEACE.

Directly above the chapel's door is engraved a replica of the Congressional Medal of Honor, our country's highest award for valor.

CHAPEL INTERIOR

On entering the chapel, one's attention is drawn immediately to the altar of black and gold Pyrenees Grand Antique marble with the inscription, I GIVE UNTO THEM ETERNAL LIFE AND THEY SHALL NEVER PERISH, engraved across its front. Directly behind the altar, a tall window with a translucent amber coating illuminates it with a soft yellow light. On the glass around the edges of the window are 48 stars representing the then 48 States. Immediately above the altar table is a Star of David with a dove in the center of the Star. Affixed to the lower-half of the window is a thin teakwood Latin cross, the sides of which are encased in gold-leafed copper. The altar sits on a two-tiered platform of travertine limestone quarried in France and is flanked on both sides by flags of the United States, France, Great Britain and Canada.

The interior walls of the chapel also are of travertine limestone quarried in France. Inscribed on the

Mosaic Ceiling of Chapel

Dove and Star of David in Window behind Chapel Altar

Garden of the Missing

south interior wall is the inscription: THROUGH THE GATE OF DEATH MAY THEY PASS TO THEIR JOYFUL RESURRECTION. Above the inscription is a Latin cross in relief carved on a circle. Separating the inscription and the cross are three small engraved stars. Directly opposite on the north interior wall of the chapel is the inscription: THINK NOT ONLY UPON THEIR PASSING REMEMBER THE GLORY OF THEIR SPIRIT. Over the inscription are the Tablets of Moses surmounted by a Star of David carved in relief on a circle. Separating the inscription and the tablets are three small engraved stars. The colorful mosaic ceiling was designed and executed by Leon Kroll of New York City. It symbolizes America blessing her sons as they depart by sea and air to fight for freedom, and a grateful France bestowing a laurel wreath upon American Dead who gave their lives to liberate Europe's oppressed peoples. The return of peace is recalled by the angel, dove and the homeward-bound ship.

THE GARDEN OF THE MISSING

Behind the memorial structure is the Garden of the Missing. Its semicircular wall, contains the names and particulars engraved on stone tablets of the 1,557 Missing in the region who gave their lives in the service of their country but whose remains have not been recovered or if recovered, have not been identified. Included among these are twin brothers. They came from forty-nine of the fifty States of the Union, the District of Columbia and Guam. The tablets are separated on the wall by large sculptured laurel leaves.

The following inscriptions in English and French appear on the wall above the names of the Missing: HERE ARE RECORDED THE NAMES OF AMERICANS WHO GAVE THEIR LIVES IN THE SERVICE OF THEIR COUNTRY AND WHO SLEEP IN UNKNOWN GRAVES. THIS IS THEIR MEMORIAL THE WHOLE EARTH THEIR SEPULCHRE. COMRADES IN ARMS WHOSE RESTING PLACE IS KNOWN ONLY TO GOD.

Graves Area

At the rear of the memorial colonnade on the western side of the garden is inscribed this extract from the dedication by General Dwight D. Eisenhower of the "Golden Book" now enshrined in St. Paul's Cathedral, London:

TO THESE WE OWE THE HIGH RESOLVE THAT THE CAUSE FOR WHICH THEY DIED SHALL LIVE.

Radiating from the memorial to the curved wall of the Missing are five paths dividing the garden into four truncated fan-shaped lawn areas. Two paths paralleling the arc of the memorial and the garden wall connect the radiating paths.

GRAVES AREA

The graves area contains ten grave plots, five on each side of the main (east-west) mall. Facing the graves area from the memorial, plots A, C, E, G and I line the left (south) side of the main mall and plots B, D, F, H and J the right. Interred within them are the remains of 9,386 servicemen and women, 307 of which are Unknowns; i.e. those which could not be identified, three Congressional Medal of Honor recipients, and four women. Each grave is marked with a white marble headstone, a Star of David for those of the Jewish faith, a Latin cross for all others. The precisely aligned headstones against the immaculately maintained, emerald green lawn convey an unforgettable feeling of peace and serenity.

The servicemen and women interred in the cemetery came from all fifty States and the District of Columbia. A small number also came from England, Scotland and Canada. Buried here side by side are a father and his son, and in over thirty instances brothers.

VISITORS' BUILDING

The visitors' building is located to the left of the parking area at the head of the path leading to the

Statue Representing the United States

Statue Representing France

One of Three Medal of Honor Recipients Buried in Cemetery

Interior of Visitors' Building

Exterior of Visitors' Building

Time Capsule

sign the register and pause to refresh themselves. During visiting hours a member of the cemetery staff is available in the building to answer questions and provide information on burials and memorializations in the Commission's cemeteries, accommodations in the vicinity, travel, local history and other items of interest.

TIME CAPSULE

Imbedded in the lawn directly opposite the entrance to the visitors' building is a time capsule in which have been sealed news reports of the June 6, 1944 Normandy landings. The capsule is covered by a Ploumanach rose granite slab upon which is engraved: TO BE OPENED JUNE 6, 2044. Affixed in the center of the slab is a bronze plaque adorned with the five stars of a General of the Army and engraved with the following inscription:

IN MEMORY OF GENERAL DWIGHT D. EISENHOWER AND THE FORCES UNDER

memorial. It contains the Superintendent's office, toilet facilities, and a comfortably furnished room where visitors may obtain information,

Spirit of American Youth Rising from the Waves

Spirit of American Youth Rising from the Waves

HIS COMMAND THIS SEALED CAPSULE CONTAINING NEWS REPORTS OF THE JUNE 6, 1944 NORMANDY LANDINGS IS PLACED HERE BY THE NEWSMEN WHO WERE THERE.

JUNE 6, 1969

PLANTINGS

The cemetery is surrounded on the east, south and west by heavy masses of Austrian pine (pinus nigra), interplanted with Whitebeam (sorbus aria), Russian olive (eleagnus augustifolia), sea buckthorn (hippophae rhamniodes), Japanese rose (rosa rugosa), and French tamarisk (tamarix galliea). Interspersed among the plots in the graves area are informal massifs of deciduous and conifer trees, shrubs and Japanese roses.

The lawn areas of the Garden of the Missing are bordered with beds of polyantha roses; European ash trees (fraxinus excelsior) grow in the lawn areas. Planting beds at the foot of the Wall of the Missing contain St. Johnswort (hypericum calycinum) and golden cypress (cupressocyparis leylandii).

𝔓𝔬𝔦𝔫𝔱𝔢 𝔇𝔲 ℌ𝔬𝔠 𝔐𝔬𝔫𝔲𝔪𝔢𝔫𝔱

Located on a cliff 8 miles west of the Normandy American Cemetery overlooking Omaha Beach, the Point du Hoc Monument was erected by the French to honor elements of the 2d Ranger Battalion under the command of LTC James E. Rudder which scaled the 100-foot cliff, seized the objective, and defended it successfully against determined German counterattacks at high cost. The monument consists of a simple granite pylon atop a concrete bunker with inscriptions in French and English on tablets at its base. It was officially turned over to the American government on January 11, 1979 for care and maintenance in perpetuity. This 30 acre battle-scarred area on the right flank of Omaha Beach remains much as the Rangers left it on June 8, 1944.

Utah Beach Monument

The site of the Utah Beach Monument is at the termination of Highway N-13D, approximately 3 kilometers northeast of Ste-Marie-du-Mont (Manche), France. This monument commemorates the achievements of the American Forces of the VII Corps who fought in the liberation of the Cotentin Peninsula from 6 June to 1 July 1944. It consists of a red granite obelisk surrounded by a small, developed park overlooking the historic sand dunes of Utah Beach, one of the two American landing beaches during the Normandy Invasion of June 1944. The site of the monument, which was under construction at the time of publication, is located in the open grassy area in the foreground of the photograph.

Rhone American Cemetery and Memorial

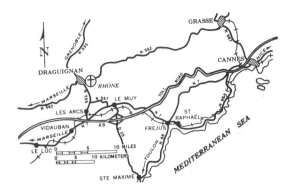

LOCATION

Rhône American Cemetery and Memorial are situated in the city of Draguignan (Var), France, 28 miles in an air line west of Cannes and 16 miles inland from the seacoast. Draguignan may be reached from Paris-Marseille-St. Raphaël-Nice by Autoroute A6/A7/A8 (toll highway) by taking the Le Muy exit onto highway N–555 to Draguignan. From Cannes the cemetery may be reached via Grasse on highway N–85 (Cannes to Grasse) and then highway D–562 to the cemetery or highway N–7 via Frejus and Le Muy or Les Arcs to the city of Draguignan as shown on the map insert.

Draguignan may also be reached by the rail line from Cannes-Nice exiting the train at Les Arcs, a stop on the main rail line from Paris to Nice. There is bus service from Les Arcs to Draguignan or taxi cabs may be hired to reach the cemetery.

Entrance Gate

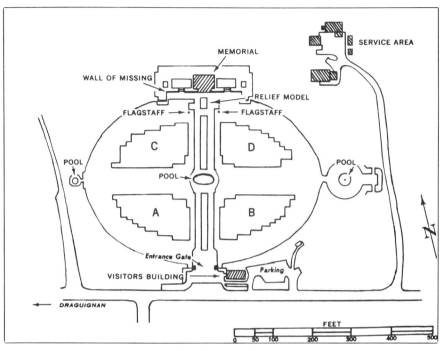

Location of Cemetery Features

Hotel accommodations are available in Draguignan and at St. Raphaël, Cannes and other towns along the Riviera.

HOURS

The cemetery is open daily to the public as shown below:

SUMMER (16 March – 30 September)
   9:00 a.m. – 6:00 p.m. — weekdays
   10:00 a.m. – 6:00 p.m. — Saturdays,
               Sundays, and holidays
WINTER (1 October – 15 March)
   9:00 a.m. – 5:00 p.m. — weekdays
   10:00 a.m. – 5:00 p.m. — Saturdays,
               Sundays, and holidays

When the cemetery is open to the public, a staff member is on duty in the Visitors' Building to answer questions and escort relatives to grave and memorial sites (except between noon and 3:00 p.m. on weekends and holidays).

HISTORY

As early as August 1943, when the campaign to seize the island of Sicily was coming to a victorious close, a landing in southern France was under active consideration by Allied war planners. They believed an amphibious assault in southern France essential, not only to relieve some of the pressure on the troops making the principal amphibious assault at Normandy, but to seize the major port of Marseille.

As planning for Normandy progressed, the desirability of launching both attacks simultaneously became apparent. When it was determined that despite the best efforts of American industry enough landing craft could not be produced to make both amphibious landings at the same time, the decision was made to undertake the southern France landings as soon as possible after the

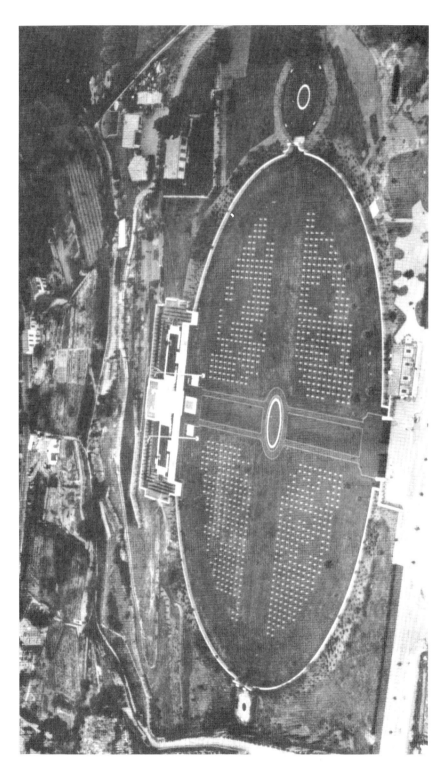

Aerial View of Cemetery

Bronze Relief Map — Operations in Southern France

Normandy landings, utilizing many of the same ships and craft. Meanwhile the threat of such landings immobilized substantial enemy forces in the south of France for over two months, preventing their deployment against Allied troops in Normandy.

Beginning in mid-June 1944, U.S. and French divisions were successively pulled from the lines in Italy, in preparation for the southern France landings. Air bombardment aimed at disrupting vital communications and installations in southern France commenced in July and increased in intensity. As the convoys assembled to bring the preponderance of the assault troops from Italy, and others from as far away as Algiers, the Twelfth and Fifteenth Air Forces struck at enemy beach defenses, and the bridges across the Rhône River in an effort to isolate the battle area.

During the night of 14 August, specially trained assault units landed to protect the flanks of the invasion areas. Then, shortly before dawn, U.S. and British troops of the 1st Airborne Task Force dropped near Le Muy to seize vital highway junctions.

At 0800 hours on 15 August 1944, under the cover of heavy naval bombardment by the Western Naval Task Force, the 3d, 36th and 45th Divisions of the U.S. VI Corps stormed ashore from St. Tropaz to St. Raphaël. Breaking through the steel and concrete fortifications, they advanced inland so rapidly that they were able to establish contact with the airborne units by nightfall. On the following day, as the U.S. troops pursued the retreating enemy, French divisions landed and began moving westward toward the ports of Toulon and Marseille.

The 3d Division on the left flank drove directly up the Rhône Valley, as the other VI Corps units of the U.S. Seventh Army advanced northward. Within ten days, Grenoble was liberated and a U.S. task force was moving westward to meet

Graves Area with Memorial in Background

the 3d Division attacking up the valley. By 28 August, the defile at Montelimar had been seized, cutting off large numbers of the retreating enemy, and Toulon and Marseille had been liberated by French troops.

The advance of the U.S. VI Corps continued without pause, while the U.S. Twelfth Air Force harassed the retreating enemy from the air. Lyon was liberated on 3 September and by 7 September U.S. troops had reached Besançon. On 11 September at Sombernon west of Dijon, U.S. Seventh Army units met patrols from the U.S. Third Army advancing from Normandy. In less than one month U.S. forces had advanced 400 miles from the beaches of southern France, isolating all remaining units in southwestern France. Ten days later the U.S. Seventh and Third Armies joined in strength near Epinal and established a solid line extending to the Swiss frontier.

THE SITE

The site covers 12 acres near the eastern edge of the city of Draguignan, at the foot of a hill clad with the characteristic cypresses, olive trees and oleanders of southern France. Across the street opposite the cemetery are schools and playgrounds. Just west of the cemetery is the civilian cemetery of the city of Draguignan.

The first U.S. troops to enter Draguignan were elements of the 1st Airborne Task Force, on the night of 16 August 1944. They were joined by units of the U.S. 36th Division on the next day. Rhône American Cemetery was first established on 19 August 1944. Here are buried 861 of our military Dead representing 39 per cent of the burials which were originally made in this region; most of these men died during the operations incident to the landings

Fountain, Memorial Garden

Memorial Interior

on the southern coast on 15 August
1944 and the advance northward.
The official name of the cemetery is
derived from the Rhône river whose
watershed was the scene of these
operations. Construction of the
cemetery and Memorial was completed in 1956.

ARCHITECTS

Architect for the cemetery and
memorial was Henry J. Toombs of
Atlanta, Georgia. The Landscape
Architect was A. F. Brinckerhoff of
New York.

GENERAL LAYOUT

The main entrance to the cemetery is
on the north side of highway D59.
Immediately to the right of the entrance gate is the Visitors' Building
— to the east (right) of it is the parking area. Beyond the gate is the
graves area within its oval wall, built
of the local limestone with a coping
of Ampilly limestone from central
France. To the north, beyond the

graves area, is the memorial. In the
northeast corner are the superintendent's quarters as well as the utilities
area and the reservoirs and water
purification system. In the southeast
corner of the reservation is the deep
well to an underground stream from
which water is pumped to the reservoirs.

Outside the oval wall, masses of
tall shrubs backed by olive and plane
trees enclose the cemetery.

MEMORIAL

To the right and left of the memorial
are the two flagstaffs 66½ feet high.
Between them is the bronze relief
map on which are portrayed the
military operations in the area beginning with the landings on the
beaches south of Draguignan on 15
August 1944 followed by the advance up the valley of the Rhône.

The bronze relief map was fabricated by Bruno Bearzi of Florence,
Italy, from data furnished by the
American Battle Monuments Commission. At the near end of the map

Wall of the Missing

is a brief description in English and French of the military operations; the English version follows:

ON 15 AUGUST 1944 THE ALLIED FORCES LAUNCHED THEIR CAMPAIGN TO ASSIST THE NORMANDY OPERATION AND LIBERATE SOUTHERN FRANCE. THE PREPARATORY AIR BOMBARDMENT HAD BEGUN IN JULY AND HAD GROWN STEADILY IN INTENSITY. AS THE ASSAULT CONVOYS ASSEMBLED, THE U. S. TWELFTH AND FIFTEENTH AIR FORCES STRUCK AT THE BEACH DEFENSES, AS WELL AS AT THE BRIDGES ASTRIDE THE RHÔNE TO ISOLATE THE BATTLE AREA.

ON THE EVE OF THE ATTACK SPECIALLY TRAINED ASSAULT UNITS LANDED TO PROTECT THE FLANKS OF THE INVASION BEACHES. BEFORE DAWN AIRBORNE TROOPS DROPPED NEAR LE MUY TO SEIZE HIGHWAY JUNCTIONS NECESSARY TO ASSURE THE ALLIED ADVANCE. AT 0800 THE U. S. VI CORPS MOVED ASHORE UNDER COVER OF BOMBARDMENT BY THE WESTERN NAVAL TASK FORCE. BREAKING THROUGH STEEL AND CONCRETE FORTIFICATIONS THE U. S. 3D, 36TH AND 45TH DIVISIONS PUSHED RAPIDLY INLAND.

IN A TWO-PRONGED ADVANCE THE U. S. SEVENTH ARMY LIBERATED GRENOBLE AND WITHIN TEN DAYS WAS ENVELOPING MONTELIMAR TO TRAP THE ENEMY. MEANWHILE FRENCH UNITS HAD LANDED AND THRUST WESTWARD TO TOULON AND MARSEILLE. BY THE END OF THE MONTH THE ALLIED GROUND TROOPS WERE APPROACHING LYON PRECEDED BY THE U. S. TWELFTH AIR FORCE WHOSE ATTACKS DISORGANIZED THE FLEEING ENEMY. BY 7 SEPTEMBER U. S. FORCES HAD REACHED BESANÇON AND WERE MOVING ON BELFORT AND EPINAL. FOUR DAYS LATER THE ALLIED FORCES FROM NORMANDY AND SOUTHERN FRANCE JOINED HANDS AT SOMBERNON, THUS ISOLATING ALL GERMAN UNITS REMAINING IN SOUTHWEST FRANCE. THE ALLIES COULD NOW DEVOTE THEIR EFFORTS TO THE DEFEAT OF THE NAZIS IN GERMANY ITSELF.

Chapel Interior

THIS CHAPEL HAS BEEN ERECTED BY THE UNITED STATES OF AMERICA
AS A SACRED RENDEZVOUS OF A GRATEFUL PEOPLE WITH ITS IMMORTAL DEAD

CETTE CHAPELLE ERIGEE PAR LES ETATS-UNIS D'AMERIQUE SYMBOLISE LE LIEN
QUI UNIT A JAMAIS UN PEUPLE RECONNAISSANT A SES HEROS IMMORTELS

Mosaic, Great Seal of the United States

The model which is 20 feet long and 11 feet wide is at a horizontal scale of 1:100,000 (1.6 miles to the inch); the vertical scale has been exaggerated three times (2,750 feet to the inch). The model is set on a base of Rocheret Clair limestone from the Jura region of eastern France.

On each side of this model, on Rocheret stone table tops between the benches, are the two sets of key maps: The War Against Germany and The War Against Japan.

On the façade of the Memorial is the heroic-size sculpture, designed by Edmund Amateis of Brewster, New York, of the Angel of Peace nurturing the new generation. Beneath is the inscription:

WE WHO LIE HERE DIED THAT FUTURE GENERATIONS MIGHT LIVE IN PEACE.

The actual carving of the sculpture was by Georges Granger of Chalon-sur-Saône.

Graves Area with Memorial in Background

West Garden Pool

THE CHAPEL

The chapel is entered from the terrace through handsome bronze grilles on the east or west sides. The memorial, like the wall of the Missing, is also built of Rocheret limestone from the Jura region.

Much of the interior of the chapel is decorated with mosaics designed by, and fabricated and installed under the supervision of, Austin Purves of Litchfield, Conn. The mosaic mural in the apse was conceived by the artist to recall the eternal care of the Almighty, understanding and transcending the personal grief of bereavement, and encouraging new hope for this and for future generations. The grief-stricken pair beneath the willow tree symbolize the mourning relatives of the dead, but apparently sleeping, youth held by the mystical figure of goodness and strength — the type of uniform, helmet and rifle characterize him as an American.

The figure of Saint Louis of France, on the right, standing on the walls of the city of Aigues-Mortes recalls an earlier crusader who set sail, as symbolized by the ship (now part of the arms of the City of Paris), from a port in this region. Behind him is the Sainte Chapelle built in Paris to enshrine the relics of his crusade. The French inscription beneath is ascribed to Saint Louis — "My faithful friends," he said — "we shall be unconquerable if we remain united in charity." (The French text was found in an ancient record.)

It will be recalled that the American crusade was symbolized by the crusader's sword which appeared in the emblem of Supreme Headquarters, Allied Expeditionary Force.

The bird in the shrub between the headstones and the central figure serves as a reminder that notwithstanding the tragic upheavals of war, nature continues its evolution unceasingly.

On the left of the apse is this extract from Cardinal Newman's prayer:

O LORD SUPPORT US ALL THE DAY LONG UNTIL OUR WORK IS DONE ☆ THEN IN THY MERCY GRANT US A HOLY REST AND PEACE AT THE LAST.

The ceiling is in blue mosaic with gold stars. The rear wall mosaic contains an adaptation of the Great Seal of the United States and this inscription (with French translation):

THIS CHAPEL HAS BEEN ERECTED BY THE UNITED STATES OF AMERICA AS A SACRED RENDEZVOUS OF A GRATEFUL PEOPLE WITH ITS IMMORTAL DEAD.

The altar is of Vert des Alpes marble from the valley of Aoste (Val d'Aoste) in the Italian Alps. At one end a Cross is engraved, at the other end the tablets of Moses. The altar cloth is of Florentine leather, the cross and candlesticks of polished brass. The prie-dieu and the pew are of teakwood. An American flag stands at each side of the altar.

Engraved in the walls flanking the apse is a list of the major units which participated in the military operations in this region:

On the left side (facing the altar):

SOUTHERN FRANCE

1944

MAJOR ARMY AND AIR FORCE UNITS ENGAGED

UNITED STATES ARMY

SEVENTH ARMY, VI CORPS
3D INFANTRY DIVISION, 36TH INFANTRY DIVISION, 45TH INFANTRY DIVISION, 1ST AIRBORNE TASK FORCE, 1ST SPECIAL SERVICE FORCE

TWELFTH AIR FORCE, FIFTEENTH AIR FORCE, XII TACTICAL AIR COMMAND, PROVISIONAL TROOP CARRIER AIR DIVISION

ARMEE FRANÇAISE

ARMEE B, 1ᵉʳ, 2ᵉ CORPS D'ARMEE 1ʳᵉ DIVISION FRANÇAISE LIBRE, 2ᵉ DIVISION D'INF MAROCAINE, 3ᵉ DIVISION D'INF ALGERIENNE, 9ᵉ DIVISION D'INF COLONIALE, 1ʳᵉ DIVISION BLINDEE, 1ʳᵉ BRIGADE DE SPAHIS, 1ᵉʳ, 2ᵉ, 3ᵉ GROUPEMENTS DE TABORS MAROCAINS, 1ᵉʳ, 2ᵉ, 3ᵉ GROUPEMENTS DE CHOC

UNITES AERIENNES

FORCES FRANÇAISES DE L'INTERIEUR

BRITISH ARMY

2 INDEPENDENT PARACHUTE BRIGADE

ROYAL AIR FORCE

202 GROUP (FIGHTER)

On the right side (facing the altar):

SOUTHERN FRANCE

1944

MAJOR NAVAL UNITS ENGAGED

WESTERN NAVAL TASK FORCE

UNITED STATES NAVY

515 SHIPS AND CRAFT
INCLUDING
BATTLESHIPS: ARKANSAS, NEVADA, TEXAS. HEAVY CRUISERS: AUGUSTA, QUINCY, TUSCALOOSA. LIGHT CRUISERS: BROOKLYN, CINCINNATI, MARBLEHEAD, OMAHA, PHILADELPHIA. ESCORT CARRIERS: KASAAN BAY, TULAGI

ROYAL NAVY

283 SHIPS AND CRAFT
INCLUDING
1 BATTLESHIP, 10 LIGHT CRUISERS
AND
7 ESCORT CARRIERS

MARINE DE GUERRE FRANÇAISE

12 SHIPS AND CRAFT
INCLUDING
1 BATTLESHIP AND 5 LIGHT CRUISERS

ROYAL HELLENIC NAVY

7 SHIPS AND CRAFT

ALLIED MERCHANT VESSELS

63 SHIPS AND CRAFT

At each end of the terrace outside the chapel is a fountain of red granite (Granit de la Clarté) from Brittany, and a pool. Behind the Memorial the hill rises steeply.

THE WALL OF THE MISSING

On the face of the retaining wall of the terrace of the Memorial are inscribed the names and particulars of 293 of our Missing:

United States Army and Army
   Air Forces[1] 256
United States Navy 37

These men gave their lives in the service of their Country but their remains have not been identified. The lists include men from every State in the Union except Arizona, Delaware, Nebraska, New Hampshire, North Dakota, Rhode Island, and Wyoming. Heading these lists is the inscription:

☆ ☆ 1941 ☆ ☆ 1945 ☆ ☆ HERE ARE RE-CORDED THE NAMES OF AMERICANS WHO GAVE THEIR LIVES IN THE SERVICE OF THEIR COUNTRY AND WHO SLEEP IN UNKNOWN GRAVES.

GRAVES AREA

The graves area is divided into four plots about the oval pool which is set at the intersection of the axes of the cemetery. The 861 headstones are arranged in straight lines; planted among them are oleanders and ancient olive trees which lend an unforgettable peacefulness to the scene.

---

[1]It will be recalled that during World War II the Air Forces still formed part of the United States Army.

The Dead who gave their lives in our Country's service came from every State in the Union except North Dakota; some came from the District of Columbia and Puerto Rico. Sixty-two of the headstones mark the graves of "Unknowns." Here, also, side by side in two instances, are the graves of two brothers.

THE GARDENS

Outside of the oval wall and on the transverse axis of the cemetery are the East and West Gardens. The East Garden is an intimate enclosure with a small circular pool which has a background of tall Italian cypress. It is surrounded with beds of broad-leaved evergreens, including oleander and crepe myrtle, as well as seasonal plants to provide color in the summer.

The West Garden is somewhat smaller; its pool is octagonal in form, and is set in a brick pavement in contrast to the green lawn of the East Garden. It is enclosed by a high sheared hedge of evergreen Japanese privet and planted with a few of the summer-flowering shrubs of the region.

PLANTINGS

The long terrace outside the Chapel is lined with a double row of closely planted Italian cypress, trimmed to a uniform height of twenty feet, which forms a green curtain behind the Chapel and across the ends of the terrace. The areas at the two sides, enclosed with low formal hedges, are planted with redbud trees (cercis canadensis) and strawberry trees (arbutus unedo).

In the graves area oleander and ancient olive trees are scattered among the headstones.

Outside of the oval walls masses of tall shrubs, olive trees (olea europaea sativa) and plane trees (platanus orientalis) soften the outline of the wall from the outside.

Interior

Exterior

VISITORS' BUILDING

Immediately to the right of the entrance gate is the Visitors' Building. The parking area is adjacent to the building on the east (right) side.

It contains the Superintendent's office, toilet facilities, and a comfortably furnished room where visitors may obtain information, sign the register and pause to refresh themselves. During visiting hours a member of the cemetery staff is available in the building to answer questions and provide information on burials and memorializations in the Commission's cemeteries, accommodations in the vicinity, travel, local history and other items of interest.

WORLD WAR II
CEMETERIES AND MEMORIALS:

ITALY

Florence American Cemetery and Memorial

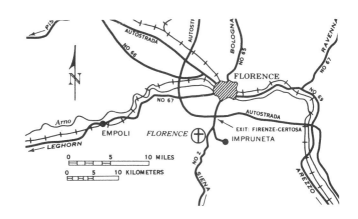

LOCATION

The Florence American Cemetery is situated approximately 7.5 miles (12 kilometers) south of Florence, Italy, on the west side of the Via Cassia, a main highway connecting Florence with Siena and Rome. The Certosa-Florence exit of the Rome-Milan autoroute is two miles south of the cemetery.

Train service to Florence from the principal cities of Italy and Europe is excellent. Bus and taxi service is available from the railroad station to the cemetery. A "SITA" bus stop is conveniently located just outside the cemetery entrance.

Hotel accommodations in Florence are ample.

HOURS

The cemetery is open daily to the public during the following hours:
SUMMER (15 May – 15 September)
    8:00 a.m. – 6:00 p.m.
WINTER (16 September – 14 May)
    8:00 a.m. – 5:00 p.m.

HISTORY

Following the capture of Rome on 4 June 1944, the Allies pursued the enemy northward toward the Po River and the Alps. For the first time since the Allies landed at Salerno in September 1943, the enemy was in full retreat.

Through June and the first half of July, Allied forces advanced rapidly

Cemetery Office and Visitors' Building

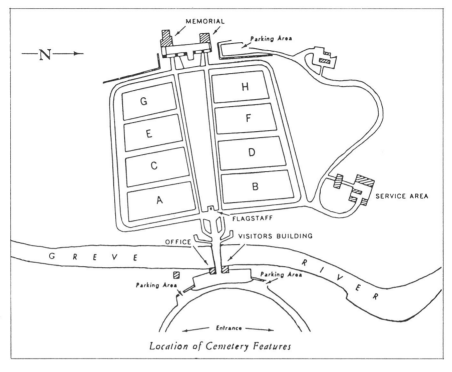

Location of Cemetery Features

northward from Rome. Pursuit was energetic even though many Allied troops were being withdrawn in preparation for the attack in southern France. Leghorn fell to U.S. troops of the Fifth Army on 18 July 1944; five days later they entered Pisa. Florence fell to British troops of the U.S. Fifth Army on 4 August 1944. By then, the Allies had crossed the Arno and reached the outposts of the Gothic Line, the last enemy defensive system in Italy. There they paused to reorganize and resupply before continuing their offensive.

On 25 August, the British Eighth Army attacked on the eastern half of the Gothic Line, driving into the mountains. Several days later, the U.S. Fifth Army penetrated the Gothic Line on the west as a prelude to outflanking and occupying the strong defenses of the Futa Pass. Continuing its advance, the Eighth Army crossed several strongly defended rivers and entered Rimini on 21 September 1944.

In October 1944, a final bid to capture Bologna brought the Fifth Army to within nine miles of that city. There with the Po Valley in sight, the Fifth Army and the Eighth Army were forced by harsh weather conditions and shortages of personnel and supplies to halt for the winter.

Preceded by massive air and artillery bombardment, the Eighth Army resumed the offensive northward on 9 April 1945. Five days later the Fifth Army joined the attack, supported by the heaviest air assault yet employed in Italy. Although the offensive met stiff opposition, within one week U.S. troops had driven into the Po Valley and were converging on Bologna from the south and west, while at the same time the Eighth Army was converging on it from the east. The city fell to the Fifth Army on 21 April 1945. With the establishment of a bridgehead across the Po River on 23 April 1945, the fleeing enemy forces were pursued rapidly northward.

Overall View of the Cemetery

The final week of the war saw wide advances throughout northern Italy. While infantry and mountain troops of the Fifth Army drove into the foothills of the Alps, its armored columns and motorized infantry raced up the Po Valley, reaching Milan on 29 April 1945. During this time, the Eighth Army swept northeast along the Adriatic coastal plain to liberate Padua and Venice.

After seizing Genoa, U.S. forces drove westward to make contact with the French as resistance began to collapse everywhere. On 2 May 1945, the enemy troops in northern Italy surrendered.

SITE

The Florence American Cemetery, 70 acres in extent, is one of fourteen permanent American World War II military cemetery memorials erected on foreign soil by the American Battle Monuments Commission.

The site was liberated on 3 August 1944 by the South African 6th Armoured Division, and later became part of the zone of the U.S. Fifth Army. It is located astride the Greve River, and is framed by wooded hills which rise several hundred feet to the west. The site was selected as a permanent cemetery after a survey of temporary cemeteries established in northern Italy during World War II revealed that there was at least one major objection in every instance to retention of any of the temporary sites as a permanent cemetery.

The 4,402 servicemen and women interred in the cemetery represent 39 percent of the temporary burials originally made between Rome and the Alps. Most died in the fighting which occurred after the capture of Rome in June 1944. Included among them are casualties of the heavy fighting in the Apennines shortly before the war's end.

ARCHITECTS

Architects for the cemetery and its memorial were McKim, Mead and White of New York. The landscape architects were Clarke and Rapuano, also of New York.

GENERAL LAYOUT

The two entrances to the cemetery are located about 250 meters apart on the Via Cassia. Connecting them is a crescent-shaped drive within the cemetery which leads to parking areas on the east or near bank of the Greve River, the cemetery office, the visitors' building and a small bridge. The office and visitors' building face each other at the near end of the bridge.

On the west bank of the Greve River are the graves area, the memorial, the service area and the superin-

The Memorial

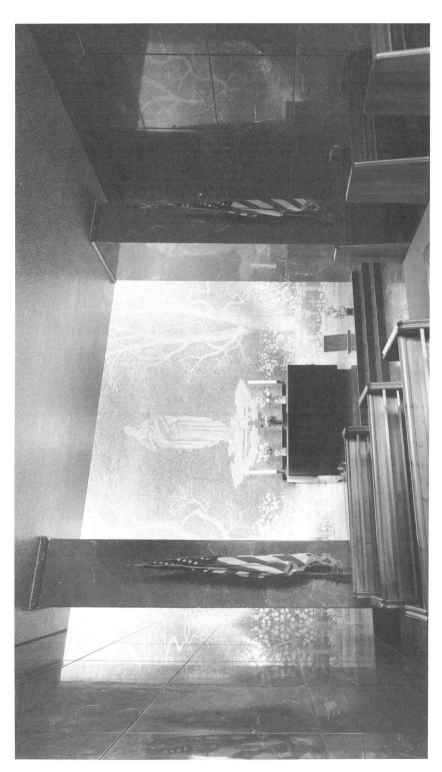

Chapel Interior

North Atrium

tendent's quarters. A wide east-west mall of fine grass separates the graves area into two parts. Overlooking it from high ground at the west end of the mall is the memorial; a large flagpole overlooks it from the east end.

Construction of the cemetery and memorial was completed in 1959.

THE MEMORIAL

The memorial consists of two open atria or courts, a connecting wall on which are affixed tablets with the names of the Missing in the region, a chapel and a stele or pylon surmounted by a sculptured figure representing the spirit of peace. The wall and chapel are on the topmost of three broad terraces overlooking the cemetery. The base of the stele is on the lower terrace.

The south atrium serves as a forecourt to the chapel. Like its counterpart on the north, it has a rectangular pool and jet in its center and it is faced with Roman travertine. The inner recessed walls of the atria are panelled in Baveno granite

from quarries at the north end of Lake Como.

Each recessed inner wall panel of the south atrium bears an inscription. Reading clockwise from its southeast corner, the inscriptions are as follows:

Panel No. 1
THEY FACED THE FOE AS THEY DREW NEAR HIM IN THE STRETCH OF THEIR OWN MANHOOD AND WHEN THE SHOCK OF BATTLE CAME THEY IN A MOMENT OF TIME AT THE CLIMAX OF THEIR LIVES WERE RAPT AWAY FROM A WORLD FILLED FOR THEIR DYING EYES NOT WITH TERROR BUT WITH GLORY

Panel No. 2
. . . SUCH WERE THE MEN WHO LIE HERE THEY RECEIVED EACH FOR HIS OWN MEMORY PRAISE THAT WILL NEVER DIE AND WITH IT THE GRANDEST OF ALL SEPULCHRES A HOME IN THE MINDS OF MEN

Panel No. 3
THEREFORE DO NOT MOURN WITH THE PARENTS OF THE DEAD WHO ARE HERE WITH US RATHER COMFORT THEM LET THEIR BURDEN BE LIGHTENED BY THE GLORY OF THE DEAD THE LOVE OF HONOR ALONE IS NOT STALED BY AGE

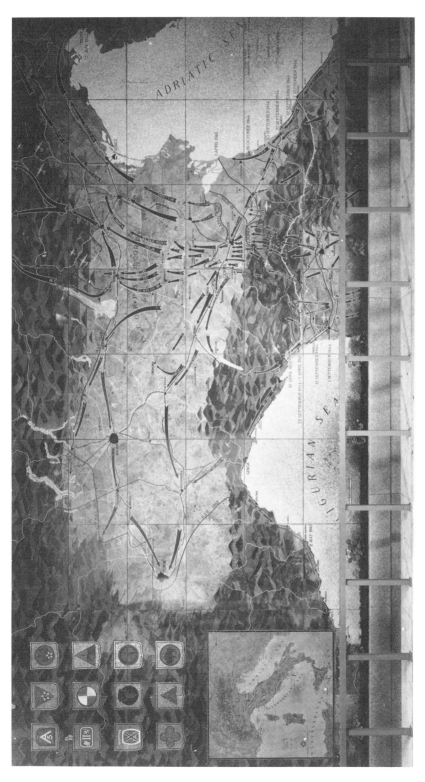

Military Operations Map

.. AND IT IS BY HONOR THAT THE END OF LIFE IS' CHEERED

(These three texts are from A. E. Zimmern's translation of Pericles' Praise of the Dead as recorded by Thucydides.)

Panel No. 4 *(to the left of the Chapel door)*
O LORD SUPPORT US ALL THE DAY LONG UNTIL THE SHADOWS LENGTHEN AND THE EVENING COMES AND THE FEVER OF LIFE IS OVER AND OUR WORK IS DONE THEN IN THY MERCY GRANT US A SAFE LODGING AND A HOLY REST AND PEACE AT THE LAST

(This is taken from Cardinal Newman's Sermon XX and is included in the Episcopal Prayer book.)

Panel No. 5 *(to the right of the Chapel door)*
O GOD WHO ART THE AUTHOR OF PEACE AND LOVER OF CONCORD DEFEND US THY HUMBLE SERVANTS IN ALL ASSAULTS OF OUR ENEMIES THAT WE SURELY TRUSTING IN THY DEFENSE MAY NOT FEAR THE POWER OF ANY ADVERSARIES

(This also is from the Episcopal prayer book.)

Panel No. 6 *(on the north wall, nearest to the Wall of the Missing)*
THEIR BODIES ARE BURIED IN PEACE THEIR NAME LIVETH FOR EVERMORE

(From Ecclesiastes 44)

Surmounting each of panels 1, 3, 4, 5 and 6 are three granite roundels in which have been carved different military insignia. Appearing clockwise from the southeast corner of the atrium are: Armor, Gunner's Mate, Aerial Gunner; Coast Artillery Corps, Boatswain's Mate, Army Air Corps; Corps of Engineers, Infantry, Christian Chaplain; Jewish Chaplain, Field Artillery, Medical Corps; and Signal Corps, Machinist's Mate and Aerial Bombardier.

A carved figure representing "The Spirit of American Youth" appears above the chapel door, while one representing an American eagle appears above panel No. 2, the center south panel. Both figures were designed by Sidney Waugh.

The bronze doors to the chapel were fabricated by the Fonderia Marinelli of Florence. From the doorway, the altar of Belgian black marble, with its bronze accouterments, can be seen at the opposite end of the chapel. Behind the altar is a mosaic, 21 feet high and 24 feet wide, designed by Barry Faulkner of New York and executed by Fabrizio Cassio of Rome. The mosaic depicts Remembrance standing on a cloud, holding in her arms the lilies of Resurrection. The figure is contemplating a crocus-strewn field of marble headstones set among trees showing the first buds of spring—symbolizing new life. At the feet of Remembrance a helmet rests on a sword. The mosaic is illuminated by a skylight.

The chapel walls and the two columns flanking the altar are of polished Rosso Collemandino marble from Versiglia, Italy. The floor is paved with Verde Serpentino marble from Sondrio, Italy; the pews are of walnut.

The north atrium is similar in general design to the south atrium. Set into its west wall are two military operations maps recalling the achievements of the American forces in the region. They were designed by Bruno Bearzi of Florence, Italy from data furnished by the American Battle Monuments Commission.

The larger of the maps pictures Northern Italy and portrays military operations to the end of the war from the vicinity of the cemetery northward. The military operations as well as the general topography of the area are depicted in a mosaic of colored marbles known as intarsia, an art form for which the Florence region is famous. The map is embellished in its upper left hand corner

South Atrium

Tablets of the Missing

by twelve shields in four rows of three, each bearing the shoulder insignia of American ground and air units which participated in the fighting in Northern Italy. From left to right, these are: Fifth Army, Twelfth Air Force, Fifteenth Air Force; II Corps, IV Corps, 1st Armored Division; 10th Mountain Division, 34th Infantry Division, 85th Infantry Division; and 88th Infantry Division, 91st Infantry Division and 92d Infantry Division.

The smaller map is an insert into the larger map just below the shields. It illustrates the broad outline of military operations which took place in Sicily and Italy beginning in July 1943. The map was executed in scagliola by Emilio Martelli of Florence, Italy, a process consisting of drawings in colored artificial compositions which are inlaid in marble and glazed.

A stone planter runs the length of the wall at the foot of the maps. In front of the planter is a low bronze railing with regularly spaced bronze uprights.

The Baveno granite panels on the side walls of the atrium are inscribed with texts in English and Italian explaining the maps. The English and Italian inscriptions on the short side wall immediately to the left of the maps apply to the insert map and read in English as follows:

ON 10 JULY 1943, AMERICAN AND BRITISH FORCES, COVERED BY GUNFIRE OF THE WESTERN NAVAL TASK FORCE AND AIRCRAFT OF THE TWELFTH AIR FORCE, LANDED ON THE SHORES OF SICILY. THE U.S. SEVENTH ARMY ADVANCED RAPIDLY OVER THE WEST AND NORTH OF THE ISLAND, WITH THE BRITISH EIGHTH ARMY ON ITS RIGHT. THIS SWIFT CAMPAIGN LIBERATED THE ISLAND IN 39 DAYS.

ON 9 SEPTEMBER, UNDER COVER OF NAVAL AND AIR BOMBARDMENT, THE U.S. FIFTH ARMY LANDED NEAR SALERNO. FIGHTING ITS WAY INLAND IT JOINED THE EIGHTH ARMY WHICH

HAD CROSSED THE STRAITS OF MESSINA. BY 1 OCTOBER, NAPLES AND THE AIRFIELDS NEAR FOGGIA HAD BEEN SEIZED; FROM THE LATTER THE U.S. FIFTEENTH AIR FORCE LAUNCHED ITS STRATEGIC ATTACKS ON AUSTRIA, THE BALKANS AND GERMANY.

AGAINST DETERMINED OPPOSITION, THE FIFTH AND EIGHTH ARMIES DROVE NORTHWARD. TO ASSIST THE ADVANCE, ALLIED TROOPS ON 22 JANUARY 1944 LANDED IN THE ANZIO REGION BUT THE ENEMY'S PROMPT REACTION PREVENTED EXPLOITATION OF THIS BEACHHEAD, ON 11 MAY THE TWO ARMIES LAUNCHED A GENERAL ATTACK; THE FIFTH ARMY AIDED BY THE TWELFTH AIR FORCE BREACHED THE ENEMY DEFENSES IN THE MOUNTAINS NORTH OF GAETA. THE TROOPS IN THE BEACHHEAD JOINED THE ATTACK AND ON 4 JUNE THE FIFTH ARMY ENTERED ROME.

The English and Italian inscriptions on the left and right panels of the north wall, respectively, apply to the large map of northern Italy and read in English as follows:

FOLLOWING THE LIBERATION OF ROME, THE ALLIES MAINTAINED THEIR PURSUIT OF THE ENEMY. BY 18 JULY 1944, THE U.S. FIFTH ARMY HAD ADVANCED 150 MILES UP THE WEST COAST AND HAD LIBERATED LEGHORN. IN CENTRAL ITALY AND ALONG THE ADRIATIC THE BRITISH EIGHTH ARMY HAD PARALLELED THIS ADVANCE. AFTER PAUSING TO REORGANIZE, THE FIFTH ARMY CROSSED THE ARNO AND PURSUED THE RETREATING ENEMY INTO THE MOUNTAINS TO THE OUTPOSTS OF THE GOTHIC LINE.

AFTER DIFFICULT FIGHTING THE FIFTH ARMY CUT THROUGH THIS STRONG DEFENSE SYSTEM TO REACH FIRENZUOLA AND THE SANTERNO VALLEY ON 21 SEPTEMBER. THE SAME DAY, BRITISH TROOPS, HAVING FORCED SUCCESSIVE DEFENDED RIVER LINES, ENTERED RIMINI. THE U.S. TWELFTH AIR FORCE AND THE DESERT AIR FORCE MATERIALLY CONTRIBUTED TO THESE ADVANCES BY THEIR CLOSE SUPPORT AND THEIR

East-West Mall

CONTINUOUS ATTACKS AGAINST REAR AREAS. THE ADVANCE TO THE SAN-TERNO VALLEY HAD OUTFLANKED THE STRONG DEFENSES OF FUTA PASS, WHICH WAS OCCUPIED ON 22 SEPTEM-BER BY AMERICAN FORCES. DURING OCTOBER, THE ALLIED ADVANCES CONTINUED AT A SLOWER PACE AGAINST STIFFENED RESISTANCE. BY THE END OF THE MONTH, HAMPERED BY BAD WEATHER AND MUD, SHORTAGES OF PERSONNEL AND DIFFICULTIES OF SUPPLY, THE FIFTH ARMY, NOW ONLY NINE MILES SHORT OF BOLOGNA AND WITHIN SIGHT OF THE PO VALLEY, PRE-PARED FOR ITS SECOND WINTER IN ITALY.

EARLY IN APRIL 1945, GAINS ALONG BOTH COASTS MARKED THE END OF THE WINTER HALT. AFTER A WEEK OF HEAVY FIGHTING OUR TROOPS BROKE INTO THE PO VALLEY. PRECEDED BY BOMBER AND FIGHTER AIRCRAFT WHICH HARASSED THE FLEEING ENEMY, THE ALLIED ADVANCE CONTINUED UN-CHECKED ACROSS THE PO, THEN SPREAD OUT TO THE NORTH, EAST AND WEST TO CLOSE THE FRONTIERS. ON 2 MAY 1945, THE ENEMY IN ITALY SUR-RENDERED UNCONDITIONALLY.

The central panel of the north wall is engraved with this extract from General Eisenhower's "Crusade in Europe": FREEDOM FROM FEAR AND INJUSTICE AND OPPRESSION IS OURS ONLY IN THE MEASURE THAT MEN WHO VALUE SUCH FREEDOM ARE READY TO SUSTAIN ITS POSSESSION, TO DEFEND IT AGAINST EVERY THRUST FROM WITHIN OR WITHOUT.

Below the inscriptions on the north wall are six key maps record-ing the development of the war against Germany and the war against Japan.

Along the frieze above the inscrip-tions are nine escutcheons of Baveno granite on which are em-bossed the names of these ground and air battles in which American forces participated: Gela-Palermo-Troina; Salerno-Altavilla-Volturno; Magnano-San Pietro-Rapido; Cas-

THIS FIGURE WAS FORMERLY PART OF A MONUMENT
ERECTED IN THE FUTA PASS BY
THE 361ST INFANTRY 91ST DIVISION
TO HONOR THE MEMORY OF THEIR FALLEN COMRADES
AND TO COMMEMORATE THE ACHIEVEMENTS OF THE REGIMENT
IN WORLD WAR II

Statue of Soldier Overlooking Plot B from the East

sino-Anzio-Cisterna; Rome-Leg-horn-Arno; Futa-Santerno-Radi-cosa; Serchio-Bologna-Po Valley; Ploesti-Vienna-Munich; Regens-burg-Budapest-Brenner.

The Wall of the Missing, which connects the north and south atria, is constructed of travertine stone and measures 17'6'' in height and 138' in length. Shaded by plane trees, the Baveno granite panels on the wall are inscribed with the names and particulars of 1,409 Missing in Action in the region or lost or buried at sea. They came from Canada, the District of Columbia and from every state of the Union except Alaska and Hawaii.

United States Army and
    Army Air Forces . . . . . . .1,397[1]
United States Navy   12

---

[1] During World War II the Air Forces were part of the Army.

Running the full length of the wall above the names is the following inscription:

HERE ARE RECORDED THE NAMES OF AMERICANS WHO GAVE THEIR LIVES IN THE SERVICE OF THEIR COUNTRY AND WHO SLEEP IN UNKNOWN GRAVES.

The pylon or stele in front of the Wall of the Missing is 69 feet high and triangular in plan. Faced in Roman travertine, it is surmounted by a sculptured figure in Baveno granite designed by Sidney Waugh of New York. The figure represents the spirit of peace hovering over the fallen, bearing olive branches. Flying beside her out of cloud-like forms is the American eagle, guardian of justice and honor. This sculpture as well as the reliefs in the two atria were executed by Polli & Cardini of Baveno, Italy. The following dedicatory inscription appears on the pylon in English and Italian:

Visitors' Room

1941-1945

IN PROUD MEMORY OF HER SONS AND IN HUMBLE TRIBUTE TO THEIR SAC-RIFICES THIS MEMORIAL HAS BEEN ERECTED BY THE UNITED STATES OF AMERICA

Protection from possible landslide damage to the memorial is provided by massive reinforced concrete walls on its sides and rear.

THE GRAVES AREA

The 4,398 headstones are separated by paths of grass into eight plots designated A to H, four on each side of the central or east-west mall.

Within the graves area, the headstones seem to radiate in gentle arcs from the memorial pylon, curving inward slightly, contributing to the harmonious relationship between the graves area and the memorial.

These honored Dead who gave their lives in our country's service came from the Philippine Islands, China, Turkey, Spain, the District of Columbia and from every state in the Union except Alaska.

Two headstones mark the multiple burials of two Unknowns whose remains could not be separated and one headstone marks the grave of three Unknowns. Five pairs of brothers are buried side-by-side within the cemetery.

PLANTINGS

The graves area is enclosed by tree and shrubbery masses in which Italian stone pines, Italian cypresses, oriental plane trees, willows, holly oaks and cedars of Lebanon predominate. There are also flowering shrubs of oleander, laurel-cherry, crepe myrtle and Chinese starjasmine. A double row of oriental plane trees flanks the mall.

On the north side of the cemetery is a road bordered with German iris which leads to the service area, the superintendent's quarters and the memorial and its parking area.

Statue of Soldier Overlooking Plot A from the East

A View of the Graves Area

Spirit of Peace atop of a Triangular Stele

Sicily-Rome American Cemetery and Memorial

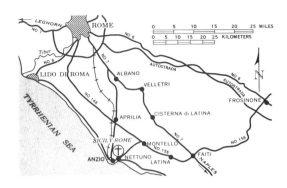

LOCATION

The Sicily-Rome American Cemetery and Memorial is situated just east of Anzio at the north edge of the town of Nettuno, 38 miles/60 kilometers south of Rome.

There is hourly train service between Rome and Nettuno. Travel one way by rail takes a little over one hour. The cemetery is located one mile north of the Nettuno railroad station, from which taxi service is available.

To travel to the cemetery from Rome by automobile, the following two routes are recommended:

(1) At Piazza di San Giovanni, bear left and pass through the old Roman wall to the Via Appia Nuova/route No. 7. About 8 miles from the Piazza di San Giovanni, after passing Ciampino airport, turn right on route No. 207 at the Sicily-Rome American Cemetery sign and follow it past Aprilia to Anzio, Nettuno and the cemetery.

(2) At Piazza di San Giovanni, bear right on the Via dell'Amba Aradam to Via delle Terme di Caracalla, pass through the old Roman wall along Viale Cristoforo Colombo and through the Exposition grounds (EUR), immediately beyond which is the first of the directional signs to the cemetery. Continue on Via Pontina/route No. 148 to overpass near Aprilia, thence take route No. 207/Via Nettunense.

Main Entrance to Cemetery

Chapel Interior

Aerial View of the Cemetery

Adequate hotel accommodations may be found in Anzio, Nettuno and Rome.

HOURS

The cemetery is open daily to the public as follows:
SUMMER (15 May – 15 September)
   8:00 a.m. – 6:00 p.m. — weekdays
   9:00 a.m. – 6:00 p.m. — Saturdays,
              Sundays, and holidays
WINTER (16 September – 14 May)
   8:00 a.m. – 5:00 p.m. — weekdays
   9:00 a.m. – 5:00 p.m. — Saturdays,
              Sundays, and holidays

During these hours, a staff member is on duty in the Visitors' Building to answer questions and escort relatives to grave and memorial sites, except between noon and 3:00 p.m. on weekends and holidays.

HISTORY

On 10 July 1943, just two months after the victorious North African campaign, Allied forces landed in strength on the southern and eastern shores of the island of Sicily. Despite vigorous resistance by the enemy, infantry and airborne troops of the U.S. Seventh Army thrust inland under cover of gunfire from the Western Naval Task Force. Five days later, the Allied beachheads were joined and a continuous line established. While the British Eighth Army on the right was advancing northeast toward Mount Etna against stiff resistance, the U.S. Seventh Army was driving rapidly to the northwest. Advancing 100 miles in four days, the Seventh Army occupied the port city of Palermo and then swung toward Messina in the northeast.

With air cover and support from the U. S. Twelfth Air Force, the Seventh and Eighth Armies drove across the difficult mountainous terrain of Sicily to seize Messina on 17 August. In just 39 days, the entire

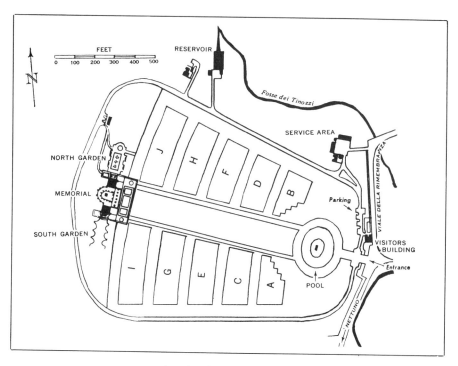

Location of Cemetery Features

island was overrun and the Sicilian campaign concluded. This resounding victory by the Allies caused the Italian government to break with the Axis and sue for peace.

In order to maintain contact with the withdrawing enemy forces, troops of the British Eighth Army crossed the Straits of Messina to the mainland. Six days later, at 0330 hours on 9 September, the major amphibious assault was launched on the Italian mainland over the beaches of Salerno by American and British troops of the U.S. Fifth Army. That same day, a British fleet landed troops at Taranto to seize the major port there and divert some enemy reserves from the main landing. Four days later, elements of two Panzer Corps mounted a powerful counterattack against Allied troops at Salerno threatening existence of the entire beachhead. After three days of bitter fighting, stubborn resistance by the Allied ground forces combined with artillery, naval gunfire and air support halted the enemy assault. Realizing that it could not dislodge the Fifth Army and fearful of not being in good defensive positions when the Eighth Army arrived in the area from Messina and Taranto, the enemy withdrew to the north as the two Allied armies joined forces at Vallo. With air support from the U.S. Twelfth Air Force, the Fifth Army seized Naples on 1 October as the Eighth Army on its right captured the airfields near Foggia. A major Allied objective of the landings on the Italian mainland was thus accomplished, obtainment of air bases from which the U.S. Fifteenth Air Force could conduct strategic bombardment of Austria, the Balkans and Germany. Together with the U.S. Eighth Air Force operating from England, it carried out numerous massive aerial attacks to destroy critical industrial targets and defeat

Graves area with Memorial in Background

the German Air Force.

Continuing its advance northward, the U. S. Fifth Army crossed the Volturno River in mid-October and attacked toward the Liri River Valley, which was considered the "gateway to Rome." Increasing resistance by the enemy, adverse weather conditions and mountainous terrain combined to slow the Fifth Army advance. In November and December, the Fifth Army fought its way across the rugged terrain in bitterly cold weather as on its right the Eighth Army crossed the Sangro River. The two Allied armies continued the breaching of the enemy's Winter Line south of Cassino, reaching the Garigliano and the Rapido Rivers in January 1944, where the advance ground to a halt at the strongly fortified Gustav Line.

To break the stalemate, an amphibious operation was planned at Anzio 40 miles south of Rome to outflank the Gustav Line and cut off the enemy from the rear. A Fifth Army attack continued to meet stubborn resistance in the heavily fortified Cassino area and failed to breach the Gustav Line. However, it was successful in drawing enemy reserves away from the landing beaches.

The amphibious landings on 22 January 1944 by American and British troops of the VI Corps at Anzio came as a surprise to the enemy. He, nevertheless, reacted forcefully and within a few days had brought reinforcements from northern Italy, France, Germany and Yugoslavia. Three major counterattacks were hurled against the VI Corps beachhead only to be stopped by a magnificent ground defense supported by tanks, artillery, airplanes and naval gunfire.

The final assault on the well entrenched enemy at the Gustav Line began on 11 May 1944. An aggressive attack by French troops of the Fifth Army successfully penetrated the Gustav Line in its area capturing

Monte Majo causing the enemy to commit its last reserves there. Soon the Allies were penetrating all along the line. Two weeks later the VI Corps broke out of the beachhead, and on 4 June 1944, the Allies entered Rome. For the first time since the landings at Salerno in September 1943, the enemy was in full retreat.

SITE

The site, 77 acres in extent, lay in the zone of advance of the U.S. 3d Infantry Division. A temporary wartime cemetery was established there on 24 January 1944, two days after the U.S. VI Corps landing on the beaches of Anzio.

After World War II, when the temporary cemeteries were disestablished by the Army, the remains of American military Dead whose next-of-kin requested permanent interment overseas were moved to one of the fourteen permanent sites on foreign soil, usually the one which was closest to the temporary cemetery. There they were reinterred by the American Graves Registration Service in the distinctive grave patterns proposed by the cemetery's architect and approved by the Commission. Design and construction of all structures and facilities at the permanent sites as well as the sculpture, landscaping and other improvements were the responsibility of the Commission.

Many of the Dead interred or commemorated here gave their lives in the liberation of Sicily (10 July to 17 August 1943); in the landings in the Salerno area (9 September 1943) and in the subsequent heavy fighting northward; in the landings at and occupation of the Anzio beachhead (22 January 1944 to May 1944); and in the air and naval operations in these regions.

The permanent cemetery and memorial were completed in 1956.

Graves Area and Peristyle of the Memorial

ARCHITECTS

Architects for the cemetery and memorial were Gugler, Kimball & Husted of New York City; the landscape architect was Ralph Griswold of Pittsburgh, Pennsylvania.

GENERAL LAYOUT

The main entrance to the cemetery is on the west side of Via della Rimembranza, 200 yards from the north edge of the town of Nettuno. Entry is through ornate bronze gates surmounted by the United States seal. The cemetery is generally trapezoidal in shape with the small end of the trapezoid near the entrance. Just inside the entrance on the right is the Visitors' Building and a limited number of parking spaces. Beyond the gate directly to the front is a large elliptical reflecting pool (82 yards by 66 yards) with a stone cenotaph of bronze-colored travertine in the shape of a sarcophagus on a small island in its center. Several Italian cypress trees flank the cenotaph on either side. Extending from the reflecting pool through the graves area to the large memorial on the west is a wide grassy mall lined with evergreen holly oak trees and a hedge of pittosporum tobira. The memorial consists of a chapel and museum connected by a peristyle and two gardens. American flags fly daily from flagpoles located on each side of the memorial.

The service road which encircles the graves area proceeds from the entrance gate past the Visitors' Building and parking area on the right at which point it curves to the left parallel to the graves area. The service area is located on the right just past the curve. A little further on the right are the pumphouse and power stations. Here water from the Fosso dei Tinozzi is directed into open reservoirs from which it is pumped into the high pressure sprinkler system. Potable water is drawn directly from city mains which pass the cemetery on the west. Along the outside of the service road to the rear of the memorial stand cedars of Lebanon, Monterey cypress and oleanders. At the top of the hill, the road turns left passing additional parking spaces and the rear entrance to the memorial. From the rear of the memorial, the road passes to the left around the west end of the graves area and returns to the entrance gate. Among the plantings beyond the road to the south of the graves area, Italian cypress, eucalyptus and oleanders predominate.

THE MEMORIAL

The memorial consists of a chapel, museum and connecting peristyle constructed largely of Roman travertine quarried near Tivoli, a few miles east of Rome.

Flanking the entrance to the peristyle are two flagstaffs 80 feet high. The peristyle contains massive columns of travertine and of Rosso Levanto marble from the vicinity of Rapallo, near Genoa. Prominently positioned in the peristyle on a pedestal of bronze-colored travertine is the "Brothers in Arms" sculpture by Paul Manship of New York, symbolizing an American soldier and sailor standing side by side with an arm around each other's shoulder. The sculpture of bronze was cast at the Battaglia Foundry in Milan. A single tall Roman pine tree shades it.

On the east facade of the chapel is a sculptured panel in relief of white Carrara marble symbolizing "Remembrance." It portrays an angel bestowing a laurel wreath upon the graves of those who gave their lives for their Country.

On the east facade of the museum is a panel symbolizing "Resurrection." It portrays a dead soldier being borne to his reward by a guardian angel. Both panels were

South Garden of the Memorial

designed by Paul Manship and carved by Pietro Bibolotti of Pietrasanta.

South of the memorial, adjacent to the chapel, is an informal garden lined on each side with connecting semi-circular planters containing beds of annual flowers. Panicled goldenrain trees and pink crepe myrtle border the planters. At the far end of the garden is a bronze statue of the legendary Thracian poet and musician Orpheus circumscribed by an armillary sphere with a sun dial.

North of the memorial, adjacent to the museum, is a more formal garden planted in parterre arrangements with beds of polyantha roses, geraniums, white oleanders, purple bougainvillea and other flowers.

At the far end of the garden is a Baveno granite fountain consisting of a large semi-circular bowl on a wide pedestal. It was carved from a single piece of granite quarried near the north end of Lake Maggiore. Cascades of water flow from the bowl into a low basin.

CHAPEL

On each side of the bronze door to the chapel (cast by the Marinelli Foundries of Florence) is the dedicatory inscription in English and Italian:

1941–1945 ☆ ☆ IN PROUD REMEMBRANCE OF THE ACHIEVEMENTS OF HER SONS AND IN HUMBLE TRIBUTE TO THEIR SACRIFICES THIS MEMORIAL HAS BEEN ERECTED BY THE UNITED STATES OF AMERICA.

INTERIOR

The chapel contains no windows. When light in addition to the artificial lighting is needed, two huge panels on the west wall, set in bronze and steel frames, can be swung open.

The floor of the chapel is of Rosso Levanto marble; the pews are of walnut.

The interior chapel walls of white Carrara marble are engraved with the name, rank, organization and State of entry into military service of 3,094 Missing in the region:

United States Army and Army
  Air Forces[1] 2,031
United States Navy 1,063

These servicemen and women, who died in the service of their Country, were Missing in Action or were lost or buried at sea. They represent every State in the Union and the District of Columbia.

Over the Apse is engraved:

HERE ARE RECORDED THE NAMES OF AMERICANS WHO GAVE THEIR LIVES IN THE SERVICE OF THEIR COUNTRY AND WHO SLEEP IN UNKNOWN GRAVES.

An Italian translation is engraved over the door.

On the altar of golden Broccatello Siena marble is a triptych of Serravezzo white marble from the Carrara region designed by Paul Manship. Carved in relief on the side

---

[1]During World War II, the Air Forces were part of the United States Army.

"Brothers in Arms" Statue,
Peristyle of the Memorial

North Garden of the Memorial

panels of the triptych are angels holding palm branches. The left panel bears this quotation from the Eighth Psalm (3-5) with reference to the sculptured ceiling dome:

WHEN I CONSIDER THY HEAVENS, THE WORKS OF THY FINGERS, THE MOON AND THE STARS, WHICH THOU HAST ORDAINED: WHAT IS MAN, THAT THOU ART MINDFUL OF HIM? AND THE SON OF MAN, THAT THOU VISITEST HIM? FOR THOU HAST MADE HIM A LITTLE LOWER THAN THE ANGELS, AND HAS CROWNED HIM WITH GLORY AND HONOR.

The right panel bears this text from T. T. Higham's translation of "The Greek Dead at Thermopylae" by Simonides:

NOBLY THEY ENDED, HIGH THEIR DESTINATION ✿ ✿ BENEATH AN ALTAR LAID, NO MORE A TOMB, WHERE NONE WITH PITY COMES OR LAMENTATIONS BUT PRAISE AND MEMORY, A SPLENDOR OF OBLATION ✿ ✿ WHO LEFT BEHIND A GEM-LIKE HERITAGE OF COURAGE AND RENOWN, A NAME THAT SHALL GO DOWN FROM AGE TO AGE.

Carved in relief on the center panel, flying against a background of clouds is the Archangel Michael sheathing his sword while four archangels below him proclaim the Victory. Beneath them is the universal prayer: "PEACE ON EARTH GOOD WILL AMONG MEN."

On the reverse of the center panel is carved the Angel of Peace. A cross in metal filigree stands before the triptych on the altar.

Engraved on the left or east end of the altar is a cross; engraved on the right end are the Tablets of Moses.

THE CEILING

The ceiling dome sculpture, 22 feet in diameter, was designed by Gugler, Kimball & Husted and executed by Paul Manship and by Bruno Bearzi of Florence. The medieval signs of the Zodiac in high-relief represent the constellations. The

planets Mars, Jupiter and Saturn occupy the same relative positions that they occupied at 0200 hours on 22 January 1944, the historic moment when the first American and British troops landed on the beaches of Anzio. The more important stars in each constellation are shown as points of light on the celestial dome. Inscribed around the base of the dome is this text:

O YE STARS OF HEAVEN BLESS YE THE LORD PRAISE HIM AND MAGNIFY HIM FOREVER.

A brief explanation of the dome is cast into the bronze cover of the large switchbox just inside the door of the chapel.

THE MUSEUM ROOM

The museum room is entered through bronze gates cast by the Marinelli Foundries, which also cast the ornamental light fixtures in the memorial.

An octagonal table of bronze-colored travertine, into which is set a circular relief map of Italy at 1:500,000 scale, occupies the center of the room. The map is of bronze inset with marble mosaic tile in various shades of blue depicting the sea areas. It was fabricated by Bruno Bearzi from information supplied by the American Battle Monuments Commission and shows in general outline the American military operations in Sicily and Italy during the period 1943-45.

The maps on the east and west walls were designed by Carlo Ciampaglia of Middle Valley, New Jersey and executed in true fresco by Leonetto Tintori of Florence. This procedure involves the mixing of pigments with the plaster as it is applied to the wall. This disappearing art was used widely in the Middle Ages in the production of many murals which have lasted through the ensuing centuries.

Altar, Triptych and Tablets of the Missing

On the west wall are three maps — "The Capture of Sicily," "The Strategic Air Assaults" and "The Naples-Foggia Campaign." To aid in understanding them, the maps bear these inscriptions:

THE CAPTURE OF SICILY

ON 10 JULY 1943, UNDER COVER OF AIR AND NAVAL BOMBARDMENT, AMERICAN AND BRITISH FORCES LANDED ON THE SOUTH AND EAST SHORES OF SICILY.

1. AIDED BY GUNFIRE OF THE WESTERN NAVAL TASK FORCE AND COVERED BY AIRCRAFT OF THE TWELFTH AIR FORCE, THE U. S. SEVENTH ARMY ADVANCED RAPIDLY INLAND, REACHING THE CENTER OF THE ISLAND IN TEN DAYS. ON 22 JULY U. S. FORCES OCCUPIED PALERMO AND ITS PORT.

2. FARTHER TO THE EAST, THE BRITISH EIGHTH ARMY, ATTACKING NORTHWARD TOWARD MOUNT ETNA, ENCOUNTERED STIFF RESISTANCE WHICH SLOWED ITS PROGRESS. THE U. S. SEVENTH ARMY, TO RELIEVE THE PRESSURE, PROMPTLY FACED TO THE NORTHEAST AND ADVANCED TOWARD MESSINA.

3. ATTACKING NORTH AND SOUTH OF MOUNT ETNA, THE SEVENTH AND EIGHTH ARMIES DROVE FORWARD OVER THE DIFFICULT MOUNTAIN TERRAIN. IN ORDER TO OUTFLANK THE ENEMY DEFENSES THE ALLIES MADE SEVERAL AMPHIBIOUS ASSAULTS ALONG THE NORTHERN AND EASTERN COASTS.

4. WITH THE OCCUPATION OF MESSINA ON 17 AUGUST THE CAMPAIGN ENDED. IN 39 DAYS THE ALLIES HAD EXPELLED THE ENEMY FROM THE ISLAND, PRECIPITATING A POLITICAL DISASTER FOR THE AXIS. ON 8 SEPTEMBER THE ITALIAN GOVERNMENT, RENOUNCING FASCIST GUIDANCE, ASKED FOR PEACE TERMS.

THE STRATEGIC AIR ASSAULTS

MAJOR OBJECTIVES IN ITALY INCLUDED THE AIR BASES IN THE NAPLES-FOGGIA AREA.

1. FROM BASES IN THE NAPLES-FOGGIA AREA THE U. S. FIFTEENTH AIR FORCE LAUNCHED ITS BOMBARDMENT OF AUSTRIA, THE BALKANS, AND GERMANY. IN COLLABORATION WITH THE DESERT AIR FORCE AND THE ALLIED AIR FLEETS ALREADY OPERATING FROM

ENGLAND, OUR BOMBERS AND FIGHT-
ERS ATTACKED INCESSANTLY. THEIR
OBJECTIVES WERE THE DEFEAT OF THE
GERMAN AIR FORCE AND THE
PROGRESSIVE DISLOCATION AND DE-
STRUCTION OF THE ENEMY'S MILITARY
AND ECONOMIC SYSTEMS.

2. THE FIFTEENTH AIR FORCE AT-
TACKED AIRCRAFT FACTORIES IN REG-
ENSBURG AND BUDAPEST, OIL RE-
FINERIES AT PLOESTI AND BRASOV,
ENEMY AIRFIELDS AND LINES OF COM-
MUNICATION IN NORTHERN ITALY,
AND TRANSPORTATION SYSTEMS CEN-
TERING IN MUNICH, VIENNA AND
BUDAPEST. ITS AIRCRAFT REACHED AS
FAR AS BERLIN ITSELF. WHILE THE
GROUND FORCES ADVANCED NORTH-
WARD, THE BOMBER OFFENSIVE PUR-
SUED WITH EVER-INCREASING INTEN-
SITY THE DESTRUCTION OF STRATEGIC
MILITARY AND INDUSTRIAL TARGETS.

THE NAPLES-FOGGIA CAMPAIGN

FOLLOWING THEIR VICTORY IN SICILY,
THE ALLIES NEXT UNDERTOOK TO
ENTER THE CONTINENT OF EUROPE.

1. THE ASSAULT ON THE SALERNO
BEACHES WAS LAUNCHED ON 9 SEP-
TEMBER 1943. AT 0330 HOURS ALLIED
TROOPS OF THE U. S. FIFTH ARMY
LANDED FROM SHIPS OF THE NORTH-
ERN AND SOUTHERN NAVAL ATTACK
FORCES. OVERCOMING THE DEFENSES
THE ALLIES FOUGHT THEIR WAY IN-
LAND. AT VALLO THEY JOINED WITH
THE BRITISH EIGHTH ARMY WHICH HAD
CROSSED FROM SICILY ON 3 SEPTEM-
BER.

2. WITH THE COOPERATION OF
FIGHTERS AND BOMBERS OF THE
TWELFTH AIR FORCE, THE FIFTH ARMY
MADE STEADY PROGRESS WHILE THE
BRITISH EIGHTH ARMY ADVANCED ON
ITS RIGHT. BY 1 OCTOBER NAPLES AND
THE FOGGIA AIRFIELDS HAD BEEN
SEIZED. FIVE DAYS LATER THE FIFTH
ARMY REACHED THE VOLTURNO RIVER,
WHICH IT CROSSED IN MID-OCTOBER

West Wall of the Museum Room

AND ADVANCED TOWARD THE LIRI RIVER VALLEY. IN NOVEMBER, MOUNTAINOUS TERRAIN, INCREASED RESISTANCE AND BAD WEATHER SLOWED THE ALLIED DRIVE. A HALT WAS CALLED ON 15 NOVEMBER TO CONSOLIDATE POSITIONS.

3. RESUMING ITS ATTACKS IN DECEMBER AND JANUARY, THE FIFTH ARMY SLOWLY BATTERED ITS WAY THROUGH THE WINTER LINE. STRUGGLING FORWARD AGAINST DETERMINED OPPOSITION, ACROSS RUGGED TERRAIN IN BITTERLY COLD WEATHER, OUR TROOPS EVENTUALLY REACHED THE GARIGLIANO AND RAPIDO RIVERS. HERE IN FRONT OF THE STRONGLY FORTIFIED GUSTAV LINE THE ATTACK WAS STOPPED, TO BE RENEWED IN COORDINATION WITH THE LANDINGS SOON TO BE MADE AT ANZIO.

Beneath the maps are two sets of key maps, "The War Against Germany" and "The War Against Japan."

On the east wall is one large map, "The Landing at Anzio and the Capture of Rome." This map portrays the landings in the vicinity of Anzio, the establishment of the Anzio beachhead, the subsequent fighting therein, and the final breach of the Gustav line on 11 May 1944 by American and Allied forces who, advancing swiftly northwards, joined hands with the troops who were breaking out of the beachhead to liberate Rome on 4 June 1944.

It is accompanied by the following explanatory text:

THE LANDING AT ANZIO AND
THE CAPTURE OF ROME

DELAYED IN THEIR ADVANCE TOWARD ROME AT THE GUSTAV LINE, THE ALLIES ATTEMPTED TO OUTFLANK IT FROM THE SEAWARD SIDE. AT 0200 HOURS ON 22 JANUARY 1944, AN ALLIED AMPHIBIOUS TASK FORCE LANDED THE U.S. VI CORPS AT ANZIO AND NETTUNO.

1. THE AMERICAN AND BRITISH LANDINGS CAME AS A SURPRISE TO THE ENEMY WHOSE REACTION, NEVERTHELESS, WAS IMMEDIATE AND EFFECTIVE. REINFORCEMENTS RUSHED TO THE AREA FROM NORTHERN ITALY, FRANCE, YUGOSLAVIA AND GERMANY PROMPTLY HALTED THE ALLIED ADVANCE. DURING FEBRUARY, THE GERMANS HURLED THREE MAJOR COUNTERATTACKS AGAINST THE BEACHHEAD. THEY REGAINED SOME GROUND BUT THE ALLIED TROOPS, WITH THE AID OF THE TWELFTH AIR FORCE AND CONCENTRATED NAVAL SUPPORT, CLUNG TO THEIR PRECARIOUS FOOTHOLD DOMINATED BY THE GERMAN POSITIONS ON THE ALBAN HILLS.

2. IN THE SOUTH, THE FIFTH ARMY ATTACKED THE GUSTAV LINE ON 17 JANUARY 1944. THIS ASSAULT, DESIGNED TO ASSIST THE ANZIO-NETTUNO LANDINGS, MET WITH LITTLE SUCCESS AGAINST THE FORMIDABLE DEFENSES OF THE CASSINO AREA. WELL ENTRENCHED, THE ENEMY WITHSTOOD HEAVY ARTILLERY FIRE AND THE ASSAULTS OF THE TWELFTH AND FIFTEENTH AIR FORCE.

3. FROM MARCH TO MAY 1944 THE ALLIES MAINTAINED THEIR CONSTANT PRESSURE ON THE ENEMY WHILE BUILDING UP THEIR STRENGTH FOR A NEW OFFENSIVE. ON 11 MAY, THE FIFTH ARMY ATTACKED AND BREACHED THE GUSTAV LINE. TWO WEEKS LATER THE FORCES IN THE BEACHHEAD BROKE OUT AND JOINED THE ADVANCE. ON 4 JUNE, THE ALLIES ENTERED ROME.

GRAVES AREA

The graves area contains ten grave plots lettered from "A" to "J", five on each side of a central mall. Plots A, C, E, G, and I are on the left (south) side of the mall and B, D, F, H and J on the right (north). Each grave plot is enclosed by a pittosporum hedge; the paths of grass between the plots are lined with Roman pines. Here are interred 7,862 of our military Dead under 7,860 headstones arranged in gentle arcs which sweep across the broad green lawns. They represent 35 per-

cent of the burials which were originally made in Sicily and southern
Italy. Each grave is marked with a
white marble headstone, a Star of
David for those of the Jewish faith —
a latin cross for others. Of the
graves, 488 contain the remains of
490 Unknowns that could not be
identified.

These Dead, who gave their lives
in their Country's service, came
from all fifty states and the District of
Columbia. A small number also
came from Canada, England, Scotland, Eire, Finland, Sweden and
Spain. In twenty-one instances, two
brothers lie buried side by side.

VISITORS BUILDING

Just inside the entrance on the right
is the Visitors' Building. It contains
the superintendent's office, toilet
facilities, and a comfortably furnished room where visitors may
rest, obtain information, sign the
register and pause to refresh themselves. Whenever the cemetery is
open to the public, a staff member is
on duty in the building to answer
questions and to escort relatives to
grave and memorialization sites (except between the hours of noon and
3:00 p.m. on weekends and holidays). He is always happy to provide
information on specific burial and
memorialization locations in any of
the Commission's cemeteries, accommodations in the vicinity, best
means and routes of travel, local history and other items that may be of
interest.

PLANTINGS

The entrance road to the cemetery is
lined with a neatly trimmed hedge of
pittosporum tobira.

Just inside the cemetery gates,
straight ahead is a large elliptical reflecting pool with a small island at its
center. Several Italian cypress trees
(cupressus sempervirens pyramidalis) and glossy abelia flank the stone

East Wall of the Museum Room

cenotaph on the island. Water lilies float in the pool. Evergreen holly oak trees (quercus ilex) and a hedge of pittosporum tobira line the wide grassy mall through the graves area from the reflecting pool to the memorial. Each grave plot is enframed by a hedge of pittosporum tobira and the grassy paths between the plots are lined with Roman pines (pinus pinea).

Within the peristyle of the memorial, a single Roman pine (pinus pinea) shades the Brothers in Arms statue. Dense plantings of Roman pine (pinus pinea) form a backdrop for the memorial.

The informal garden south of the memorial contains planters filled with annual flowers and surrounded by panicled goldenrain trees (koetreuteria paniculata) and pink crepe myrtle (lagerstroemia indica rosea). Gazanca Varicolor compliments the Orpheus statue. The more formal garden north of the memorial is planted with beds of polyantha roses, geraniums, white oleander, purple bougainvillea and other flowers in parterre arrangements.

Cedars of Lebanon, Monterey cypress (cupressus macrocarpa), eucalyptus and oleanders predominate the plantings outside of the service road around the perimeter of the cemetery.

Headstone of Medal of Honor Recipient

Visitors' Room

Graves Area with Memorial in Background

"Remembrance"

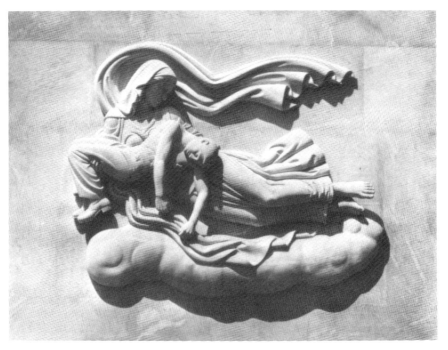

"Resurrection"

WORLD WAR II
CEMETERIES AND MEMORIALS:

LUXEMBOURG

Luxembourg American Cemetery and Memorial

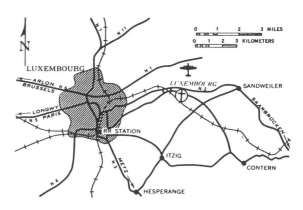

LOCATION

The Luxembourg American Cemetery and Memorial is situated within the capital city of Luxembourg, 3 miles east of its center in the section of the city called Hamm. It lies 2 miles/3 kilometers southwest of the airport. The cemetery can be reached by train from Paris (Gare de l'Est) in approximately 5 hours; from Liege, Belgium in about 3 hours and from Germany. Taxicabs to the cemetery are available at the railroad station.

Luxembourg City can be reached by automobile from Paris (215 miles/346 kilometers) via N-3/N-33 to Verdun, then northeast on N-18 to Longwy, and finally N-5/N-52A to Luxembourg City. Once in the city, one should take E-42 southeast toward Saarbrucken. The road is well marked and passes within 300 yards of the cemetery. To reach Luxem-

Entrance to the Cemetery

Altar against Back Wall of Chapel

Aerial View of Cemetery

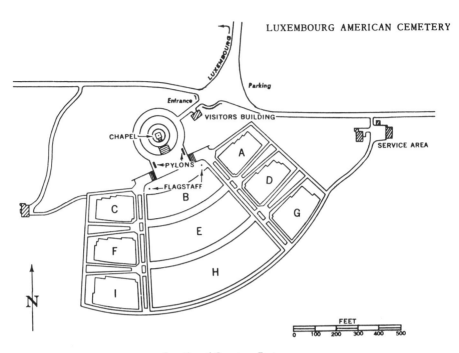

Location of Cemetery Features

bourg City from Brussels (135 miles/ 218 kilometers), take N-4/E-40 southeast to Arlon, then N-4/E-9 east to the city. The airport in Luxembourg City is serviced by frequent international flights daily. Taxicabs and rental cars are available at the airport. Hotel accommodations in the city are adequate.

HOURS

The cemetery is open daily to the public as shown below:
SUMMER (16 March – 30 September)
    9:00 a.m. – 6:00 p.m. — weekdays
    10:00 a.m. – 6:00 p.m. — Saturdays,
        Sundays, and holidays
WINTER (1 October – 15 March)
    9:00 a.m. – 5:00 p.m. — weekdays
    10:00 a.m. – 5:00 p.m. — Saturdays,
        Sundays, and holidays

When the cemetery is open to the public, a staff member is on duty in the Visitors' building to answer questions, and to escort relatives to grave and memorial sites (except between noon and 3:00 p.m. on weekends and holidays).

HISTORY

On 16 December 1944, the enemy in Europe launched his last major counteroffensive of the war. For the location of his attack, he chose the Ardennes Forest where his first breakthrough had achieved such tremendous success in 1940. Prepared in the greatest of secrecy, the plan called for three armies abreast to attack on a narrow front toward the west with Antwerp as its objective. The attack was timed to coincide with inclement weather in order to limit the use of Allied air power. The assault began at 5:30 a.m. under the cover of fog and rain and initially was quite successful as the enemy broke through on a 45 mile front. American soldiers resisted valiantly, however, and with heroic effort were able to hold the shoulders of the salient, blocking all attempts to expand the width of the penetration.

Available U.S. reserves were rushed to the scene of battle. At St. Vith, a furious struggle prevented the enemy's use of its vital road junction for a crucial period. In Bastogne, at the other vital road junction, American defenders clung tenaciously to their positions even though they had been surrounded for five days. Despite a penetration by some units of over 60 miles, the enemy was unable to exploit the breakthrough.

On 22 September 1944, the U.S. Third Army launched a strong counterattack against the southern flank of the penetration. The next day the skies cleared sufficiently to permit the U.S. Eighth and Ninth Air Forces to join the battle and to drop supplies to the defenders at Bastogne. Driving relentlessly forward despite strong opposition and bitterly cold weather, the U.S. Third Army broke through the enemy cordon around Bastogne on 26 December. The U.S. First Army counterattacked from the north on 3 January 1945 and ten days later met with the U.S. Third Army at Houffalize. By 25 January, the enemy salient no longer existed.

In February, the U.S. Third Army drove the enemy from Luxembourg and breached the Siegfried Line. After capturing Trier, it continued its advance, seizing bridgeheads across the Kyll River and launching an attack to reach the Rhine. The Third Army units north of the Moselle River advanced first, covered by fighters and bombers of the U.S. Ninth Air Force. In just five days, they swept forward to join the First Army. By 10 March, all enemy units were cleared from the west bank of the Rhine north of its junction with the Moselle at Koblenz.

On 13 March, Third Army troops north of the Moselle River turned to the Southeast to attack in coordination with the Third Army troops advancing south of the river. By 21 March, the entire west bank of the Rhine had been cleared in the Third Army sector. The next night, in a surprise assault, the Third Army crossed the Rhine at Oppenheim, a prelude to the final offensive of the war.

SITE

The Luxembourg American Cemetery and Memorial, 50.5 acres in extent, is situated in a glade enframed by spruce, beech, oak and other trees. It is one of fourteen permanent World War II American military cemeteries erected on foreign soil by the American Battle Monuments Commission. The site was liberated by the U.S. 5th Armored Division on 10 September 1944 and a temporary military burial ground was established there nineteen days later. At the time, Allied forces were engaged in stemming the enemy's Ardennes offensive known as the "Battle of the Bulge." The site subsequently was selected to be the location of one of the permanent World War II American military cemeteries to be erected on foreign soil. Free use of the site as a permanent military burial ground for American World War II Dead was granted by the Grand Ducal government of Luxembourg in perpetuity without charge or taxation. Later, the Grand Ducal government developed a parking area for the cemetery and modified its agreement with the United States to include it.

After the war, when the temporary burial grounds were being disestablished by the American Graves Registration Service (AGRS), the remains of American military Dead, whose next of kin had directed permanent interment on foreign soil in a cemetery memorial designed especially to honor them, were moved by the AGRS to a permanent cemetery site, usually the one closest to the

The Memorial with Graves Area in Foreground

temporary burial location. They were interred by the AGRS in the distinctive grave patterns proposed by the cemetery's architect and approved by the Commission. Interment of the 5,076 permanent burials in the Luxembourg American Cemetery and Memorial was completed on 16 December 1949. They represented 39% of the original burials in the region. Most lost their lives in the enemy's Ardennes offensive, the "Battle of the Bulge;" in air operations over the general region; and in the fighting eastward to the Rhine and beyond during the winter of 1944 and the spring of 1945.

Design and construction of all facilities at permanent American military cemeteries on foreign soil were the responsibilities of the American Battle Monuments Commission, i.e., the memorial, the chapel, the visitors' building, superintendent's quarters, paths, roads, perimeter walls and service facilities. The Commission also was responsible for the sculpture, landscaping and other improvements on the site. Construction of the permanent cemetery at Luxembourg was completed in the spring of 1960; it was dedicated on 4 July 1960.

ARCHITECTS

Architects for the cemetery and memorial were KealXy and Patterson of New York City. The landscape architect was Alfred Geiffert, Jr., also of New York City.

GENERAL LAYOUT

The cemetery's parking area comes into one's view immediately after turning south from highway E-42. At the far side of the parking area is the tall wrought iron entrance gate at the northeastern edge of the cemetery. Its massive stone pillars, each weighing more than a ton, are surmounted by gilded bronze eagles

East Facade of Chapel with Dedicatory Inscription

bearing laurel wreaths, the ancient award for valor. Engraved in relief on each pillar is a cluster of 13 stars representing the original thirteen states. Climbing hydrangea adorn the walls adjacent to the entrance. Inside the gate immediately to the left is the Visitors' Building, laced with Virginia Creeper, resembling a small cottage.

A short wide path leads from the entrance gate past the Visitors' building to the memorial, where it intersects the circular path around the chapel. Facing southeast, the chapel, flanked by massifs of Japanese holly, overlooks a terrace paved with stone on which are two pylons containing operations maps and the names of the Missing in Action in the region and two bronze frames holding three key maps abreast, depicting the course of the war around the world. At the edge of the terrace adjacent to the graves area is a long bronze balustrade, constructed by the H. H. Martyn Company of Cheltenham, England. The terrace itself is encircled by a hedge and a broad border of

Cotoneaster horizontalis. A flight of steps paved in Vosges stone at each end of the terrace leads down to a flag pole and the fan shaped graves area beyond.

THE MEMORIAL

The memorial consists of a tall, columnar, square chapel of stone set upon a podium, reached by two flights of steps, and a terrace overlooking the graves area with two pylons and two bronze stands holding key maps. The pylons are faced with operations maps on one side and stone tablets with the names of the Missing in the region on the other. The six key maps depict the course of the war throughout the world.

Set into the granite paving at the center of the memorial terrace in bronze letters is the following inscription from General Eisenhower's dedication of the Roll of Honor in St. Paul's Cathedral in London: ALL WHO SHALL HEREAFTER LIVE IN FREEDOM WILL BE HERE REMINDED THAT TO THESE MEN AND THEIR COMRADES WE OWE A DEBT TO BE PAID WITH GRATEFUL RE-

MEMBRANCE OF THEIR SACRIFICE AND WITH THE HIGH RESOLVE THAT THE CAUSE FOR WHICH THEY DIED SHALL LIVE ETERNALLY.

THE CHAPEL

The chapel, of white Valore stone from the Jura Mountain region of central France, rises 50 feet above its podium. As one approaches it from the cemetery entrance, a carving in high relief of the obverse of the seal of the United States of America is clearly visible on the east facade of the chapel. Engraved below the seal is the dedicatory inscription: 1941–1945 ✩ ✩ IN PROUD REMEMBRANCE OF THE ACHIEVEMENTS OF HER SONS AND IN HUMBLE TRIBUTE TO THEIR SACRIFICES THIS MEMORIAL HAS bEEN ERECTED BY THE UNITED STATES OF AMERICA. On the opposite or west facade of the chapel is a carving in high relief of the coat of arms of the Grand Duchy of Luxembourg. Engraved below it is a translation of the dedicatory inscription in French.

Above the entrance to the chapel on the south face, which is reached by a short flight of stairs, is a 23-foot sculpture of the Angel of Peace carved in Swedish Orchid Red granite. His right hand is raised in blessing and his left hand holds a laurel branch. Above the Angel of Peace is a dove against a cloud. The sculpture was designed by Leo Friedlander of White Plains, New York and executed by Cirla & Figlio of Babena, Italy. Beneath the sculpture on the lintel over the entrance door is carved: HERE IS ENSHRINED THE MEMORY OF VALOR AND SACRIFICE.

The bronze door of the chapel, also designed by Leo Friedlander, was cast by H. H. Martyn of Cheltenham, England. Each of its eight panels symbolizes a different military virtue or attribute of a good soldier. They are:

Physical Fitness	Fidelity
Proficiency	Sacrifice
Valor	Family Ties
Fortitude	Faith

Entrance Door to Chapel

CHAPEL INTERIOR

The interior walls of the chapel are of Hauteville Perle stone from the Jura Mountain region of France.

Above the door inside the chapel is the inscription: SOME THERE BE WHICH HAVE NO SEPULCHRE THEIR NAME LIVETH FOR EVERMORE. On the west wall left of the entrance is the inscription: GRANT US GRACE FEARLESSLY TO CONTEND AGAINST EVIL AND TO MAKE NO PEACE WITH OPPRESSION. Over the inscription is a roundel containing a latin cross. On the east wall to the right of the entrance is the inscription: TAKE UNTO THYSELF O LORD THE SOULS OF THE VALOROUS THAT THEY MAY DWELL IN THY GLORY. Over that inscription is a roundel featuring the Tablets of Moses surmounted by the Star of David.

Against the north wall opposite the entrance is the altar flanked by United States flags. It is of Bleu Belg marble from southern Belgium and bears this inscription from St. John X, 28: I GIVE UNTO THEM ETERNAL LIFE AND THEY SHALL NEVER PERISH. Above the

Chapel Interior

altar is a tall narrow window of stained glass portraying the insignia of the five major U.S. commands that operated in the region, the 12th Army Group, First Army, Third Army, Eighth Air Force and the Ninth Air Force. It was designed by Allyn Cox of New York City and fabricated by Morris Singer of London, who also made the massive bronze light fixtures. The pews and priedieu of ebony-stained birchwood were made by Patriarca of Rome, Italy. The floor is of four different marbles from Italy, Bianco Carrara Chiaro, Giallo di Sienna Scuro, Nero Assoluto Italiano and Bardiglio Capella. Inset in the floor is a bronze circular plaque containing the thirteen stars of the seal of the United States of America wreathed in oak, pine and laurel. In the center of the mosaic ceiling is a dove, representing the Holy Spirit, on a background of clouds within a nimbus, held by four angels, from which emanates the sun's rays. At the feet of the angels is this running inscription encircling the ceiling: IN PROUD AND GRATEFUL MEMORY OF THOSE MEN OF THE ARMED SERVICES OF THE UNITED STATES OF AMERICA WHO IN THIS REGION AND IN THE SKIES ABOVE IT ENDURED ALL AND GAVE ALL THAT JUSTICE AMONG NATIONS MIGHT PREVAIL AND THAT MANKIND MIGHT ENJOY FREEDOM AND INHERIT PEACE. The mosaic was designed by Allyn Cox and fabricated by Fabrizio Cassio of Rome.

PYLONS

The two memorial pylons of Valore stone on the terrace are rectangular in shape. Inscribed on the outer faces of these pylons are the name, rank, organization and state of entry into the military service of 370 Missing in Action of the United States Army and the Army Air Forces*, whose remains were never recovered, or if recovered, never identified. Above the names on each

*During World War II, the Air Force was part of the United States Army

pylon is the inscription: HERE ARE RE-CORDED THE NAMES OF AMERICANS WHO GAVE THEIR LIVES IN THE SERVICE OF THEIR COUNTRY AND WHO SLEEP IN UNKNOWN GRAVES. These men came from 42 states and the District of Columbia.

A large operations map is set into the inner face of each pylon. The west pylon on the right side of the terrace contains a map of military operations in western Europe from the landings in Normandy to the end of the war. The east pylon on the left side of the terrace contains a map of the Ardennes and Rhineland campaigns to include the "Battle of the Bulge," subsequent fighting to clear the west bank of the Rhine, and the crossing of the Rhine River at Oppenheim. Flanking the map of operations in Western Europe are explanatory inscriptions in English and French of which the following is the English version: ON 6 JUNE 1944, PRECEDED BY AIRBORNE UNITS AND COVERED BY NAVAL AND AIR BOMBARDMENT, UNITED STATES AND BRITISH COMMONWEALTH FORCES LANDED ON THE COAST OF NORMANDY. PUSHING SOUTHWARD THEY ESTABLISHED A BEACHHEAD SOME 20 MILES IN DEPTH. ON 25 JULY, IN THE WAKE OF A PARALYZING AIR BOMBARDMENT, THE U.S. FIRST ARMY BROKE OUT OF THE BEACHHEAD AND WAS SOON JOINED BY THE U.S. THIRD ARMY. TOGETHER THEY REPULSED A POWERFUL COUNTERATTACK TOWARDS AV-

Inscription and Roundel, East Wall of Chapel

RANCHES. CRUSHED BETWEEN THE AMERICANS ON THE SOUTH AND WEST AND THE BRITISH ON THE NORTH, ATTACKED CONTINUOUSLY BY THE U.S. EIGHTH AND NINTH AIR FORCES AND THE ROYAL AIR FORCE, THE ENEMY RETREATED ACROSS THE SEINE.

SUSTAINED BY THE HERCULEAN ACHIEVEMENTS OF ARMY AND NAVY SUPPLY PERSONNEL, THE ALLIED ARMIES AND AIR FORCES PURSUED VIGOROUSLY. BY MIDSEPTEMBER THE U.S. NINTH ARMY HAD LIBERATED BREST; THE FIRST ARMY WAS STANDING ON THE THRESHOLD OF GERMANY; THE THIRD ARMY HAD REACHED THE MOSELLE AND HAD JOINED THE U.S. SEVENTH AND FRENCH FIRST ARMIES ADVANCING NORTHWARD FROM THE MEDITERRANEAN. PROGRESS IN THE NEXT THREE MONTHS WAS SLOW, THE FIGHTING BITTER. METZ FELL AS THE THIRD ARMY MOVED INTO THE SAAR.

THE ENEMY LAUNCHED, IN THE ARDENNES, HIS FINAL MAJOR COUNTEROFFENSIVE ON 16 DECEMBER 1944. PROMPT TACTICAL COUNTERMEASURES AND THE SUPERB FIGHTING QUALITIES OF AMERICAN SOLDIERS AND AIRMEN HALTED THIS DRIVE. DURING FEBRUARY AND MARCH THE WEST BANK OF THE RHINE WAS CLEARED. IN RAPID SUCCESSION AMERICAN FORCES SEIZED A BRIDGE AT REMAGEN, CROSSED AT OPPENHEIM, THEN JOINED THE BRITISH IN THE MAJOR ASSAULT NORTH OF THE RUHR. SWEEPING ACROSS GERMANY THE ALLIES MET THE ADVANCING TROOPS OF THE U.S.S.R. TO FORCE THE COMPLETE SURRENDER OF THE ENEMY ON 8 MAY 1945, 337 DAYS AFTER THE INITIAL LANDING IN FRANCE.

Similarly, flanking the map of the Ardennes and Rhineland campaigns

Mosaic Ceiling of Chapel

Military Operations in Western Europe – West Pylon

in both languages, is this explanatory inscription: ON 16 DECEMBER 1944 THE ENEMY MADE HIS LAST CONCERTED EFFORT TO STAVE OFF DEFEAT BY UNLEASHING THREE ARMIES ON A NARROW FRONT. PREPARED IN GREATEST SECRECY AND LAUNCHED UNDER COVER OF FOG AND RAIN, HIS ATTACK IN THE ARDENNES WAS INITIALLY SUCCESSFUL. BREAKING THROUGH ON A 45-MILE FRONT, HIS FORCES PENETRATED OVER 60 MILES, BUT AMERICAN SOLDIERS, FIGHTING VALIANTLY, HELD THE CRITICAL SHOULDERS OF THE SALIENT.

REACTING PROMPTLY AND DECISIVELY, THE ALLIES RUSHED ALL AVAILABLE RESERVES TO THE SCENE. A FURIOUS STRUGGLE DEVELOPED AT ST. VITH WHERE THE ENEMY ADVANCE WAS STUBBORNLY DELAYED. AT BASTOGNE, ALTHOUGH SURROUNDED FOR FIVE DAYS, AMERICAN TROOPS, WITH THE HELP OF SUPPLIES DROPPED BY IX TROOP CARRIER COMMAND AIRCRAFT, MAINTAINED THEIR DEFENSE. ON 22 DECEMBER THE THIRD ARMY COUNTERATTACKED THE SOUTHERN FLANK OF THE PENETRATION. THE NEXT DAY THE SKIES CLEARED AND THE EIGHTH AND NINTH AIR FORCES PLUNGED INTO THE BATTLE. THE THIRD ARMY CONTINUED ITS AD-

VANCE THROUGH BITTERLY COLD WEATHER, REACHING BASTOGNE ON 26 DECEMBER. THE FIRST ARMY'S COUNTERATTACK CAME ON 3 JANUARY 1945; ON THE 16TH THE TWO ARMIES MET AT HOUFFALIZE. THE SALIENT WAS REDUCED BY 25 JANUARY.

IN FEBRUARY THE THIRD ARMY FORCED ITS WAY THROUGH THE SIEGFRIED LINE, CAPTURED TRIER, AND BY 5 MARCH HAD ESTABLISHED BRIDGEHEADS ACROSS THE KYLL. THE NEXT DAY IT LAUNCHED ITS ATTACK NORTH OF THE MOSELLE. PRECEDED BY AIRCRAFT OF THE NINTH AIR FORCE, ITS GROUND TROOPS SWEPT FORWARD TO JOIN THE FIRST ARMY ON THE RHINE. THEN, ON 13 MARCH, AMERICAN FORCES SOUTH OF THE MOSELLE ADVANCED; THOSE WEST OF KOBLENZ SWUNG TO THE SOUTHEAST TO JOIN THIS ASSAULT. HAVING CLEARED THE WEST BANK BY 21 MARCH, THE THIRD ARMY RUSHED ACROSS THE RHINE AT OPPENHEIM THE NEXT NIGHT.

The operations maps were carved and fitted together from slabs of several granites: Rosso Vanga and Verde Svezia from Sweden, and Verde Mergozzo Chiaro, Nero

Ardennes and Rhineland Campaigns – East Pylon

Biella, Rosa Baveno Chiaro, Bianco Montorfano and Verde Blauco from the Alpine regions of northwest Italy. Allyn Cox, an American artist, designed the maps utilizing information provided by the American Battle Monuments Commission. Military data are shown on the map by bronze letters, enamel-bronze arrows and other devices. All engraving was accomplished by sandblasting. M. C. Bargna of Milan, Italy performed the granite work. Stefano Johnson, also of Milan, performed the bronze work.

Carved on the ends of each pylòn is a flaming sword under a rainbow, the insignia of Supreme Headquarters, Allied Expeditionary Forces. The 48 stars around the capstones represent the then 48 states of the Union.

Behind each pylon is a bronze frame with three key maps, one set depicting "The War Against Germany," the other "The War Against Japan."

GRAVES AREA

There are 5,076 American military Dead who lost their lives in the service of their country buried in the cemetery. These honored Dead came from the 50 states and the District of Columbia. In 22 instances, two brothers rest side-by-side in adjacent graves. Among those interred in the cemetery are 101 "Unknowns" whose remains could not be identified. Their headstones are inscribed: HERE RESTS IN HONORED GLORY A COMRADE IN ARMS KNOWN BUT TO GOD. White marble shafts surmounted by a Star of David mark the graves of 117 of the Jewish faith, white marble latin crosses mark the others.

The 5,076 headstones are set in nine plots of fine grass lettered from A to I. Separating the plots are two malls radiating from the memorial and two transverse paths. Two flag poles overlook the graves area at its northern end in front of the memorial. Centered between the flag poles is the grave of General George S.

Grave site of General George S. Patton, Jr.

Fountain in Radial Mall

Visitors' Room

Visitors' Building and Office

Graves Area from the Rear facing Northwest

*Emblem of Evangelist St. Luke –
Reverse Side of Fountain Pylon*

Patton, Jr. Originally, General Patton was buried with the other men. However, so many people came to view his grave each year that all the fine grass on his and nearby graves was killed by the heavy foot traffic. The problem was solved by moving his grave to the area between the flag poles and paving in front of it with stone.

Each radial mall contains two fountains consisting of a pylon of Valore stone overlooking three jet pools on descending levels. High on the obverse side of the pylon is a bronze sea shell from which water flows into the pools. Carved on the reverse side of the pylons is a symbol of one of the four evangelists — an angel for St. Matthew, a lion for St. Mark, a bull for St. Luke and an eagle for St. John. The pools themselves are decorated with bronze dolphins symbolizing Resurrection and bronze turtles symbolizing Everlasting Life. Both the carved and the bronze symbols were designed by Nathaniel Choate of New York.

At the southern end of the graves area are three platforms that afford excellent positions to view the cemetery and take photographs.

VISITORS' BUILDING

Just inside the entrance on the left is the Visitors' Building. It contains the superintendent's office, toilet facilities, and a comfortably furnished room with easy chairs where visitors may obtain information, sign the register and pause to refresh themselves. Whenever the cemetery is open to the public, a staff member is on duty in the building to answer questions and to escort relatives to grave and memorialization sites (except between the hours of noon and 3:00 p.m. on weekends and holidays). He is always happy to provide information on specific burial and memorialization locations in any of the Commission's cemeteries, accommodations in the vicinity, best means and routes of travel, local history and other items that may be of interest.

PLANTINGS

The cemetery lies in a glade surrounded by woods of spruce, beech, oak and other trees of the forest. Climbing Hydrangea (Hydrangea quercifolia) adorns the walls near the entrance to the cemetery and Virginia Creeper covers the Visitors' Building just inside the entrance. Within the enframement of the cemetery are large-scale plantings of Rhododendrons. A hedge of Beech (Fagus sylvatica) and a broad band of Cotoneaster (Cotoneaster horizontalis) encircle the chapel which is flanked on either side by massifs of Japanese Holly (Ilex crenata). Below the terrace, a border of low growing Yew (Taxus baccata repandens) and Cotoneaster (Cotoneaster horizontalis) link the two flag poles.

Color is provided in the spring by the Rhododendrons in the enframement of the cemetery and in the summer by long planters of Polyantha and tree roses in the radial paths.

WORLD WAR II
CEMETERIES AND MEMORIALS:

THE NETHERLANDS

Netherlands American Cemetery and Memorial

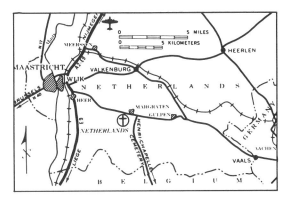

LOCATION

Netherlands Cemetery, the only American military cemetery in the Netherlands, is situated near the southeast limit of the country in the village of Margraten, 6 miles (10 km) east of Maastricht, on the main highway to Aachen, Germany, which is 14 miles (22 km) farther east. Margraten is 70 miles (112 km) east of Brussels and 252 miles (405 km) northeast of Paris.

Maastricht may be reached by train from Brussels, from Paris (Gare du Nord — in approximately 7 hours), any city in Holland, or from Germany via Aachen. A bus service from Maastricht railroad station passes the cemetery entrance.

To reach Margraten by automobile from the north, west or south, follow the appropriate highway to Maastricht, thence east along the Cadier en Keer/Vaals highway (N278); if driving from Aachen, follow the Maastricht highway (N278) west for 11 miles (18 km) after passing the Netherlands frontier post.

There are good hotels at Maas-

Memorial and Court of Honor

Chapel Interior

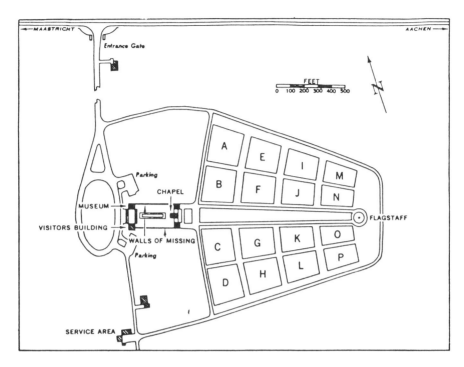

Location of Cemetery Features

tricht, Valkenburg, 4.5 miles (7 km), Aachen and at other towns in the vicinity.

HOURS

The cemetery is open daily to the public as shown below:

SUMMER (16 March–30 September)
9:00 a.m.–6:00 p.m. — weekdays
10:00 a.m.–6:00 p.m. — Saturdays, Sundays and holidays

WINTER (1 October–15 March)
9:00 a.m.–5:00 p.m. — weekdays
10:00 a.m.–5:00 p.m. — Saturdays, Sundays and holidays

When the cemetery is open to the public, a staff member is on duty in the Visitors' Building to answer questions and escort relatives to grave and memorial sites (except between noon and 3:00 p.m. on weekends and holidays).

HISTORY

Three months after successfully landing on the beaches of Normandy, Allied forces had advanced farther than they had thought possible. By mid-September 1944, the U.S. First Army had crossed Luxembourg; captured Liege, Belgium; reached the German frontier near Aachen; and entered the Netherlands near Maastricht. The U.S. Third Army sweeping across France on the right had reached the Moselle River and made contact with the U.S. Seventh Army driving northward from southern France. The British Second Army on the left had liberated Brussels and Antwerp, as the Canadian First Army kept pace with it along the coast liberating Ostend and Bruges; both Armies then found themselves astride the Netherlands frontier.

At this point, enemy defenses began to stabilize around the Siegfried Line, the heavily fortified cities in front of that line to the west, and the more easily defensible natural barriers provided by the numerous rivers and canals in the Netherlands to the east.

In an attempt to outflank the north end of the Siegfried Line, the Allies launched a combined airborne–ground assault along a narrow corridor across three major rivers (the Meuse, the Rhine and the Neder Rijn) and several canals, the success of which among other things depended heavily upon surprise. At 1400 hours on 17 September 1944, elements of three divisions of the First Airborne Army were landed by parachute and glider in column along the main road from Eindhoven to Nijmegen to Arnhem, a distance of 64 miles from the starting point of the supporting British 30 Corps. Almost immediately, 30 Corps, consisting of one Armored and two Infantry Divisions, encountered stronger resistance than was anticipated. Therefore, its progress was much slower than planned.

Aided by air cover from the U.S. Eighth and Ninth Air Forces and the Royal Air Force, the landings on the drop zones were extraordinarily successful. In the Eindhoven area, the U.S. 101st Airborne Division captured all bridges except one that was destroyed by the enemy. Contrary to plans, the supporting ground column, did not reach Eindhoven until the second day and it was early on the third day before the destroyed bridge was replaced.

South of Nijmegen, the U.S. 82d Airborne Division quickly seized the bridge over the Maas (Meuse) River. It was not until the 4th day (20 September), however, that the bridge over the Waal (Rhine) River was captured and not until the 5th day that all defenders were cleared from the area and ground troops were able to

cross. The most important bridge of all over the Neder Rijn (lower Rhine) was still ten miles away.

Enemy reaction at Arnhem was swift and telling, as it quickly separated the battalion of the British 1st Airborne Division that had seized the north end of the Arnhem bridge from the remainder of the division and encircled the drop zones west of the city. Harsh weather further complicated the problem by preventing the cutoff battalion from being supported from the air. On the 5th day, a Polish Parachute Brigade made a valiant but unsuccessful attempt to reinforce it. Even when ground troops arrived on 23 September (the 7th day), all attempts to send reinforcements north of the river failed. After dark on 25 September, the battalion's remnants, less than one-quarter of those who had landed, were evacuated to the south bank.

Allied progress during the next three months was slow as opposition stiffened in all areas. The British Second Army concentrated on widening the sides of the Nijmegen corridor, while the Canadian First Army performed the difficult task of opening the Schelde estuary, so that the port of Antwerp could begin to operate on 28 November and ease the logistical burden. The main Allied offensive effort during this period was shifted to the center of the enemy defenses. There, the U.S. First Army with strong air support from the U.S. Ninth Air Force, broke through the Siegfried Line and encircled Aachen which surrendered on 21 October. The U.S. Ninth Army, which had been organized at Brest in Brittany, was shifted from the U.S. First Army's right flank to its left. Together, the two Armies continued the assault to the Roer River. On their right, the U.S. Third Army and the U.S. Seventh Army, with the French First Army on the extreme right, made substantial

View of Graves Area and Tower

gains toward the German frontier.

Suddenly on 16 December 1944, the Allied advance was interrupted as the enemy launched its final major counteroffensive of the war in the Ardennes, followed by a second assault in Alsace to the south. By the end of January 1945, these offensives were halted and all ground retaken. The Allies then resumed their advance, which was planned in two stages. The first stage was to clear all enemy units west of the Rhine; the second was to invade Germany itself.

The advance to the Rhine in the north was scheduled to begin on 8 February 1945, with the Canadian First Army attacking to the southeast, followed in two days by a converging attack to the northeast by the U.S. Ninth and First Armies. When the V Corps of the First Army seized control of the upstream dams of the Roer on 10 February, it discovered that the enemy had wrecked the discharge valves the evening before. The resultant heavy flow of water halted the attack there for two weeks.

At 0245 hours on 23 February, following a short but intensive air and artillery bombardment, the U.S. Ninth Army lowered its assault boats into the swirling waters and began to cross the Roer River before the flood waters had completely subsided. Despite heavy enemy artillery fire, Julich was captured on the first day, with the support of fighters and medium bombers of the U.S. Ninth Air Force.

By 25 February, all four corps of the U.S. Ninth Army had crossed the Roer and were advancing. As the advance turned northward, the armored units were committed. By 1 March 1945, the industrial city of Monchen-Gladbach had been captured. It was the largest German city taken to date. Now the advance became a race to destroy as many units as possible before they could retreat across the Rhine. Despite constant harrassment by our aircraft, the enemy was able to demolish all bridges across the Rhine. On 10 March, the entire west bank of the Rhine from Dusseldorf northward was in Allied hands.

The major assault crossing of the Rhine occurred on 23–24 March, when the U.S. Ninth Army crossed at Rheinberg, a city it had captured on 6 March. Advancing Allied armies by-passed the northern Netherlands, encircled the Ruhr, then pursued the retreating enemy throughout Germany and Austria. All enemy forces in Europe surrendered on 8 May 1945.

SITE

The cemetery occupies 65½ acres of gently rolling farmland just south of the highway. The site was liberated on 13 September 1944 by troops of the U.S. 30th Infantry Division which were advancing northeastward toward the Roer River in Germany, as part of the U.S. First Army. A battlefield cemetery, one of the first to be used for the interment of American soldiers who fell on German soil, was established here on 10 November 1944 by the U.S. Ninth Army.

Here rest 8,301 of our military Dead, representing 43 percent of those who were originally buried in this and in other temporary cemeteries in this region. Most of them gave their lives in the airborne and ground operations to liberate eastern Holland, during the advances into Germany over the Roer and across the Rhine and in air operations over these regions.

ARCHITECTS

Architects for the cemetery and memorial were Shepley, Bulfinch, Richardson and Abbott, of Boston, Mass.; the landscape architects were

Clarke, Rapuano and Halleran of New York City.

GENERAL LAYOUT

From the entrance gate on the south side of the Maastricht–Aachen highway the approach drive leads to the right, around a grassed oval, to the steps leading to the Court of Honor. Immediately north and south of these steps are the parking areas; farther to the south is the service area.

The Court of Honor of the memorial leads to the tower containing the chapel. Beyond the chapel is the burial area. The cemetery and memorial were completed in 1960.

THE MEMORIAL

Flanking the entrance to the Court of Honor on the south side is the Visitors' Building. On the north side is the museum room.

On the exterior wall of the museum is this inscription taken from General Eisenhower's dedication of the Golden Book in St. Paul's Cathedral in London:

HERE WE AND ALL WHO SHALL HERE-AFTER LIVE IN FREEDOM WILL BE RE-MINDED THAT TO THESE MEN AND THEIR COMRADES WE OWE A DEBT TO BE PAID WITH GRATEFUL REMEMBRANCE OF THEIR SACRIFICE AND WITH THE HIGH RESOLVE THAT THE CAUSE FOR WHICH THEY DIED SHALL LIVE.

Engraved on the Roman Travertine walls within the museum are three maps embellished with mosaic and bronze and enamel appliques. The large map on the north wall records the progress of the military operations from the landings in Normandy until the end of the war. Mention is also made of the strategic air attacks which started in 1942. Accompanying the map is a descriptive text in English and Dutch of which this is the English version:

ON 6 JUNE 1944, PRECEDED BY AIRBORNE UNITS AND COVERED BY NAVAL AND AIR BOMBARDMENT, UNITED STATES

Aerial View of Cemetery

AND BRITISH COMMONWEALTH FORCES LANDED ON THE COAST OF NORMANDY. PUSHING SOUTHWARD THEY ESTABLISHED A BEACHHEAD SOME 20 MILES IN DEPTH. ON 25 JULY, IN THE WAKE OF A PARALYZING AIR BOMBARDMENT BY THE U.S. EIGHTH AND NINTH AIR FORCES AND THE ROYAL AIR FORCE, THE U.S. FIRST ARMY BROKE OUT OF THE BEACHHEAD WEST OF ST. LO. ON 1 AUGUST IT WAS JOINED BY THE U.S. THIRD ARMY. TOGETHER THEY REPULSED A POWERFUL COUNTERATTACK TOWARD AVRANCHES. CRUSHED BETWEEN THE AMERICANS ON THE SOUTH AND WEST AND THE BRITISH ON THE NORTH, AND ATTACKED CONTINUOUSLY BY THE ALLIED AIR FORCES, THE ENEMY RETREATED ACROSS THE SEINE.

SUSTAINED BY THE HERCULEAN ACHIEVEMENTS OF ARMY AND NAVY SUPPLY PERSONNEL, THE ALLIED ARMIES AND AIR FORCES PURSUED VIGOROUSLY. BY MID-SEPTEMBER THE U.S. NINTH ARMY HAD LIBERATED BREST; THE FIRST ARMY HAD SWEPT THROUGH FRANCE, BELGIUM AND LUXEMBOURG AND WAS STANDING ON THE THRESHOLD OF GERMANY; THE THIRD ARMY HAD REACHED THE MOSELLE AND HAD JOINED FORCES WITH THE U.S. SEVENTH AND THE FRENCH FIRST ARMIES ADVANCING NORTHWARD FROM THE MEDITERRANEAN. ON THE LEFT FLANK, BRITISH AND CANADIAN TROOPS HAD ENTERED THE NETHERLANDS. ON 17 SEPTEMBER THREE AIRBORNE DIVISIONS DROPPED IN THE EINDHOVEN–ARNHEM AREA IN A BOLD BUT UNSUCCESSFUL ATTEMPT TO OUTFLANK THE FORTIFIED SIEGFRIED LINE.

PROGRESS DURING THE NEXT THREE MONTHS WAS SLOW, THE FIGHTING BITTER AS OPPOSITION STIFFENED. THE OPENING OF THE PORT OF ANTWERP ON 28 NOVEMBER MATERIALLY EASED THE LOGISTICAL BURDEN. IN THE CENTER THE FIRST AND NINTH ARMIES SEIZED AACHEN AND FOUGHT THEIR WAY TO THE ROER. METZ FELL AS THE THIRD ARMY PUSHED TO THE SAAR. ON ITS RIGHT, THE SEVENTH ARMY AIDED BY THE FIRST TACTICAL AIR FORCE DROVE TO THE RHINE AT STRASBOURG, WHILE FRENCH TROOPS FREED MULHOUSE.

IN THE ARDENNES, ON 16 DECEMBER, THE ENEMY LAUNCHED HIS FINAL

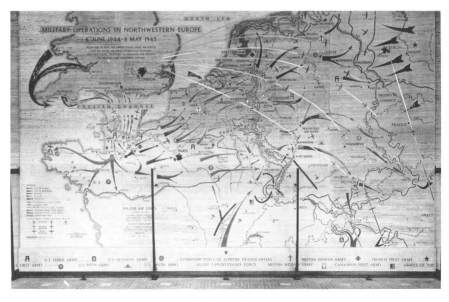

The Large Map

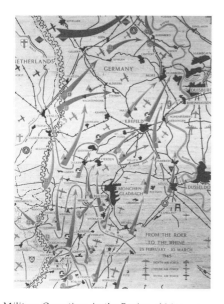

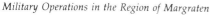

Military Operations in the Region of Margraten

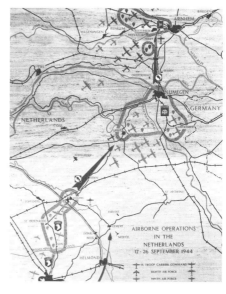

Airborne Operations Map

MAJOR COUNTEROFFENSIVE. PROMPT TACTICAL COUNTERMEASURES AND THE SUPERB FIGHTING QUALITIES OF AMERICAN SOLDIERS AND AIRMEN FINALLY HALTED THIS DRIVE. DURING FEBRUARY AND MARCH THE WEST BANK OF THE RHINE WAS CLEARED IN A SERIES OF HIGHLY SUCCESSFUL OPERATIONS. IN RAPID SUCCESSION, AMERICAN FORCES SEIZED A BRIDGE AT REMAGEN, CROSSED THE RHINE AT OPPENHEIM, THEN ON 23–24 MARCH STAGED WITH THE BRITISH THEIR MAJOR ASSAULT CROSSING NEAR WESEL. PUSHING RAPIDLY EASTWARD OUR ARMIES ENCIRCLED THE ENTIRE RUHR VALLEY IN A GIGANTIC DOUBLE ENVELOPMENT. WITH THE AIR AND GROUND FORCES OPERATING AS A TEAM, THE ALLIES SWEPT ACROSS GERMANY TO MEET THE ADVANCING TROOPS OF THE U.S.S.R. AND FORCE THE COMPLETE SURRENDER OF THE ENEMY ON 8 MAY 1945, 337 DAYS AFTER THEIR INITIAL LANDINGS IN FRANCE.

On the west wall the map portrays the daring large-scale airborne operation which was intended to outflank the fortified Siegfried Line and seize the crossings of the Lower Rhine. It, too, is accompanied by an inscription in both languages of which this is the English version:

IN EARLY SEPTEMBER 1944, THE ALLIED FORCES WERE MOVING NORTHEAST-WARD IN A SWEEPING ADVANCE. PROGRESS THROUGH FRANCE AND BELGIUM WAS RAPID, BUT AS OUR TROOPS APPROACHED THE GERMAN FRONTIER THE OPPOSITION STIFFENED. TO OUTFLANK THE SIEGFRIED LINE AND THUS TO OBTAIN IMMEDIATELY A BRIDGEHEAD OVER THE RHINE, THE AL-LIES LAUNCHED A STRONG AIRBORNE AND GROUND ASSAULT IN THE EAST-ERN NETHERLANDS.

ON 17 SEPTEMBER 1944 ELEMENTS OF THE U.S. 101ST AND 82D AIRBORNE DIVI-SIONS AND THE BRITISH 1 AIRBORNE DIVISION DROPPED IN COLUMN ALONG THE MAIN ROAD FROM EINDHOVEN TO ARNHEM. THEIR MISSION WAS TO CAP-TURE THE BRIDGES OVER THE MAJOR CANALS AND OVER THE MAAS, THE WAAL AND THE NEDER RIJN, THUS ES-TABLISHING A CORRIDOR THROUGH WHICH THE BRITISH 30 CORPS WOULD ADVANCE RAPIDLY AND ESTABLISH IT-SELF NORTH OF THE NEDER RIJN. ON THAT DAY MORE THAN 1,500 TROOP-

CARRYING AIRCRAFT AND 478 GLIDERS OF THE U.S. IX TROOP CARRIER COMMAND AND THE ROYAL AIR FORCE, PROTECTED BY 2,200 COMBAT AIRPLANES OF THE U.S. EIGHTH AND NINTH AIR FORCES AND THE ROYAL AIR FORCE, CARRIED APPROXIMATELY 50% OF THE STRENGTH OF THE THREE AIRBORNE DIVISIONS. INTENSIVE AIR BOMBARDMENT OF ANTIAIRCRAFT GUN POSITIONS AND AIRFIELDS, AND THE ACHIEVEMENT OF SURPRISE CONTRIBUTED TO THE SUCCESS OF THE INITIAL OPERATIONS.

IMMEDIATELY AFTER LANDING, THE 101ST AIRBORNE DIVISION SECURED THE BRIDGES IN ITS AREA EXCEPT THAT AT SON WHICH THE ENEMY DESTROYED. THE 82D AIRBORNE DIVISION CAPTURED INTACT THE BRIDGE ACROSS THE MAAS AT GRAVE BUT FOUND NIJMEGEN TOO STRONGLY HELD. A BATTALION OF THE BRITISH 1 AIRBORNE DIVISION REACHED ARNHEM AND SEIZED THE NORTHERN EDGE OF THE HIGHWAY BRIDGE ACROSS THE NEDER RIJN, BUT OVERPOWERING ENEMY FORCES HELD THE REMAINDER OF THE DIVISION WITHIN A SMALL PERIMETER WEST OF THE CITY. ON SUCCEEDING DAYS, BAD WEATHER DELAYED AIRBORNE REINFORCEMENTS AND SUPPLIES AND THUS PREVENTED EFFECTIVE AIR ASSISTANCE TO THE FORCES FIGHTING TO ESTABLISH AND MAINTAIN THE CORRIDOR.

MEANWHILE THE ADVANCING 30 CORPS PASSED THROUGH THE 101ST AIRBORNE DIVISION WHICH HAD CAPTURED EINDHOVEN. IT THEN JOINED THE 82D AIRBORNE DIVISION IN ITS ATTACK ON THE NIJMEGEN BRIDGES, BOTH OF WHICH WERE FINALLY SIEZED INTACT ON THE EVENING OF 20 SEPTEMBER BY THE 82D AIRBORNE DIVISION IN COOPERATION WITH BRITISH ARMORED UNITS; BUT BRITISH INFANTRY COULD NOT REACH THE SOUTH BANK OF THE NEDER RIJN IN FORCE UNTIL 24 SEPTEMBER. THE ENEMY PREVENTED ALL ATTEMPTS TO REINFORCE THE TROOPS BEYOND THE RIVER, AND AFTER DARK ON 25 SEPTEMBER THE REMNANTS OF THE DECIMATED 1 AIRBORNE DIVISION WERE EVACUATED.

On the east wall the map records the operations in the crossing of the Roer and the advance to the Rhine; this is the English version of its inscription:

UPON THE VICTORIOUS CONCLUSION OF THE ARDENNES CAMPAIGN ON 25 JANUARY 1945 THE ALLIES UNDERTOOK THE TASK OF DESTROYING THE ENEMY ARMIES WEST OF THE RHINE. THE FIRST ATTACK WAS TO BE MADE ON THE NORTHERN FLANK BY THE CANADIAN FIRST ARMY AND THE U.S. NINTH ARMY; THE U.S. FIRST ARMY WAS TO ADVANCE ON THEIR RIGHT. THE CANADIANS OPENED THE OFFENSIVE ON 8 FEBRUARY BUT ON THE NEXT DAY THE ENEMY FLOODED THE ROER VALLEY BY RELEASING THE WATER FROM AN UPSTREAM DAM. THIS CREATED AN IMPASSABLE OBSTACLE BEFORE THE NINTH ARMY, WHICH THEN POSTPONED ITS ASSAULT FOR NEARLY TWO WEEKS. DURING THE RESULTING DELAY THE U.S. EIGHTH AND NINTH AIR FORCES CONTINUOUSLY ATTACKED BRIDGES, RAILROAD TRACKS AND MARSHALLING YARDS ON BOTH SIDES OF THE RHINE TO ISOLATE THE BATTLEFIELD. REACHING A CLIMAX ON 22 FEBRUARY, THE BOMBARDMENT SYSTEMATICALLY DISRUPTED THE ENEMY COMMUNICATIONS AND TRANSPORTATION SYSTEMS THROUGHOUT GERMANY.

IN THE EARLY MORNING HOURS OF 23 FEBRUARY, FOLLOWING AN INTENSIVE ARTILLERY PREPARATION, THE LEADING UNITS OF THE NINTH ARMY LOWERED THEIR ASSAULT BOATS INTO THE SWIRLING WATERS OF THE STILL FLOODED ROER. THE SWIFT CURRENT AND ENEMY ARTILLERY FIRE ON THE CROSSING SITES MADE PASSAGE OF THE RIVER MOST HAZARDOUS, BUT THE XIX CORPS ADVANCED AND CAPTURED JULICH ON THE FIRST DAY WHILE THE XIII CORPS MADE SUBSTANTIAL GAINS IN THE LINNICH AREA. FIGHTERS AND MEDIUM BOMBERS OF THE NINTH AIR FORCE CLOSELY SUPPORTED THE FORWARD UNITS, DESTROYING ENEMY

TANKS AND EQUIPMENT; THE BRIDGE-HEADS ON THE EAST BANK WERE MADE SECURE BY THE END OF THE SECOND DAY.

ONCE ACROSS THE RIVER, THE U.S. NINTH ARMY OFFENSIVE RAPIDLY GATHERED MOMENTUM. ON 25 FEBRU-ARY THE XVI CORPS CROSSED ON THE LEFT FLANK. ARMORED UNITS WERE COMMITTED AS THE DIRECTION OF AD-VANCE TURNED NORTHWARD AND BROKE THROUGH THE ENEMY LINES. BY 1 MARCH THE INDUSTRIAL CENTER OF MONCHEN–GLADBACH HAD BEEN CLEARED, THE LARGEST GERMAN CITY YET CAPTURED BY ALLIED FORCES.

THE BATTLE BECAME A PURSUIT; THE OBJECTIVE NOW WAS TO PREVENT AS MANY ENEMY AS POSSIBLE FROM ESCAPING. THE XIX CORPS REACHED THE RHINE NEAR NEUSS ON 2 MARCH WHILE THE XIII CORPS ENTERED KRE-FELD; EARLY THE NEXT DAY THE XVI CORPS MADE CONTACT WITH THE CANADIAN FIRST ARMY AT GELDERN. CONSTANTLY HARASSED BY THE FIGHTER–BOMBERS OF THE NINTH AIR FORCE, THE ENEMY WITHDREW, DEMOLISHING THE BRIDGES AS HE RE-TREATED ACROSS THE RIVER. BY 6 MARCH RHEINBERG, THE FUTURE CROSSING SITE FOR THE NINTH ARMY, HAD BEEN TAKEN. FOUR DAYS LATER THE WEST BANK OF THE RHINE FROM DUSSELDORF NORTHWARD WAS IN ALLIED HANDS.

Below the maps are insignia of the principal major units which partici-pated in these operations.

These maps were designed by Lewis York of New Haven, Conn., from data prepared by the American Battle Monuments Commission, and were executed by the Dura Company of Heerlen, Holland. The enamel-bronze appliques were fab-ricated by the Morris Singer Com-pany of London.

On the exterior east wall of the museum are mounted the two series of key maps "The War Against Ger-many" and "The War Against Ja-pan."

Chapel Lights

COURT OF HONOR

Extending from the steps to the tower is the Court of Honor with its reflecting pool. Engraved on the north and south walls of the Court are the names, rank, organization and the State of 1,722 of our Missing of the Army and Army Air Forces*. These men gave their lives in the service of their Country in this region, but their remains have not been recovered or identified. Their names include men from every State of the Union (except Alaska) and the District of Columbia.

Over these names is carved this heading, with a Dutch translation:

HERE ARE RECORDED THE NAMES OF AMERICANS WHO GAVE THEIR LIVES IN THE SERVICE OF THEIR COUNTRY AND WHO SLEEP IN UNKNOWN GRAVES.

Toward the east ends of the walls

---

*It will be recalled that during World War II the Air Forces still formed part of the United States Army.

are these inscriptions also:

NORTH WALL:

TO YOU FROM FAILING HANDS WE THROW THE TORCH — BE YOURS TO HOLD IT HIGH (from John McCrae's "In Flanders Fields").

SOUTH WALL:

HONOR IS THEIRS WHO KNEW THE PATH OF HONOR.

The trees planted in lawns before the Walls of the Missing are Japanese Cherries (Prunus serrulata Sekiyama).

THE TOWER AND CHAPEL

The bronze group standing before the tower at the east end of the Court of Honor was designed by Joseph Kiselewski, of New York City and cast in Milan by the Battaglia foundries. The mourning figure, the doves, the new shoot from the war-destroyed tree are appositely described by the inscription on the stone base:

NEW LIFE FROM WAR'S DESTRUCTION PROCLAIMS MAN'S IMMORTALITY AND HOPE FOR PEACE.

The west face of the tower bears this inscription from a free translation of Pericles' oration as recorded by Thucydides:

EACH FOR HIS OWN MEMORIAL EARNED PRAISE THAT WILL NEVER DIE AND WITH IT THE GRANDEST OF ALL SEPULCHRES NOT THAT IN WHICH HIS MORTAL BONES ARE LAID BUT A HOME IN THE MINDS OF MEN

The tower rises 101 ft. above the Court of Honor. Its exterior walls, like those of the Court of Honor and the entrance pavilions, are built of English Portland stone. On the walls flanking it to the left and right are the names of significant battles fought by the soldiers and airmen commemorated:

MAASTRICHT ☆ EINDHOVEN ☆ GRAVE ☆ NIJMEGEN ☆ ARNHEM ☆ JULICH ☆ LINNICH ☆ GEILENKIRCHEN ☆ KREFELD ☆

View of Wall of the Missing

Chapel Entrance

VENLO ☆ RHEINBERG ☆ COLOGNE ☆ WESEL ☆ RUHR

On the north side of the tower is the entrance to the observation platform, reached by 149 steps, which affords a wide panorama of the countryside, as well as a comprehensive view of the pattern of the burial area.

The entrance to the chapel, reached after mounting a few steps, is on the east, the burial area side, of the tower. The doors are of bronze fabricated by H. H. Martyn of Cheltenham, England, and bear in outline a Tree of Life. Above them is engraved:

IN MEMORY OF THE VALOR AND THE SACRIFICES WHICH HALLOW THIS SOIL

The interior of the chapel is 52 feet high. Suspended from the ceiling is the handsome lighting fixture presented by the Dutch people and consisting of a royal crown surrounded by tiny lights recalling the firmament above.

The silver flower vase on the altar,

also a gift of the Dutch people, bears the inscription:

PRO MUNDI LIBERTATE MORTUIS
(To those who died for a free world)

Another gift of the Dutch people is the wrought iron candelabrum next to the altar.

A tablet near the door records these donations in the following terms (with a Dutch version):

THE LIGHTS AND ALTAR ORNAMENTS ARE THE GENEROUS GIFTS OF THE GOVERNMENT OF THE NETHERLANDS AND THE ADMINISTRATION & PEOPLE OF THE PROVINCE OF LIMBURG.

The altar, itself of oak, bears the inscription:

HONOR ☆ FAITH ☆ VALOR

Mounted on the south wall of the chapel are three U.S. National flags, a Christian Chapel flag and a Jewish Chapel flag.

Following are the inscriptions in the interior of the memorial:

EAST WALL:

1941–1945 ☆ IN PROUD REMEMBRANCE OF THE ACHIEVEMENTS OF HER SONS AND IN HUMBLE TRIBUTE TO THEIR SACRIFICES THIS MEMORIAL HAS BEEN ERECTED BY THE UNITED STATES OF AMERICA

NORTH WALL:

O GOD WHO ART THE AUTHOR OF PEACE AND LOVER OF CONCORD DEFEND US THY HUMBLE SERVANTS IN ALL ASSAULTS OF OUR ENEMIES THAT WE SURELY TRUSTING IN THY DEFENSE MAY NOT FEAR THE POWER OF ANY ADVERSARIES
(Peace Prayer from the Episcopal Book of Common Prayer.)

SOUTH WALL:

O LORD SUPPORT US ALL THE DAY LONG UNTIL THE SHADOWS LENGTHEN AND THE EVENING COMES AND THE FEVER OF LIFE IS OVER AND OUR WORK IS DONE THEN IN THY MERCY GRANT US

A SAFE LODGING AND A HOLY REST AND PEACE AT THE LAST

(From the "Works of Cardinal Newman.")

GRAVES AREA

The burial area is divided into 16 plots, lettered from A to P, separated by the broad central mall and by grass paths. The 8,300 headstones are arranged in parallel arcs sweeping across the broad green lawn.

Of the 8,301 Dead who gave their lives in their Country's service, from every State in the Union, The District of Columbia, England, Canada and Mexico, 106 are Unknowns. In no less than 40 instances two brothers lie buried side by side, while one headstone marks the common grave of two Unknowns.

At the top of the hill, on the axis of the mall, is the flagstaff.

VISITORS' BUILDING

The Visitors' Building is located on the south side of the Court of Honor. Within it is a comfortably furnished lounge where visitors may obtain burial locations or other information from the cemetery staff or simply pause to relax and refresh themselves.

PLANTINGS

Characteristically American tulip poplars (Liriodendron Tulipifera) line the central mall. Prominent are beds of rhododendron which produce their wealth of blossom just before Memorial Day each year. Among the other plants at the cemetery are the hawthorn hedges (crataegus oxycantha), as well as the forested areas of various species of oak, maple and hawthorn.

The wide curved borders north and south of the memorial are filled with Polyantha Roses framed within a coping of dwarf box and backed with a holly hedge.

View of Graves Area and Tower

Visitors' Building

Interior of Visitors' Building

"The Mourning Woman"

WORLD WAR II
CEMETERIES AND MEMORIALS:

THE PACIFIC ISLANDS

𝔖𝔞𝔦𝔭𝔞𝔫
𝔐𝔬𝔫𝔲𝔪𝔢𝔫𝔱

Saipan Monument is situated near the beach overlooking Tanapag Harbor on the Island of Saipan, Commonwealth of the Northern Mariana Islands. It is part of an American memorial park commemorating the American and Marianas Dead in the Marianas Campaign of World War II. The monument honors specifically the 24,000 American Marines and Soldiers who died recapturing the volcanic islands of Saipan, Tinian and Guam during the period of 15 June 1944–11 August 1944.

It is a twelve-foot rectangular obelisk of rose granite in a landscaped area of local flora. Inscribed upon the monument are these words: "THIS MEMORIAL HAS BEEN ERECTED BY THE UNITED STATES OF AMERICA IN HUMBLE TRIBUTE TO THE SONS WHO PAID THE ULTIMATE SACRIFICE FOR LIBERATION OF THE MARIANAS. 1941-1945."

WORLD WAR II
CEMETERIES AND MEMORIALS:

THE PHILIPPINES

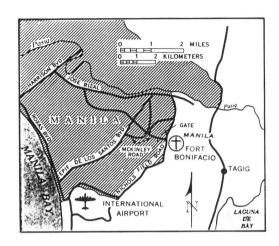

Manila American Cemetery and Memorial

LOCATION

Manila American Cemetery is situated about six miles southeast of the center of the city of Manila, Republic of the Philippines, within the limits of the former U.S. Army reservation of Fort William McKinley, now Fort Bonifacio. It can be reached most easily from the city by taxicab or other automobile via Epifanio de los Santos Avenue (Highway 54) and McKinley Road. The Nichols Field Road connects the Manila International Airport with the cemetery. The cemetery is open daily to the public from 6:30 a.m. to 4:45 p.m.

HISTORY

Several months before the Japanese attack on Pearl Harbor, a strategic policy was adopted with respect to the United States priority of effort, should it be forced into war against the Axis powers (Germany and Italy) and simultaneously find itself at war with Japan. The policy was that the stronger European enemy would be defeated first.

With the surprise Japanese attack on Pearl Harbor on 7 December 1941 and the bombing attacks on 8 De-cember on Wake Island, Guam, Hong Kong, Singapore and the Philippine Islands, the United States found itself thrust into a global war. (History records the other attacks as occurring on 8 December because of the international date line; actually they all occurred during the same daylight period.) The day after the Pearl Harbor attack, the United States declared war against Japan. Within the short span of two days, Japanese troops had landed on the Malay Peninsula and Tarawa and Makin in the Gilbert Islands, forced Guam to surrender, and made their principal landing on the island of Luzon in the Philippines. On 11 December, Germany and Italy declared war on the United States.

Despite the fact that Japan had dealt a grievous blow to the strength of the United States Navy in the Pacific and was advancing on all fronts in the southwest Pacific, the basic decision of "Europe First" was reaffirmed promptly by President Roosevelt and British Prime Minister Churchill.

At the same meeting, in concert with their military advisors, formation of the Combined Chiefs of Staff

Altar in the Chapel

was approved to coordinate the operations of all Allied Forces; however, actual control of operations in the Pacific remained with the U.S. Joint Chiefs of Staff. For all practical purposes, the war against Japan was relegated to second place, except for the early months of the war when it was essential to reinforce our Pacific forces which now were so much smaller than those of the Japanese. There was little hope of saving the Philippines, but it was decided that the line of communications to Australia must be kept open as it was considered essential to the defense of that continent. At first, it seemed there was nothing that could stop the Japanese advance. Hong Kong fell on Christmas Day. Shortly thereafter, U.S. and Philippine troops evacuated Manila and withdrew to the Bataan Peninsula. In January, the Japanese landed in the East Indies, and simultaneously crossed over into Burma. Singapore capitulated in mid-February. The only bright spot at this time was the magnificent resistance by the American and Filipino forces on Bataan. But even that bright spot became a fading light as there was no way for us to bring help to those gallant defenders, whereas the enemy was pouring reinforcements into Bataan. On 9 April 1942, Bataan surrendered; it was followed by Corregidor on 6 May. The superb defense of Bataan and Corregidor, however, threw the enemy off its timetable as many Japanese reinforcements that had been scheduled for deployment to other areas had to be diverted to Bataan. This delayed the Japanese advance in New Guinea and the Solomon Islands.

At the end of March 1942, the Joint Chiefs of Staff divided the Pacific into two commands — the Pacific Ocean Area and the Southwest Pacific Area. The latter command included New Guinea and the Solomon Islands which were the major objectives of the Japanese in their advance toward Australia. Anxious to make up for lost time, the Japanese occupied Tulagi, just north of Guadalcanal, and dispatched a strong force to invade Port Moresby on the south coast of New Guinea, as that territory was considered essential to the defense of northern Australia. This led to the battle of the Coral Sea on 4–8 May where U.S. and Allied naval forces won a major and strategic victory. The Port Moresby invasion force was forced to turn back and two large enemy aircraft carriers were put out of action for an extended period of time.

With their advance checked in the Coral Sea, the Japanese shifted their main offensive toward the Hawaiian Islands and the Aleutians. The decisive battle of Midway on 3–7 June 1942 restored to balance Allied and enemy sea power in the Pacific. It proved to be the last great enemy offensive against American territory.

Following their defeat at Midway, the Japanese launched a determined effort to capture Port Moresby in the southwest Pacific by attacking overland across the Huon Peninsula, the long tail of New Guinea stretching to the southeast. On 21 July the enemy seized Buna and Gona on the northeast coast, then crossed the Owen Stanley Range to within 30 miles of Port Moresby where they were stopped by Australian troops and driven back.

In order to bring more forces to bear against the enemy in the Solomons, the boundary of the Southwest Pacific Area was shifted westward to put the southern Solomons in the Pacific Ocean Area (whose command had more forces readily available); the northern Solomons continued to be a part of the Southwest Pacific Area.

U.S. forces undertook their first offensive in the Pacific on 7 August 1942, when U.S. Marines landed on Guadalcanal. Subsequently, a succession of hard-fought naval battles and grim struggles by U.S. Marine, Army and Navy forces on land and in the air led to the turning point of the war in the Pacific. The bitter struggle for Guadalcanal and other islands in the southern Solomons lasted six months until February 1943 and was extremely costly to both sides. Simultaneously, in New Guinea, after defeating another Japanese force at Milne Bay, Australian and American troops eliminated the Buna-Gona beachhead on 22 January 1943.

From this point onward, the character of the war in the Pacific began to change. The enemy's next attack on the Huon Peninsula was repulsed by Australian troops who were transported to the battle area by American aircraft. A Japanese attempt to reinforce garrisons on the peninsula ended in disaster at the battle of the Bismarck Sea, 2–4 March 1943, when the U.S. Fifth Air Force and Royal Australian Air Force together with U.S. Navy small craft sank eight transports and four destroyers. During the summer, additional U.S. Army forces were transferred to the southwest Pacific command.

At two conferences, one in May 1943 and the other in August, the Combined Chiefs of Staff agreed to accelerate the pace of the war against Japan and selected the specific routes of advance. The Joint Chiefs of Staff directed the commander of the Pacific Ocean Area to begin a series of amphibious operations across the Central Pacific. In the Southwest Pacific Area, initially there were two axes of operations.

Under the strategic direction of the Southwest Pacific Commander, advances along both axes had already begun.

Late in June 1943, the U.S. Third Fleet's Amphibious Force landed Army troops and Marines on Rendova Island and then on New Georgia in the northern Solomons. The Army completed the capture of New Georgia in August. Bypassing the strongly held island of Kolombangara, Valla Lavella was attacked and captured by U.S. Army and New Zealand troops. The Treasury Islands were then occupied by New Zealand troops. Preceded by diversionary landings on Choiseul, a large force of U.S. Marines landed at Empress Augusta Bay, Bougainville, on 1 November 1943. This attack, reinforced by Army troops, permitted the establishment of a naval base and airfields from which the U.S. Thirteenth Air Force, together with the aircraft of the U.S. Third Fleet, could neutralize the strong Japanese base at Rabaul, New Britain Island.

On the other axis of advance, the U.S. Sixth Army seized the islands of Kiriwina and Woodlark in June as bases from which air support could be provided for future operations. Then three attacks were launched by U.S. Army and Australian troops in rapid succession on the eastern coast of New Guinea; an overland advance and an amphibious assault against Salamaua that was completed on 11 September; a combined parachute drop and an airborne assault which resulted in the occupation of Lae on 16 September; and an advance on Finschaffen which was occupied completely by 2 October.

The next objective was the western end of the island of New Britain. On 15 December, three Army landings were made in the Arawe area

Entrance to Cemetery

followed on 26 December by a larger landing of U.S. Marines which captured the important air base at Cape Gloucester. Then on 2 January 1944, U.S. Sixth Army troops landed at Saidor on the northern New Guinea coast to cut the enemy escape route along the coastal road. Throughout these operations and those that followed, continuing air attacks against the enemy's supply lines and airfields by Army and Naval forces contributed materially to the success of ground operations.

Although fighting still continued on Bougainville and on western New Britain, a decision was made to bypass the enemy bases at Rabaul and at Kavieng, New Ireland, as they were being systematically neutralized by intensive bombardment. It was the plan of the Southwest Pacific Area Commander to land troops where the Japanese were weakest and confine the stronger Japanese forces to pockets from which, because of incredibly difficult terrain and Allied air and sea superiority, they could not break out. The next nine months of 1944 were devoted to a continuation of this strategy on an increasing scale.

The operation against the Admiralty Islands, strategically important because of their airfields and harbors, was scheduled initially for April 1944. But on 29 February, as a result of a reconnaissance by the Southwest Pacific Area Commander, U.S. Sixth Army troops landed on Los Negros from ships of the U.S. Seventh Fleet. During March and April, the larger island of Manus was occupied.

The next advance was along the New Guinea coast. It came so swiftly and was so far forward that the enemy was completely taken by surprise. The strongly held Japanese base at Wewak was bypassed in favor of the Hollandia-Humboldt Bay area which would provide us with excellent airfields and a good naval base.

As the 350 mile distance was beyond the effective range of many of our land-based aircraft, the fast carrier task force of the U.S. Fifth Fleet was used to provide additional fire support on the target areas and bomb other targets to the westward. On 22 April, three landings were made by the U.S. Sixth Army, two in the Hollandia area and one to the east at Aitape.

These landings were so successful that in May two more landings were made farther to the west at Arara and on Wakde Island. At the end of May, another leap of over 300 miles was made to seize airfields on the island of Biak where fierce enemy resistance was encountered. Despite this hold up, the advance continued to Noemfoor in early July, to Sansapor on 30 July, and to the island of Morotai on 15 September 1944.

On the same day, 15 September 1944, Pacific Ocean Area forces, having completed their long series of advances across the Central Pacific via the Gilbert and Marshall Islands to seize Saipan, Tinian and Guam, invaded the Palau Islands. Simultaneously, as the result of successful fast carrier strikes on the Philippine Islands, the commander of the Third Fleet recommended that several intermediate operations be cancelled and that U.S. forces land in the Philippines as soon as possible.

The Pacific Ocean Area Commander concurred and offered to place additional forces at the disposal of the Southwest Pacific Area Commander, who promptly replied that he would be prepared to land on Leyte on 20 October instead of on 20 December as previously planned. Immediate approval by the Joint Chiefs of Staff advanced the long-awaited return to the Philippines by two months.

On 20 October 1944, the date agreed on so quickly over a month before, the U.S. Sixth Army, under cover of naval gunfire and air bombardment by the U.S. Seventh Fleet, with aircraft of the U.S. Third Fleet furnishing long-range support, landed on the eastern shores of Leyte.

In a desperate effort to destroy the landing forces and prevent the United States from returning to the Philippines, the Japanese decided to risk a major sea battle. The resultant Battle of Leyte Gulf, fought on 23–26 October, was one of the most decisive naval battles in history and almost eliminated Japan as a major sea power.

The U.S. Sixth Army continued its advance, as the Japanese rushed reinforcements to Leyte, mostly in the Ormoc Bay area on the western side of the island, where they were repeatedly attacked by the U.S. Fifth Air Force. In turn the U.S. Sixth Army was reinforced. Despite torrential rains and difficult terrain, the advance continued and spread to the neighboring island of Samar to the north. In December, Army units supported by Army, Navy and Marine Corps aircraft, landed at Ormoc Bay to cut the last major Japanese line of communications to the island of Leyte. By the end of the month, command of operations on Leyte was turned over to the U.S. Eighth Army. Severe fighting on Leyte continued in isolated areas for several more months.

Meanwhile, in December, landings also were made on southern Mindoro to provide support for the major landings scheduled on Luzon. On 9 January 1945, the U.S. Seventh Fleet landed units of the U.S. Sixth Army on the south shore of Lingayen Gulf. Supported by the U.S.

Fifth Air Force, and by Marine Corps and Navy aircraft, the U.S. Sixth Army drove inland. By the end of the month, Clark Field was recaptured, a large number of enemy troops were driven into the mountains, an additional landing was made to cut off the Bataan Peninsula, and a third landing, that included a parachute drop, was made south of Manila.

As the advance on Manila continued from the north and the south, the Bataan Peninsula was rapidly secured. On 16 February, airborne and amphibious units assaulted Corregidor; resistance ended there on 27 February. On 3 March, the city of Manila was finally cleared of all Japanese troops. With the exception of Fort Drum, which held out until April, U.S. forces accomplished in less than two months what took the Japanese six months to accomplish.

While the U.S. Sixth Army continued its campaign against the remainder of the Japanese on Luzon, the U.S. Eighth Army and the U.S. Seventh Fleet was already embarked on a series of more than fifty amphibious assaults to free the other islands. On 19 February, forces of the Pacific Ocean Area landed U.S. Marines on the island of Iwo Jima to begin a fierce 26 day struggle to capture that island fortress. The assault on Okinawa commenced on 26 March and lasted almost until the end of June 1945.

During this same period, after securing Palawan Island, the U.S. Eighth Army made its first landing on Mindanao, and then occupied Panay, Cebu, Negros and several islands in the Sulu Archipelago, providing bases for the U.S. Fifth and Thirteenth Air Forces from which to attack targets throughout the Philippines and the South China Sea. Following additional landings on Mindanao, U.S. Eighth Army troops continued their steady advance against stubborn resistance. By the end of June the enemy was compressed into isolated pockets on Mindanao and Luzon where fighting continued until the end of the war. During these last months, Australian troops also seized important strategic installations on the island of Borneo. By this time, a complete reorganization of U.S. Forces had been made in preparation for the projected invasion of Japan. The two Area Commands were replaced by Army, Navy and Air Force commands, the latter was increased greatly in size by the transfer of the U.S. Eighth Air Force from Europe and creation of the U.S. Twentieth Air Force. During the last two months of the war, the aerial and naval bombardment of the Japanese home islands intensified. Hostilities ceased on 15 August 1945.

THE SITE

The cemetery site covers 152 acres of gently rising ground which culminates at the memorial. It is the largest in area of the cemeteries built and administered by the American Battle Monuments Commission, and the largest in point of the number of graves and of those Missing who are recorded upon the walls of the memorial.

Major objections having been found to all of the sites of temporary cemeteries which had been established during World War II, the Government of the Philippines on 1 April 1948 granted permission to the United States to establish a memorial cemetery on part of the former U.S. reservation of Fort William McKinley. A tremendous amount of grading, draining and landscaping was required in order to convert the rough terrain to the beautiful and regular forms of the present cemetery. Visitors may note that some areas among the burial plots are merely grassed, without headstones; generally this is because in these areas the underlying rock is so close to the surface as to make them unsuitable for burials.

In this cemetery are buried 17,206 of our military Dead representing 40 percent of the burials which were originally made in temporary cemeteries in New Guinea, the Philippines and other islands of the Southwest Pacific Area, and also in the Palau Islands of the Central Pacific Area. Most of these lost their lives in the epic defense of the

The Memorial Chapel With Hemicycles

Aerial View of the Cemetery

Philippines and the East Indies in 1941 and 1942 or in the long but victorious return of the American forces through the vast island chain. The cemetery and memorial was completed in 1960. The cemetery was dedicated on 8 December 1960.

ARCHITECT

Architect for the cemetery was Gardener A. Dailey of San Francisco, who also designed most of the landscape development.

GENERAL LAYOUT

The entrance to the cemetery is at the far (south) side of the large grassed circle just beyond the military sentinel's post which is at the junction of the McKinley and Nichols Field Roads. Immediately beyond the gate is the plaza with its circular fountain; at the right is the Visitors' Building.

Stretching from the plaza to the memorial is the central mall which is lined with mahogany trees (Swietenia Macrophylla); circular roads leading eastward and westward through the graves area join the straight roads along the edges of the mall.

To the east of, and lower than, the graves area are the service area, deep wells and reservoirs. A purification system provides potable water within the cemetery.

THE GRAVES AREA

The graves area is divided into eleven curved lettered plots of varying sizes forming concentric bands around the high ground on which the memorial stands. The 17,100 headstones within the plots form segments of concentric circles and mark the graves of 16,636 U.S. military and 570 Philippine Nationals

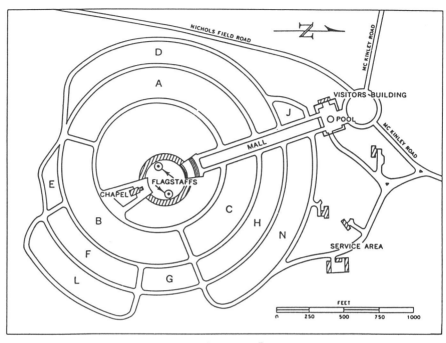

Location of Cemetery Features

who were serving with U.S. Forces in the Southwest Pacific. Of these headstones, 13,434 mark the graves of single identified remains; six mark the graves of 28 identified remains which could not be separated individually; 3,644 mark the graves of single unidentified remains (Unknowns); and 16 mark the graves of 100 unidentified remains which could not be separated individually. The heroic Dead interred in the cemetery represent all of the then 48 States of the Union, as well as the District of Columbia, Panama, Guam, Philippines, Puerto Rico, Australia, Canada, China, England, Mexico, Costa Rica, Honduras, Finland, Jamaica, Burma and Peru. In 20 instances, two brothers lie side by side.

Most of the white marble headstones were quarried in Lasa or Carrara, Italy; however, more than 100 were quarried and fabricated on the Island of Romblon in the Philippines.

THE MEMORIAL

The memorial is faced with Travertine limestone quarried near Tivoli, a few miles east of Rome, Italy. It consists of the tower containing the small devotional chapel, and the two extensive hemicycles to its front which embrace the Memorial Court. The principal entrance to the memorial area is by the monumental staircase at the south end of the mall. At the top of these steps the Great Seal of the Commonwealth of the Philippines has been carved into the paving; this is the seal which was authorized for use during World War II and until the Republic had been established. To the right and left stretch the hemicycles; on the end facade of each is the dedicatory inscription:

IN PROUD REMEMBRANCE OF THE
ACHIEVEMENTS OF HER SONS AND IN
HUMBLE TRIBUTE TO THEIR SACRIFICES
THIS MEMORIAL HAS BEEN ERECTED BY
THE UNITED STATES OF AMERICA ☆
1941-1945.

Each hemicycle contains 24 pairs of fin walls upon the four faces of which are inscribed the names and particulars of 36,280 of our Missing:

United States Army and Army
   Air Forces[1] 16,913
United States Navy................ 17,582
United States Marine Corps 1,727
United States Coast Guard 58

These gave their lives in the service of their Country in the regions from Australia northward to Japan, eastward to the Palau Islands and westward to China, Burma and India but their remains have not been identified, or they were lost or buried at sea. Their names include men from every State in the Union, also from the District of Columbia, Panama, Guam, Philippines, Puerto Rico, Australia, Canada and New Zealand. At each end of each hemicycle is a map room. The memorial area offers many magnificent prospects — over Manila toward Mount Arayat to the north, and over the Laguna de Bay toward Mount Makiling to the southeast and Tagaytay Ridge to the south.

Without confirmed information to the contrary, a War Department Administrative Review Board established the official date of death of those commemorated on the Tablets of the Missing as one year and a day from the date on which the individual was placed in Missing in action status.

---

[1] It will be recalled that during World War II the Air Forces still formed part of the United States Army.

THE WEST HEMICYCLE

The west hemicycle is entered from the Memorial Court. At the extreme north end is a map room which is described in detail beginning on page 33.

On the partition wall of each map room facing the lists of the Missing are these inscriptions:

HERE ARE RECORDED THE NAMES OF AMERICANS WHO GAVE THEIR LIVES IN THE SERVICE OF THEIR COUNTRY AND WHO SLEEP IN UNKNOWN GRAVES ☆ 1941-1945.

INCLUDED ON THESE ROLLS ARE THE NAMES OF PHILIPPINE SCOUTS WHO SHARED WITH THEIR AMERICAN COMRADES IN THE DEFENSE AND LIBERATION OF THE PHILIPPINES ☆ 1941-1945.

The lists of the Missing are arranged according to the four Armed Services, and alphabetically beginning at the far (south) end. In the west hemicycle are the Missing of the United States Navy, and part of the Missing of the United States Marine Corps. The names are engraved in Trani, a marble quarried near Bari on the east coast of Italy.

In the Travertine floor of each section of the hemicycles and the map rooms are carved the Great Seal of the United States, obverse or reverse, the Seal of one of the States of the Union, the District of Columbia and Puerto Rico; the 48 states (as of 1945) are in alphabetical order.

Along the frieze of this hemicycle, facing the Memorial Court, are engraved the names of World War II battles of particular significance in the Navy's and Marine Corps' proud record: MAKASSAR STRAIT; JAVA SEA; CORAL SEA; SAVO; EASTERN SOLOMONS; CAPE ESPERANCE; SANTA CRUZ; TASSAFARONGA; KULA GULF; VELLA GULF; EMPRESS AUGUSTA BAY; LEYTE GULF; GUADALCANAL; PELELIU. The facade of the hemicycle nearest to the chapel bears these inscriptions:

SOME THERE BE WHICH HAVE NO SEP-ULCHRE ☆ THEIR NAME LIVETH FOR EV-ERMCRE.

GRANT UNTO THEM O LORD ETERNAL REST WHO SLEEP IN UNKNOWN GRAVES.

Much of the paving at the Memorial is of Travertine; there are also many panels of bluish pebbles (from Luna, La Union, in the Philippines) set in mortar.

THE CHAPEL

The chapel stands between the south ends of the hemicycles. In front of the steps leading to the door is the obverse of the Great Seal of the United States, carved in the Travertine paving. The facade of the tower which rises 60 feet above its podium is decorated with sculpture in high relief designed by Boris Lovet-Lorski of New York City and executed by Filippo Cecchetti of Tivoli, Italy, who furnished all of the stone for the Memorial. The sculpture consists of a series of superimposed groups, representing, from bottom to top, the young American warrior symbolized by St. George, fighting his enemy, the dragon, in the jungle. Above them are the ideals for which he fought — Liberty, Justice, Country. Columbia, with the child symbolizing the future, stands at the zenith.

On the rear (south) facade of the tower is this inscription:

TAKE UNTO THYSELF O LORD THE SOULS OF THE VALIANT.

Beyond the bronze grille doors of the chapel the entrance is lined with blue glass mosaic; on the left this prayer, abridged from that in the Episcopal Book of Common Prayer, is inset in gold tesserae:

O GOD WHO ART THE AUTHOR OF PEACE AND LOVER OF CONCORD DEFEND US THY HUMBLE SERVANTS IN ALL AS-SAULTS OF OUR ENEMIES THAT WE SURELY TRUSTING IN THY DEFENSE MAY NOT FEAR THE POWER OF ANY ADVER-SARIES.

Opposite, on the right side, is this prayer abridged from that ascribed to Cardinal Newman:

O LORD SUPPORT US ALL THE DAY LONG UNTIL THE SHADOWS LENGTHEN AND OUR WORK IS DONE THEN IN THY MERCY GRANT US A SAFE LODGING AND A HOLY REST AND PEACE AT THE LAST.

The altar, against the rear wall, is of Perlato di Sicilia marble from the west coast of that island. The entire wall behind the altar is decorated with mosaic; on a predominantly blue background a tall, graceful female figure scatters flowers — an inscription proclaiming: TO THEIR MEMORY THEIR COUNTRY BRINGS ITS GRATITUDE AS FLOWERS FOREVER LIV-ING. The chapel mosaics were designed by Boris Lovet-Lorski of New York City and fabricated and installed by Fabrizio Cassio of Rome, Italy. The chapel is lighted through tall stone unglazed grilleworks. The priedieu and benches are of Philippine Narra wood, the altar ornaments of bronze.

Located at the Chapel is a carillon which on 3 February 1985 was presented and dedicated by the American Veterans of World War II, Korea and Vietnam (AMVETS) as a memorial to the Americans and Filipinos who fought and died together for the cause of freedom. Between the hours of 9:00 a.m. and 4:30 p.m. daily the carillon tolls the hour and half hour. This is followed by two patriotic songs. At 5:00 p.m., the carillon plays the national anthems of the Republic of the Philippines and the United States, followed by a rifle volley and then taps "AS THESE BELLS RING . . . HONORED DEAD REST . . . FREEDOM LIVES".

THE EAST HEMICYCLE

On the facade of the hemicycle nearest to the chapel are these inscriptions:

COMRADES IN ARMS WHOSE EARTHLY RESTING PLACE IS KNOWN ONLY TO GOD.
LET US HERE HIGHLY RESOLVE THAT THE CAUSE FOR WHICH THEY DIED SHALL LIVE.

Beyond the map room are the lists of the Missing of the United States Army and Army Air Forces, the United States Coast Guard, and part of the Missing of the United States Marine Corps. Along the frieze facing the Memorial Court are these names of battles which are particularly significant in the achievements of the the United States Army and Army Air Forces and the United States Marines: BATAAN; CORREGIDOR; PAPULA; BISMARCK SEA; HUON GULF; ADMIRALTIES; AITAPE; HOLLANDIA; WAKDE; BIAK; NOEMFOOR; BURMA; ANGAUR; LEYTE; MANILA; NEW BRITAIN; BOUGAINVILLE; NEW GEORGIA.

THE MAPS

The maps were designed by Margaret Bruton of Carmel, California, from data supplied by the American Battle Monuments Commission, and fabricated by the P. Grassi American Terrazzo Company of South San Francisco. They are of tinted concretes with brilliantly colored fine aggregates. Military data are expressed by mosaic or ceramic inserts; the borders and compasses recall the art patterns of the Pacific Islands. The descriptive texts which amplify the maps and which were cast with them are of plastic.

SOUTHWEST ROOM

This room has seven maps; the descriptive texts thereon are printed after the title of each:

1. DEFENSE OF LUZON — 8 DECEMBER 1941-6 MAY 1942

ON 7 DECEMBER 1941 (HAWAII TIME) THE JAPANESE LAUNCHED A SURPRISE ATTACK ON PEARL HARBOR, THEN SEVERAL HOURS LATER BOMBED FROM THE AIR U.S. MILITARY INSTALLATIONS IN THE PHILIPPINES. TWO DAYS LATER THE ENEMY LANDED ON LUZON ANTICIPATING AN EASY CONQUEST, BUT STUBBORN RESISTANCE BY U.S. AND PHILIPPINE FORCES SLOWED THE ADVANCE. MANNING SUCCESSIVE DEFENSIVE POSITIONS OUR TROOPS DELAYED THE ONCOMING ENEMY, THEN EVACUATED MANILA AND WITHDREW TO THE BATAAN PENINSULA. ON 2 JANUARY 1942 THE JAPANESE OCCUPIED THE CAPITAL.

UNITED STATES FORCES INCLUDING PHILIPPINE SCOUTS AS WELL AS THE PHILIPPINE ARMY STEMMED THE JAPANESE OFFENSIVE DURING JANUARY 1942 AND DEFEATED AN ATTEMPTED AMPHIBIOUS ENVELOPMENT ON THE SOUTHWESTERN SHORE OF THE PENINSULA. THE ENEMY THEN POURED REINFORCEMENTS INTO BATAAN, WITHHOLDING THEM FROM OFFENSIVE OPERATIONS AGAINST NEW GUINEA AND THE SOLOMON ISLANDS.

UNTIL APRIL THE JAPANESE CONTINUED TO BUILD UP THEIR STRENGTH WHILE THE BELEAGUERED AMERICANS AND FILIPINOS ON BATAAN WASTED AWAY FOR WANT OF ADEQUATE FOOD AND MEDICINE. CIVILIAN NEEDS AGGRAVATED THESE SHORTAGES.

ON 3 APRIL, FOLLOWING A DEVASTATING AIR BOMBARDMENT AND A THREE-DAY ARTILLERY BARRAGE, THE ENEMY LAUNCHED AN ASSAULT UTILIZ-

View From Inside Chapel Entrance

ING EVERY ELEMENT OF HIS OVER-
WHELMING FORCES. RELENTLESS PRES-
SURE CONTINUED DAY BY DAY, AND
COUNTERATTACKS FAILED TO HALT THE
JAPANESE ONSLAUGHT. NO LONGER
ABLE TO INFLICT DAMAGE UPON THE
ENEMY, THE BATAAN FORCES SURREN-
DERED ON 9 APRIL.

ON CORREGIDOR AND AT OTHER
FORTS IN MANILA BAY A COMPOSITE
FORCE OF U.S. MARINES, ARMY AND
NAVY PERSONNEL, TOGETHER WITH THE
COAST ARTILLERY GARRISONS, CONTIN-
UED TO RESIST. SUBMARINES DELIVERED
AMMUNITION AND FOOD AND MAIN-
TAINED TENUOUS COMMUNICATIONS.
BUT, PROGRESSIVELY, THE BATTERIES
AND BEACH DEFENSES OF CORREGIDOR
WERE DEMOLISHED BY CONTINUOUS
BOMBING AND SHELLING. ON 5 MAY THE
JAPANESE LAUNCHED THEIR FINAL AS-
SAULT. THE FOLLOWING DAY U.S. AND
PHILIPPINE FORCES SURRENDERED THE
ISLAND FORTRESS.

OF ALMOST 30,000 AMERICAN MILI-
TARY PRISONERS OF WAR, SOME 11,000
DIED BEFORE THE WAR ENDED. MANY
THOUSANDS OF AMERICAN CIVILIANS
OF ALL AGES WERE ALSO HELD IN HARSH
CAPTIVITY AS WERE UNTOLD NUMBERS
OF FILIPINO CITIZENS.

FOR OVER THREE YEARS THE PHILIP-
PINE ISLANDS SUFFERED UNDER ENEMY
OCCUPATION WHILE THE UNITED STATES
FORCES FOUGHT THEIR WAY BACK. DUR-
ING THESE LONG YEARS THE COURA-
GEOUS GUERRILLAS FOUGHT UNCEAS-
INGLY TO KEEP ALIVE THE FLAME OF
HOPE IN THE OPPRESSED BUT LOYAL CI-
VILIAN POPULATION.

2. DEFENSE OF SOUTHEAST ASIA— DECEMBER 1941-MAY 1942

IN DECEMBER 1941, THE NAVAL,
GROUND AND AIR FORCES OF THE JAPA-
NESE EMPIRE ATTACKED AMERICAN,
BRITISH, DUTCH AND AUSTRALIAN

UNITS AND INSTALLATIONS IN THE PA-
CIFIC. IN JANUARY 1942 THE U.S. ASI-
ATIC FLEET AND THE U.S. FAR EAST AIR
FORCE UNITED WITH THE LAND, SEA
AND AIR FORCES OF THESE ALLIES TO
FORM THE ABDA COMMAND IN JAVA.

PITTING THEIR LIMITED DEFENSIVE
MEANS AGAINST OVERWHELMING
ODDS, THE ALLIES RESISTED THE SUC-
CESSIVE JAPANESE ASSAULTS. BUT AS
RESOURCES DIMINISHED THIS DEFENSE
WAS CONDUCTED WITH INCREASING
DIFFICULTY. UNDER PROGRESSIVELY
MOUNTING ODDS THE ALLIES SUFFERED
HEAVY LOSSES OF GALLANT DEFENDERS
AND VALUABLE NAVAL AND AIR CRAFT.

AMERICAN MILITARY PERSONNEL IN
CHINA, BURMA AND INDIA HELPED OR-
GANIZE AND CONSOLIDATE LOCAL RE-
SISTANCE TO THE JAPANESE ON-
SLAUGHT. BY 1 MAY 1942 THE ALLIED
FORCES IN BURMA HAD WITHDRAWN TO
THE MANDALAY-LASHIO LINE. LATER
THEY WITHDREW TO CHINA AND INDIA
WHERE CHINESE TROOPS WERE TRAINED
AND REARMED UNDER U.S. GUIDANCE.

BY MAY 1942, THE ENEMY HAD
GAINED CONTROL OF THE VAST EXPANSE
FROM BURMA IN THE WEST TO THE SO-
LOMON SEA IN THE EAST AND WAS
THREATENING AUSTRALIA. IN THE
MEANTIME THE AUSTRALIANS HAD RE-
INFORCED PORT MORESBY AND MADE A
DETERMINED EFFORT TO HOLD THE NEW
GUINEA BARRIER. IN THE DECISIVE BAT-
TLE OF THE CORAL SEA ON 4-8 MAY U.S.
NAVAL FORCES DEFEATED THE JAPANESE
AND TURNED BACK THEIR PORT
MORESBY INVASION FORCE. THIS
MARKED THE HIGH TIDE OF THE JAPA-
NESE ADVANCE.

3. BATTLE FOR LEYTE GULF—23-26
   OCTOBER 1944

ON 20 OCTOBER 1944, THE U.S. SEV-
ENTH FLEET COMMENCED LANDING THE
SIXTH ARMY ON THE EASTERN SHORE OF
LEYTE. THEREUPON THE JAPANESE DE-
CIDED TO RISK A MAJOR SEA BATTLE IN
A DETERMINED EFFORT TO DESTROY THE
AMERICAN FORCES.

THREE JAPANESE FLEETS WERE CON-
CENTRATED. THE LARGEST, THE CENTER
FORCE, MOVED TOWARD LEYTE FROM
ITS BASE NEAR SINGAPORE. THE FIRST
SECTION OF THE SOUTHERN FORCE PRO-
CEEDED SOUTH OF PALAWAN, THROUGH
THE SULU SEA, TO JOIN THE SECOND
SECTION IN ATTACKING THE AMERICAN
FORCES AT LEYTE GULF. THE NORTHERN
FORCE, WHICH INCLUDED THE ENEMY'S
MAIN CARRIER STRENGTH, ADVANCED
TOWARD THE PHILIPPINES FROM JAPA-
NESE HOME WATERS.

ON 23 OCTOBER AMERICAN SUBMA-
RINES ATTACKED THE ENEMY'S CENTER
FORCE IN PALAWAN PASSAGE, SINKING
TWO CRUISERS AND CRIPPLING A THIRD.
ON 24 OCTOBER THE U.S. THIRD FLEET,
ITS STRENGTH PREPONDERANT IN FAST
CARRIERS, ATTACKED THIS CENTER
FORCE IN THE SIBUYAN SEA; AIRCRAFT
INFLICTED SUCH HEAVY LOSSES AS TO
CAUSE THIS FORCE TO TURN BACK. JAPA-
NESE AIRCRAFT BASED ON LUZON THEN
COUNTERATTACKED, DESTROYING A
U.S. CARRIER.

DURING THE NIGHT OF 24-25 OCTO-
BER, THE ENEMY'S SOUTHERN FORCE
STEAMED INTO SURIGAO STRAIT DI-
RECTLY TOWARD THE WAITING U.S. SEV-
ENTH FLEET. THE JAPANESE WERE DECI-
SIVELY DEFEATED BY TORPEDO ATTACKS
FROM PT BOATS AND DESTROYERS AND
GUNFIRE FROM THE HEAVIER SHIPS
WHICH SANK TWO BATTLESHIPS, A
CRUISER AND THREE DESTROYERS.

MEANWHILE THE THIRD FLEET
MOVED NORTHWARD TO INTERCEPT THE
ENEMY'S NORTHERN FORCE WHICH WAS
APPROACHING THE TIP OF LUZON. IN
THE ENSUING BATTLE OFF CAPE ENGANO
ON 25-26 OCTOBER U.S. CARRIER BASED
AIRCRAFT, GUNFIRE, AND SUBMARINES
SANK FOUR JAPANESE CARRIERS, TWO
CRUISERS AND THREE DESTROYERS.

EARLY ON THE MORNING OF 25 OCTO-
BER, THE JAPANESE CENTER FORCE,
HAVING AGAIN REVERSED COURSE,
PUSHED THROUGH SAN BERNARDINO
STRAIT, TURNED SOUTH AND ATTACKED
THE ESCORT CARRIERS OF THE SEVENTH

FLEET OPERATING OFF SAMAR TO PRO-
TECT THE AMERICAN FORCES IN LEYTE
GULF. ALTHOUGH OUTNUMBERED AND
OUTGUNNED, THE ESCORT CARRIERS
AND THEIR SCREEN OF DESTROYERS
FOUGHT COURAGEOUSLY AND SANK
THREE JAPANESE CRUISERS; TWO AMER-
ICAN ESCORT CARRIERS AND THREE DE-
STROYERS WERE LOST. THEREUPON THE
SURVIVORS OF ALL THREE ENEMY FLEETS
WITHDREW.

ELIMINATING THE JAPANESE EMPIRE
AS A SEA POWER, LEYTE GULF BECAME
ONE OF THE DECISIVE NAVAL BATTLES
OF HISTORY.

4. RETURN TO THE PHILIPPINES— OCTOBER 1944

ON 20 OCTOBER 1944, UNDER COVER
OF NAVAL GUNFIRE AND AIR BOMBARD-
MENT OF THE SEVENTH FLEET, THE U.S.
SIXTH ARMY LANDED ON THE EASTERN
SHORES OF LEYTE; AIRCRAFT OF THE
THIRD FLEET FURNISHED LONG-RANGE
SUPPORT. THE 7TH DIVISION OF THE
XXIV CORPS ON THE LEFT TOOK THE DU-
LAG AIRFIELD THEN DROVE WEST AND
SOUTH, WHILE THE 96TH DIVISION CAP-
TURED SAN JOSE AND MOVED AGAINST
THE ENEMY TO THE NORTHWEST. THE
24TH DIVISION OF THE X CORPS ON THE
RIGHT, OVERCOMING STRONG RESIST-
ANCE ON THE BEACHES, FOUGHT ITS
WAY INLAND. THE 1ST CAVALRY DIVI-
SION ON THE RIGHT FLANK SEIZED TAC-
LOBAN AND ITS AIRFIELD, THEN AD-
VANCING NORTH IN COORDINATED AM-
PHIBIOUS AND LAND OPERATIONS SE-
CURED SAN JUANICO STRAIT, THE WEST
COAST OF SAMAR AND THE SHORE OF
CARIGARA BAY ON THE NORTHERN
COAST OF LEYTE.

THE JAPANESE RUSHED REINFORCE-
MENTS FROM THE NEIGHBORING IS-
LANDS AND FROM THE ASIATIC MAIN-
LAND. MOST OF THESE LANDED AT
ORMOC BAY WHERE THEY WERE REPEAT-
EDLY ATTACKED BY THE U.S. FIFTH AIR
FORCE. NEVERTHELESS, THE ENEMY WAS
ABLE TO CONCENTRATE POWERFUL

FORCES IN THE ORMOC VALLEY AND, BY
7 NOVEMBER, HAD ORGANIZED STRONG
POSITIONS IN THE MOUNTAINS TO THE
EAST. THE SIXTH ARMY IN TURN WAS
REINFORCED BY THREE ADDITIONAL DI-
VISIONS BUT DESPERATE RESISTANCE,
THE RUGGED TERRAIN AND TORRENTIAL
RAINS SLOWED THE ADVANCE.

IN DECEMBER THE 77TH DIVISION OF
XXIV CORPS LANDED ALONG THE EAST
COAST OF ORMOC BAY IN THE REAR OF
THE JAPANESE. SUPPORTED BY ARMY,
NAVY AND MARINE CORPS AIRCRAFT, IT
ADVANCED NORTHWARD TO SEIZE OR-
MOC AFTER FIERCE FIGHTING, THUS
CUTTING THE LAST MAJOR LINE OF EN-
EMY COMMUNICATIONS.

IN THE CARIGARA BAY AREA TO THE
NORTH, THE X CORPS FOUGHT THROUGH
THE MOUNTAINOUS TERRAIN NEAR LI-
MON AND DROVE SOUTHWARD TO UNITE
WITH THE XXIV CORPS ADVANCING UP
THE VALLEY. ON 21 DECEMBER THEY
BROKE THROUGH THE OPPOSING LINES
AND MET NEAR KANANGA, THUS ISO-
LATING THE JAPANESE TO THE EAST;
FOUR DAYS LATER THE ISLAND WAS DE-
CLARED SECURE. MANY OF THE ISO-
LATED JAPANESE HAD ESCAPED TO THE
NORTH AND WEST TO JOIN OTHER EN-
EMY UNITS; SEVERE FIGHTING CONTIN-
UED AGAINST THE EIGHTH ARMY, NOW
IN CONTROL, UNTIL MAY 1945.

5. LUZON CAMPAIGN—15 DECEMBER 1944-15 AUGUST 1945

BY THE END OF 1944 PROGRESSIVELY
LARGER PROPORTIONS OF AMERICA'S
GREATLY AUGMENTED MILITARY RE-
SOURCES HAD BEEN CONCENTRATED IN
THE PACIFIC THEATERS OF WAR. WHILE
THE LEYTE CAMPAIGN WAS STILL IN
PROGRESS, POWERFUL U.S. FORCES
STRUCK AT THE NEXT TARGET, LUZON.
AIRCRAFT OF THE NAVY AND ARMY AIR
FORCES CONDUCTED DEVASTATING AT-
TACKS AGAINST ENEMY AIRFIELDS, SUP-
PLY CENTERS AND TRANSPORTATION
SYSTEMS THERE AND IN SURROUNDING
AREAS. THE INTENSITY AND ACCURACY

Memorial Hemicycles from the Rear

OF THESE BOMBARDMENTS AND THE TREMENDOUS POTENTIAL FIRE POWER OF THE THIRD AND SEVENTH FLEETS INDUCED THE JAPANESE ON LUZON TO WITHDRAW THEIR MAIN FORCES FROM THE BEACHES AND CONCENTRATE THEM IN DEFENSIVE POSITIONS IN MOUNTAINOUS AREAS OF THE INTERIOR.

IN DECEMBER, THE U.S. SIXTH ARMY CONVOYED BY THE SEVENTH FLEET SEIZED MINDORO, ESTABLISHING BASES AND AIRFIELDS TO PROVIDE CLOSE SUPPORT FOR THE IMPENDING LUZON OPERATION. MEANWHILE THE JAPANESE MASSED OVER A QUARTER OF A MILLION MEN TO DEFEND LUZON AND UNLEASHED DAMAGING SUICIDAL AIR ATTACKS AGAINST ALLIED NAVAL FORCES.

ON 9 JANUARY 1945, THE SEVENTH FLEET LANDED TWO DIVISIONS FROM EACH OF THE I AND XIV CORPS ON THE SOUTH SHORE OF LINGAYEN GULF. SUPPORTED BY THE FIFTH AIR FORCE AND BY MARINE CORPS AND NAVAL AIRCRAFT, THE SIXTH ARMY PUSHED INLAND. INITIALLY RESISTANCE WAS ENCOUNTERED ALONG THE LEFT FLANK, WHERE THE MASS OF THE JAPANESE STRENGTH HAD BEEN CONCENTRATED IN THE MOUNTAINS NEAR BAGUIO. ON THE RIGHT THE AMERICAN FORCES CAPTURED CLARK FIELD, DROVE THE ENEMY INTO THE ZAMBALES MOUNTAINS, THEN ADVANCED TOWARD MANILA, WHERE HEAVY FIGHTING ENSUED.

ON THE WEST COAST OF LUZON THE XI CORPS LANDED ON 29 JANUARY AND MOVED EASTWARD TO CUT OFF THE BATAAN PENINSULA; SOUTH OF MANILA OTHER UNITS OF THE EIGHTH ARMY LANDED ON 31 JANUARY AND SWUNG NORTHWARD. ALL PASSED TO THE CONTROL OF THE SIXTH ARMY. AFTER FIERCE AND PROLONGED FIGHTING, MANILA, BATAAN AND CORREGIDOR WERE CLEARED OF THE ENEMY, AND MANILA BAY WAS OPENED.

EAST OF MANILA THE FIGHTING WENT ON FOR MANY WEEKS. CONSTANT PRESSURE FORCED THE ENEMY DEEPER INTO THE MOUNTAINS WHERE HE WAS HELD ISOLATED UNTIL THE END OF HOSTILITIES. OTHER AMERICAN UNITS CLEARED THE AREA SOUTH OF LAGUNA DE BAY AND LIBERATED THE BICOL PENINSULA, ASSISTED BY AMPHIBIOUS FORCES LANDED AT LEGASPI.

IN CENTRAL AND NORTHERN LUZON U.S. TROOPS AND PHILIPPINE GUERRILLA FORCES CONTINUED THEIR PRESSURE NORTHWARD FROM THE CENTRAL PLAIN THROUGH DIFFICULT TERRAIN DEFENDED BY A DETERMINED ENEMY; CONSTANT ATTACKS BY AIR AND GROUND FORCES FINALLY BROKE JAPANESE RESISTANCE AT BALETE PASS IN MAY. ON 1 JULY THE EIGHTH ARMY ASSUMED RESPONSIBILITY FOR DESTROYING THE REMAINING ENEMY FORCES ON LUZON, RELIEVING THE SIXTH ARMY FOR THE PROJECTED INVASION OF JAPAN.

6. REOCCUPATION OF MANILA

BY 31 JANUARY 1945, THREE WEEKS AFTER THE INITIAL LANDINGS ON LUZON, THE U.S. SIXTH ARMY WAS READY TO LAUNCH ITS OFFENSIVE TO LIBERATE MANILA AND THE BATAAN PENINSULA. THE 1ST CAVALRY AND 37TH INFANTRY DIVISIONS ADVANCED ON THE CITY FROM THE NORTH, WHILE THE 40TH DIVISION FOUGHT WESTWARD INTO THE ZAMBALES MOUNTAINS TO SECURE THE RIGHT FLANK AND MEET THE 38TH DIVISION PUSHING EASTWARD TO CUT OFF BATAAN. SIMULTANEOUSLY THE 11TH AIRBORNE DIVISION ADVANCED ON MANILA FROM THE SOUTH.

WITHIN THE CITY THE 1ST CAVALRY DIVISION, IN A NIGHT ATTACK, CAPTURED SANTO TOMAS UNIVERSITY AND LIBERATED 3,700 AMERICAN AND ALLIED PRISONERS INTERNED THERE. ON 4 FEBRUARY THE 37TH INFANTRY DIVISION FREED OVER A THOUSAND MORE FROM BILIBID PRISON. THESE TWO DIVISIONS THEN CROSSED THE PASIG RIVER AGAINST STIFFENING RESISTANCE WHILE THE 11TH AIRBORNE DIVISION OVERCAME SIMILAR RESISTANCE IN ITS ATTACK UPON NICHOLS FIELD. THE 1ST

CAVALRY AND 37TH INFANTRY DIVISIONS FORCED THEIR WAY THROUGH THE CITY, EVENTUALLY REACHING THE STRONGHOLD AT INTRAMUROS WHERE THE FIGHTING WAS ESPECIALLY BITTER. ON 3 MARCH MANILA WAS FINALLY CLEARED OF JAPANESE TROOPS WHO, IN DEFENDING THE CITY, HAD CAUSED INCALCULABLE DEVASTATION.

MEANWHILE THE 38TH INFANTRY DIVISION, TOGETHER WITH ELEMENTS OF THE 6TH AND 24TH DIVISIONS, SUPPORTED BY AERIAL BOMBARDMENT AND NAVAL GUNFIRE, CLEARED THE BATAAN PENINSULA. ON 16 FEBRUARY AIRBORNE AND AMPHIBIOUS UNITS LAUNCHED ASSAULTS AGAINST CORREGIDOR; JAPANESE RESISTED DESPERATELY FROM CAVES, TUNNELS AND CONCRETE MORTAR PITS UNTIL 27 FEBRUARY. FORT DRUM HELD OUT UNTIL APRIL.

ON 28 FEBRUARY 1945, BEFORE THE JAPANESE HAD BEEN COMPLETELY ELIMINATED FROM MANILA AND ITS OUTLYING FORTS, THE COMMONWEALTH GOVERNMENT OF THE PHILIPPINES WAS CEREMONIALLY REINSTALLED AT MALACANAN PALACE.

7. LIBERATION OF THE PHILIPPINES — 20 OCTOBER 1944–15 AUGUST 1945

DURING THE LONG ENEMY OCCUPATION OF THE PHILIPPINES, THE UNITED STATES PERSISTENTLY FOUGHT HER WAY BACK. BY THE FALL OF 1944 SUCCESS WAS IN SIGHT.

THE FIRST STEP IN LIBERATING THE ISLANDS WAS THE INVASION OF LEYTE IN OCTOBER 1944. THE DECISIVE DEFEAT OF THE JAPANESE FLEET AT THE BATTLE FOR LEYTE GULF RENDERED IT POWERLESS TO PREVENT FUTURE AMPHIBIOUS OPERATIONS. TWO MONTHS OF HARD FIGHTING FREED MOST OF LEYTE WHICH THEN BECAME THE CENTRAL BASE OF OPERATIONS FOR THE LIBERATION OF THE ARCHIPELAGO. THE NEXT STEP ESTABLISHED OUR FORCES ON MINDORO IN DECEMBER.

IN JANUARY 1945, UNDER COVER OF NAVAL AND AIR BOMBARDMENT, THE SIXTH ARMY LANDED ON LUZON AND ADVANCED DOWN THE CENTRAL PLAINS FROM LINGAYEN GULF TO MANILA. OTHER UNITS LANDED ON THE WEST COAST OF THE ISLAND AND SEIZED BATAAN PENINSULA AND CORREGIDOR. MANILA BAY WAS OPENED IN EARLY MARCH. AFTER HEAVY FIGHTING THE SIXTH ARMY DROVE THE ENEMY INTO THE MOUNTAINS OF NORTH AND EAST LUZON.

THE EIGHTH ARMY AND UNITS OF THE SEVENTH FLEET HAD ALREADY EMBARKED ON A SERIES OF MORE THAN FIFTY AMPHIBIOUS ASSAULTS TO FREE THE OTHER ISLANDS. DURING FEBRUARY AND MARCH U.S. FORCES SECURED AIRFIELDS ON PALAWAN AND ZAMBOANGA, THEN EXTENDED THEIR CONTROL OVER THE SULU ARCHIPELAGO, ENABLING THE FIFTH AND THIRTEENTH AIR FORCES TO PROJECT THEIR STRENGTH FAR OVER THE WATERS OF THE SOUTH CHINA SEA. U.S. SEA AND AIR POWER BLOCKED ENEMY TRAFFIC BETWEEN THE SOUTHERN ISLANDS AND THE JAPANESE HOMELAND, THUS ISOLATING THE JAPANESE REMAINING ON EACH OF THE ISLANDS.

SIMULTANEOUSLY THE EIGHTH ARMY OVERPOWERED THE ENEMY IN THE VISAYAN SEA AREA, THEREBY OPENING A SHORTER SUPPLY ROUTE FROM LEYTE TO LUZON. ON 17 APRIL SOME OF ITS UNITS LANDED ON THE COAST OF MINDANAO AND ADVANCED TOWARD DAVAO GULF; OTHERS FOLLOWED AND FOUGHT THEIR WAY NORTHWARD TOWARD MALAYBALAY TO MEET ADDITIONAL AMPHIBIOUS FORCES WHICH LANDED IN MAY. RESISTANCE WAS STUBBORN BUT THE TROOPS PUSHED STEADILY FORWARD INTO THE MOUNTAINS, PRECEDED BY MARINE CORPS AND ARMY AIR FORCES AIRCRAFT WHICH DEMORALIZED THE RETREATING ENEMY.

BY THE END OF JUNE, ON BOTH MINDANAO AND LUZON AMERICAN SOLDIERS AND FILIPINO GUERRILLAS HAD

COMPRESSED THE ENEMY INTO ISO-LATED MOUNTAINOUS AREAS. THERE HE WAS SUBJECTED TO INTENSIVE AERIAL BOMBARDMENT AND TO CONSTANT PRESSURE UNTIL 15 AUGUST 1945 WHEN HOSTILITIES CEASED. ON 1 JULY THE EIGHTH ARMY ASSUMED RESPONSIBIL-ITY FOR LAND OPERATIONS IN THE PHILIPPINES; THE SIXTH ARMY RE-GROUPED FORCES IN PREPARATION FOR AN INVASION OF JAPAN.

SOUTHEAST ROOM

This room has seven maps:

1. BATTLE OF THE CORAL SEA—4-8 MAY 1942

THE BATTLE OF THE CORAL SEA WAS THE FIRST NAVAL BATTLE IN WHICH ALL LOSSES WERE INFLICTED BY CARRIER-BASED AIRCRAFT, AND NO SHIP ON EI-THER SIDE SIGHTED A SURFACE ENEMY.

BY MID-APRIL 1942 THE JAPANESE HAD ESTABLISHED BASES IN THE NEW GUINEA–SOLOMON ISLAND AREA, THUS MENACING AUSTRALIA ITSELF. ON 3 MAY THEY OCCUPIED TULAGI, A SMALL ISLAND IN THE SOLOMONS. PART OF A U.S. NAVAL TASK FORCE CONSISTING OF THE AIRCRAFT CARRIER YORKTOWN, FOUR CRUISERS AND SIX DESTROYERS MOVED NORTH TO CHECK THE INVA-SION. AIRCRAFT FROM THE USS YORKTOWN ATTACKED TULAGI ON 4 MAY SINKING AN ENEMY DESTROYER, SEVERAL MINESWEEPERS, SMALLER CRAFT AND SEAPLANES.

FOLLOWING THE TULAGI STRIKE, YORKTOWN AND HER ESCORTS TURNED SOUTH TO RENDEZVOUS WITH USS LEX-INGTON EARLY ON THE MORNING OF 5 MAY. THE ALLIED TASK FORCE MOVED NORTHWEST TO INTERCEPT THE JAPA-NESE PORT MORESBY INVASION GROUP AND A POWERFUL CARRIER STRIKING FORCE. THEIR STRONG AMPHIBIOUS FORCE, INCLUDING 11 TROOP-LADEN TRANSPORTS PROTECTED BY A DE-STROYER SCREEN, HAD LEFT RABAUL AND WAS HEADING FOR A DASH THROUGH JOMARD PASS.

ON 7 MAY LEXINGTON AND YORK-TOWN AIRCRAFT SANK THE ENEMY CAR-RIER SHOHO WHICH WAS CLOSELY SUP-PORTING THE PORT MORESBY AMPHIBI-OUS ATTACK FORCE. THE JAPANESE WITHDREW THIS INVASION FORCE THUS MAKING THEIR FIRST SIGNIFICANT RE-TREAT IN WORLD WAR II. THE SAME MORNING JAPANESE CARRIER AIRCRAFT SANK USS SIMS AND THE TANKER NEOSHO, WHICH HAD BEEN MISTAKEN FOR A CARRIER AND CRUISER.

ON 8 MAY OCCURRED THE CLIMACTIC CARRIER BATTLE. NAVAL CARRIER AIR-CRAFT LOCATED TWO LARGE JAPANESE CARRIERS PROTECTED BY FOUR HEAVY CRUISERS AND SEVERAL DESTROYERS. THE AIRPLANES HEAVILY DAMAGED THE LARGE JAPANESE CARRIER SHOKAKU. THE ENEMY IN TURN DAMAGED YORKTOWN AND LEXINGTON, THE LAT-TER SO SERIOUSLY THAT SHE HAD TO BE ABANDONED AND SUNK.

THE BATTLE OF THE CORAL SEA WAS A STRATEGIC VICTORY OF THE FIRST MAG-NITUDE FOR THE U.S. NAVY. WHEN THE PORT MORESBY INVASION WAS THWARTED, THE HERETOFORE UNINTER-RUPTED JAPANESE PUSH INTO THE SOUTH PACIFIC WAS HALTED FOR THE FIRST TIME. OCCURRING IMMEDIATELY AFTER THE SURRENDER OF CORREGIDOR, ITS MORAL VALUE TO ALL ALLIED NA-TIONS WAS IMMEASURABLE. FURTHER-MORE, DAMAGE TO SHOKAKU AND A LARGE LOSS OF AIRCRAFT BY ZUIKAKU PREVENTED THESE POWERFUL JAPANESE AIRCRAFT CARRIERS FROM TAKING PART IN THE BATTLE OF MIDWAY WHERE THEIR PRESENCE MIGHT HAVE MADE A CRITICAL DIFFERENCE IN THE OUT-COME.

2. CHINA-BURMA-INDIA THEATER— 1942-1945

AFTER THE LOSS OF BURMA IN 1942 THE PEOPLE OF CHINA, WHO FOR MORE THAN A DECADE HAD BEEN RESISTING JAPANESE ENCROACHMENT UPON THEIR TERRITORY, WERE ISOLATED FROM

THEIR ALLIES. A UNITED STATES AIR ROUTE WAS ESTABLISHED OVER THE SOUTHEASTERN RANGES OF THE HIMALAYAS AND FOR MANY MONTHS WAS THE SOLE MEANS OF SENDING EFFECTIVE SUPPORT TO THE CHINESE WAR EFFORT. THE U.S. TENTH AIR FORCE PROTECTED THIS ROUTE FROM ASSAM AND, WITH THE ROYAL AIR FORCE, ESTABLISHED AIR SUPREMACY OVER BURMA BY THE END OF 1943.

AT RAMGARH AN AMERICAN STAFF TRAINED CHINESE TROOPS AND PROVIDED THEM WITH MILITARY EQUIPMENT. LATER THESE TROOPS FOUGHT AGAINST THE JAPANESE IN BURMA AND WERE THEN AIRLIFTED TO CHINA TO CONTINUE THE STRUGGLE.

TO INCREASE THE FLOW OF SUPPLIES TO CHINA IT WAS ESSENTIAL TO REOPEN SURFACE COMMUNICATIONS ACROSS BURMA. BETWEEN DECEMBER 1943 AND MARCH 1945 ALLIED GROUND FORCES, WHO WERE TRANSPORTED, SUPPLIED AND SUPPORTED BY AIR, DROVE THE JAPANESE OUT OF NORTH AND CENTRAL BURMA. ON THE HEELS OF THE COMBAT FORCES U.S. ENGINEERS BUILT THE LEDO ROAD, AN OUTSTANDING FEAT OF MILITARY CONSTRUCTION AND CONNECTED IT TO THE BURMA ROAD NEAR THE CHINESE BORDER.

OVER CHINA THE U.S. FOURTEENTH AIR FORCE PROTECTED THE AIRLIFT OF URGENTLY NEEDED SUPPLIES UPON WHICH THE AMERICAN AND CHINESE FORCES DEPENDED. IN SPITE OF ITS LIMITED RESOURCES IT EFFECTIVELY SUPPORTED CHINESE GROUND OPERATIONS, AND THROUGH ADVANCE BASES IN EAST CHINA STRUCK AT ENEMY SHIPPING IN ASIATIC WATERS. A WIDESPREAD NAVAL INTELLIGENCE NETWORK BASED AT CHUNGKING PLAYED ITS PART IN THESE ACTIVITIES.

BEHIND THE VICTORIES IN CHINA, THE RECONQUEST OF BURMA, AND THE TRIUMPH OF OUR AIR AND GROUND FORCES, LAY CONTROL OF THE SEA BY THE ALLIED NAVIES AND THE TREMENDOUS EFFORTS OF THE SERVICES OF SUPPLY WHICH MADE THE CONTINUOUS FLOW OF VITAL SUPPLIES POSSIBLE. AFTER BEING SHIPPED HALF-WAY AROUND THE WORLD ACROSS TWO OCEANS AND PAST THREE CONTINENTS, SUPPLIES WERE UNLOADED AT INDIAN PORTS, THEN TRANSPORTED BY ROAD, RAILROAD, FERRY, BARGE OR PIPELINE TO ASSAM AIRFIELDS BEFORE BEING AIRLIFTED IN HAZARDOUS FLIGHT OVER THE MOUNTAINS FOR ULTIMATE DISTRIBUTION WITHIN CHINA. BY FEBRUARY 1945, PIPELINES WERE BEING EXTENDED FROM ASSAM TO KUNMING, AND TRUCKS WERE ROLLING ALONG THE LEDO-BURMA ROAD. THESE EFFORTS ENABLED THE CHINESE TO MAKE MATERIAL CONTRIBUTION TO THE DEFEAT OF THE JAPANESE.

3. AMERICAN AIR FERRY ROUTES — SUPPLY TO THE U.S.S.R. — 1941–1945

THE UNITED STATES OF AMERICA, WHILE CONTRIBUTING ITS LAND, SEA AND AIR FORCES TO THE PROSECUTION OF WORLD WAR II, ALSO AIDED ITS MANY ALLIES BY FURNISHING MILITARY EQUIPMENT AND SUPPLIES. ITEMS OF ALL KINDS WERE CARRIED BY VAST FLEETS OF STEAMSHIPS TO EVERY AVAILABLE PORT. ALSO IN THIS EFFORT THOUSANDS OF AIRCRAFT WERE FERRIED FROM THE UNITED STATES ACROSS THE ATLANTIC OCEAN AND CENTRAL AFRICA TO CAIRO, BASRA AND KARACHI.

THROUGH THE PERSIAN GULF COMMAND AREA THE UNITED STATES DELIVERED, FROM 1942 TO 1945, NEARLY 4½ MILLION TONS OF SUPPLIES TO THE U.S.S.R. THESE INCLUDED 4,874 AIRCRAFT OF WHICH 995 WERE FLOWN IN; OVER 160,000 TANKS, ARMORED CARS AND TRUCKS; 140,000 TONS OF GUNS, AMMUNITION AND EXPLOSIVES; 550,000 TONS OF PETROLEUM PRODUCTS; 950,000 TONS OF FOOD; AND 1,000,000 TONS OF METAL AND METAL PRODUCTS. THE UNITED STATES ALSO FURNISHED TO THE U.S.S.R., THROUGH OTHER PORTS,

MORE THAN 13 MILLION TONS OF ADDITIONAL SUPPLIES.

4. UNITED STATES SUBMARINE OPERATIONS IN THE PACIFIC

UNITED STATES SUBMARINES CONTRIBUTED MATERIALLY TO THE ALLIED VICTORY IN THE PACIFIC. THEY DESTROYED NEARLY A THIRD OF THE JAPANESE COMBAT SHIPS AND FIFTY PERCENT OF THE JAPANESE MERCHANT MARINE. THE COST WAS THE LOSS OF FORTY-NINE SUBMARINES WITH THEIR GALLANT CREWS.

IMMEDIATELY FOLLOWING THE ATTACK ON PEARL HARBOR THE SUBMARINES BEGAN THEIR CAMPAIGN AGAINST JAPANESE SHIPPING. OPERATING THOUSANDS OF MILES FROM THEIR BASES AND DEEP WITHIN ENEMY-CONTROLLED WATERS THEY STRUCK WITH DEVASTATING EFFECTIVENESS. DURING THE EARLY PART OF 1942, WHILE SURFACE FORCES WERE RECOVERING FROM JAPANESE SURPRISE ATTACKS, AMERICAN SUBMARINES CONTINUED TO PRESS THE WAR BY LONG-RANGE OFFENSIVE OPERATIONS.

AT THE OUTBREAK OF THE WAR THE U.S. HAD 39 FLEET SUBMARINES IN THE PACIFIC. THE NUMBER NEVER EXCEEDED 169, YET THEIR ATTACKS PRODUCED IMMEDIATE AND DAMAGING RESULTS. THEY MADE IT MORE DIFFICULT FOR THE ENEMY TO HOLD HIS FORWARD POSITIONS, TO SUPPLY AND REINFORCE THREATENED AREAS, AND TO MAINTAIN IN JAPAN AN ADEQUATE RESERVE OF FUEL OIL, RUBBER, IRON AND OTHER ESSENTIAL MATERIALS. AS U.S. DOMINANCE EXTENDED ACROSS THE PACIFIC SUBMARINE ATTACKS BECAME INCREASINGLY EFFECTIVE.

SUBMARINES PERFORMED SPECIAL MISSIONS OF RECONNAISSANCE, SUPPLY AND RESCUE. THEY EVACUATED PERSONNEL FROM BELEAGUERED AREAS, NOTABLY FROM CORREGIDOR. THE SUPPLIES AND EQUIPMENT DELIVERED BY

Interior of East Hemicycle Showing Inscribed Names

SUBMARINES TO FRIENDLY GUERRILLA FORCES DID MUCH TO KEEP ALIVE THE SPIRIT OF RESISTANCE IN THE PHILIPPINES. IN ADDITION U.S. SUBMARINES RESCUED MORE THAN FIVE HUNDRED ALLIED AIRMEN DURING THE COURSE OF THE WAR.

THROUGHOUT THE ENTIRE PERIOD OF THE WAR AMERICAN SUBMARINES ALSO PLAYED A SIGNIFICIANT PART IN THE ALLIED WAR EFFORT BY SUCCESSFUL OPERATIONS IN THE ATLANTIC AND INDIAN OCEANS AND IN THE MEDITERRANEAN AND CARIBBEAN SEAS.

5. THE MARIANAS—15 JUNE-10 AUGUST 1944

TO PENETRATE THE ENEMY'S DEFENSES AND GAIN BASES FROM WHICH AIRCRAFT COULD STRIKE AT THE JAPANESE HOME ISLANDS, THE UNITED STATES UNDERTOOK TO SEIZE THE MARIANA ISLANDS IN THE SUMMER OF 1944. FOR SEVERAL MONTHS PRIOR TO THE LANDINGS, FAST CARRIER TASK FORCES AND AIRCRAFT OF THE SEVENTH AIR FORCE CONDUCTED PRELIMINARY BOMBARDMENTS OF THE TARGET AREA.

ON 15 JUNE 1944, UNDER COVER OF NAVAL AND AIR BOMBARDMENT BY THE FIFTH FLEET, THE 2D AND 4TH MARINE DIVISIONS OF THE V AMPHIBIOUS CORPS LANDED ON SAIPAN. THE JAPANESE REACTION WAS IMMEDIATE AND VIGOROUS; THEIR CARRIER TASK FORCE STEAMED TOWARD THE MARIANAS TO MEET THE AMERICAN AMPHIBIOUS EFFORT. IN THE ACTION THAT FOLLOWED, THE BATTLE OF THE PHILIPPINE SEA ON 19-20 JUNE, JAPANESE CARRIER AVIATION WAS SUBSTANTIALLY IMPAIRED AS A MAJOR FORCE IN THE WAR.

MEANWHILE THE MARINES AND THE ARMY'S 27TH INFANTRY DIVISION FOUGHT THEIR WAY ACROSS THE ISLAND AGAINST DETERMINED RESISTANCE. THEY THEN TURNED NORTHWARD AND SEIZED THE DOMINATING HEIGHTS OF MT. TAPOTCHAU ON 25 AND 26 JUNE. ON THE LATTER NIGHT AN ENEMY ATTEMPT TO BREAK OUT OF HIS ISOLATED POSI-

TION ON NAFUTAN POINT WAS DECISIVELY DEFEATED. AMERICAN FORCES CONTINUED TO PRESS THE ATTACK AGAINST THE MASS OF THE ENEMY, SLOWLY FORCING HIM NORTHWARD. FINALLY, ON THE NIGHT OF 6-7 JULY, THE JAPANESE MADE A DESPERATE LAST EFFORT; THEIR FURIOUS ASSAULT WAS REPULSED AND TWO DAYS LATER THE ISLAND WAS DECLARED SECURE.

ON 24 JULY, AFTER A LENGTHY PREPARATORY BOMBARDMENT BY U.S. SHIPS, AIRCRAFT, AND ARTILLERY FIRING FROM SAIPAN, THE 4TH MARINE DIVISION FOLLOWED BY THE 2D MARINE DIVISION LANDED ON NORTHERN TINIAN. AFTER NINE DAYS OF SEVERE FIGHTING, WITH CONTINUOUS SUPPORT BY SEVENTH AIR FORCE AND CARRIER AIRCRAFT AND BY NAVAL GUNFIRE, THE MARINES SECURED THE ISLAND.

PRECEDED BY ONE OF THE HEAVIEST SUSTAINED NAVAL AND AIR BOMBARDMENTS CONDUCTED IN THE PACIFIC, THE 3D MARINE DIVISION AND THE 1ST MARINE BRIGADE OF THE III AMPHIBIOUS CORPS MADE TWO SEPARATE LANDINGS ON THE WESTERN SHORES OF GUAM ON 21 JULY. ON 24 JULY THE 77TH INFANTRY DIVISION ASSUMED CONTROL OF THE SOUTHERN BEACHHEAD. THE NEXT DAY, WHILE THE 3D MARINE DIVISION CONTINUED ITS ASSAULT TO GAIN THE HIGH GROUND TO ITS FRONT, THE 1ST MARINE BRIGADE BEGAN CLEARING THE OROTE PENINSULA. THAT NIGHT THE CRISIS CAME ON BOTH FRONTS WHEN THE JAPANESE LAUNCHED SPIRITED BUT UNSUCCESSFUL COUNTERATTACKS AGAINST BOTH UNITS.

THE INDIVIDUAL BEACHHEADS WERE THEN LINKED TOGETHER AND AMERICAN LINES CONSOLIDATED. SUPPORTED BY ARMY, NAVY AND MARINE CORPS AIRCRAFT, THE 77TH INFANTRY DIVISION AND THE 3D MARINE DIVISION LAUNCHED A COORDINATED ATTACK TOWARD THE NORTH END OF THE ISLAND WHERE THE JAPANESE HAD CONCENTRATED THEIR FORCES. BY 10 AUGUST ORGANIZED RESISTANCE HAD CEASED.

6. BATTLE OF MIDWAY—3–7 JUNE 1942

AFTER THEIR ADVANCE TOWARD AUSTRALIA WAS CHECKED AT THE BATTLE OF THE CORAL SEA IN MAY 1942, THE JAPANESE SHIFTED THEIR MAIN OFFENSIVE NORTHWARD TOWARD THE HAWAIIAN ISLANDS AND THE ALEUTIANS.

IN JUNE, JAPANESE OCCUPATION FORCES, SUPPORTED BY THE JAPANESE COMBINED FLEET, MOVED AGAINST MIDWAY ISLAND, WEST OF HAWAII, AND KISKA AND ATTU IN THE WESTERN ALEUTIANS.

MEANWHILE, THE UNITED STATES REINFORCED THE MARINE GARRISON ON MIDWAY AND ALERTED THE PACIFIC FLEET FOR THE DEFENSE OF THAT ISLAND. ON 4 JUNE AIRCRAFT FROM FOUR JAPANESE FLEET CARRIERS ATTACKED MIDWAY. IN ITS DEFENSE U.S. MARINE ANTI-AIRCRAFT BATTERIES, AND LAND-BASED AIRCRAFT MANNED BY MARINE, NAVY AND ARMY AIR FORCES PILOTS, DESTROYED MORE THAN 40 JAPANESE AIRPLANES. THEREUPON NAVAL AIRCRAFT FROM THE U.S. CARRIERS ENTERPRISE, YORKTOWN AND HORNET ATTACKED THE JAPANESE CARRIERS AND SANK FOUR OF THEM. JAPANESE CARRIER-BASED AIRCRAFT AND A SUBMARINE ATTACKED OUR CARRIERS AND SANK YORKTOWN. DISCOMFITED BY THE AMERICAN AIR RESISTANCE THE JAPANESE MIDWAY OCCUPATION FORCE WITHDREW WITHOUT ATTEMPTING TO LAND, LOSING A CRUISER IN THE OPERATION.

FAR TO THE NORTH, JAPANESE AIRPLANES FROM TWO OTHER CARRIERS BOMBED DUTCH HARBOR ON 3 AND 4 JUNE, MEETING RESISTANCE FROM U.S. NAVY AND ARMY AIR FORCES AIRCRAFT. UNDER COVER OF THIS DIVERSION THE JAPANESE, WITHOUT OPPOSITION, OCCUPIED THE ISLANDS OF ATTU AND KISKA ON 7 JUNE.

THE JAPANESE LOSS OF FOUR AIRCRAFT CARRIERS AND THEIR COMPLEMENT OF 250 AIRCRAFT WITH MANY FIRST-LINE PILOTS COMPLETELY REVERSED THE STRATEGIC SITUATION IN THE PACIFIC. THIS WAS THEIR LAST GREAT OFFENSIVE AGAINST AMERICAN TERRITORY. THEREAFTER THE UNITED STATES TOOK THE OFFENSIVE AND STARTED THE LONG ADVANCE TOWARD THE JAPANESE HOMELAND AND FINAL VICTORY.

7. BATTLE OF THE PHILIPPINE SEA— 15–20 JUNE 1944

WHEN, ON 15 JUNE 1944, THE U.S. FIFTH FLEET LANDED THE 2D AND 4TH MARINE DIVISIONS OF THE V AMPHIBIOUS CORPS ON SAIPAN, THE JAPANESE REACTION WAS IMMEDIATE AND VIGOROUS. BY THE VERY NEXT DAY THE JAPANESE MOBILE FLEET, WHICH INCLUDED NINE FAST CARRIERS, HAD SET UNITS IN MOTION FROM MANY WIDELY SEPARATED AREAS, EFFECTED A RENDEZVOUS IN THE PHILIPPINE SEA, AND MOVED TO THE ATTACK. THE COMBAT ELEMENTS OF THE FIFTH FLEET, INCLUDING FIFTEEN FAST CARRIERS, IMMEDIATELY MOVED INTO POSITION TO COVER THE SAIPAN AMPHIBIOUS OPERATION WHILE ITS CARRIER-BASED AIRCRAFT CONTINUED THEIR DESTRUCTIVE ATTACKS UPON THE JAPANESE AIR BASES IN THE MARIANAS.

THE JAPANESE, EARLY ON THE MORNING OF 19 JUNE, BEGAN LAUNCHING AIRCRAFT AT EXTREME RANGE, PLANNING THAT THESE SHOULD SUCCESSFULLY ATTACK THE AMERICAN SHIPS, THEN LAND AND REFUEL AT GUAM. FOUR SEPARATE ATTACKS WERE INTERCEPTED BY AIRCRAFT OF THE FIFTH FLEET; OVER 300 JAPANESE AIRCRAFT BEING SHOT DOWN BY AMERICAN INTERCEPTORS AND ANTIAIRCRAFT FIRE, DESTROYED ON THE GROUND OR LOST AT SEA.

ONLY A FEW JAPANESE AIRCRAFT WERE ABLE TO RETURN TO THEIR CARRIERS, WHICH IN THE MEANTIME BEGAN TO WITHDRAW TO THE NORTHWEST. THE FIFTH FLEET PURSUED BUT DID NOT LOCATE THE RETREATING ENEMY UNTIL THE AFTERNOON OF 20 JUNE WHEN

Graves Area with West Hemicycle in Background

AMERICAN AIRCRAFT WERE LAUNCHED AT SUCH LONG RANGE, SO LATE IN THE DAY, THAT A PERILOUS NIGHT RECOVERY WAS INEVITABLE. NEVERTHELESS, THE AMERICAN PILOTS BOLDLY PRESSED THEIR ATTACK AND SANK A CARRIER AND TWO TANKERS. MANY AIRCRAFT FAILED TO RETURN.

IN ADDITION TO THE DESTRUCTION INFLICTED BY U.S. NAVAL AIRCRAFT, SUBMARINES OF THE PACIFIC FLEET SANK TWO OTHER JAPANESE AIRCRAFT CARRIERS ON 19 JUNE.

NORTHEAST ROOM

This room has six maps:

1. GENERAL STRATEGY IN THE PACIFIC 1942–1945

EXPLOITING THEIR SUCCESSFUL ATTACK UPON PEARL HARBOR ON 7 DECEMBER 1941, THE JAPANESE STRUCK AT AMERICAN, BRITISH, CHINESE AND DUTCH TERRITORIES. THE UNITED STATES, FORCED INITIALLY UPON THE DEFENSIVE, NEVERTHELESS DETER-MINED TO HOLD OPEN THE LINE OF COMMUNICATIONS TO AUSTRALIA, TO AID IN THE DEFENSE OF THAT CONTINENT AND TO DO ITS UTMOST TO REINFORCE THE PHILIPPINES. IN MAY AND JUNE 1942 THE ENEMY OFFENSIVE WAS CHECKED AT THE BATTLES OF THE CORAL SEA AND MIDWAY WHICH RESTORED THE BALANCE OF SEA POWER IN THE PACIFIC.

TO STOP THE JAPANESE ADVANCE IN THE SOLOMONS WHICH THREATENED THE VITAL SUPPLY LINE TO AUSTRALIA, U.S. FORCES TOOK THE OFFENSIVE, LANDING ON GUADALCANAL ON 7 AUGUST 1942. THE SUCCESSION OF HARD-FOUGHT NAVAL BATTLES AND GRIM STRUGGLES ON LAND AND IN THE AIR WHICH FOLLOWED MARKED THE TURNING POINT OF THE PACIFIC WAR. IN NEW GUINEA, U.S. AND AUSTRALIAN FORCES REPULSED THE JAPANESE THRUST TOWARD PORT MORESBY AND ADVANCED ON THE LONG ROAD BACK TO THE PHILIPPINES. THE CHINESE EFFORT WAS AIDED BY SUPPLIES FLOWN OVER THE HIMALAYAS FROM INDIA.

MEANWHILE SUBMARINES HAD BEEN CONTINUOUSLY ATTACKING JAPANESE SHIPS CARRYING OIL, RUBBER AND OTHER MATERIALS ESSENTIAL TO THE ENEMY'S INDUSTRY. THE RELENTLESS ASSAULT AGAINST HIS COMBAT AND MERCHANT SHIPS WAS TO CONTINUE, FROM THE SEA AND FROM THE AIR, WITH EVER-INCREASING ATTRITION THROUGHOUT THE WAR.

TO PENETRATE THE ENEMY'S DEFENSES AND GAIN BASES FROM WHICH AIRCRAFT COULD STRIKE AT THE JAPANESE HOME ISLANDS, THE UNITED STATES COMMITTED ITS MAJOR FORCES ALONG TWO MAIN AXES OF ADVANCE. ONE THRUST WAS TO CONTINUE THE ATTACK NORTHWESTWARD SIMULTANEOUSLY THROUGH THE SOLOMON ISLANDS AND ALONG THE COAST OF NEW GUINEA; THE OTHER WOULD CROSS THE TREMENDOUS REACHES OF THE CENTRAL PACIFIC VIA THE GILBERT AND MARSHALL ISLANDS AND THE STRONGLY DEFENDED MARIANA AND PALAU ISLANDS. BY MID-SEPTEMBER 1944 ALL THESE MISSIONS HAD BEEN ACCOMPLISHED, WHILE, SIMULTANEOUSLY, CONTROL OF THE SEA AND AIR HAD BEEN WRESTED FROM THE ENEMY, THUS DENYING ESCAPE TO HUNDREDS OF THOUSANDS OF JAPANESE TROOPS ON BY-PASSED BASES SUCH AS RABAUL AND TRUK. MEANWHILE FAR TO THE NORTH OTHER AMERICAN FORCES HAD EXPELLED THE ENEMY FROM THE ALEUTIANS. IN BURMA ALLIED FORCES WERE DRIVING FORWARD TO REOPEN THE OVERLAND SUPPLY ROUTE TO CHINA AND STIMULATE HER EFFORTS TO EJECT THE JAPANESE INVADERS.

IN JUNE 1944 THE STRATEGIC AIR BOMBARDMENT OF JAPAN HAD BEGUN FROM AIRFIELDS IN CHINA. WITH THE CAPTURE OF THE MARIANAS, BOMBERS FROM THESE ISLANDS JOINED THE ASSAULT WHICH DEVELOPED BY WAR'S END INTO A PROLONGED AND VIOLENT BOMBARDMENT AIMED AT THE DESTRUCTION OF THE JAPANESE MILITARY AND INDUSTRIAL SYSTEMS.

TO LIBERATE THE PHILIPPINES AND TO OBTAIN FORWARD BASES CLOSER TO JAPAN, U.S. ARMY, NAVY, MARINE AND AIR FORCES CONTINUED THEIR SUCCESSIVE AMPHIBIOUS ASSAULTS. THE LANDING AT LEYTE IN OCTOBER 1944 BROUGHT ON THE DECISIVE NAVAL BATTLES FOR LEYTE GULF. AMPHIBIOUS LANDINGS ON LUZON, IWO JIMA AND OKINAWA FOLLOWED IN RAPID SUCCESSION. FAST CARRIER TASK FORCES JOINED IN THE STRATEGIC BOMBARDMENT OF JAPAN; U.S. WARSHIPS SHELLED THE COASTAL STATIONS DENYING TO THE REMNANTS OF THE JAPANESE FLEET THE SAFETY OF ITS HOME HARBORS.

AFTER THE DEVASTATION FROM THE AIR OF HIROSHIMA AND NAGASAKI, THE JAPANESE GOVERNMENT SUED FOR PEACE; THE SURRENDER TERMS WERE SIGNED IN TOKYO BAY ON 2 SEPTEMBER 1945.

2. GUADALCANAL—7 AUGUST 1942– 9 FEBRUARY 1943

FOLLOWING THE NAVAL VICTORY IN THE CORAL SEA, THE UNITED STATES LAUNCHED AN OFFENSIVE IN THE SOLOMON ISLANDS TO HALT THE JAPANESE ADVANCE ON LAND. SUPPORTED BY NAVAL AIRCRAFT, THE SOUTH PACIFIC FORCE OF THE U.S. PACIFIC FLEET LANDED THE 1ST MARINE DIVISION AT GUADALCANAL AND TULAGI ON 7 AUGUST 1942.

THE JAPANESE REACTION WAS PROMPT AND VIGOROUS, BOMBERS FROM RABAUL ATTACKED TROOPS ASHORE AND THE SUPPORTING NAVAL VESSELS. ON 9 AUGUST A STRONG JAPANESE FLEET CAME DOWN "THE SLOT" AND ENGAGED U.S. AND AUSTRALIAN NAVAL FORCES OFF SAVO ISLAND. ALLIED LOSSES WERE HEAVY. ASHORE THE MARINES FOUGHT HEROICALLY TO CONSOLIDATE THEIR BEACHHEAD AND COMPLETE THE AIR BASE AT HENDERSON FIELD.

FROM THEIR ADVANCE BASES BOTH OPPONENTS STROVE TO BUILD UP THEIR

OWN STRENGTH ON GUADALCANAL. ATTENTION WAS FOCUSSED ON HENDERSON FIELD. AMERICAN EFFORTS TO DEVELOP AND KEEP IT OPERATING COULD NOT BE RELAXED NOTWITHSTANDING CONTINUOUS SURFACE AND AIR BOMBARDMENT. A SERIES OF HARD-FOUGHT SEA BATTLES ENSUED WITH SEVERE LOSSES ON BOTH SIDES — THE BATTLE OF THE EASTERN SOLOMONS IN AUGUST, THE BATTLES OF CAPE ESPERANCE AND THE SANTA CRUZ ISLANDS IN OCTOBER, FOLLOWED BY GUADALCANAL AND TASSAFARONGA IN NOVEMBER AND RENNELL ISLAND IN JANUARY 1943. THE SEA BATTLE OF GUADALCANAL WHEN OUTNUMBERED U.S. CRUISERS AND DESTROYERS ENGAGED THE JAPANESE BATTLESHIP FORCE WAS ESPECIALLY FURIOUS.

ON LAND THE JAPANESE, SUPPORTED BY STRONG AIR COVER, ON THE NIGHTS OF 12 AND 13 SEPTEMBER ATTACKED BOTH FLANKS, AS WELL AS THE CENTER OF THE MARINE POSITION ON THE RIDGE SOUTH OF HENDERSON FIELD, BUT WERE DECISIVELY DEFEATED. IN TURN, THE AMERICANS, HAVING BEEN REINFORCED BY ADDITIONAL MARINE AND ARMY UNITS, ATTACKED THE JAPANESE POSITIONS TO THE WEST ALONG THE MATANIKAU RIVER FROM 23 TO 27 SEPTEMBER BUT WERE FORCED TO WITHDRAW; THEY RENEWED THE ATTACK ON 7 OCTOBER AND SECURED THE EAST BANK OF THE RIVER TWO DAYS LATER.

THE JAPANESE BROUGHT IN REINFORCEMENTS INCLUDING HEAVIER ARTILLERY. ON 23 OCTOBER STRONG JAPANESE INFANTRY FORCES SUPPORTED BY TANKS, ARTILLERY FIRE AND AIR AND NAVAL BOMBARDMENT, ATTACKED ACROSS THE MATANIKAU BUT WERE REPULSED BY THE 1ST AND 7TH MARINE REGIMENTS. ON 24-25 OCTOBER THE ENEMY LAUNCHED TWO POWERFUL ATTACKS AGAINST THE SOUTHERN PERIMETER. THE FIRST ATTACK AGAINST HENDERSON FIELD WAS REPULSED AFTER DESPERATE FIGHTING BY THE 7TH MARINE REGIMENT AND THE 164TH INFANTRY REGIMENT. THE OTHER ATTACK, NORTH OF MOUNT AUSTEN, AFTER A BRIEF INITIAL SUCCESS WAS ALSO REPULSED.

THE TENACIOUS OPPOSITION OF THE JAPANESE MADE IT NECESSARY TO REINFORCE OUR LAND, SEA AND AIR FORCES HEAVILY. THE ARMY'S 25TH AND AMERICAL DIVISIONS, AS WELL AS THE 2D MARINE DIVISION, NOW RELIEVED THE 1ST MARINE DIVISION. ON 17 DECEMBER THESE DIVISIONS LAUNCHED A DETERMINED ATTACK AGAINST THE JAPANESE POSITION ON MOUNT AUSTEN WHICH THEY CAPTURED A WEEK LATER. ON 10 JANUARY THE ATTACK WAS RESUMED AND AFTER HARD FIGHTING THE STRONGLY DEFENDED JAPANESE POSITIONS FARTHER TO THE WEST WERE SEIZED.

RECOGNIZING THEIR PERIL, THE JAPANESE, BETWEEN THE 1ST AND 8TH OF FEBRUARY, EVACUATED ABOUT 13,000 MEN FROM GUADALCANAL UNDER COVER OF DARKNESS. BY 9 FEBRUARY 1943 THE AMERICAN TROOPS HAD OVERRUN THE LAST OF THE JAPANESE POSITIONS AND THE HARD-FOUGHT CAMPAIGN FOR GUADALCANAL WAS WON.

3. FAST CARRIER STRIKES IN THE PACIFIC — 1942–1945

BECAUSE THE ATTACK ON PEARL HARBOR FORCED THE U.S. NAVAL FORCES TO THE DEFENSIVE THROUGHOUT THE PACIFIC, THEIR FIRST OFFENSIVE EFFORTS WERE LIMITED STRIKES AGAINST SUPERIOR ENEMY CONCENTRATIONS BY THE NAVAL AIR FORCES.

IN MAY AND JUNE 1942, U.S. FORCES FOUGHT THE SUCCESSFUL BATTLES OF THE CORAL SEA AND MIDWAY. THEN, AT GUADALCANAL, THERE FOLLOWED A SERIES OF HARD-FOUGHT NAVAL BATTLES AND GRIM STRUGGLES ON THE LAND AND IN THE AIR WHICH MARKED THE TURNING POINT OF THE PACIFIC WAR.

THE LONG ADVANCE TOWARD THE JAPANESE HOMELAND BEGAN IN 1943. THE VOLUME AND EFFECTIVENESS OF

AIR STRIKES WAS INTENSIFIED; DURING THE FIRST TWO YEARS OF THE WAR THE NUMBER OF AIRCRAFT CARRIERS WAS INCREASED FROM NINE TO MORE THAN FIFTY. THESE FORMED THE SPEARHEAD OF THE TRIPHIBIOUS OFFENSIVES IN THE GILBERT ISLANDS, THEN IN EARLY 1944, THROUGH THE MARSHALL ISLANDS. IN JUNE THE AMERICAN ATTACK ON THE MARIANAS BROUGHT ON THE BATTLE OF THE PHILIPPINE SEA IN WHICH THE JAPANESE NAVAL AIR ARM WAS ELIMINATED AS A DECISIVE FACTOR IN THE WAR.

AIRCRAFT CARRIERS SUPPORTED THE LANDINGS IN THE PHILIPPINES IN 1944, AND ON IWO JIMA AND OKINAWA IN 1945. FAST CARRIER TASK FORCES JOINED IN THE STRATEGIC BOMBARDMENT OF JAPAN, RANGING AT WILL OFF THE COAST OF THE JAPANESE HOME ISLANDS, SINKING SHIPS AND RENDERING HARBORS UNTENABLE. THE ROLE OF THESE MOBILE CARRIERS WAS OF MAJOR IMPORTANCE IN THE PROSECUTION OF THE WAR.

4. AIR ASSAULT ON JAPAN —
   1942–1945

ON 15 JUNE 1944 U.S. ARMY HEAVY BOMBERS FROM AIRFIELDS IN CHINA LAUNCHED THE FIRST STRATEGIC AIR ATTACKS AGAINST THE JAPANESE HOMELAND. ON THE SAME DAY U.S. AMPHIBIOUS FORCES ASSAULTED THE MARIANA ISLANDS SO AS TO GAIN AIR BASES CLOSER TO JAPAN. IN JANUARY 1945 AIRCRAFT FROM CHINA WERE REDEPLOYED TO THESE NEW BASES.

EVEN BEFORE THE CAPTURE OF THE MARIANAS WAS COMPLETE, AIRFIELDS WERE BEING BUILT FROM WHICH THE U.S. TWENTIETH AIR FORCE WAS LATER TO CONDUCT ITS DEVASTATING BOMBARDMENT CAMPAIGN. FROM THE FIRST MAJOR STRIKE ON 24 NOVEMBER 1944 UNTIL THE END OF HOSTILITIES IN AUGUST 1945 THE OFFENSIVE CONTINUED WITH EVER MOUNTING INTENSITY. THE OBJECTIVE WAS THE PROGRESSIVE DESTRUCTION OF THE

Interior of Chapel, Altar and Mosaic

ENEMY'S MILITARY, INDUSTRIAL AND ECONOMIC SYSTEMS. IN MARCH 1945 HEAVY BOMBERS ENGAGED ALSO IN AERIAL MINE LAYING TO INTENSIFY THE BLOCKADE OF JAPAN ALREADY ESTABLISHED BY U.S. SUBMARINES.

THE CAPTURE OF IWO JIMA IN FEBRUARY AND MARCH 1945 WAS OF VITAL IMPORTANCE TO THE AIR ASSAULTS ON JAPAN. THE AIRFIELDS THERE ESTABLISHED SERVED AS A BASE FOR FIGHTER ESCORTS AND A HAVEN FOR DAMAGED

Visitors Building at Entrance Plaza

BOMBERS MAKING THE LONG OVER-
WATER RETURN TO THE MARIANAS.

IN JULY 1945 THE U.S. TWENTIETH AIR
FORCE, IN THE MARIANAS, AND THE
U.S. EIGHTH AIR FORCE, STATIONED ON
OKINAWA, COMBINED TO OPERATE AS
THE U.S. ARMY STRATEGIC AIR FORCES.
DURING JULY AND AUGUST THE U.S. FAR
EAST AIR FORCES AND MARINE CORPS
AIRCRAFT BASED ON OKINAWA PAR-
TICIPATED IN THE STRATEGIC ASSAULT.
AFTER THE DEVASTATION FROM THE AIR
OF HIROSHIMA AND NAGASAKI IN
AUGUST 1945, THE JAPANESE GOVERN-
MENT SUED FOR PEACE.

5. OKINAWA — 26 MARCH–22 JUNE 1945

EARLY IN 1945 THE GREAT CONCEN-
TRATION OF U.S. SEA, LAND AND AIR
POWER IN THE PACIFIC ENABLED OUR
FORCES TO CHALLENGE JAPAN IN HER
OWN WATERS. FOR MONTHS AIRCRAFT
FROM THE NAVY'S FAST CARRIERS AND
ARMY AIR FORCE BOMBERS FROM THE
SOUTHWEST PACIFIC AREA AND THE
MARIANAS HAD BOMBED THE IMPOR-

TANT BASES IN THE RYUKYUS. THE AM-
PHIBIOUS INVASION WAS INITIATED
WHEN A DIVISION OF THE TENTH ARMY
LANDED ON KERAMA RETTO WEST OF
OKINAWA ON 26 MARCH. THERE FOL-
LOWED A DESPERATE THREE MONTHS
STRUGGLE ON LAND, ON SEA, AND IN
THE AIR.

ON 1 APRIL, UNDER COVER OF AN IN-
TENSIVE NAVAL AND AIR BOMBARD-
MENT BY THE U.S. FIFTH FLEET, TWO DI-
VISIONS OF THE U.S. ARMY XXIV CORPS
AND TWO DIVISIONS OF THE MARINE III
AMPHIBIOUS CORPS LANDED ON
OKINAWA ITSELF. THE TWO CORPS, AT-
TACKING ABREAST, PUSHED RAPIDLY
ACROSS THE ISLAND, THUS SPLITTING
THE JAPANESE FORCES. THE III AM-
PHIBIOUS CORPS THEN TURNED NORTH,
WHILE THE XXIV CORPS TURNED SOUTH
TO ATTACK THE JAPANESE MAIN DE-
FENSIVE POSITIONS.

TO INSURE EARLY WARNING OF THE
EXPECTED ENEMY AIR OFFENSIVE FROM
AIRFIELDS IN JAPAN, CHINA AND FOR-
MOSA, THE FIFTH FLEET ESTABLISHED A
RING OF DESTROYERS AND ESCORT VES-

SELS AROUND OKINAWA. INITIALLY THE SUICIDAL ATTACKS OF THE JAPANESE LAND-BASED KAMIKAZE AIRPLANES WHICH CAUSED HEAVY LOSSES WERE FOUGHT OFF BY THE CARRIER-BASED AIRCRAFT AND ANTIAIRCRAFT FIRE OF THE SURFACE SHIPS. ON THE NIGHT OF 6-7 APRIL, THE ENEMY SURFACE FLEET MADE ITS LAST SORTIE FROM ITS HOME WATERS. U.S. CARRIER AIRCRAFT ATTACKED THIS FORCE, SINKING A BATTLESHIP, A CRUISER AND FOUR DESTROYERS. COMMENCING ON 9 APRIL LAND-BASED AIRCRAFT OF THE U.S. MARINES AND THE ARMY AIR FORCES RAPIDLY AUGMENTED THE CARRIER-BASED AIRCRAFT AND ULTIMATELY CHECKED THE KAMIKAZES.

ASSISTED BY LAND-BASED AIRCRAFT OF THE MARINES AND THE ARMY AIR FORCES, AND BY NAVAL GUNFIRE, OUR MARINE AND ARMY DIVISIONS ADVANCED SOUTHWARD AGAINST FANATICAL RESISTANCE AND FURIOUS COUNTERATTACKS. EACH SUCCESSIVE ENEMY STRONGPOINT WAS CLEARED ONLY BY PERSISTENT AND HEROIC EFFORT. BY THE MIDDLE OF JUNE OUR GROUND FORCES HAD BATTERED THEIR WAY THROUGH THE FORTIFIED NAHA-SHURI LINE. BY 22 JUNE 1945 THE LAST ORGANIZED UNIT OF THE JAPANESE GARRISON HAD BEEN DESTROYED. OKINAWA THEN BECAME THE FIRST AMERICAN STRATEGIC BASE WITHIN EASY RANGE OF THE JAPANESE HOMELAND.

6. IWO JIMA—16 FEBRUARY–16 MARCH 1945

BEFORE THE CAPTURE OF THE MARIANA ISLANDS HAD BEEN COMPLETED IN AUGUST 1944 AIRFIELDS WERE UNDER CONSTRUCTION ON SAIPAN AND GUAM. FROM THESE, IN NOVEMBER, THE U.S. ARMY AIR FORCES BEGAN INTENSIVE AIR ASSAULTS AGAINST THE JAPANESE HOMELAND. THE PROMPT SEIZURE OF THE ISLAND OF IWO JIMA BECAME OF VITAL IMPORTANCE BECAUSE IT COULD PROVIDE THE ONLY EMERGENCY LANDING FIELD FOR RETURNING AIRCRAFT IN DISTRESS AS WELL AS A BASE FOR FIGHTER ESCORTS.

SENSING THE PERIL TO THEIR EMPIRE THE JAPANESE CONCENTRATED ON MAKING IWO JIMA IMPREGNABLE, GARRISONING THIS FORTIFIED ISLAND OF ABOUT SEVEN SQUARE MILES WITH MORE THAN 20,000 TROOPS IN CAREFULLY PREPARED DEFENSIVE POSITIONS. AGAINST THESE, FOR SEVEN MONTHS PRIOR TO THE AMPHIBIOUS ASSAULT, THE U.S. SEVENTH AIR FORCE AS WELL AS FAST CARRIER AIRCRAFT SQUADRONS AND NAVAL SURFACE SHIPS DIRECTED BOMBARDMENTS OF INCREASING FREQUENCY AND INTENSITY.

ON 16 FEBRUARY 1945 UNITS OF THE FIFTH FLEET BEGAN A CONCENTRATED GUNFIRE AND AERIAL BOMBARDMENT OF IWO JIMA WHILE THE FAST CARRIERS, IN A COVERING ACTION, STRUCK AT TARGETS IN JAPAN, THEN RETURNED THREE DAYS LATER TO JOIN IN THE ATTACK. ON THE MORNING OF 19 FEBRUARY, UNDER COVER OF A HEAVY BOMBARDMENT, THE FIFTH FLEET LANDED THE 4TH AND 5TH MARINE DIVISIONS ON THE SOUTHEAST COAST OF THE ISLAND. THE ENEMY REACTED VIOLENTLY, POURING CONCENTRATED FIRE FROM PREVIOUSLY UNDETECTED POSITIONS. AS THE MARINES ADVANCED ACROSS OPEN GROUND THEY WERE RAKED BY HEAVY FIRE FROM THE HIGH GROUND ON THE FLANKS. THE 4TH MARINE DIVISION ON THE RIGHT SUFFERED SEVERE CASUALTIES AND THE ESCORT CARRIER BISMARCK SEA WAS SUNK OFF-SHORE BY ENEMY AIR ATTACK.

BY THE END OF THE DAY THE MARINES HAD FOUGHT THEIR WAY ACROSS THE ISLAND AND HAD ISOLATED THE JAPANESE ON MOUNT SURIBACHI FROM THE MAIN FORCES IN THE NORTH. ON THE FOLLOWING DAY OUR TROOPS CAPTURED AIRFIELD NO. 1. THE 3D MARINE DIVISION LANDED ON THE THIRD DAY.

AIRFIELD NO. 2 WAS REACHED ON 23 FEBRUARY. SIMULTANEOUSLY THE 5TH DIVISION STORMED THE STEEP SLOPES

Interior of Visitors Building

OF MOUNT SURIBACHI, CAPTURING THE SUMMIT. AN ASSAULT UP TO THE MOTO-YAMA PLATEAU BROUGHT THE MARINES DIRECTLY INTO THE FACE OF THE HEAVIEST ENEMY DEFENSES. THEN AS THE 4TH DIVISION ATTACKED ON THE RIGHT AND THE 5TH DIVISION ON THE LEFT, THE 3D DIVISION IN THE CENTER CRACKED THE MAIN LINE OF JAPANESE RESISTANCE.

FOR NEARLY TWO WEEKS MORE, WITH CONTINUOUS SUPPORT BY SEVENTH AIR FORCE AND CARRIER AIRCRAFT AND NA-VAL GUNFIRE, THE MARINES PRESSED FORWARD AGAINST A DETERMINED RE-SISTANCE CONDUCTED BY A WELL-TRAINED, WELL-EQUIPPED ENEMY, FIGHTING FROM THOUSANDS OF DEFEN-SIVE INSTALLATIONS AND DEEP CAVES. DESPITE HEAVY AND CONTINUOUS LOSSES THE MARINES MAINTAINED THEIR DRIVE UNTIL FINALLY, AFTER 26 DAYS OF BITTER ASSAULT, THE ISLAND WAS SECURED.

NORTHWEST ROOM

This room has five maps:

1. THE WAR AGAINST GERMANY— 1941-1945

THROUGHOUT THE WAR IN EUROPE WHICH BEGAN IN 1939 THE PROTECTION AND CONTROL OF THE SEA AND AIR ROUTES TO THE BRITISH ISLES WERE VI-TAL TO THE ALLIES' HOPES OF VICTORY. FOLLOWING THE JAPANESE ATTACK ON PEARL HARBOR, THE UNITED STATES NAVY ACTIVELY JOINED THE ALLIED FORCES ENGAGED IN THE BITTERLY CON-TESTED BATTLE OF THE ATLANTIC, FIGHTING TO KEEP THE SEA LANES OPEN.

IN AUGUST 1942 THE U.S. ARMY AIR FORCES JOINED THEIR BRITISH COM-RADES IN THE STRATEGIC BOMBARD-MENT OF GERMANY. FOR NEARLY THREE YEARS THIS AERIAL ASSAULT CONTIN-UED WITH EVER-INCREASING VIO-LENCE, STRIKING DEEP INTO ENEMY TERRITORY TO DISLOCATE AND DESTROY

HIS MILITARY AND INDUSTRIAL SYS-TEMS.

IN NOVEMBER 1942 AMERICAN AND BRITISH FORCES LANDED ON THE SHORES OF NORTH AFRICA BUT WERE CHECKED JUST 16 MILES FROM TUNIS. A COUNTERATTACK NEAR KASSERINE WAS HALTED ON 22 FEBRUARY. THE FINAL CAMPAIGN IN NORTH AFRICA OPENED ON 22 APRIL 1943. BY 13 MAY ONE QUAR-TER OF A MILLION AXIS TROOPS RE-MAINING IN TUNISIA BECAME PRIS-ONERS OF WAR.

ON 10 JULY 1943, UNDER COVER OF NAVAL AND AIR BOMBARDMENT, THE ALLIES LANDED ON THE SHORES OF SIC-ILY. IN A SWIFT CAMPAIGN, LASTING ONLY 39 DAYS, THEY EXPELLED THE EN-EMY FROM THE ISLAND.

IN SEPTEMBER U.S. AND BRITISH FORCES LANDED IN SOUTHERN ITALY, SEIZING THE AIRFIELDS NEAR FOGGIA. FROM THESE, U.S. ARMY AIR FORCES LAUNCHED STRATEGIC AIR ATTACKS, IN COORDINATION WITH THE ALLIED AIR FLEETS ALREADY OPERATING FROM ENGLAND, ON AUSTRIA, THE BALKANS AND GERMANY. TO ASSIST THE GROUND ADVANCE, A LANDING WAS MADE IN THE ANZIO REGION BUT THE ENEMY'S PROMPT REACTION PREVENTED EXPLOI-TATION OF THIS BEACHHEAD. ON 11 MAY THE ALLIES LAUNCHED A GENERAL ASSAULT, BROKE THROUGH THE ENEMY DEFENSES AND ON 4 JUNE 1944 AMERI-CAN TROOPS ENTERED ROME.

DRIVING NORTHWARD, THE ALLIES BREACHED THE ENEMY'S "GOTHIC" MOUNTAIN DEFENSE LINE BUT STIFFEN-ING RESISTANCE HALTED THE AD-VANCE. RESUMING THE OFFENSIVE IN THE SPRING OF 1945 OUR TROOPS CROSSED THE PO THEN SPREAD OUT TO CLOSE THE NORTHERN FRONTIERS. ON 2 MAY 1945 THE ENEMY IN ITALY SURREN-DERED UNCONDITIONALLY.

ON 6 JUNE 1944 UNITED STATES AND BRITISH COMMONWEALTH FORCES LANDED ON THE NORTHERN COAST OF FRANCE. ON 25 JULY THEY BROKE OUT OF THEIR BEACHHEAD, REPULSED A

POWERFUL COUNTERATTACK AND THEN DROVE EASTWARD ACROSS THE SEINE. BY MID-SEPTEMBER, JOINED BY THOSE WHO HAD LANDED IN SOUTHERN FRANCE, THEY WERE STANDING ON THE THRESHOLD OF GERMANY.

ON 16 DECEMBER THE ENEMY LAUNCHED HIS FINAL MAJOR COUNTER-OFFENSIVE. THE SUPERB FIGHTING QUALITIES OF AMERICAN SOLDIERS AND AIRMEN HURLED BACK THIS ASSAULT AND CARRIED THEM TO THE RHINE. U.S. FORCES SEIZED A BRIDGE AT REMAGEN, CROSSED AT OPPENHEIM, THEN JOINED THE BRITISH IN THE MAJOR ASSAULT CROSSING NORTH OF THE RUHR. SWEEP-ING ACROSS GERMANY THE ALLIES MET THE TROOPS OF THE U.S.S.R., WHO HAD BEEN ADVANCING WESTWARD FOR TWO YEARS, AND FORCED THE COMPLETE SURRENDER OF THE ENEMY ON 8 MAY 1945.

2. SUPPLY ROUTES ACROSS THE PACIFIC OCEAN—1941-1945

THE VAST DISTANCES OF THE PACIFIC OCEAN IMPOSED ENORMOUS PROBLEMS UPON THE UNITED STATES NAVY AND THE SHIPPING WHICH IT PROTECTED. IN THIS HEMISPHERE, THE LOGISTIC SUP-PORT OF OUR MILITARY, NAVAL AND AIR OPERATIONS INVOLVED THE BROAD-EST WATER-DISTANCES ON EARTH. THE AMERICAN ARMY AND NAVY WERE RE-QUIRED TO SUPPLY THEIR FORCES, NOT ONLY ACROSS THE CENTRAL PACIFIC, BUT ALSO TO AUSTRALIA AND NEW GUINEA BELOW THE EQUATOR. IN ADDI-TION, SHIPPING FROM THE UNITED STATES SAILED BOTH EASTWARD AND WESTWARD TO INDIAN OCEAN PORTS WITH CARGOES FOR THE CHINA-BURMA-INDIA THEATER.

NOTWITHSTANDING HER INTENSE PREOCCUPATION WITH THE CAMPAIGNS IN EUROPE AND NORTH AFRICA THE UNITED STATES STEADILY BUILT UP HER SUPPLY RESOURCES IN THE PACIFIC. OVER THREE MILLION AMERICAN FIGHTING MEN AND MORE THAN SIXTY MILLION TONS OF CARGO WERE TRANS-PORTED TO PACIFIC OCEAN AREAS FROM THE UNITED STATES. AT THE MOMENT OF THE GERMAN COLLAPSE AMERICAN SUPPLY BASES HAD BEEN PUSHED FOR-WARD TO THE RYUKYUS ON THE THRESH-OLD OF THE JAPANESE HOMELAND. THE UNITED STATES NAVY BORE THE HEAVY RESPONSIBILITY OF SAFE-GUARDING THE CONTINUOUS FLOW OF TROOPS AND SUPPLIES OVER SEA LANES WHICH IT DE-NIED TO THE ENEMY, ATTACKING HIM WHENEVER AND WHEREVER HE COULD BE FOUND.

SUPPLEMENTING THE NAVY, THE ARMY AIR FORCES ESTABLISHED AIR ROUTES ACROSS THE PACIFIC. THE AIR TRANSPORT COMMAND EARLY ESTAB-LISHED BOTH PASSENGER AND AIR EX-PRESS ROUTES FROM CALIFORNIA TO AUSTRALIA AND THE FAR EAST. AS THE WAR ADVANCED, HEAVY BOMBERS WERE FLOWN FROM CALIFORNIA TO GUAM, SAIPAN AND OTHER PACIFIC BASES.

LOGISTIC SERVICES ASHORE AND AFLOAT REPLENISHED OUR FIGHTING SHIPS AND PROVIDED FOR THE SHELTER, SUPPLY, HOSPITALIZATION AND EVACU-ATION OF OUR SOLDIERS, SAILORS, MA-RINES AND AIRMEN. THEY PREPARED AIRFIELDS AND SUPPORTED THE STRATE-GIC AND TACTICAL AIR ASSAULTS UPON THE ENEMY. ON THE HEELS OF AMPHIBI-OUS ASSAULTS AGAINST HOSTILE BEACHES THEY LANDED AMMUNITION, ARTILLERY, COMBAT VEHICLES, FOOD, WATER, FUEL AND EQUIPMENT.

THE EFFORTS OF OUR MEDICAL PER-SONNEL IN COMBAT AID STATIONS AND HOSPITALS, BOTH AFLOAT AND ASHORE, WERE OF PRIMARY IMPORTANCE IN MAINTAINING THE MORAL AND COM-BAT EFFICIENCY OF OUR ARMY, NAVAL AND AIR FORCES. THE DEVOTED EFFORTS OF ALL OF THE OTHER MULTI-SKILLED PERSONNEL OF SUPPLY AND TECHNICAL ORGANIZATIONS ASHORE AND AFLOAT WERE REQUIRED TO ENABLE OUR COM-BAT FORCES TO FIGHT THEIR WAY TO VICTORY OVER IMPERIAL JAPAN.

THE UNITED STATES OF AMERICA, WHILE CONTRIBUTING HER LAND, SEA

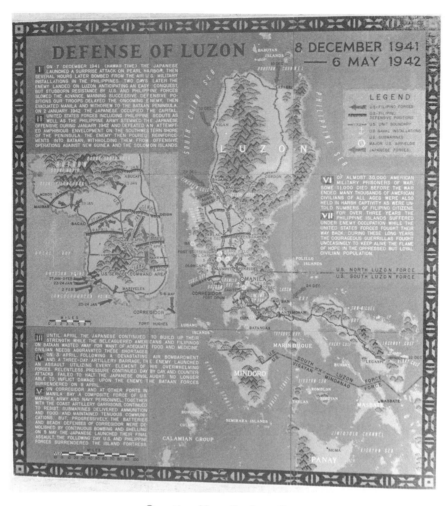

Operations Map—Southwest Room

AND AIR FORCES TO THE PROSECUTION OF WORLD WAR II, ALSO AIDED THE U.S.S.R. BY FURNISHING OVER SEVENTEEN AND A HALF MILLION TONS OF EQUIPMENT AND SUPPLIES. OF THESE MORE THAN EIGHT MILLION TONS WERE SHIPPED ACROSS THE PACIFIC TO SIBERIA OR FLOWN ACROSS VIA THE ALEUTIANS.

3. NEW GUINEA—21 JULY 1942–11 MAY 1945

DURING 1942 NEW GUINEA WAS A MAJOR OBJECTIVE OF THE JAPANESE. A U.S.

NAVAL TASK FORCE BLOCKED THEIR FIRST THREAT TO PORT MORESBY, KEY TO AUSTRALIA, ON 4-8 MAY IN THE DECISIVE BATTLE OF THE CORAL SEA. ON 21 JULY JAPANESE FORCES SEIZED BUNA AND GONA, THEN CROSSED THE OWEN STANLEY RANGE TO WITHIN 30 MILES OF PORT MORESBY, TO BE DRIVEN BACK TO THEIR BEACHHEAD BY AUSTRALIAN TROOPS. ANOTHER JAPANESE FORCE, DEFEATED AT MILNE BAY, WITHDREW ON 5 SEPTEMBER. ON 16 NOVEMBER ALLIED FORCES OPENED THEIR ATTACKS AGAINST THE BUNA-GONA BEACHHEAD

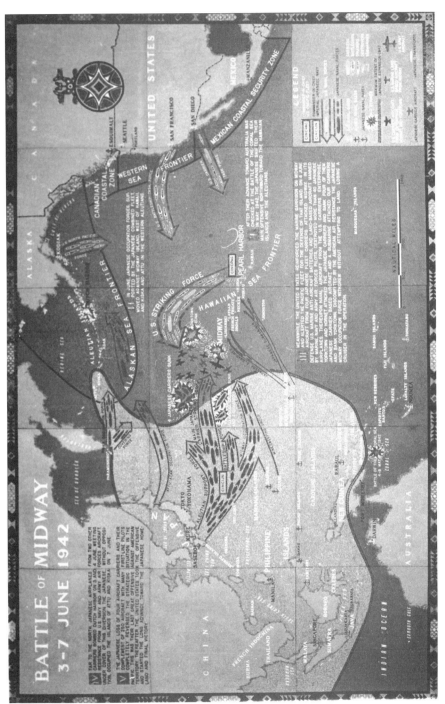

Operations Map—Southeast Room

AND EXPELLED THE JAPANESE ON 22 JANUARY 1943.

THE ENEMY NEXT ATTACKED WAU BUT AUSTRALIAN TROOPS TRANSPORTED BY AMERICAN AIRCRAFT REPULSED HIM. ON 2–4 MARCH, IN THE BATTLE OF THE BISMARCK SEA, THE U.S. FIFTH, AND ROYAL AUSTRALIAN AIR FORCES TOGETHER WITH U.S. NAVY SMALL CRAFT STOPPED HIS ATTEMPT TO REINFORCE HIS HUON PENINSULA GARRISONS. THE ALLIED FORCES CONTINUED THEIR OFFENSIVE ALONG THE NORTHERN COAST; AMERICAN AND AUSTRALIAN TROOPS CAPTURED SALAMAUA ON 11 SEPTEMBER AND ON 16 SEPTEMBER THE AUSTRALIANS, ASSISTED BY BOMBARDMENTS BY THE U.S. VII AMPHIBIOUS FORCE AND THE FIFTH AIR FORCE, AND AN AIRDROP BY THE 503D PARACHUTE INFANTRY REGIMENT UPON THE NADZAB AIRFIELD, CAPTURED LAE.

THE AUSTRALIANS EXTENDED THE ADVANCE BY A DOUBLE ENVELOPMENT OF THE HUON PENINSULA. ADDED IMPETUS WAS GIVEN TO THEIR ATTACK BY A U.S. REGIMENTAL COMBAT TEAM WHICH LANDED AT SAIDOR AND CUT THE JAPANESE LINE OF RETREAT ALONG THE COAST.

MEANWHILE ELEMENTS OF THE U.S. SIXTH ARMY SUPPORTED BY THE U.S. SEVENTH FLEET LAUNCHED AN OFFENSIVE AGAINST THE JAPANESE STRONGHOLD OF RABAUL ON NEW BRITAIN. THEY FIRST OCCUPIED WOODLARK AND KIRIWINA ISLANDS; THEREUPON, SUPPORTED BY AIR AND NAVY BOMBARDMENT, THEY CAPTURED ARAWE AND THE CAPE GLOUCESTER AREA.

THE DECISION WAS THEN MADE TO BY-PASS BOTH RABAUL AND KAVIENG, NEW IRELAND. THESE STRONG BASES WERE FIRST NEUTRALIZED BY INTENSIVE BOMBARDMENTS FROM THE SEA AND AIR; THEN THE ADMIRALTY ISLANDS AND EMIRAU WERE OCCUPIED IN RAPID SUCCESSION.

IN ORDER TO SPEED THE GENERAL ADVANCE IT WAS NOW DECIDED TO BY-PASS THE STRONG JAPANESE BASE AT WEWAK BY LEAPFROGGING SOME 350 MILES TO HOLLANDIA, WITH A SECONDARY LANDING AT AITAPE TO THE EAST. AS HOLLANDIA WAS BEYOND THE EFFECTIVE RANGE OF MANY OF OUR LAND-BASED AIRCRAFT, THE FAST CARRIER TASK FORCE FROM THE U.S. FIFTH FLEET HELPED THE U.S. FIFTH AIR FORCE TO DESTROY ITS AIR INSTALLATIONS, ALSO THOSE TO THE WESTWARD. THEN, IN RAPID SUCCESSION, THE U.S. SIXTH ARMY SEIZED WAKDE, BIAK, NOEMFOOR, SANSAPOR AND MOROTAI. BY THE END OF SEPTEMBER 1944 THE FORCES OF THE SOUTHWEST PACIFIC AREA WERE POISED FOR THE ADVANCE TO THE PHILIPPINES.

THROUGHOUT THE NEW GUINEA CAMPAIGN CONTINUOUS SUPPORT WAS RENDERED BY U.S. NAVAL FORCES.

4. NORTHERN SOLOMONS — 6 MARCH 1943–27 MARCH 1944

IN FEBRUARY 1942 THE AIR FORCES OF THE SOUTHWEST AND SOUTH PACIFIC COMMANDS BEGAN THEIR ATTACKS ON THE JAPANESE AIR AND NAVAL INSTALLATIONS IN THE NORTHERN SOLOMONS AND THE IMPORTANT BASE OF RABAUL TO THE WEST. IN JANUARY 1943 ALLIED SURFACE SHIPS JOINED IN THE NEUTRALIZATION OF SHORE TARGETS; MINES PLANTED BY MARINE CORPS AND NAVAL AIRCRAFT AND MINELAYERS IN HARBORS OF KOLOMBANGARA AND BOUGAINVILLE CAUSED HEAVY LOSSES OF JAPANESE SHIPS.

LATE IN JUNE 1943 THE 43D DIVISION AND THE 1ST MARINE RAIDER REGIMENT, PROTECTED BY ALLIED FIGHTERS, LANDED ON RENDOVA AND NEW GEORGIA WITH THE MUNDA AIRFIELD AS A PRIME OBJECTIVE. THE ENEMY'S EFFORTS TO REINFORCE HIS GROUND TROOPS BROUGHT ON THE NAVAL ENGAGEMENTS OF KULA GULF AND KOLOMBANGARA. THE REST OF THE U.S. XIV CORPS (37TH AND 25TH DIVISIONS) THEN MOVED INTO NEW GEORGIA, AND

AFTER FIERCE FIGHTING CAPTURED MUNDA AIRFIELD ON 5 AUGUST. JAPANESE ATTEMPTS TO REINFORCE THEIR GARRISONS RESULTED IN THEIR DEFEAT IN THE BATTLE OF VELLA GULF.

BY-PASSING STRONGLY DEFENDED KOLOMBANGARA, THE U.S. 25TH DIVISION AND 3D NEW ZEALAND DIVISION CAPTURED VELLA LAVELLA. EFFORTS TO PREVENT THE JAPANESE WITHDRAWAL OF MORE THAN 10,000 MEN FROM THESE TWO ISLANDS LED TO THE NAVAL BATTLE OF VELLA LAVELLA.

THE STRENGTH OF ALLIED AIR, GROUND AND NAVAL FORCES HAD NOW SO INCREASED AS TO PROMISE SUCCESS IN THE ASSAULT ON BOUGAINVILLE ALTHOUGH IT WAS WITHIN CLOSE FIGHTER SUPPORT DISTANCE OF RABAUL. IN PREPARATION FOR, AND IN SUPPORT OF, THIS ASSAULT THE FIFTH AIR FORCE FROM THE SOUTHWEST PACIFIC COMMAND MADE SEVERAL LARGE-SCALE ATTACKS ON THAT BASE, WHILE THE AIR SOLOMONS COMMAND, OPERATING FROM BASES ON NEW GEORGIA AND GUADALCANAL BOMBED THE JAPANESE AIRFIELDS ON BOUGAINVILLE — ANOTHER NOTEWORTHY EXAMPLE OF SKILLFUL COORDINATION OF THE EFFORTS OF TWO WIDELY SEPARATED COMMANDS.

PRECEDED BY DIVERSIONARY LANDINGS ON THE TREASURY ISLANDS AND CHOISEUL, THE 3D MARINE DIVISION, UNDER COVER OF AIR BOMBARDMENT AND NAVAL GUNFIRE, LANDED AT BOUGAINVILLE ON 1 NOVEMBER 1943. IN THE BATTLE OF EMPRESS AUGUSTA BAY THAT NIGHT A JAPANESE CRUISER AND A DESTROYER WERE SUNK. U.S. ARMY AIR FORCES, MARINE CORPS, AND NAVAL CARRIER-BASED AIRCRAFT CONTINUED TO FIGHT A SERIES OF BATTLES WITH THE JAPANESE WHICH EVENTUALLY RESULTED IN THE ELIMINATION OF RABAUL AS AN IMPORTANT AIR AND NAVAL BASE.

ON 25 NOVEMBER FIVE U.S. DESTROYERS ENGAGED AN EQUAL NUMBER OF JAPANESE DESTROYERS REINFORCING BUKA AND, IN THE BATTLE OF CAPE ST. GEORGE, SANK THREE. IN FEBRUARY 1944 THE 37TH AND THE AMERICAL DIVISIONS COMPLETED RELIEF OF THE 3D MARINE DIVISION. ON 9 MARCH TWO JAPANESE DIVISIONS UNSUCCESSFULLY LAUNCHED MAJOR COUNTERATTACKS AGAINST THESE TWO DIVISIONS. HOWEVER THE ENEMY CONTINUED TO HARASS THE PERIMETER FOR SEVERAL MONTHS THEREAFTER.

ON 15 FEBRUARY 1944 THE 3D NEW ZEALAND DIVISION OCCUPIED THE GREEN ISLANDS, ONLY 140 MILES FROM RABAUL. THIS COMPLETED THE LONG NORTHWESTWARD ADVANCE IN THE SOLOMONS.

5. INVASION OF THE PALAU ISLANDS

COINCIDING WITH THE FINAL OPERATIONS IN NEW GUINEA TO THE SOUTH AND FOLLOWING CLOSELY THE CAPTURE OF THE MARIANA ISLANDS TO THE NORTH, UNITED STATES FORCES INVADED THE PALAU ISLANDS. DURING THE WEEKS IMMEDIATELY PRECEDING THIS INVASION, AIRCRAFT OF THE FIFTH AND THIRTEENTH AIR FORCES BASED ON NEW GUINEA HEAVILY BOMBED THE PALAUS; CARRIER-BASED AIRCRAFT OF THE THIRD FLEET AND LAND-BASED AIRPLANES OF THE SEVENTH AIR FORCE STRUCK WITH DEVASTATING EFFECT AT FARFLUNG TARGETS TO THE NORTH, EAST AND WEST. THEN THE AIRPLANES OF THE THIRD FLEET PROVIDED DIRECT AIR SUPPORT FOR THE ATTACKING TROOPS. ITS WARSHIPS SUPPORTED THE ASSAULT WITH GUNFIRE.

ON 15 SEPTEMBER 1944 THE THIRD AMPHIBIOUS FORCE LANDED THE 1ST MARINE DIVISION ON PELELIU. AS IT ADVANCED FROM THE BEACHHEAD STRONG OPPOSITION DEVELOPED; THE ENEMY LAUNCHED ESPECIALLY FIERCE COUNTERATTACKS ACROSS THE AIRFIELD AGAINST POSITIONS REACHED BY THE 1ST AND 5TH MARINE REGIMENTS. REPULSING THESE ASSAULTS THE

MARINES PUSHED INLAND AND CAP-
TURED THE AIRFIELD ON THE FOLLOW-
ING DAY. THEIR PROGRESS WAS COSTLY
BUT THEY CONTINUED THE ATTACK
NORTHWARD AND WITHIN A WEEK
DROVE THE JAPANESE INTO THE ROUGH
TERRAIN TO THE NORTH. AT THE SAME
TIME, THE 7TH MARINE REGIMENT
OVERCAME STRONG OPPOSITION AND
SECURED THE SOUTHERN SECTOR OF
THE ISLAND.

ON 17 SEPTEMBER THE 321ST AND 322D
REGIMENTS OF THE U.S. ARMY'S 81ST
INFANTRY DIVISION LANDED ON AN-
GAUR, SIX MILES TO THE SOUTHWEST.
AFTER SUFFERING HEAVY CASUALTIES
FROM NUMEROUS PILLBOXES AND
DUGOUTS, THE TROOPS OVERRAN OR-
GANIZED OPPOSITION. WHILE ISO-
LATED POCKETS OF THE ENEMY WERE
STILL HOLDING OUT, U.S. ARMY EN-
GINEERS BEGAN TO DEVELOP A HEAVY
BOMBER BASE.

THE 321ST REGIMENT MOVED TO
PELELIU, WHERE IT RELIEVED THE 1ST
MARINE REGIMENT. AIDED BY MARINE
AIRCRAFT FLOWN FROM THE CAPTURED
AIRSTRIP ON PELELIU, INFANTRYMEN
AND MARINES PUSHED NORTHWARD
ALONG THE COAST AND FORCED THE
ENEMY INTO A SMALL POCKET ON MT.
UMURBROGOL. THERE HE STUBBORNLY
DEFENDED CAVE FORTIFICATIONS FOR
ANOTHER TWO MONTHS.

IN THE MEANTIME THE 323D INFAN-
TRY HAD OCCUPIED ULITHI, 300 MILES
TO THE NORTH, AND RETURNED TO
FIGHT ON PELELIU. THESE ISLANDS
WERE THEN DEVELOPED INTO NAVAL
AND AIR BASES WHICH WERE TO PROVE
THEIR VALUE AS SUPPORT AND STAG-
ING POINTS DURING THE LIBERATION
OF THE PHILIPPINES.

VISITORS' BUILDING

The Visitors' Building is located just
inside the main gate at the right of
the plaza. It contains the Superintendent's office, toilet facilities
and a comfortably furnished room
where visitors may obtain information, sign the register and pause to
refresh themselves. During visiting
hours a member of the cemetery
staff is available in the building to
answer questions and provide information on burials and memorializations in the Commission's
cemeteries, accommodations in the
vicinity, travel, local history and
other items of interest.

There is parking space in the Visitors' Building plaza and also immediately in rear of the memorial. In
the interest of visitors, of whom
many take photographs, parking is
not permitted in front of the memorial.

PLANTINGS

In his design for the layout of the
cemetery the landscape architect
visualized a park-like background
for the Memorial and graves plots
which would assure a rotation of
bloom to embellish perpetually this
resting place of the honored Dead.
In so doing he achieved in effect the
creation of a large botanical garden
with stately stretches of broad lawns
and magnificent vistas, using gen-
era and species which are representative of the great wealth of flowering trees, shrubs, palms and foliage
plants of the Philippines, the East
Indies, and the warmer climates of
Southern Asia, Africa and Tropical
America.

It is impracticable to include in
this booklet the entire plant-list of
the cemetery, but visitors are invited to refer to a copy of the plant-
list which is available at the Visitors'
Building.

The grass covering most of the
cemetery is Zoysia Matrella. All of it
has been propagated from two
square yards of sod shipped in 1951
from the United States Department
of Agriculture Experimental Station
at Beltsville, Maryland.

The Graves Area

The Memorial Tower

WORLD WAR II
CEMETERIES AND MEMORIALS:

TUNISIA

North Africa American Cemetery and Memorial

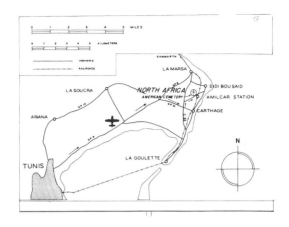

LOCATION

North Africa American Cemetery and Memorial is situated 10 miles northeast of the city of Tunis, Tunisia, and 5 miles northeast of its airport (El Aouina). It may be reached by taxicab from the city or the airport. There is an electric commuter train from Tunis — the nearest stop is at Amilcar station, from which the cemetery is only two or three hundred yards distant. Hotels are available in Tunis, Carthage, Amilcar and Gammarth. The weather is likely to be quite hot during the summer months and cold on occasion during the winter.

HOURS

The cemetery is open daily to the public as shown below:

SUMMER (15 May–15 September):
    8:00 a.m.–6:00 p.m.
WINTER (16 September–14 May)
    8:00 a.m.–5:00 p.m.

Cemetery Entrance

"Honor" at the Wall of the Missing

Aerial View of Cemetery

HISTORY

Prior to entry into World War II, the United States adopted a strategic policy regarding how it would conduct combat operations, should it be forced into war against the Axis powers (Germany and Italy) and Japan at the same time. The policy was to defeat the stronger enemy in Europe first, while simultaneously maintaining a vigorous defensive posture against Japan. It was not altered by the surprise Japanese attack at Pearl Harbor on 7 December 1941.

The basic plan of action advocated by U.S. war planners was to concentrate forces, supplies and materiel in the British Isles, and after a period of training, to launch a powerful amphibious assault across the English Channel in the summer of 1943. Although the German advance against Moscow had been stopped in December 1941 and the enemy had been forced backward by a strong Russian winter offensive, the Germans again began advancing rapidly in 1942. The Crimea was overrun, Sevastopol was captured and German forces were moving against Stalingrad on the Volga River. Even greater advances were being made in the Caucasus Mountains to the southeast.

Matters also were going badly for the British in the Mediterranean area along the coast of North Africa in Libya and Egypt, the area known as the Western Desert. There, where the fighting had been seesawing back and forth for nearly two years, the combined German–Italian force known as the Afrika Korps had forced the British Eighth Army back further into Egypt, and was closer to Alexandria than ever before. Additional Axis advances in Egypt and

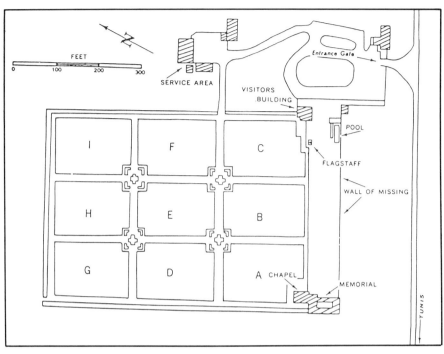

Location of Cemetery Features

the Caucasus posed a threat to the entire Middle East.

The Allies sorely needed an offensive operation that would lessen the pressure on the British Eighth Army in Egypt. The only operation that could be undertaken with a reasonable chance of success was an assault in French Morocco and Algiers in northwest Africa. It had the advantage of getting American forces into action in 1942, although it would probably delay the cross-Channel assault planned for 1943.

The Allies hoped that French forces defending northwest Africa, which were operating under the control of the portion of France which had not been occupied by the Germans after the armistice of 1940, might welcome them or offer only token resistance. Some of these forces were loyal to Vichy, France; others were sympathetic to the Allied cause.

The invasion plan of northwest Africa provided for three naval task forces to land before dawn on 8 November 1942 in three widely separated areas. The U.S. Western Naval Task Force, composed entirely of American ships sailing from the United States at the height of the Battle of the Atlantic against German submarines, arrived unsuspected and undetected. Its landings in French Morocco encountered the strongest resistance of any of the landing forces. In the center, the U.S. 3d Infantry Division landing at Fedala near Casablanca, found both army and naval forces opposing it. As it fought its way inland, fire from U.S. naval forces neutralized the shore batteries and sank several French warships. By 1500 hours, Fedala had fallen. The 3d Division then closed on Casablanca where it met strong resistance, until the French surrendered on 11 November upon orders from Algiers.

"Memory" at the Wall of the Missing

Further to the south, the 47th Regimental Combat Team of the U.S. 9th Infantry Division and Combat Command B of the U.S. 2d Armored Division established a bridgehead at Safi, against heavy ground and air resistance. When U.S. carrier planes joined the attack, Combat Command B drove northward toward Casablanca, halting only when it was informed that resistance had ceased. To the north, the 60th Regimental Combat Team of the 9th Division captured the Port Lyautey airfield late on 10 November, with the support of naval and armored units.

When the British Center and Eastern Naval Forces coming from the United Kingdom passed through the Straits of Gibraltar, their presence was immediately reported to the enemy by spies. As the British Eighth Army had won a great victory at El Alamein just a few days before and now was pursuing the Afrika Korps westward toward Libya and Tunisia, the enemy assumed falsely that the task forces were en route to block the retreat of the Afrika Korps.

Although the war and troop ships of the British Central Naval Task Force were British, the assault troops at Oran, as in French Morocco, were entirely American. Landing on both sides of the city, the U.S. 1st Infantry Division, elements of the U.S. 1st Armored Division and a battalion of Rangers met only sporadic resistance as they came ashore. Quickly, the infantry advanced toward the city while the armored units seized the airfields, where a U.S. parachute battalion had previously been dropped nearby. The French capitulated at 1230 hours on 10 November.

The landing at Algiers from the ships of the British Eastern Naval Task Force encountered the least resistance. Debarking on both sides of the city, the force consisted of the U.S. 34th Infantry Division, the 39th

Regimental Combat Team of the U.S. 9th Infantry Division, British Commandos and elements of the British 78 Infantry Division. Opposition ended that same day, as orders from Algiers were issued to cease all hostilities in North Africa.

Meanwhile the race for Tunisia had begun. Anticipating that the Allies next would move into Tunisia to seize the Tunis–Bizerte area, the enemy began moving troops as rapidly as possible into northern Tunisia by sea and air, even though fighting was still in progress at Oran and in French Morocco. The following day, the floating reserve of the Eastern Naval Task Force, a brigade group of the British 78 Division, was dispatched eastward to the port of Bougie, in the first step of the Allied advance toward Tunisia. That evening, German and Italian forces moved into southern France as Italy prepared to seize Corsica.

At this stage of the war, it was clear to almost all Frenchmen that the future of France depended upon whether or not it joined with the Allies. Among the first to take this action was the French army commander in Tunisia. Although his forces were greatly outnumbered by the enemy, he slowly withdrew them into the mountains to establish contact with Allied troops moving eastward. As the number of troops on each side gradually strengthened, both the Allies and the Axis launched a series of attacks on Tunisia with indifferent success. By advent of the winter rains, it was clear that the British First Army and its attached French and American units were unable to oust the stronger Fifth Panzer Army from Tunisia. A major factor was the enemy's superiority of air power.

In January 1943, the U.S. II Corps began arriving in southern Tunisia with some additional troops. At that time, the British First Army was organized from north to south into three corps; the British 5 Corps in the north, the French XIX Corps in the center, the U.S. II Corps in the

Wall of the Missing with Statue of "Honor" in foreground

Statue of "Recollection" at Wall of the Missing

south. Throughout the next month and a half, the stronger enemy air and ground forces hammered away at the Allies in central and southern Tunisia. To reduce the effects of these attacks, U.S. units were dispersed throughout their area as were units of the French XIX Corps to the north.

Meanwhile, by early February the Afrika Korps had retreated across Libya and reached the Mareth Line, a series of old French fortifications in southern Tunisia. There it began to prepare a defense against the approaching British Eighth Army, whose pursuit had been slowed by major logistical problems.

Before the British Eighth Army arrived in strength, the Fifth Panzer Army and the Afrika Korps launched a heavy armored assault against the widely dispersed U.S. II Corps. In a series of sharp actions, the enemy forced a withdrawal, broke through the mountains near the Kasserine Pass into the valley beyond and achieved spectacular success. They were not halted until 22 February when combined American and British armored and infantry units and the U.S. 9th Division Artillery, which had been rushed to the scene from as far away as Oran, arrived in the nick of time to stem the assault.

Two more enemy attacks were repulsed, one in the north, the other against the British Eighth Army, of which only a few of its units had arrived. From that point onward, the initiative passed to the Allies. As the reorganized U.S. II Corps threatened the Mareth Line from the flank and rear, the Eighth Army attacked frontally. Success was achieved when New Zealand and British troops outflanked the Afrika Korps' position and drove northward. During this same March period, the Allies gained control of the air. By mid-April, the enemy had been driven northward and was confined to a small area in northeast Tunisia consisting of Bizerte, Tunis and the Cape Bon Peninsula.

In preparation for the final Allied attacks, the U.S. II Corps was moved

Entrance to the Memorial

north opposite Bizerte. The First Army's main effort was to be made in the center by the British 5 and 9 Corps, the latter corps having been organized when reinforcements were transferred from the Eighth Army. On 19 April, the Eighth Army began to attack in the south, but made little gain at great cost. Three days later the First Army's main attack was launched and was met by a vigorous defense. In the center, very little progress was being made. However, the U.S. II Corps in the north and the French XIX Corps further south were making substantial gains.

Two additional divisions at this time were transferred from the Eighth Army to strengthen the First Army's British 5 and 9 Corps. Utilizing the reinforcements, the attack resumed on 4 May, preceded by a devastating air bombardment. Little could be done to counter the bombardment as the enemy had withdrawn almost all its aircraft to Sicily. The U.S. II Corps captured Bizerte on 7 May and the British 5 and 9

Corps drove down the Medjerda River to capture Tunis that same day. On 9 May, the enemy in the II Corps area capitulated. By 13 May 1943 over one quarter of a million Axis troops had been taken prisoner.

THE SITE

The cemetery site covers 27 acres of the plateau lying between the Mediterranean and the Bay of Tunis, both of which are a mile or so distant. It is located near the site of the ancient Carthaginian city destroyed by the Romans in 146 B.C. and lies over part of the site of Roman Carthage. Some 200 yards to the east are remnants of Roman houses and streets — the entire region thereabouts contains vestiges of the Roman city as well as some remains of the Carthaginian era.

After the end of World War II a survey made jointly by representatives of the Secretary of War and the American Battle Monuments Commission revealed that all of the sites of the temporary cemeteries estab-

Cloister with Stone of Remembrance

Statue of "Honor"

lished in North Africa during the war had major disadvantages. The present site was established in 1948. It lies in the sector of the British First Army which liberated the Tunis area in May 1943. Construction of the cemetery and memorial was completed in 1960.

Here rest 2,841 of our Military Dead, representing 39 percent of the burials which were originally made in North Africa and in Iran. A high proportion of these gave their lives in the landings in, and occupation of, Morocco and Algeria and in subsequent fighting which culminated in the liberation of Tunisia. Others died as a result of accident or sickness in these and other parts of North Africa, or while serving in the Persian Gulf Command in Iran.

ARCHITECTS

Architects for the cemetery and memorial were Moore and Hutchins of New York. The landscape architect was Bryan J. Lynch also of New York.

GENERAL LAYOUT

The main entrance from the eucalyptus-bordered highway is at the southeast corner of the cemetery. To the right of the entrance is one of the superintendents' houses; beyond is the oval forecourt. Beneath the green plot in the center of the forecourt is the reservoir which stores the water for the cemetery needs, as well as the pumps which operate the high pressure sprinkling system. All of the water comes from the municipal supply for which the storage area is located some miles to the south of the city of Tunis. Down the hill and beyond the forecourt is the utilities area.

In the forecourt are rows of eucalyptus and ornamental India laurel fig (Ficus nitida) trees; the beds include Pittosporum tobira, scarlet hibiscus, Lantana camara, English ivy, Cassia floribunda, orangeberry pittosporum and other shrubs and vines.

Extending to the left (west) of the forecourt and parking area is the

*Map — American and Allied Forces in North Africa
1942–1943*

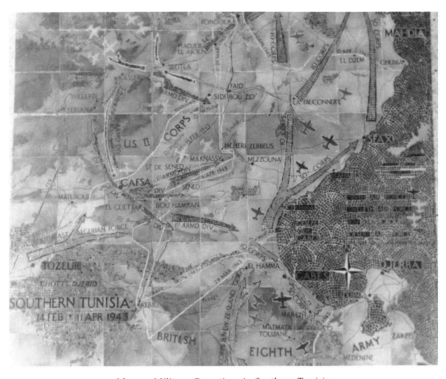

Map — Military Operations in Southern Tunisia

mall. At the head of the steps leading to the mall, and at the right (north) is the Visitors' building, built of Roman travertine imported from Italy; west of it is the flagpole.

On the south side of the mall is the Wall of the Missing; at its far (west) end is the memorial chapel. North of the mall is the graves area which it overlooks. South of the highway is an additional area used for service purposes.

THE WALL OF THE MISSING

This wall, 364 feet long, is of local Nahli limestone, with local Gathouna limestone copings. Built into it are panels of Trani limestone imported from Italy on which are inscribed the names and particulars of 3,724 of the Missing:

United States Army and Army Air Forces (3,095)*
United States Navy (615)
United States Coast Guard (14)

These men gave their lives in the service of their Country; but their remains either were not identified or they were lost or buried at sea in the waters surrounding the African continent. They include men from all of the States, except Alaska and Hawaii, and from the District of Columbia.

At each end of the wall is this inscription:

HERE ARE RECORDED THE NAMES OF AMERICANS WHO GAVE THEIR LIVES IN THE SERVICE OF THEIR COUNTRY AND WHO SLEEP IN UNKNOWN GRAVES 1941–45 ☆ INTO THEY HANDS O LORD.

---

*It will be recalled that during World War II the Air Forces still formed part of the United States Army.

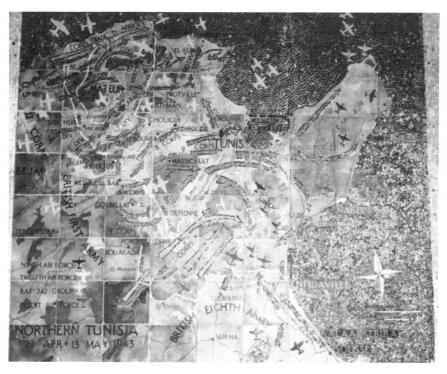

Map — Military Operations in Northern Tunisia

Near the foot of the steps leading down from the forecourt is a pool and figure of HONOR about to bestow a laurel branch upon those who gave their lives. The figure's pedestal bears this inscription:
HONOR TO THEM THAT TROD THE PATH OF HONOR.

Along the wall are two other sculptured figures: MEMORY and RECOLLECTION, the latter holding a book with the inscription PRO PATRIA. Between these figures are oak leaf wreaths within which are engraved the names of battles on land, sea and in the air, in which the American forces participated: ORAN, CASABLANCA, ALGIERS, KASSERINE, EL GUETTAR, SIDI NSIR, BIZERTE, SICILY, PLOESTI. All of this sculpture is of Bianco Caldo stone from near Foggia, Italy; it was designed by Henry Kreis of Essex, Connecticut, and executed by Pietro Bibolotti, Pietrasanta, Italy.

Planted in front of the Wall of the Missing are rows of India laurel fig trees (Ficus nitida) in beds of English ivy. On the north side of the terrace are rows of holly oaks (Quercus ilex) and potted pink geraniums adjacent to beds of ivy.

THE MEMORIAL

The memorial consists of the court of honor and the chapel. The court of honor is in the form of a cloister. Within it is a large rectangular stone of remembrance of black Diorite d'Anzola quarried in northwest Italy; this inscription, adapted from Ecclesiasticus XLIV, is worked into the design of the mosaic panel surrounding the base:
SOME THERE BE WHICH HAVE NO SEPULCHRE. THEIR NAME LIVETH FOR EVERMORE.

The rectangular pylons of the cloister are of San Gottardo lime-

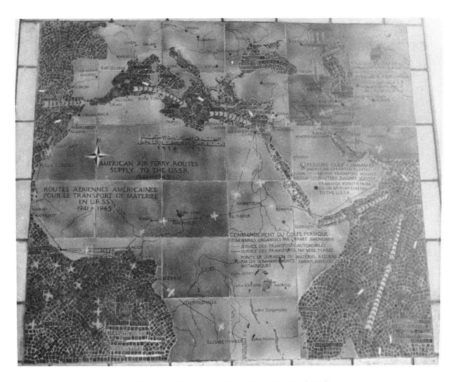

Map — Air Transport and Supplies to Russia

stone from the vicinity of Vicenza in Italy; the main part of the structure of the memorial is faced with Roman travertine. The pavement is of Sienite della Balma granite from northwest Italy. In the southwest corner is a Russian olive tree (Elaeagnus angustifolia). On the west wall of the cloister facing the mall is this inscription, with translations in French and Arabic:

1941–1945

IN PROUD REMEMBRANCE OF THE ACHIEVEMENTS OF HER SONS AND IN HUMBLE TRIBUTE TO THEIR SACRIFICES THIS MEMORIAL HAS BEEN ERECTED BY THE UNITED STATES OF AMERICA.

At the south end of the cloister are the maps. These are of ceramic, designed and fabricated by Paul D. Holleman of Roxbury, Massachusetts, from information supplied by the American Battle Monuments Commission.

The large map on the end (south)

wall records the military operations of the American forces and those of the Allies in Morocco, Algeria and Tunisia from the initial "Torch" landings on 8 November 1942 to the Axis surrender on 13 May 1943. The descriptive text is in English, Arabic and French, of which this is the English version:

ON 8 NOVEMBER 1942, IN A MAJOR OPERATION COVERED BY NAVAL GUN-FIRE AND AIRCRAFT, UNITED STATES AND BRITISH TROOPS WERE LANDED SIMULTANEOUSLY IN THREE WIDELY SEPARATED AREAS ON THE SHORES OF NORTH AFRICA. THE AMERICAN WEST-ERN NAVAL TASK FORCE, SAILING FROM THE UNITED STATES, LANDED AMERICAN TROOPS AT FEDALA, MEHDIA AND SAFI FOR THE ASSAULT ON CASABLANCA. OTHER AMERICAN UNITS ESCORTED FROM THE UNITED KINGDOM BY THE BRITISH CENTER NAVAL TASK FORCE WENT ASHORE NEAR ORAN AND IN TWO DAYS OC-

CUPIED THAT CITY. SHIPS OF THE BRITISH EASTERN NAVAL TASK FORCE, COMING ALSO FROM THE BRITISH ISLES, LANDED UNITED STATES AND BRITISH TROOPS NEAR ALGIERS WHICH WAS OCCUPIED THAT DAY. FOLLOWING THE LANDINGS, THE ALLIED NAVAL FORCES KEPT THE SEA LANES OPEN FOR AN UNINTERRUPTED FLOW OF SUPPLIES AND ALSO PROVIDED FIRE SUPPORT TO THE TROOPS ASHORE. ON 11 NOVEMBER AN ARMISTICE PROCLAMATION ENDED VICHY FRENCH RESISTANCE THROUGHOUT ALGERIA AND MOROCCO.

THE ALLIED FORCES THEN TURNED EASTWARD TOWARD TUNISIA INTO WHICH AXIS TROOPS WERE STEADILY STREAMING. MOVING RAPIDLY, AMERICAN AND BRITISH UNITS ADVANCED ACROSS THE FRONTIER TOWARD TUNIS. STRONG RESISTANCE, COUPLED WITH UNFAVORABLE WEATHER AND DIFFICULT SUPPLY CONDITIONS, CHECKED THIS ADVANCE JUST 16 MILES FROM ITS GOAL. DURING THE FIRST WEEK OF DECEMBER A COUNTEROFFENSIVE IN THE TEBOURBA-CHOUIGUI AREA PUSHED BACK THE ALLIED LINE BETWEEN JEFNA AND MEDJEZ EL BAB.

IMMEDIATELY AFTER THE LANDINGS, ALLIED AIR UNITS HAD OCCUPIED EXISTING NORTH AFRICA BASES AND HAD AIDED THE EASTWARD ADVANCE, BUT LACK OF SUITABLE FORWARD AIRFIELDS AND SHORTAGES OF PERSONNEL AND AIRCRAFT HAMPERED THEIR OPERATIONS.

DURING DECEMBER AND JANUARY AXIS FORCES, WHICH HAD BEEN STRONGLY REINFORCED BY SEA AND AIR, WERE AGGRESSIVE IN CENTRAL AND SOUTHERN TUNISIA. IN MID-FEBRUARY THEY LAUNCHED A PINCERS ATTACK AIMED AT EL KEF WHICH PENETRATED UNITED STATES II CORPS POSITIONS, PUSHED THROUGH A PASS NORTHWEST OF KASSERINE BUT WAS HALTED ON 22 FEBRUARY BEFORE THALA. ONE MONTH LATER THE BRITISH EIGHTH ARMY TURNED THE WESTERN FLANK OF THE MARETH LINE

AND DROVE THE ENEMY NORTHWARD TO ENFIDAVILLE. THE FRENCH XIX CORPS HELD FAST IN ITS MOUNTAIN POSITIONS NEAR MAKTAR.

BY MARCH 1943 THE ALLIES HAD GAINED CONTROL OF THE SKIES OVER AFRICA. THE FINAL CAMPAIGN OPENED IN NORTHWEST TUNISIA ON 22 APRIL 1943. THE UNITED STATES II CORPS, NOW ON THE ALLIED LEFT FLANK, PUSHED EASTWARD, REDUCING SUCCESSIVE DEFENSIVE POSITIONS IN DIFFICULT HILLY TERRAIN, LIBERATING MATEUR, FERRYVILLE AND BIZERTE. MEANWHILE THE BRITISH 5 AND 9 CORPS WERE ENGAGED IN A DETERMINED ASSAULT DOWN THE MEDJERDA RIVER WHICH CULMINATED IN FREEING THE CITY OF TUNIS. IN THE II CORPS AREA THE ENEMY CAPITULATED ON 9 MAY. BY 13 MAY, DENIED ESCAPE BY ALLIED MASTERY OF THE SEA AND AIR, ONE QUARTER OF A MILLION AXIS TROOPS THEN REMAINING IN TUNISIA BECAME PRISONERS OF WAR.

On this wall also are the two series of key maps — The War Against Germany and The War Against Japan.

As indicated by the texts, the map on the east wall records in greater detail the operations in central and southern Tunisia, while the one on the opposite (west) wall covers the final stages in northern Tunisia.

The map on the west pylon portrays most of Africa, the Mediterranean and the Middle East. It records the air ferry routes across Africa as well as the operations of the Persian Gulf Command.

The descriptive text for this map, also in English, French and Arabic, is on the face of the corresponding east pylon. The English text follows:

THE UNITED STATES OF AMERICA, WHILE CONTRIBUTING ITS LAND, SEA, AND AIR FORCES TO THE PROSECUTION OF WORLD WAR II, ALSO AIDED ITS MANY ALLIES BY FURNISHING MILITARY EQUIPMENT AND SUPPLIES. ITEMS OF ALL KINDS WERE CARRIED BY VAST

FLEETS OF STEAMSHIPS TO EVERY AVAILABLE PORT. IN THIS EFFORT ALSO AIRCRAFT WERE FERRIED FROM THE UNITED STATES ACROSS THE ATLANTIC OCEAN AND CENTRAL AFRICA TO CAIRO, KARACHI AND BASRA.

THROUGH THE PERSIAN GULF COMMAND AREA, THE UNITED STATES DELIVERED, FROM 1942 TO 1945, NEARLY 4½ MILLION TONS OF SUPPLIES TO THE U.S.S.R. THESE INCLUDED 4,874 AIRCRAFT OF WHICH 995 WERE FLOWN IN; OVER 160,000 TANKS, ARMORED CARS AND TRUCKS; 140,000 TONS OF GUNS, AMMUNITION AND EXPLOSIVES; 550,000 TONS OF PETROLEUM PRODUCTS; 950,000 TONS OF FOOD; AND 1,000,000 TONS OF METAL AND METAL PRODUCTS. THE UNITED STATES ALSO FURNISHED TO THE U.S.S.R., THROUGH OTHER PORTS, MORE THAN 13 MILLION TONS OF ADDITIONAL SUPPLIES.

THE CHAPEL

The bronze doors and the windows of the chapel were fabricated by the Morris Singer Company of London, England. At the far end of the chapel, which is lighted by the tall window on the right and a row of lower windows on the left is the altar of white Carrara marble, with this inscription from St. John X, 28: I GIVE UNTO THEM ETERNAL LIFE AND THEY SHALL NEVER PERISH. ☆☆☆ The wall behind the altar is of polished Rosso Porfirico marble from near Udine in northeastern Italy.

Facing the door, on the wing wall projecting from the right, is the sculpture SACRIFICE carved in Italian Bianco Caldo stone, designed by Henry Kreis and executed by Pietro Bibolotti. Below and to its left is this inscription from Shelly's ode

Oasis with Cemetery and Memorial in Background

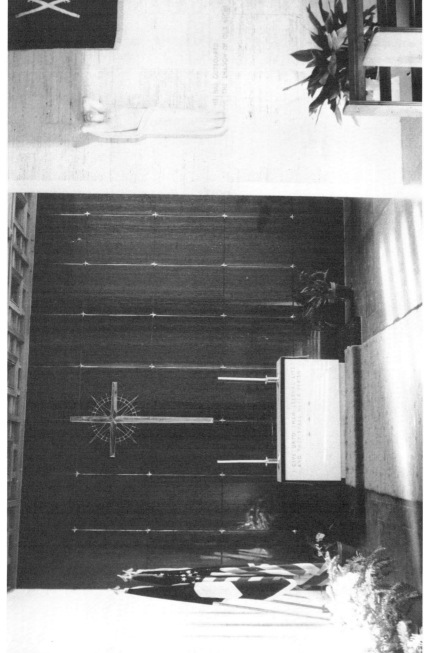

Chapel Interior

"Adonais": "HE HAS OUTSOARED THE SHADOW OF OUR NIGHT."

To the left of the altar are the United States national flag and Christian and Jewish chapel flags. Projecting from the east wall above the pews are the flags of combat arms, viz.: Infantry, Field Artillery, Navy Infantry Battalion, Air Corps and Armor. Beneath the flags is this prayer: ALMIGHTY GOD, RECEIVE THESE THY HEROIC SERVANTS INTO THY KINGDOM.

The ceiling is of Moroccan cedar; the pews and prie-dieu are of walnut. Three flower boxes of teakwood, with bronze appurtenances, are located under the west windows of the chapel.

North of the chapel, down a flight of steps from the cloister, is the memorial garden with its pool; the plants include latana, poinciana, pink geraniums and a Jerusalem thorn tree (Parkinsonia aculeata). Beyond is the graves area.

THE GRAVES AREA

The 2,833 headstones in the rectangular graves area are divided into nine plots designated A to I. They are arranged in rectangular lines harmonizing with the rectangular composition of the cemetery and memorial. The 2,841 burials in the cemetery, include 240 Unknowns.

These Dead who gave their lives in their Country's service came from all of the States except Alaska and Hawaii and from the District of Columbia; a few came from foreign countries. Among the headstones is one which marks the tomb of seven Americans whose identity is unknown; also two adjacent headstones mark the graves of four men whose names are known but whose remains could not be separately

Roman Mosaic donated by President Bourguiba

Interior of Visitors' Center

identified; a bronze tablet between these graves records their names. In this cemetery also, in three instances, two brothers are buried side by side.

In the burial area are four fountains and pools of Roman travertine, which with their surrounding vegetation of rosemary, oleander, and pink geraniums form small and welcome oases in this frequently hot climate.

The paths are lined either by Ficus nitida or California pepper trees (Schinus molle). The border massifs contain a wide variety of trees and shrubs in which oleanders and hibiscus are predominant.

VISITORS' BUILDING

On the west facade of the Visitors' building is this inscription taken from General Eisenhower's dedication of the Golden Book now enshrined in St. Paul's Cathedral in London:

HERE WE AND ALL WHO SHALL HERE-AFTER LIVE IN FREEDOM WILL BE RE-MINDED THAT TO THESE MEN AND THEIR COMRADES WE OWE A DEBT TO BE PAID WITH GRATEFUL REMEMBRANCE OF THEIR SACRIFICE AND WITH THE HIGH RESOLVE THAT THE CAUSE FOR WHICH THEY DIED SHALL LIVE.

Within the Visitors' building is a Roman mosaic discovered in the region and donated in 1959 by President Bourguiba of Tunisia to Ambassador G. Lewis Jones, who in turn presented it to the Cemetery.

PLANTINGS

The grass in the cemetery is kikuyu (Pennisetum clandestinum). It can sustain the heat of this region with minimum water.

The entire graves and memorial areas are surrounded beyond the inner walls by massifs of trees and shrubbery in which these predominate: pyramidal cypress (C. pyramidalis), aleppo pine (P. halepensis), eucalyptus (E. gomocephala), Casuarina tenuissima, Ficus macrophylla, Acacia pycnantha, as well as weaver's broom (Spartium junceum) and some 3,000 oleanders.

WORLD WAR II
CEMETERIES AND MEMORIALS:

UNITED KINGDOM

Cambridge American Cemetery and Memorial

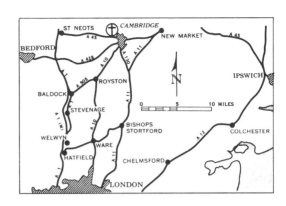

LOCATION

The Cambridge American Cemetery is situated three miles west of the university city of Cambridge, on highway A-1303 and 60 miles north of London, England.

There is frequent train service between Cambridge and London's King's Cross or Liverpool Street stations. Travel time is about 1½ hours. Taxicab service is available at the Cambridge Station.

The cemetery may be reached in about 2¼ hours from London by automobile. There are excellent hotels in the city of Cambridge.

HOURS

The cemetery is open daily to the public during the following hours
SUMMER (16 April–30 September)
    8:00 a.m.–6:00 p.m.
WINTER (1 October–15 April)
    8:00 a.m.–5:00 p.m.

During these hours, a staff member is on duty at the visitors' building to escort relatives to the gravesites.

HISTORY

When the United States entered World War II, it was apparent that Germany, with its great military and

Chapel Interior

Memorial Interior

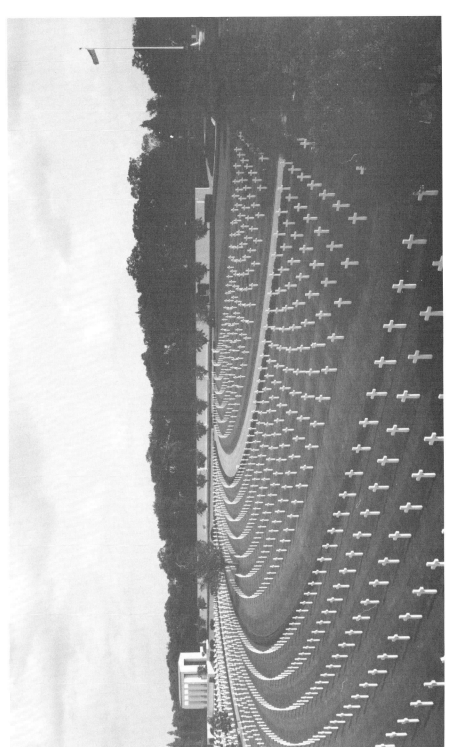

View of Graves Area and Memorial

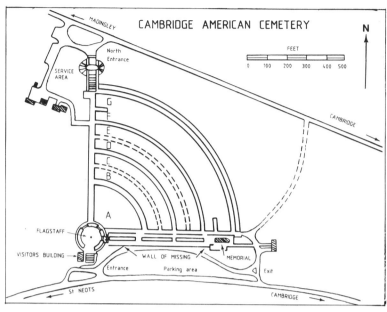

Location of Cemetery Features

industrial strength, posed the strongest threat of the Axis powers and should be dealt with first. Her defeat hinged on achieving four major objectives, for each of which effective use of Great Britain was a key factor. In the attainment of these objectives, the country became a vast supply depot, military base, air base and training and staging facility. During the war, more than 17 million tons of cargo and nearly two million servicemen and women from the United States passed through British ports. Many military bases and training areas were established throughout the British Isles to receive the forces which later were to achieve such spectacular results on the beaches of Normandy. At the same time, airfields were enlarged and additional bases constructed for use by U. S. Army Air Forces.

The first objective in the war against Germany was to provide the United Kingdom with the resources needed to carry on until sufficient men, materials and supplies could be assembled for a cross-channel invasion of Europe. To do so, the Atlantic sea lanes had to be made safe for the passage of Allied convoys between Great Britain and the United States. The battle for the Atlantic continued from 1939 to 1945, when the last German U-Boats surrendered. This costly but generally successful struggle gave the Allies control of the sea lanes between United States and Great Britain, which was essential to the success of Allied operations in Europe.

The second objective was to aid and sustain other nations actively engaged against the Axis, particularly the U. S. S. R., which at the time was receiving the brunt of the enemy's land assaults. A "second front" was opened in North Africa in November 1942 to relieve the pressure against the U. S. S. R. Allied forces from bases in both Great Britain and the United States landed in North Africa and fought their way inland in the face of determined enemy resistance. Six months later, victory in North Africa was achieved when all enemy forces there surrendered. The operations in North Africa were followed by Allied landings in Sicily, Salerno and Anzio during 1943 and 1944. Victories in

Sicily and Italy were paralleled by Soviet successes in the East, with the winning of the battle for Stalingrad in February 1943 and the liberation of Sevastopol in May 1944. One month later, Allied forces entered Rome, and the landings in Normandy commenced.

The third objective during the war against Germany was to conduct an intensive strategic bombardment of Germany in order to destroy its military, industrial and economic systems. Achievement of this objective depended on the use of air bases within the British Isles. As the airfields were constructed and expanded, the air war against Germany intensified. The first American strategic bombing against a target in Europe took place in August 1942. By the end of the war, more than one-half million sorties against targets in Western Europe were flown by British-based American aircraft.

The final objective was to invade the European continent and defeat the enemy on its historic battlefields. U. S. and British Commonwealth forces landed on the beaches of Normandy on 6 June 1944 in what was to be the greatest amphibious operation in the history of warfare. Supported by U. S. and British aircraft, the Allied ground forces fought their way across France and crossed into Germany in September of 1944.

With the Allied victory in Europe on 8 May 1945, the struggle against the enemy in the Pacific was intensified. Confronted by overwhelming military superiority, its major cities devastated and weakened by the defeat of the Axis in Europe, Japan surrendered on 2 September 1945.

THE SITE

The Cambridge American Cemetery, 30.5 acres in extent, is one of fourteen permanent American World War II military cemetery memorials erected on foreign soil by the American Battle Monuments Commission.

It was established as a temporary military cemetery in 1943 on land donated by the University of Cambridge. The site was later selected as the only permanent American World War II military cemetery in the British Isles and was dedicated

Great Mall, Facing West

A View of Reflecting Pool through the Memorial Door

16 July 1956. About 42 percent of those temporarily interred in England and Northern Ireland during the war were reinterred in the Cambridge American Cemetery. A high proportion of these 3,811 American servicemen and women were crew members of British-based American aircraft. Most of the others interred at the cemetery died in the invasions of North Africa and France, in the training areas of the United Kingdom and in the waters of the Atlantic.

The cemetery is situated on the north slope of a hill from which Ely Cathedral, 14 miles distant, can be seen on clear days. It is framed by woodland on the west and south; the road to Madingley runs along the cemetery's northern boundary.

ARCHITECTS

Architects for the cemetery were Perry, Shaw, Hepburn and Dean of Boston, Massachusetts. The landscape architects were Olmsted Brothers of Brookline, Massachusetts.

GENERAL LAYOUT

The main entrance is at the southwest corner of the cemetery. Immediately inside it is the Visitors' Building. On the porch wall of the Visitors' Building is a bronze tablet from the grateful people of the English communities of Cheshunt and Waltham Cross which honors the members of an American bomber crew who sacrificed themselves in order to avoid abandoning their disabled aircraft over these communities.

Just beyond the Visitors' Building is a 72-foot flagpole on a tall platform whose base is inscribed with the following quotation from John McCrae's poem, *In Flanders Fields:* "TO YOU FROM FAILING HANDS WE THROW THE TORCH — BE YOURS TO HOLD IT HIGH!" The platform affords an excellent view of the cemetery.

The great mall, with its reflecting pool bordered by polyantha roses, stretches eastward from the flagpole platform to the Memorial at the opposite end. Along the south side of the mall is the Wall of the Missing. The north side, toward the graves area, is lined with a single row of double-pink hawthorn trees.

The west mall stretches northward from the flagpole platform to the lower gates of the cemetery and the service area. This broad walk

passes between rows of Japanese pagoda trees. The grave plots lie between the two malls. From the lower end of the west mall, a gravel walk turns to the right and follows the curve of the lower plot toward the Memorial. In this area are planted rose of Sharon, firethorn, forsythia and cotoneaster.

THE MEMORIAL

The Memorial structure is of Portland stone, as are St. Paul's Cathedral and many other monumental buildings in London. It is 85 feet long, 30 feet wide and 28 feet high. On the north face of the Memorial are five pylons, each inscribed with one of the years from 1941 to 1945, during which the United States participated in World War II. Above these pylons runs the inscription: GRANT UNTO THEM O LORD ETERNAL REST. Below the bronze rope railing on the north face balcony is inscribed: IN GRATEFUL TRIBUTE TO THEIR SACRIFICE AND IN PROUD MEMORY OF THEIR VALOR.

The entrance to the Memorial at the west end is framed by two pylons. On the pediment above them is the dedication: TO THE GLORY OF GOD AND IN MEMORY OF THOSE WHO DIED FOR THEIR COUNTRY 1941–1945.

The main entrance doors are of teakwood. They bear bronze models of the following military equipment and naval vessels:

Military Equipment

Armored Scout Car M8
Truck ¼ Ton 4×4
90 Millimeter Antiaircraft Gun
155 Millimeter Gun M2
Medium Tank M4
Motor Carriage, Multiple Gun M16
Amphibious Truck 2½ Ton DUKW
105 Millimeter Howitzer

Naval Vessels

Destroyer
Light Cruiser
Attack Transport
Landing Ship, Tank
Battleship
Escort Carrier

On the south exterior wall of the Memorial is a great map of the United Kingdom with the inscription: THESE AND MANY OTHER SITES WERE LENT BY THE PEOPLE OF THE UNITED KINGDOM TO THE ARMED FORCES OF THE UNITED STATES OF AMERICA IN ORDER THAT THEY MIGHT PREPARE AND SUPPORT THEIR GREAT MILITARY ASSAULTS 1941–1945. It depicts each location in the United Kingdom where an American unit of battalion or larger size was stationed during World War II. The places where units of brigade size or larger were stationed are indicated by name. The map also shows the principal air and sea approach routes to Great Britain from the United States, and the invasion routes to North Africa in 1942 and to Normandy in 1944. It is embellished with the sculptured coats of arms of the United States and the United Kingdom. The significance of the signs and colors used is explained in the legend. Worksheets for the map were furnished by the American Battle Monuments Commission; execution was by the English artist David Kindersley.

The interior of the Memorial is separated into a large museum room and a small devotional chapel at the far end. The outstanding feature of the museum room is its impressive map "The Mastery of the Atlantic — The Great Air Assault." The map was designed by the American artist Herbert Gute from data prepared by the American Battle Monuments Commission and indicates the principal sea routes across the Atlantic and the types of naval and commercial craft which bore men and munitions to Europe from the United States. It also recalls the aircraft which operated in the anti-

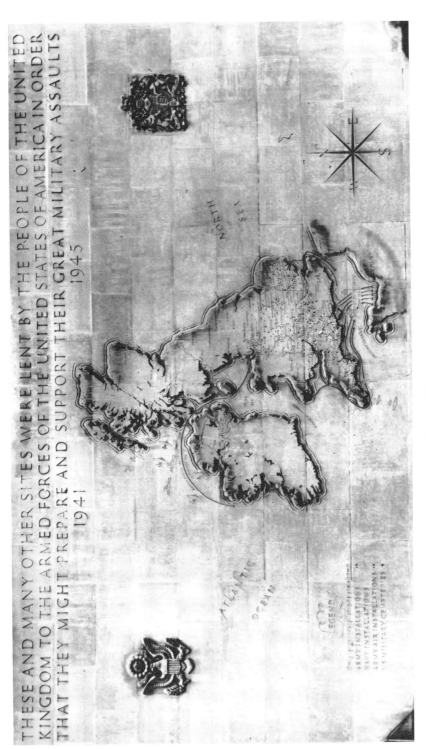

THESE AND MANY OTHER SITES WERE LENT BY THE PEOPLE OF THE UNITED KINGDOM TO THE ARMED FORCES OF THE UNITED STATES OF AMERICA IN ORDER THAT THEY MIGHT PREPARE AND SUPPORT THEIR GREAT MILITARY ASSAULTS
1941   1945

Exterior Map

submarine campaign. The continuous air assaults by the U. S. and Royal Air Forces over Europe are also depicted. Symbolic air lanes indicate their routes from both England and Italy to the various targets, whose nature — military, industrial, transportation — are explained in the legend. The map is 30 feet long, 18 feet high.

The wall bearing the map is of Portland stone. On the map, the lower land elevations are indicated in polished Portland stone, while the higher elevations are in polished Hauteville marble, Lunel Clair marble and Lunel Fonce marble, respectively. This unusual work of art was executed by David Kindersley's workshop.

Below the map are seven plates, six of which contain key maps recording the development of the war against Germany and the war against Japan. The seventh, a bronze plaque in the center, bears the following description of the operations portrayed by the great map: THRUST INTO A GLOBAL WAR WITH THE AXIS POWERS, THE UNITED STATES, AT THE CLOSE OF 1941, MOVED TO STRENGTHEN ITS DEFENSE POSITIONS IN THE ATLANTIC AND PACIFIC OCEANS. THE PROTECTION AND CONTROL OF THE SEA AND AIR ROUTES ACROSS THE ATLANTIC, SO VITAL TO THE ALLIES' HOPES OF VICTORY, WERE CONCERNS OF UNCEASING URGENCY. THE UNITED STATES NAVY JOINED WITH THE ROYAL NAVY IN THIS BITTERLY CONTESTED BATTLE; U. S. ARMY AND MARINE CORPS UNITS WERE DISPATCHED TO STRENGTHEN KEY OUTPOSTS IN THE NORTH ATLANTIC AND TO REINFORCE THE DEFENSE OF THE UNITED KINGDOM. WHILE THE ENEMY MADE EVERY EFFORT TO SEVER THE LIFELINES TO THE BRITISH ISLES, THE ALLIED NAVIES FOUGHT TO KEEP THE SEA LANES OPEN, TO CONVOY TROOPS AND MILITARY AND CIVILIAN SUPPLIES ACROSS THE ATLANTIC AND TO MAINTAIN THE LONG RUN TO NORTH RUSSIA TO SUSTAIN THE SOVIET FORCES.

CONTINUOUSLY THE ALLIES STROVE TO DEVELOP AND IMPROVE THEIR ANTISUBMARINE TACTICS, TO PROVIDE ADEQUATE ESCORT AND AIR COVERAGE TO THEIR CONVOYS. THE COORDINATED EMPLOYMENT OF LAND-BASED AIRPOWER AND OF ESCORT CARRIER AND DESTROYER GROUPS, TOGETHER WITH DEVELOPMENTS IN DETECTION DEVICES, GRADUALLY DROVE THE ENEMY'S SUBMARINES FROM THE PRINCIPAL SEA ROUTES.

THIS WAR OF ATTRITION ON, ABOVE, AND BELOW THE WATERS OF THE ATLANTIC STEADILY TURNED IN FAVOR OF THE ALLIES.

IN NOVEMBER 1942, ALLIED FORCES LANDED ON THE SHORES OF NORTH AFRICA. THIS SUCCESSFUL OPERATION INVOLVED THE SIMULTANEOUS DEBARKMENT OF ATTACK TEAMS TRANSPORTED FROM THE UNITED STATES AND THE UNITED KINGDOM.

THROUGHOUT THE BATTLE OF THE ATLANTIC THE UNITED STATES ARMY AIR FORCES OVERSEAS CONTINUED TO GROW IN THE URGENT EFFORT TO BUILD OVERWHELMING AIR STRENGTH. THE FIRST AMERICAN STRATEGIC BOMBING MISSION WAS UNDERTAKEN IN AUGUST 1942. BY THE SUMMER OF 1943 THE U. S. EIGHTH AIR FORCE WAS CONDUCTING LARGE-SCALE DAYLIGHT BOMBING ATTACKS; THE ROYAL AIR FORCE CONTINUED TO FLY MISSIONS AT NIGHT. THE OBJECTIVE WAS THE PROGRESSIVE DISLOCATION AND DESTRUCTION OF THE ENEMY'S MILITARY, INDUSTRIAL AND ECONOMIC SYSTEM. EVER PRESENT WAS THE NECESSITY OF BEATING DOWN THE GERMAN FIGHTERS WHICH ATTACKED OUR HEAVY BOMBERS FIERCELY AND PERSISTENTLY.

WITH THE ALLIED LANDINGS IN ITALY IN SEPTEMBER 1943 CAME OPPORTUNITY FOR ATTACK FROM ANOTHER DIRECTION. THE U. S. FIFTEENTH AIR FORCE JOINED WITH THE EIGHTH TO FORM THE U. S. STRATEGIC AIR FORCES IN EUROPE. MASSIVE ATTACKS ON CRITICAL INDUSTRIAL TARGETS FORCED

Exterior of Visitors' Building

THE GERMAN AIR FORCE TO FIGHT FOR THEIR PROTECTION. IN A SERIES OF VIOLENT BATTLES THE ENEMY AIR ARM WAS BROKEN, NEVER AGAIN TO BE A SERIOUS MENACE. IN MARCH 1944 THE U. S. NINTH AIR FORCE AND THE BRITISH SECOND TACTICAL AIR FORCE INITIATED CONCENTRATED ATTACKS ON THE ENEMY'S TRANSPORTATION SYSTEMS AND COASTAL DEFENSES IN BELGIUM AND NORTHERN FRANCE. THE U. S. EIGHTH AIR FORCE, WHILE CONTINUING ITS STRATEGIC ATTACK, AUGMENTED THIS ASSAULT.

ON 6 JUNE 1944, ALLIED FORCES CROSSED THE ENGLISH CHANNEL TO STORM THE BEACHES OF NORMANDY IN THE GREATEST AMPHIBIOUS OPERATION RECORDED IN HISTORY. THE ABSENCE OF SERIOUS NAVAL AND AIR OPPOSITION ATTESTED TO THE EFFECTIVENESS OF ALLIED OPERATIONS DURING THE LONG MONTHS OF PREPARATION THAT HAD PRECEDED THE LANDINGS. FOLLOWING THE SUCCESS OF THIS ASSAULT, THOUSANDS OF MEN AND MILLIONS OF TONS OF SUPPLIES WERE MOVED OVER THESE BEACHES THROUGH ARTIFICIALLY CREATED HARBORS. WITH NAVAL GUNFIRE AND AIR SUPPORT, BEACHHEADS WERE CONSOLIDATED AND THE ALLIED ARMIES MOVED FORWARD.

THROUGH THE REMAINING MONTHS OF THE WAR THE ALLIED MILITARY STRENGTH GREW STEADILY AS TROOPS, EQUIPMENT AND SUPPLIES FLOWED ACROSS THE ATLANTIC. THE COMBINED BOMBER OFFENSIVE CONTINUED TO STRIKE AT STRATEGIC MILITARY AND INDUSTRIAL TARGETS WITH EVER-MOUNTING INTENSITY AS THE GROUND FORCES PUSHED ONWARD INTO GERMANY.

ON 8 MAY 1945, 337 DAYS AFTER THE LANDINGS IN NORMANDY, CAME VICTORY IN EUROPE.

The seals of the War and Navy Departments as well as the principal decorations awarded by our Armed Services are depicted in glass panels beside and above the main door to the Memorial. The decorations shown are listed below:

War Department

Air Medal
Distinguished Flying Cross
Silver Star
Distinguished Service Cross
Medal of Honor — Army
Distinguished Service Medal — Army
Soldier's Medal

Navy Department

Purple Heart
Bronze Star
Legion of Merit
Navy Cross
Medal of Honor — Navy
Distinguished Service Medal — Navy
Navy and Marine Corps Medal

The other windows of the Memorial contain stained-glass replicas of the seals of the States of the Union arranged from left to right, in the order in which they entered the Union. Above them are the seals of the United States (obverse and reverse), the District of Columbia, Alaska, Hawaii and Puerto Rico. Over the teakwood doorway to the chapel is the following inscription in bronze characters: INTO THY HANDS O LORD.

The words FAITH and HOPE in bronze letters are set into the chancel rail in the chapel. A cloth of mail is spread over the Portland stone altar on which rests a large bronze cross. Flanking the altar are two large ornamental candelabra, also embellished with mosaic.

A mosaic by Francis Scott Bradford depicting the Archangel trumpeting the arrival of the Resurrection and the Last Judgment covers the wall above the altar and continues across the entire ceiling of the Memorial, with pictures of ghostly aircraft, accompanied by mourning

Interior of Visitors' Building

angels, making their final flight. The deep blue of the ceiling denotes the depth of infinity, while the lighter colors reflect the light of Heaven breaking through the earthly layers of the sky. The lighter nimbus surrounding each of the single-engine, twin-engine and four-engine aircraft separates them from earthly forces while they carry the souls of the men who perished in the skies. Around the ceiling is the following inscription: IN PROUD AND GRATEFUL MEMORY OF THOSE MEN OF THE UNITED STATES ARMY AIR FORCE WHO FROM THESE FRIENDLY ISLES FLEW THEIR FINAL FLIGHT AND MET THEIR GOD. THEY KNEW NOT THE HOUR THE DAY NOR THE MANNER OF THEIR PASSING. WHEN FAR FROM HOME THEY WERE CALLED TO JOIN THAT HEROIC BAND OF AIRMEN WHO HAD GONE BEFORE. MAY THEY REST IN PEACE.

The ship and aircraft depicted above the altar memorialize the members of the Naval sea and air forces who are buried or commemorated at the cemetery. The Crosses and Star of David symbolize those who are buried beneath the ground. Mourning angels and the inscription from the 23rd Psalm: HE RESTORETH MY SOUL — HE MAKETH ME TO LIE DOWN IN GREEN PASTURES, also enter into the design.

THE WALL OF THE MISSING

The wall is of Portland stone, a limestone quarried on the south coast of England, and is 472 feet in length. Recorded on it are the names and particulars of 5,126 Missing in Action or lost or buried at sea. They come from every State of the Union and the District of Columbia.

United States Army and Army
  Air Forces[1] 3,524
United Sates Navy 1,371
United States Coast Guard   201
United States Marine Corps   30

---

[1] During World War II the Air Forces were part of the Army.

The names of the twenty-four "Unknowns" interred in the cemetery are probably included among those listed on the Wall of the Missing.

At the top of the wall above the names, running its full length, is the following extract from the dedication by President Eisenhower of the *Golden Book* enshrined in St. Paul's Cathedral, London. "THE AMERICANS, WHOSE NAMES HERE APPEAR, WERE PART OF THE PRICE THAT FREE MEN FOR THE SECOND TIME IN THIS CENTURY HAVE BEEN FORCED TO PAY TO DEFEND HUMAN LIBERTY AND RIGHTS. ALL WHO SHALL HEREAFTER LIVE IN FREEDOM WILL BE HERE REMINDED THAT TO THESE MEN AND THEIR COMRADES WE OWE A DEBT TO BE PAID WITH GRATEFUL REMEMBRANCE OF THEIR SACRIFICE AND THE HIGH RESOLVE THAT THE CAUSE FOR WHICH THEY DIED SHALL LIVE ETERNALLY."

Along the wall are four statues designed by Wheeler Williams of New York and carved by English craftsmen, a soldier, a sailor, an airman and a Coast Guardsman. The paving is of English York sandstone.

THE GRAVES AREA

The 3,811 headstones in the fan-shaped graves area are arranged in seven curved grave plots, A-G. The headstones within the plots are aligned in seven rows of concentric arcs whose wide sweep across the green lawns may be best viewed from the mall near the Memorial. From the north edge of the flagpole platform another feature of the pattern is evident — the headstones are also aligned like the spokes of a wheel. Each grave plot is enclosed by a boxwood hedge with tulip trees, catalpa, beech, oak and liquidambar (sweetgum) also present.

These Dead, who gave their lives in our country's service, came from every State in the Union, the District of Columbia, Puerto Rico and the

Philippines. Some also entered the Services from Canada, Chile, Denmark, England, Greece, Holland, Malta, Norway, Panama, Portugal and Scotland. Twenty-four of the headstones mark the graves of "Unknowns."

Among the headstones are two which represent burials of two and three servicemen, respectively, whose names are known but could not be separately identified. Their remains are buried together; bronze tablets over the graves record their names.

VISITORS' BUILDING

Immediately inside the main entrance to the cemetery is the Visitors' Building. It contains the Superintendent's office, toilet facilities and a comfortably furnished room where visitors may obtain information, sign the register and pause to refresh themselves. During visiting hours a member of the cemetery staff is available in the building to answer questions and provide information on burials and memorializations in the Commission's cemeteries, accommodations in the vicinity, travel, local history and other items of interest.

Mosaic Ceiling of Chapel

Soldier

Sailor

Airman

Coast Guardsman

WORLD WAR II
CEMETERIES AND MEMORIALS:

UNITED STATES

East Coast Memorial

LOCATION

The East Coast Memorial is situated in Battery Park near the southern tip of Manhattan Island, New York City. Automobiles may approach to a distance of about 200 yards from the south side of the memorial. The South Ferry subway station some 300 yards distant.

THE SITE

The site covers three-quarters of an acre at the south (New York Bay) edge of Battery Park, between the circular stone structure of Fort Clinton and the United States Coast Guard Headquarters at the tip of the island.

Use of the site was granted to the

East Coast Memorial

East Coast Memorial

American Battle Monuments Commission by the New York City Department of Parks.

ARCHITECTS

Architects for the memorial were Gehron & Seltzer of New York.

GENERAL LAYOUT

The memorial may be reached either by one of the paths running generally parallel with the river, or by following the promenade along the water's edge. The longitudinal axis of the memorial passes through the Statue of Liberty about two miles distant in the upper Bay.

On each side of the Court of Honor are four granite stelae, 19 feet high, of Chelmsford (Massachusetts) gray granite. On these eight slabs are engraved the names, rank, organization and state of 4,596 men of our Armed Services who lost

their lives in the western waters of the Atlantic Ocean during World War II:

United States Army and
  Army Air Forces[1] 1,262
United States Navy 2,985
United States Marine Corps .. 7
United States Coast Guard ... 342

These men gave their lives in the service of their Country, but their remains have not been recovered and identified. Among them are at least four pairs of brothers. The lists include men from every state in the Union except Alaska and Hawaii; the District of Columbia, the Canal Zone, Guam, the Virgin Islands and Canada are also represented.

Near the landward end of the Court of Honor is a bronze eagle 18½ feet high symbolically placing a wreath upon the waters. This eagle which weighs about 5 tons was designed by Albino Manca of New York. The Massachusetts Peerless

A Wreath Laid Upon a Wave

polished black granite base beneath it bears this inscription:

1941–1945 ★ ERECTED BY THE UNITED STATES OF AMERICA IN PROUD AND GRATEFUL REMEMBRANCE OF HER SONS WHO GAVE THEIR LIVES IN HER SERVICE AND WHO SLEEP IN THE AMERICAN COASTAL WATERS OF THE ATLANTIC OCEAN ★ INTO THY HANDS O LORD.

The memorial is enframed by formal planting of London Plane (*Platanus acerifolia*) trees and Euonymus patens hedges; the area is bounded on three sides by Battery Park. A broad flight of steps leads from the Court of Honor to the seawall promenade.

The memorial was completed in 1963 and was dedicated by President John F. Kennedy on 23 May of that year.

Honolulu Memorial,
National
Memorial Cemetery
of the Pacific,
Honolulu, Hawaii

The Honolulu Memorial was erected by the American Battle Monuments Commission at the National Memorial Cemetery of the Pacific, Honolulu, Hawaii in 1964; it was dedicated on 1 May 1966. The Veterans' Administration, Washington, D.C. 20420 administers the cemetery; the American Battle Monuments Commission, Washington, D.C. 20314 administers the Memorial.

LOCATION

The Honolulu Memorial and the National Memorial Cemetery of the Pacific are co-located at 2177 Puowaina Drive, Honolulu, Hawaii 96813. The telephone number at the cemetery is (808) 546-3190. These shrines are easily accessible from the city of Honolulu via bus No. 15, taxi or private or rental car. As the local bus stops outside of the cemetery gate, anyone who has difficulty in walking distances should travel by automobile.

HOURS

The memorial and cemetery are open daily to the public as shown below:
SUMMER (2 March–29 September) 8:00 a.m.–6:30 p.m.
WINTER (30 September–1 March) 8:00 a.m.–5:30 p.m.
Office hours for the cemetery are

Honolulu Memorial

Dedicatory Stone

from 8:00 a.m.–4:30 p.m. weekdays. The office is closed on weekends and holidays. Personnel on duty in the office are available to answer questions concerning the cemetery and the memorial.

THE SITE

The memorial and cemetery, 112.5 acres in extent, are located in Puowaina Crater, an extinct volcano referred to locally as the Punchbowl because of its shape. Roughly translated, Puowaina means "Consecrated Hill" or "Hill of Sacrifice." The Punchbowl was the site of many secret Alii (Royal) burials. It was also the place where offenders of certain kapas (taboos) were sacrificed. In the early 1800's, the crater was an important stronghold for Oahu natives who tried in vain to resist the invading Army of Kamehameha when he unified the Hawaiian Islands in 1810. The kingdom established by Kamehameha existed until Queen Lilioukalani was deposed in 1893.

Puowaina Crater was selected as a permanent cemetery site when major objections were made to the temporary World War II cemetery sites in the central and south Pacific areas. It is one of two hallowed resting places in the vast Pacific for the recovered remains of World War II Dead whose next of kin did not request return of the remains to the continental United States. Nearly 13,000 World War II Dead from the Pacific are buried here. They came from such battle sites as Guadalcanal, China, Burma, Saipan, Guam and Iwo Jima and from the prisoner of war camps in Japan. Also interred in the cemetery are the unidentified remains of 800 U.S. servicemen who died fighting in Korea and the Dead of World War II and the Korean and Vietnam Wars whose next of kin requested that they be buried here.

The other hallowed resting place in the Pacific for World War II Dead is the Manila American Cemetery and Memorial, Fort Bonifacio, Manila, Republic of the Philippines, which is administered by the American Battle Monuments Commission.

ARCHITECTS

Architects for the memorial were Weihe, Frick & Kruse of San Fran-

Interior of Chapel

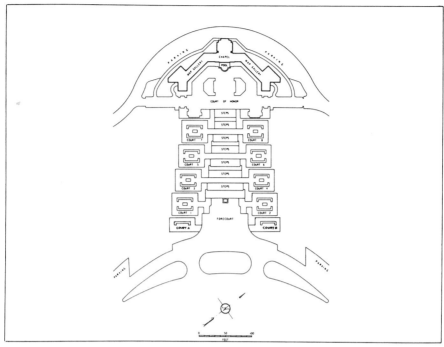

Location of Memorial Features

cisco, assisted locally by Theodore A. Vierra, Architects of Honolulu. The landscape architects were Thompson and Thompson of Honolulu.

THE MEMORIAL

The Honolulu Memorial was erected to honor the sacrifices and achievements of American Armed Forces in the Pacific during World War II and in the Korean War. In 1980, it was enlarged to encompass the Missing of the Vietnam War. Commemorated individually by name on Tablets of the Missing at the memorial are the Missing in Action or lost or buried at sea in the Pacific during World War II, other than the southwest Pacific, and those who were Missing in Action or lost or buried at sea during the Korean and Vietnam Wars. This impressive memorial sits high on the wall of Puowaina Crater overlooking the graves area of the National Memorial Cemetery of the Pacific. It consists of a nonsectarian chapel, two map galleries — one extending laterally from each side of the chapel and two flagpoles in a Court of Honor; a monumental stairway leading from the crater floor to the Court of Honor; ten courts of the Missing, five flanking each side of the stairway and a Dedicatory Stone centered at the base of the stairway. Engraved upon the Dedicatory Stone is this inscription:

IN THESE GARDENS ARE RECORDED THE NAMES OF AMERICANS WHO GAVE THEIR LIVES IN THE SERVICE OF THEIR COUNTRY AND WHOSE EARTHLY RESTING PLACE IS KNOWN ONLY TO GOD.

THE COURTS OF THE MISSING

On the tablets of the Courts of the Missing (eight full courts and two

Courts of the Missing

half courts) are engraved the names of 28,778 American heroes. Each of them was Missing in Action (MIA) or lost or buried at sea in the Pacific during World War II (but not the southwest Pacific — its Missing in Action are commemorated by name at the Manila American Cemetery and Memorial, Republic of the Philippines), in the Korean War or in the Vietnam War. Unlike the MIA's of World War II, the names of all of the Missing in Action or lost or buried at sea of the Korean and Vietnam Wars are recorded here in one place. These MIA's came from every State of the Union and the District of Columbia, Puerto Rico, the Panama Canal Zone, Guam, the Philippines, Mexico, Canada and Samoa. It is noted that the names of those identified servicemen and women whose remains are buried in the cemetery do not appear on the Courts of the Missing.

The names of the Missing are arranged in alphabetical order by military service as follows (Courts are numbered 1 through 8 and A and B as shown on the plan of the memorial):

World War II	Courts	Names
United States Army and Air Forces[1]	7, 5	3,947
United States Navy	5, 3, 1, 2	11,743
United States Marine Corps	2, 4	2,370
United States Coast Guard	4	34
		18,094
Korea		
United States Army	4, 6, 8	6,324
United States Navy	8	289
United States Marine Corps	8	663
United States Air Force	8	919
		8,195
Vietnam		
United States Army	B	706
United States Navy	B	516
United States Marine Corps	A	295
United States Air Force	A	971
United States Coast Guard	B	1
		2,489

[1] During World War II the Air Forces still formed part of the United States Army.

Half Court "A", Vietnam War

The Trani stone tablets of the eight full Courts where the names of the Missing appear were quarried in southeastern Italy. In the center of each Court is a frangipani tree *(Plumeria acuminata)* surrounded by low *Ficus ramentacea.* On the stairway side of the Courts are allspice *(Pimenta acres)* trees surrounded by allamanda *(Allamanda cathartica);* on the outer sides of the Courts is a hedge of orange jessimine *(Murraya exotica)* and rainbow shower *(Cassia fistula* and *javanica)* and Chinese banyan *(Ficus retusa)* trees. At the top of the slope are beds of cup of gold *(Solandra guttata)* and star jasmine *(Jasminum pubescens).* Flanking the open area at the base of the stairway below the full Courts of the Missing are two half Courts on which are engraved the names of the MIA's of the Vietnam War. Centered on the wall of the half Court on the right facing the graves area (B Court) is the following inscription:

IN PROUD MEMORY OF THE ACHIEVEMENTS OF HER SONS AND IN HUMBLE TRIBUTE TO THEIR SACRIFICES THIS MEMORIAL HAS BEEN ERECTED BY THE UNITED STATES OF AMERICA.

* * *

THESE MEN WERE PART OF THE PRICE THAT FREE MEN HAVE BEEN FORCED TO PAY TO DEFEND HUMAN LIBERTY AND RIGHTS. TO THESE MEN WE OWE A DEBT TO BE PAID WITH GRATEFUL REMEMBRANCE OF THEIR HEROISM.

On the wall above the inscription are two sculptured angels holding a laurel wreath in the center of which is a replica of the Great Seal of the United States.

To the left of the central inscription on B Court appear these words:

1950 ⋆ 1953
DURING THE KOREAN CONFLICT 36,923 AMERICANS GAVE THEIR LIVES IN THE CAUSE OF LIBERTY FOR OTHER PEOPLE. GRANT UNTO THEM O LORD ETERNAL

Central Inscription, Half Court "B", Vietnam War

REST WHO SLEEP IN UNKNOWN GRAVES. OUR RELIANCE IS IN THE LOVE OF LIBERTY WHICH GOD HAS PLANTED IN US.

To the right of the central inscription on B Court appears these words:

1961 ★ 1973

IN THE LONGEST CONFLICT IN AMERICAN HISTORY 57,704 PAID THE LAST SACRIFICE SERVING THEIR COUNTRY IN VIETNAM IN THE CAUSE OF FREEDOM

★

THIS MEMORIAL IS A SACRED RENDEZVOUS OF A GRATEFUL PEOPLE WITH ITS IMMORTAL DEAD

★

TIME SHALL NOT DIM THE GLORY OF THEIR DEEDS

Centered on the wall of the half Court facing the graves area on the left (A Court) is the following inscription:

THIS MEMORIAL HAS BEEN ERECTED BY THE UNITED STATES OF AMERICA IN PROUD AND GRATEFUL MEMORY OF HER SOLDIERS SAILORS MARINES AND AIRMEN WHO LAID DOWN THEIR LIVES IN ALL QUARTERS OF THE EARTH THAT OTHER PEOPLES MIGHT BE FREED FROM OPPRESSION

To the left of the central inscription on A Court appear these words:

★ IN 1923 ★

THE CONGRESS OF THE UNITED STATES CREATED THE AMERICAN BATTLE MONUMENTS COMMISSION TO WORTHILY HONOR HER SONS WHO PAID THE LAST SACRIFICE IN THE SERVICE OF THEIR COUNTRY ON FOREIGN SOIL

★

LET US HERE HIGHLY RESOLVE THAT THESE HONORED DEAD SHALL NOT HAVE DIED IN VAIN

Interior of Court of the Missing

To the right of the central inscription on A Court appear these words:

1941 ★ 1945
IN WORLD WAR II 360,845 AMERICANS GAVE THEIR LIVES IN THE SERVICE OF THEIR COUNTRY

★

THEY FACED THE FOE AS THEY DREW NEAR HIM IN THE STRENGTH OF THEIR MANHOOD AND WHEN THE SHOCK OF BATTLE CAME THEY IN A MOMENT OF TIME AT THE CLIMAX OF THEIR LIVES WERE RAPT AWAY FROM A WORLD FILLED FOR THEIR DYING EYES NOT WITH TERROR BUT WITH GLORY

COURT OF HONOR

The Court of Honor contains the chapel; two map galleries, one extending laterally from each side of the central tower housing the chapel; two flagpoles; two planting pockets in the center of the forecourt containing *Filicium decepiens* trees and *Allamanda* ground cover; a small pool with water jets at the foot of the tower housing the chapel; and two planting pockets flanking the pool. The floor of the court is paved with porphyry stone.

On the front of the tower housing the chapel is a 30-foot female figure standing on the symbolized prow of a U.S. Navy carrier with a laurel branch in her left hand. Engraved below the figure is the poignant sympathy expressed by President Lincoln to Mrs. Bixby, mother of five sons who had died in battle; . . . "THE SOLEMN PRIDE THAT MUST BE YOURS TO HAVE LAID SO COSTLY A SACRIFICE UPON THE ALTAR OF FREEDOM." The female figure was designed by Bruce Moore of Washington, D.C. as were the eagles over the entrances to the structure. Fillippo Cecchetti of Tivoli and Ugo Quaglieri of Rome, Italy carved the sculpture under the direction of Mr. Moore.

MAP GALLERIES

The map galleries extend from the right and left sides of the tower. Inscribed upon the frieze of the galleries are the names of places which attained notable significance in the proud record of our Armed Forces: PEARL HARBOR ★ WAKE ★ CORAL SEA ★

MIDWAY ★ ATTU ★ SOLOMONS ★ GILBERTS ★ MARSHALLS ★ MARIANAS ★ LEYTE ★ IWO JIMA ★ OKINAWA ★ TOKYO ★ KOREA.

The original maps in the galleries, each ten feet high, were designed by Richard and Carlotta (Gonzales) Lahey of Vienna, Virginia from data prepared for that purpose by the American Battle Monuments Commission. They were of scagliola, i.e. paintings on a special composition applied to Carrara marble surface and glazed. Although scagliola had been used for centuries as one of the decorative fine arts in Italy, it did not withstand the humid climate in Hawaii and the maps were replaced during the period 1968-1972. The new maps of precast tinted mosaic concrete and colored glass aggregate were designed by Mrs. Mary Morse Hamilton Jacobs of Glenelg, Maryland. Early Studios of Manassas, Virginia fabricated the maps under

Chapel Tower

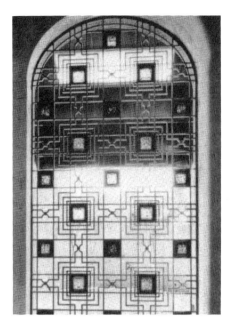

Chapel Window Grill with Cabochons

Mrs. Jacobs' supervision. The titles of the maps and their amplifying inscriptions are as follows:

OPERATIONS IN THE PACIFIC
1942–1945

1. EXPLOITING THEIR SUCCESSFUL ATTACK UPON PEARL HARBOR ON 7 DECEMBER 1941, THE JAPANESE STRUCK AT AMERICAN, BRITISH, CHINESE AND DUTCH TERRITORIES. THE UNITED STATES, FORCED INITIALLY UPON THE DEFENSIVE, NEVERTHELESS DETERMINED TO HOLD OPEN THE LINE OF COMMUNICATIONS TO AUSTRALIA, TO AID IN ITS DEFENSE, AND TO REGAIN HER STATUS IN THE PHILIPPINES. IN MAY AND JUNE 1942 THE ENEMY WAS CHECKED AT THE BATTLES OF THE CORAL SEA AND MIDWAY AND THE BALANCE OF SEA POWER IN THE PACIFIC WAS RESTORED.

2. TO HALT THE JAPANESE ADVANCE IN THE SOLOMONS, U.S. FORCES TOOK THE OFFENSIVE, LANDING ON GUADALCANAL ON 7 AUGUST 1942. THE SUCCESSION OF HARD-FOUGHT NAVAL BATTLES AND GRIM STRUGGLES ON LAND AND IN THE AIR WHICH FOLLOWED MARKED THE TURNING POINT OF THE PACIFIC WAR. IN SOUTHEASTERN NEW GUINEA, U.S. AND AUSTRALIAN FORCES REPULSED THE JAPANESE AND STARTED ON THE LONG ROAD BACK TO THE PHILIPPINES. SUPPLIES FLOWN FROM INDIA OVER THE HIMALAYAS AIDED THE CHINESE EFFORT AGAINST THE INVADERS.

3. SUBMARINES PERSISTENTLY ATTACKED JAPANESE SHIPS CARRYING OIL, RUBBER AND OTHER MATERIALS ESSENTIAL TO THE ENEMY'S INDUSTRY. RELENTLESS ASSAULT AGAINST HIS COMBAT AND MERCHANT SHIPS, FROM THE SEA AND FROM THE AIR, CONTINUED WITH EVER-INCREASING ATTRITION THROUGHOUT THE WAR.

4. TO PENETRATE THE ENEMY'S DEFENSES AND GAIN BASES FROM WHICH AIRCRAFT COULD STRIKE AT THE JAPANESE HOME ISLANDS, THE UNITED STATES IN 1943 COMMITTED ITS FORCES IN A SUCCESSION OF TRIPHIBIOUS ASSAULTS ALONG TWO MAIN AXES OF ADVANCE. ONE THRUST CONTINUED THE ATTACKS NORTHWESTWARD SIMULTANEOUSLY THROUGH THE SOLOMONS AND ALONG THE COAST OF NEW GUINEA; THE OTHER CROSSED THE VAST REACHES OF THE CENTRAL PACIFIC VIA THE GILBERT AND MARSHALL ISLANDS, THEN THE MARIANAS (BRINGING ON THE BATTLE OF THE PHILIPPINE SEA) AND THE PALAUS. FAR TO THE NORTH OTHER AMERICAN FORCES EXPELLED THE ENEMY FROM THE ALEUTIANS. IN BURMA ALLIED FORCES FOUGHT TO REOPEN THE OVERLAND SUPPLY ROUTE TO CHINA AND STIMULATE HER EFFORTS TO EJECT THE JAPANESE.

5. AFTER THE CAPTURE OF THE MARIANAS, BOMBERS FROM THESE ISLANDS JOINED THE ASSAULT ON JAPAN, ALREADY STARTED FROM AIRFIELDS IN CHINA, WHICH DEVELOPED INTO CONTINUAL AND VIOLENT BOMBARDMENT AIMED AT THE DESTRUCTION OF THE ENEMY'S MILITARY AND INDUSTRIAL SYSTEMS.

6. THE LANDING AT LEYTE IN OC-

Map Gallery

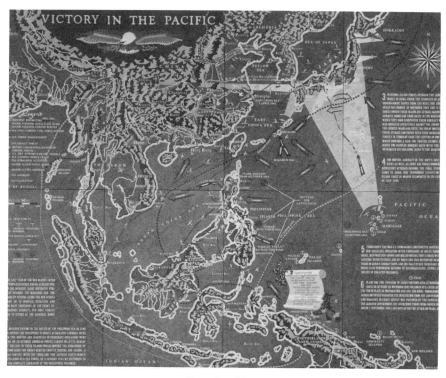

Operations Map

TOBER 1944 LED TO THE DECISIVE NAVAL VICTORIES AT LEYTE GULF. LANDINGS ON LUZON, IWO JIMA AND OKINAWA FOLLOWED IN RAPID SUCCESSION CARRYING AMERICAN FORCES TO THE ENEMY'S THRESHOLD. FAST CARRIER TASK FORCES COMING FROM THE CENTRAL PACIFIC JOINED IN THE BOMBARDMENT OF JAPAN WHILE WARSHIPS SHELLED HER COASTAL STATIONS. FOLLOWING THE DEVASTATION FROM THE AIR OF HIROSHIMA AND NAGASAKI, THE JAPANESE GOVERNMENT SUED FOR PEACE; THE SURRENDER TERMS WERE SIGNED IN TOKYO BAY ON 2 SEPTEMBER 1945.

BATTLE OF THE CORAL SEA
4–8 MAY 1942

BY MID-APRIL 1942, THE JAPANESE HAD ESTABLISHED BASES IN THE NEW GUINEA–SOLOMON ISLANDS AREA, THUS MENACING AUSTRALIA ITSELF. ON 3 MAY THEY OCCUPIED TULAGI, IN THE SOLOMONS. AIRCRAFT FROM THE U.S. CARRIER YORKTOWN ATTACKED TULAGI THE NEXT DAY SINKING AN ENEMY DESTROYER, SEVERAL MINESWEEPERS, SMALLER CRAFT AND SEAPLANES. THE YORKTOWN TASK FORCE THEN TURNED SOUTH TO RENDEZVOUS WITH U.S.S. LEXINGTON. ON 5 MAY THE ALLIED TASK FORCE MOVED NORTHWEST TO INTERCEPT THE JAPANESE PORT MORESBY INVASION GROUP WHICH WAS COVERED BY A POWERFUL AIRCRAFT CARRIER STRIKING FORCE.

ON 7 MAY, LEXINGTON AND YORKTOWN AIRCRAFT SANK THE ENEMY CARRIER SHOHO; THE JAPANESE THEN WITHDREW THEIR AMPHIBIOUS INVASION FORCE. THAT SAME MORNING JAPANESE CARRIER AIRCRAFT SANK DESTROYER SIMS AND DAMAGED OILER NEOSHO SO BADLY THAT SHE HAD TO BE SCUTTLED. THE CLIMACTIC CARRIER BATTLE OCCURRED ON 8 MAY. AMERICAN CARRIER AIRCRAFT, HAVING LOCATED TWO LARGE JAPANESE

CARRIERS, SHOKAKU AND ZUIKAKU, PROTECTED BY FOUR HEAVY CRUISERS, SEVERELY DAMAGED THE SHOKAKU. THE ENEMY IN TURN DAMAGED YORKTOWN AND LEXINGTON, THE LATTER BEING ABANDONED AND SUNK.

THE BATTLE OF THE CORAL SEA, THE FIRST MAJOR NAVAL BATTLE IN WHICH ALL LOSSES WERE INFLICTED BY CARRIER-BASED AIRCRAFT WAS A STRATEGIC VICTORY OF THE FIRST MAGNITUDE FOR THE U.S. NAVY. WHEN THE PORT MORESBY INVASION WAS THWARTED THE JAPANESE PUSH SOUTHWARDS WAS HALTED FOR THE FIRST TIME. OCCURRING IMMEDIATELY AFTER THE SURRENDER OF COR-REGIDOR, THE MORAL VALUE OF THE VICTORY WAS IMMEASURABLE. FURTHERMORE, DAMAGE TO SHOKAKU AND LARGE LOSS OF AIRCRAFT BY ZUIKAKU PREVENTED THESE POWERFUL JAPANESE CARRIERS FROM PARTICIPAT-ING IN THE CRUCIAL BATTLE OF MID-WAY.

BATTLE OF MIDWAY ★ 3–7 JUNE 1942

WHEN THEIR ADVANCE TOWARD AUSTRALIA WAS CHECKED AT THE BAT-TLE OF THE CORAL SEA, THE JAPANESE SHIFTED THE DIRECTION OF THEIR MAIN OFFENSIVE. ENEMY OCCUPATION FORCES, SUPPORTED BY THE JAPANESE COMBINED FLEET, MOVED AGAINST MIDWAY ISLAND, AND KISKA AND ATTU IN THE WESTERN ALEUTIANS. ON 4 JUNE AIRCRAFT FROM FOUR JAPANESE FLEET CARRIERS ATTACKED MIDWAY. IN ITS DEFENSE U.S. MARINE CORPS AN-TIAIRCRAFT BATTERIES, AND LAND-BASED AIRCRAFT MANNED BY MARINE, NAVY AND ARMY AIR FORCE PILOTS, DESTROYED MORE THAN 40 JAPANESE AIRPLANES, THEREUPON NAVAL AIR-CRAFT FROM U.S. CARRIERS ENTER-PRISE, YORKTOWN AND HORNET AT-TACKED THE JAPANESE CARRIERS AND SANK FOUR OF THEM. ENEMY CARRIER-BASED AIRCRAFT AND A SUB-MARINE IN TURN ATTACKED OUR CAR-RIERS AND SANK YORKTOWN AND DE-STROYER HAMMANN. THE AGGRESSIVE

AMERICAN AIR RESISTANCE CAUSED THE JAPANESE MIDWAY OCCUPATION FORCE TO WITHDRAW WITHOUT AT-TEMPTING TO LAND, LOSING A CRUISER IN THE OPERATION.

FAR TO THE NORTH, JAPANESE AIR-PLANES FROM TWO OTHER CARRIERS BOMBED DUTCH HARBOR ON 3 and 4 JUNE, MEETING RESISTANCE FROM U.S. NAVAL AND ARMY AIR FORCES AIR-CRAFT. UNDER COVER OF THIS DIVER-SION THE JAPANESE, WITHOUT OPPOSI-TION, OCCUPIED THE ISLANDS OF ATTU AND KISKA ON 7 JUNE.

THE JAPANESE LOSS OF FOUR LARGE AIRCRAFT CARRIERS AND THEIR COM-PLEMENT OF 250 AIRCRAFT WITH MANY FIRST-LINE PILOTS REVERSED THE STRATEGIC SITUATION IN THE PACIFIC. THIS WAS THE ENEMY'S LAST GREAT OFFENSIVE AGAINST AMERICAN TER-RITORY. THEREAFTER THE UNITED STATES TOOK THE OFFENSIVE AND STARTED THE LONG ADVANCE TO-WARD THE JAPANESE HOMELAND AND FINAL VICTORY.

NEW GUINEA AND THE SOLOMONS
4 MAY 1942–30 SEPTEMBER 1944

REACTING TO THEIR DEFEATS AT THE BATTLES OF THE CORAL SEA AND MID-WAY IN MAY AND JUNE 1942 WHICH RE-STORED THE BALANCE OF SEA POWER IN THE PACIFIC OCEAN, THE JAPANESE AIMED AT NEW GUINEA AND THE SOL-OMONS AS THEIR NEW OBJECTIVES. ON 21 JULY, THEY SEIZED BUNA AND GONA IN EASTERN NEW GUINEA, THEN CROSSED THE OWEN STANLEY RANGE TO WITHIN 30 MILES OF PORT MORESBY. THE JAPANESE ALSO STARTED TO BUILD AN AIRFIELD ON GUADALCANAL.

TO BLOCK THE ADVANCE IN THE SOLOMONS WHICH THREATENED OUR VITAL SUPPLY LINE TO AUSTRALIA, U.S. FORCES TOOK THE OFFENSIVE, LAND-ING ON GUADALCANAL AND TULAGI ON 7 AUGUST 1942. THE ENEMY RE-SPONSE WAS PROMPT AND VIGOROUS. THE SERIES OF HARD-FOUGHT NAVAL BATTLES AND GRIM STRUGGLES ON LAND AND IN THE AIR WHICH FOL-LOWED MARKED THE EBBING OF THE

JAPANESE ONSLAUGHT, ALTHOUGH THEIR TENACIOUS OPPOSITION FORCED US TO REINFORCE OUR LAND, SEA, AND AIR FORCES HEAVILY. SIX LONG MONTHS PASSED BEFORE AMERICAN TROOPS OVERRAN THE LAST JAPANESE POSITIONS ON GUADALCANAL.

SIMULTANEOUSLY, IN NEW GUINEA, THE AUSTRALIANS DROVE THE ENEMY BACK TO HIS BUNA-GONA BEACHHEAD AND DEFEATED ANOTHER JAPANESE FORCE AT MILNE BAY. AUSTRALIAN AND AMERICAN TROOPS THEN EX-PELLED THE JAPANESE FROM THEIR BEACHHEAD, AIDED BY THE ALLIED AIR FORCES WHICH BOTH TRANSPORTED TROOPS AND SUPPLIES AND ALSO CONSTANTLY BOMBARDED THE ENEMY.

DURING THE LAST WEEK OF JANUARY 1943, AIR-TRANSPORTED AUSTRALIAN TROOPS REPULSED A THRUST AT WAU. IN MARCH, IN THE BATTLE OF THE BIS-MARCK SEA, U.S. AND AUSTRALIAN AIRCRAFT EXECUTED AN ANNIHILAT-ING ATTACK ON A JAPANESE CONVOY ATTEMPTING TO REINFORCE THEIR NEW GUINEA GARRISONS. IN JUNE, THE AL-LIES LAUNCHED HEAVY AIR ASSAULTS AGAINST THE STRONGHOLDS OF RABAUL AND KAVIENG; AFTER OCCUPY-ING WOODLARK AND KIRIWINA IS-LANDS THEY OPENED SIMULTANEOUS AMPHIBIOUS OFFENSIVES IN THE SOL-OMONS AND NEW GUINEA. SEIZING RENDOVA, U.S. FORCES ASSAULTED NEW GEORGIA AND, AFTER A SEVERE STRUGGLE, CAPTURED THE ENEMY AIR-FIELD AT MUNDA, THEN MOVED ON VELLA LAVELLA. IN NEW GUINEA AUS-TRALIAN AND U.S. FORCES CAPTURED SALAMAUA, LAE, AND FINSCHHAFEN. PRECEDED BY DIVERSIONARY ATTACKS ON CHOISEUL AND THE TREASURY IS-LANDS, AMERICAN FORCES NEXT LANDED ON BOUGAINVILLE; LAND-INGS ON NEW BRITAIN AND AT SAIDOR, NEW GUINEA FOLLOWED. THE ENCIR-CLEMENT OF RABAUL WAS COMPLETED WHEN OUR TROOPS SEIZED THE AD-MIRALTIES IN FEBRUARY AND OC-CUPIED EMIRAU IN MARCH 1944. MEANWHILE A MAJOR COUNTEROF-FENSIVE AGAINST OUR BOUGAINVILLE BEACHHEAD WAS REPULSED.

IN ORDER TO SPEED THE WESTWARD ADVANCE IN NEW GUINEA IT WAS NOW DECIDED TO BYPASS THE STRONG JAPANESE BASE AT WEWAK BY LEAP-FROGGING SOME 350 MILES TO HOL-LANDIA, WITH A SECONDARY LANDING AT AITAPE TO THE EAST; HERE A SEVERE STRUGGLE ENSUED. THEN, WHILE AUS-TRALIAN TROOPS CONTINUED THE AD-VANCE ON LAND, U.S. ARMY TROOPS, IN CLOSE TEAMWORK WITH U.S. NAVAL AND AIR FORCES, SEIZED WAKDE, BIAK, NOEMFOOR, SANSAPOR, AND MORO-TAI IN RAPID SUCCESSION. BY THE END OF SEPTEMBER 1944, OUR FORCES WERE POISED FOR THE RETURN TO THE PHILIPPINES.

ATTU ★ 11–30 MAY 1943

DURING THE BATTLE OF MIDWAY IN JUNE 1942 JAPANESE AIRCRAFT AT-TACKED DUTCH HARBOR; THE ENEMY THEN OCCUPIED ATTU AND KISKA TO BLOCK A POSSIBLE AMERICAN AD-VANCE. IN AUGUST AMERICAN FORCES STARTED WESTWARD ALONG THE ALEUTIAN CHAIN, CONSTRUCTING AIRFIELDS AND NAVAL BASES. DESPITE PERSISTENTLY HAZARDOUS WEATHER U.S. NAVAL FORCES, THE ELEVENTH AIR FORCE, AND CANADIAN AIRCRAFT AT-TACKED THE ENEMY AT EVERY OPPOR-TUNITY. JAPANESE EFFORTS TO SEND REINFORCEMENTS WERE HALTED AT THE NAVAL BATTLE OF THE KOMAN-DORSKI ISLANDS, WEST OF ATTU, ON 26 MARCH 1943.

BYPASSING KISKA, THE U.S. NAVY NORTH PACIFIC FORCE SAILED FOR ATTU, A MOUNTAINOUS ISLAND 40 MILES LONG BY 15 MILES WIDE. ON 11 MAY THE REINFORCED 7TH INFANTRY DIVISION LANDED NORTH AND SOUTH OF THE JAPANESE, WHO HELD ONLY THE EAST END OF THE ISLAND. THE TROOPS MADE GOOD PROGRESS ASHORE IN SPITE OF FOG, TREACHER-OUS TUNDRA, AND PRECIPITOUS SNOW-COVERED MOUNTAINS, UNTIL THEY ENCOUNTERED STIFF RESISTANCE ON BOTH FRONTS. ALTHOUGH SUP-PORTED BY NAVAL GUNFIRE, AND BY ARMY AND NAVY AIRCRAFT WHENEVER THE WEATHER PERMITTED, THE AD-VANCE WAS COSTLY AND DIFFICULT.

FINALLY ON 16 MAY THE NORTHERN FORCE BROKE THROUGH THE SKILLFUL, DETERMINED DEFENSE. THEREUPON OUR INFANTRY CAPTURED PRENDER-GAST AND GILBERT RIDGES, THEN SEIZED POSITIONS ON FISHHOOK RIDGE. ON THE NIGHT OF 28–29 MAY, THE ENEMY PUSHED A SUICIDAL COUN-TERATTACK 3½ MILES THROUGH A GAP IN THE LINES UNTIL HALTED BY U.S. ARMY ENGINEERS AND ARTILLERYMEN; ORGANIZED RESISTANCE ENDED ON 30 MAY.

THE STRATEGIC SOUNDNESS OF BYPASSING KISKA WAS THEN DEMON-STRATED. WHEN AMERICANS AND CANADIANS LANDED ON THAT ISLAND ON 15 AUGUST, THE JAPANESE HAD AL-READY DEPARTED.

BATTLE FOR TARAWA ATOLL
20–23 NOVEMBER 1943

TOWARD THE END OF 1943 THE UNITED STATES COMMITTED ITS FORCES IN AN ADVANCE ACROSS THE CENTRAL PACIFIC TO CONVERGE WITH ITS THRUSTS THROUGH NEW GUINEA AND THE SOLOMONS. THE INITIAL EF-FORT WAS AGAINST MAKIN AND TARAWA IN THE GILBERT ISLANDS, TO GAIN BASES FOR AN ATTACK ON THE MARSHALLS. FAST CARRIER STRIKES BY THE FIFTH FLEET AND BOMBING AT-TACKS BY THE SEVENTH AIR FORCE, WHICH HAD BEEN STARTED DURING THE SUMMER, WERE INTENSIFIED IN PREPARATION FOR THE ASSAULT. ON 20 NOVEMBER, USING ITS FIRE SUPPORT, THE NORTHERN ATTACK FORCE LANDED THE 165TH AND ELEMENTS OF THE 105TH INFANTRY REGIMENTS OF THE ARMY'S 27TH DIVISION ON MAKIN. OVERCOMING STUBBORN DEFENSE THE TROOPS SECURED THE ATOLL.

SIMULTANEOUSLY THE SOUTHERN ATTACK FORCE, LIKEWISE COVERED BY NAVAL AND AERIAL BOMBARDMENT, LANDED FIVE BATTALIONS OF THE 2D AND 8TH REGIMENTS OF THE 2D MARINE DIVISION ON BETIO, THE STRONGHOLD OF TARAWA ATOLL. THE CHAIN OF PILLBOXES, GUN EMPLACEMENTS AND

RIFLE PITS HAD NOT BEEN DESTROYED BY THE BOMBARDMENT AND THE DE-FENDERS TOOK A HEAVY TOLL OF ALL WHO APPROACHED THE ISLAND. BY NIGHTFALL TWO SMALL BEACHHEADS HAD BEEN ESTABLISHED ON THE NORTH SHORE.

REINFORCED ON 21 NOVEMBER, THE MARINES FOUGHT THEIR WAY ACROSS THE ISLAND. ON THE FOLLOWING DAY THE 6TH MARINES, FROM THEIR WEST-ERN LANDING BEACH, ADVANCED ALONG THE SOUTH SHORE TO LINK UP WITH THE 2D, AND THEN IN COOPERA-TION WITH THE 8TH, TO EXTEND THE FRONTLINE TO THE EASTERN EDGE OF THE AIRFIELD. ON 23 NOVEMBER, THE 2D DIVISION CLEARED THE REMAINDER OF THE ISLAND.

ROI-NAMUR ★ 1–2 FEBRUARY 1944

EVEN BEFORE THE AMPHIBIOUS AS-SAULTS UPON THE GILBERT ISLANDS WERE LAUNCHED, THE NEXT STEP IN THE CENTRAL PACIFIC ADVANCE, THE AIR ATTACK UPON THE MARSHALL IS-LANDS, WAS INITIATED. AS EARLY AS NOVEMBER 1943 AIRCRAFT OF THE SEVENTH AIR FORCE AND CARRIER-BASED AIRPLANES OF THE FIFTH FLEET STARTED THE PRELIMINARY BOM-BARDMENT OF THE MARSHALLS; IN DE-CEMBER AND JANUARY THE ATTACKS WERE PROGRESSIVELY INTENSIFIED.

ON 29 JANUARY 1944 FIRE SUPPORT UNITS OF THE FIFTH FLEET JOINED IN THE BOMBARDMENT OF ROI AND NAMUR, THE TWIN NORTHERNMOST IS-LANDS OF KWAJALEIN ATOLL. THEN ON 31 JANUARY THE SIX ISLETS TO THE SOUTH OF, AND CLOSEST TO ROI AND NAMUR, WERE SEIZED BY THE 25TH MARINES OF THE 4TH MARINE DIVISION WHICH EMPLACED ARTILLERY TO FIRE IN SUPPORT OF THE MAIN ATTACK.

ON 1 FEBRUARY, THE 23D MARINES LANDED ON ROI WHILE THE 24TH MARINES LANDED ON NAMUR. OVER-COMING THE JAPANESE GARRISON THE 23D MARINES PUSHED FORWARD AND CAPTURED ROI BEFORE NIGHTFALL. THE 24TH MARINES ENCOUNTERED

MUCH STRONGER RESISTANCE ON NAMUR AND THEIR ADVANCE WAS STOPPED AFTER THEY HAD ESTABLISHED A BEACHHEAD 500 YARDS DEEP. ON 2 FEBRUARY, THEY RESUMED THE ATTACK WITH RENEWED AGGRESSIVENESS AND EARLY IN THE AFTERNOON NAMUR WAS DECLARED SECURE.

KWAJALEIN ISLAND
1–4 FEBRUARY 1944

TO THE SOUTH, ARMY AND NAVAL AIRCRAFT COOPERATED IN THE PRELIMINARY BOMBARDMENT OF KWAJALEIN, THE LARGEST ISLAND IN THE ATOLL, AS THEY HAD AGAINST ROI AND NAMUR IN THE NORTH. HERE, TOO, THE SHIPS OF THE FIFTH FLEET TOOK THE ISLAND UNDER HEAVY FIRE COMMENCING ON 30 JANUARY 1944. THE NEXT DAY THE 17TH INFANTRY OF THE 7TH DIVISION SEIZED FOUR ISLETS TO THE NORTH OF KWAJALEIN, AND ARTILLERY WAS EMPLACED.

ON 1 FEBRUARY, COVERED BY ARMY AND NAVAL AIR SUPPORT, GUNFIRE OF THE SHIPS, AND BY ITS OWN ARTILLERY, THE 7TH DIVISION LANDED ITS 32D AND 184TH INFANTRY REGIMENTS ON THE NARROW WESTERN END OF KWAJALEIN. THE TWO REGIMENTS ADVANCED STEADILY AND BY NIGHTFALL HAD ESTABLISHED A BEACHHEAD ALMOST A MILE DEEP. THE ATTACK CONTINUED ON THE TWO SUCCEEDING DAYS AGAINST INCREASING RESISTANCE, WHICH WAS FINALLY BEATEN DOWN; CAPTURE OF THE ISLAND WAS COMPLETED ON THE AFTERNOON OF 4 FEBRUARY. THE REMAINING ISLETS COMPRISING KWAJALEIN ATOLL WERE TAKEN BY 5 FEBRUARY. IN THE MEANTIME OUR FORCES LANDED ON MAJURO ATOLL IN THE SOUTHEASTERN PART OF THE GROUP.

IN THE WESTERN MARSHALLS, BETWEEN 17 AND 22 FEBRUARY, THE 22D MARINES WITH THE 106TH INFANTRY OF THE 27TH DIVISION TOOK ENIWETOK ATOLL, BRINGING OUR FORCES CLOSER TO THE NEXT OBJECTIVE, THE MARIANAS. THE JALUIT, MILLE, MALOELAP, AND WOTJE ATOLLS OF THE MARSHALL ISLANDS WERE BYPASSED AND REMAINED IN JAPANESE HANDS UNTIL THE END OF THE WAR.

THE MARIANAS
15 JUNE–10 AUGUST 1944

1. TO PENETRATE THE ENEMY'S DEFENSES AND GAIN BASES FROM WHICH AIRCRAFT COULD STRIKE AT THE JAPANESE HOME ISLANDS, THE UNITED STATES UNDERTOOK TO SEIZE THE MARIANA ISLANDS IN THE SUMMER OF 1944. FOR SEVERAL MONTHS PRIOR TO THE LANDINGS, FAST CARRIER TASK FORCES AND AIRCRAFT OF THE SEVENTH AIR FORCE CONDUCTED PRELIMINARY BOMBARDMENTS OF THE TARGET AREA.

2. ON 15 JUNE 1944, UNDER COVER OF AIR AND NAVAL BOMBARDMENT BY THE FIFTH FLEET, THE 2D AND 4TH MARINE DIVISIONS OF THE V AMPHIBIOUS CORPS LANDED ON SAIPAN. THE JAPANESE REACTION WAS IMMEDIATE AND VIGOROUS; THEIR CARRIER TASK FORCE STEAMED TOWARD THE MARIANAS TO MEET THE AMERICAN AMPHIBIOUS EFFORT. IN THE ACTION THAT FOLLOWED, THE BATTLE OF THE PHILIPPINE SEA ON 19–20 JUNE, JAPANESE CARRIER AVIATION WAS SUBSTANTIALLY IMPAIRED AS A MAJOR FORCE IN THE WAR.

3. MEANWHILE THE MARINES AND THE ARMY'S 27TH INFANTRY DIVISION FOUGHT THEIR WAY ACROSS THE ISLAND AGAINST DETERMINED RESISTANCE. THEY THEN TURNED NORTHWARD AND SEIZED THE DOMINATING HEIGHTS OF MT. TAPOTCHAU ON 25 AND 26 JUNE. ON THE LATTER NIGHT AN ENEMY ATTEMPT TO BREAK OUT OF HIS ISOLATED POSITION ON NAFUTAN POINT WAS DECISIVELY DEFEATED. AMERICAN FORCES CONTINUED TO PRESS THE ATTACK AGAINST THE MASS OF THE ENEMY, SLOWLY FORCING HIM NORTHWARD. FINALLY, ON THE NIGHT OF 6–7 JULY, THE JAPANESE MADE A DESPERATE LAST EFFORT; THEIR FURIOUS ASSAULT WAS REPULSED AND

TWO DAYS LATER THE ISLAND WAS DE-
CLARED SECURE.

4. ON 24 JULY, AFTER A LENGTHY
PREPARATORY BOMBARDMENT BY U.S.
SHIPS, AIRCRAFT, AND ARTILLERY FIR-
ING FROM SAIPAN, THE 4TH MARINE
DIVISION FOLLOWED BY THE 2D MARINE
DIVISION LANDED ON NORTHERN TIN-
IAN. AFTER NINE DAYS OF SEVERE
FIGHTING, WITH CONTINUOUS SUP-
PORT BY SEVENTH AIR FORCE AND CAR-
RIER AIRCRAFT AND BY NAVAL GUN-
FIRE, THE MARINES SECURED THE IS-
LAND.

5. PRECEDED BY ONE OF THE
HEAVIEST SUSTAINED NAVAL AND AIR
BOMBARDMENTS CONDUCTED IN THE
PACIFIC, THE 3D MARINE DIVISION AND
THE 1ST MARINE BRIGADE OF THE III
AMPHIBIOUS CORPS MADE TWO SEPA-
RATE LANDINGS ON THE WESTERN
SHORES OF GUAM ON 21 JULY. ON 24
JULY THE 77TH INFANTRY DIVISION AS-
SUMED CONTROL OF THE SOUTHERN
BEACHHEAD. THE NEXT DAY, WHILE
THE 3D MARINE DIVISION CONTINUED
ITS ASSAULT TO GAIN THE HIGH
GROUND TO ITS FRONT, THE 1ST
MARINE BRIGADE BEGAN TO CLEAR THE
OROTE PENINSULA. THAT NIGHT THE
CRISIS CAME ON BOTH FRONTS WHEN
THE JAPANESE LAUNCHED SPIRITED
BUT UNSUCCESSFUL COUNTERAT-
TACKS AGAINST BOTH UNITS.

6. THE INDIVIDUAL BEACHHEADS
WERE THEN LINKED TOGETHER AND
AMERICAN LINES CONSOLIDATED.
SUPPORTED BY ARMY, NAVY, AND
MARINE CORPS AIRCRAFT, THE 77TH IN-
FANTRY DIVISION AND THE 3D MARINE
DIVISION LAUNCHED A COORDINATED
ATTACK TOWARD THE NORTH END OF
THE ISLAND WHERE THE JAPANESE HAD
CONCENTRATED THEIR FORCES. BY 10
AUGUST ORGANIZED RESISTANCE HAD
CEASED.

VICTORY IN THE PACIFIC

1. IN THE LAST YEAR OF THE WAR
AGAINST JAPAN THE TEMPO QUICK-
ENED. HAVING ALREADY PENETRATED
THE JAPANESE BASIC DEFENSIVE
PERIMETER BY INVADING THE
MARIANAS AND THE PALAUS AND BY
PUSHING ALONG THE NEW GUINEA
COAST AND ON TO MOROTAI, BYPASS-
ING AND ISOLATING MANY THOU-
SANDS OF THE ENEMY BY THEIR LEAP-
FROG ASSAULTS, OUR JOINT FORCES
PREPARED TO STRIKE AT THE JAPANESE
HOME ISLANDS.

2. THE DECISIVE VICTORY IN THE
BATTLE OF THE PHILIPPINE SEA IN JUNE
1944 OPENED THE PHILIPPINES TO DI-
RECT ATTACK; OUR LANDINGS WERE
ADVANCED TWO MONTHS AND
SCHEDULED INTERMEDIATE OPER-
ATIONS WERE CANCELLED. ON 20 OC-
TOBER AMERICAN FORCES LANDED ON
LEYTE. REALIZING THAT THE LOSS OF
THESE ISLANDS WOULD IMPERIL THE
REMAINDER OF HIS WARTIME GAINS
THE ENEMY REACTED SWIFTLY, RISK-
ING, AND LOSING, A MAJOR SEA CON-
TEST WITH THE THIRD AND SEVENTH
FLEETS WHICH ELIMINATED JAPAN AS A
SEAPOWER. ON 9 JANUARY 1945 WE RE-
TURNED TO LUZON—THE COMPLETE
LIBERATION OF THE PHILIPPINES FOL-
LOWED.

3. IN BURMA, ALLIED FORCES OVER-
RAN THE JAPANESE, WHILE IN CHINA,
UNDER THE STIMULUS OF AIR- AND
GROUND-BORNE SUPPLY FROM THE
WEST, THE ENEMY'S GRASP WAS BRO-
KEN. IN NOVEMBER 1944 THE U.S. AIR
FORCES OPENED THEIR MAJOR AIR AT-
TACKS AGAINST THE JAPANESE HOME-
LAND FROM BASES IN THE MARIANAS,
TO WHICH THEY SOON REDEPLOYED
THEIR AIRCRAFT WHICH HAD OPER-
ATED EFFECTIVELY AGAINST THE
ENEMY FROM THE CHINESE MAINLAND.
UNTIL THE END OF HOSTILITIES THESE
ATTACKS CONTINUED WITH EVER IN-
CREASING INTENSITY. IN FEBRUARY
CAME THE CAPTURE OF IWO JIMA
WHICH PROVIDED A BASE FOR FIGHTER
ESCORTS AND A HAVEN FOR CRIPPLED
BOMBERS FACED WITH THE LONG
OVERWATER RETURN FROM JAPAN TO
THE MARIANAS.

4. FOR MONTHS, AIRCRAFT OF THE
NAVY'S FAST CARRIERS AS WELL AS
ARMY AIR FORCE BOMBERS HAD RE-

PEATEDLY ATTACKED OKINAWA, THE FINAL STEPPING STONE TO JAPAN; OUR TRIPHIBIOUS ASSAULT ON THAT IS-LAND EARLY IN MARCH CULMINATED IN ITS CAPTURE BY LATE JUNE.

5. THROUGHOUT THE WAR U.S. SUBMARINES CONTRIBUTED MATE-RIALLY TO OUR SUCCESS. OPERATING OFTEN THOUSANDS OF MILES FROM THEIR BASES, DEEP WITHIN ENEMY-CONTROLLED WATERS, THEY STRUCK WITH DEVASTATING EFFECTIVENESS AND, BY WAR'S END, HAD DESTROYED NEARLY ONE-THIRD OF JAPAN'S COM-BAT SHIPS AND ONE-HALF OF HER MER-CHANT MARINE, WHILE ALSO PER-FORMING MISSIONS OF RECONNAI-SANCE, SUPPLY, AND THE RESCUE OF ISOLATED PERSONNEL.

6. PLANS FOR THE INVASION OF JAPAN CONTEMPLATED A TRIPHIBIOUS ASSAULT ON KYUSHU IN NOVEMBER 1945, FOLLOWED BY A LATER ATTACK ON THE TOKYO PLAIN. IN PREPARA-TION, OUR AIR AND NAVAL BOMBARD-MENTS OF JAPAN CONTINUED UN-ABATED. THE DEVASTATION FROM THE AIR OF HIROSHIMA AND NAGASAKI IN EARLY AUGUST WAS FOLLOWED BY THE CAPITULATION OF THE JAPANESE GOV-ERNMENT, THE SURRENDER TERMS BEING SIGNED IN TOKYO BAY ON 2 SEP-TEMBER 1945, 1,365 DAYS AFTER THE ATTACK ON PEARL HARBOR.

LIBERATION OF THE PHILIPPINES
OCTOBER 1944–15 AUGUST 1945

FROM THE EARLY DAYS OF THE LONG ENEMY OCCUPATION OF THE PHILIP-PINES, UNITED STATES FORCES PERSISTENTLY FOUGHT THEIR WAY BACK. EVENTUALLY, ON 20 OCTOBER 1944, UNDER COVER OF NAVAL GUN-FIRE AND AIR BOMBARDMENT OF THE SEVENTH FLEET AND WITH LONG-RANGE SUPPORT BY AIRCRAFT OF THE THIRD FLEET, THE SIXTH ARMY LANDED ON THE EASTERN SHORES OF LEYTE.

THEREUPON THE JAPANESE DECIDED TO RISK A MAJOR SEA BATTLE IN A DE-TERMINED EFFORT TO DESTROY THE AMERICAN FORCES; THREE FLEETS MOVED TOWARD THE PHILIPPINES. ON 23 OCTOBER AMERICAN SUBMARINES ATTACKED THE CENTER FORCE IN PALAWAN PASSAGE. ON THE FOLLOW-ING DAY AIRCRAFT FROM THE THIRD FLEET INFLICTED HEAVY LOSSES ON THIS FORCE IN THE SIBUYAN SEA WHILE JAPANESE AIRCRAFT FROM LUZON DE-STROYED A U.S. CARRIER.

DURING THE NIGHT OF 24–25 OC-TOBER THE ENEMY'S SOUTHERN FORCE STEAMED INTO SURIGAO STRAIT DI-RECTLY TOWARD THE WAITING SEVENTH FLEET AND WAS DECISIVELY DEFEATED BY TORPEDO ATTACKS AND GUNFIRE. MEANWHILE THE THIRD FLEET MOVED TO INTERCEPT THE NORTHERN FORCE AND ON 25–26 OC-TOBER WON A MAJOR VICTORY OFF CAPE ENGANO.

ON THE MORNING OF 25 OCTOBER THE CENTER FORCE PUSHED THROUGH SAN BERNARDINO STRAIT AND AT-TACKED THE ESCORT CARRIERS OF THE SEVENTH FLEET OFF SAMAR. AL-THOUGH OUTNUMBERED AND OUT-GUNNED, THE ESCORT CARRIERS AND THEIR SCREEN OF DESTROYERS FORCED THE ENEMY TO WITHDRAW. RELIEVING OUR GROUND FORCES FROM THE MENACE OF ISOLATION, THE DECISIVE DEFEAT OF THE JAPANESE FLEET AT THESE BATTLES FOR LEYTE GULF ALSO RENDERED IT POWERLESS TO PREVENT FUTURE AMPHIBIOUS OPERATIONS.

TWO MONTHS OF HARD FIGHTING FREED MOST OF LEYTE, ALTHOUGH MANY JAPANESE ESCAPING TO THE NORTH AND WEST RESISTED THE PUR-SUING EIGHTH ARMY, NOW IN CON-TROL ON THE ISLAND. IN DECEMBER THE SIXTH ARMY SEIZED MINDORO; MEANWHILE THE JAPANESE MASSED A QUARTER OF A MILLION MEN TO DE-FEND LUZON.

ON 9 JANUARY 1945, THE SEVENTH FLEET LANDED THE SIXTH ARMY AT LINGAYEN GULF. SUPPORTED BY THE FIFTH AIR FORCE AND BY MARINE CORPS AND NAVAL AIRCRAFT, THE TROOPS PUSHED INLAND. INITIALLY, RESISTANCE WAS ENCOUNTERED ALONG THE LEFT FLANK; ON THE RIGHT

AMERICAN FORCES ADVANCED DOWN THE CENTRAL PLAINS TOWARD MANILA. AFTER FIERCE FIGHTING MANILA, BATAAN, AND CORREGIDOR WERE CLEARED OF THE ENEMY. U.S. TROOPS AND PHILIPPINE GUERRILLA FORCES, CONTINUOUSLY SUPPORTED BY AERIAL BOMBARDMENT, THEN FORCED THE ENEMY DEEP INTO THE MOUNTAINS. ON 1 JULY, THE EIGHTH ARMY ASSUMED RESPONSIBILITY FOR LAND OPERATIONS; THE SIXTH ARMY REGROUPED IN PREPARATION FOR AN INVASION OF JAPAN.

WITH THE COOPERATION OF THE SEVENTH AND THIRTEENTH AIR FORCES THE EIGHTH ARMY AND THE SEVENTH FLEET HAD ALREADY EMBARKED ON A SERIES OF AMPHIBIOUS ASSAULTS TO FREE THE OTHER ISLANDS. DURING FEBRUARY AND MARCH THEY SECURED AIRFIELDS IN PALAWAN AND ZAMBOANGA AND OVERPOWERED THE ENEMY IN THE VISAYAN SEA AREA. IN APRIL THEY LANDED UNITS ON THE SOUTHERN COAST OF MINDANAO AND ADVANCED TOWARD DAVAO GULF; OTHERS FOLLOWED AND FOUGHT THEIR WAY NORTHWARD TO MEET ADDITIONAL FORCES WHICH LANDED IN MAY. BY THE END OF JUNE, AMERICAN SOLDIERS AND FILIPINO GUERRILLAS HAD COMPRESSED THE ENEMY INTO ISOLATED MOUNTAIN AREAS. THERE HE WAS SUBJECTED TO INTENSIVE AERIAL BOMBARDMENT AND TO CONSTANT PRESSURE UNTIL 15 AUGUST 1945 WHEN HOSTILITIES CEASED.

IWO JIMA
16 FEBRUARY–16 MARCH 1945

BEFORE THE CAPTURE OF THE MARIANA ISLANDS HAD BEEN COMPLETED IN AUGUST 1944, AIRFIELDS WERE UNDER CONSTRUCTION. FROM THESE, IN NOVEMBER, THE U.S. ARMY AIR FORCES BEGAN MASSIVE AIR ASSAULTS AGAINST THE JAPANESE HOMELAND. THE PROMPT SEIZURE OF THE ISLAND OF IWO JIMA BECAME OF VITAL IMPORTANCE BECAUSE IT COULD PROVIDE THE ONLY EMERGENCY LANDING FIELD FOR RETURNING AIRCRAFT IN DISTRESS AS WELL AS A BASE FOR FIGHTER ESCORTS.

SENSING THE PERIL TO THEIR EMPIRE THE JAPANESE CONCENTRATED THEIR EFFORTS ON MAKING IWO JIMA IMPREGNABLE, GARRISONING THIS FORTIFIED ISLAND OF ABOUT SEVEN SQUARE MILES WITH MORE THAN 20,000 TROOPS IN CAREFULLY PREPARED DEFENSIVE POSITIONS. AGAINST THESE, FOR SEVEN MONTHS PRIOR TO THE AMPHIBIOUS ASSAULT, THE U.S. SEVENTH AIR FORCE AS WELL AS FAST CARRIER AIRCRAFT SQUADRONS AND NAVAL SURFACE SHIPS DIRECTED BOMBARDMENTS OF INCREASING FREQUENCY AND INTENSITY.

ON 16 FEBRUARY 1945, UNITS OF THE FIFTH FLEET BEGAN A CONCENTRATED GUNFIRE AND AERIAL BOMBARDMENT OF IWO JIMA WHILE THE FAST CARRIERS, IN A COVERING ACTION, STRUCK AT TARGETS IN JAPAN, THEN RETURNED THREE DAYS LATER TO JOIN IN THE ATTACK. ON THE MORNING OF 19 FEBRUARY, UNDER COVER OF A HEAVY BOMBARDMENT, THE FIFTH FLEET LANDED THE 4TH AND 5TH MARINE DIVISIONS ON THE SOUTHEAST COAST OF THE ISLAND. THE ENEMY REACTED VIOLENTLY, POURING CONCENTRATED FIRE FROM PREVIOUSLY UNDETECTED POSITIONS. AS THE MARINES ADVANCED ACROSS OPEN GROUND THEY WERE RAKED BY HEAVY FIRE FROM THE HIGH GROUND ON THE FLANKS. THE 4TH MARINE DIVISION ON THE RIGHT SUFFERED SEVERE CASUALTIES AND THE ESCORT CARRIER BISMARCK SEA WAS SUNK OFFSHORE BY ENEMY AIR ATTACK.

BY THE END OF THE DAY THE MARINES HAD FOUGHT THEIR WAY ACROSS THE ISLAND AND HAD ISOLATED THE JAPANESE ON MOUNT SURIBACHI FROM THE MAIN FORCES IN THE NORTH. ON THE FOLLOWING DAY OUR TROOPS CAPTURED AIRFIELD NO. 1. THE 3D MARINE DIVISION LANDED ON THE THIRD DAY.

AIRFIELD NO. 2 WAS REACHED ON 23 FEBRUARY. SIMULTANEOUSLY THE 5TH

DIVISION STORMED THE STEEP SLOPES OF MOUNT SURIBACHI, CAPTURING THE SUMMIT. AN ASSAULT UP TO THE MOTOYAMA PLATEAU BROUGHT THE MARINES DIRECTLY INTO THE FACE OF THE HEAVIEST ENEMY DEFENSES. THEN AS THE 4TH DIVISION ATTACKED ON THE RIGHT AND THE 5TH DIVISION ON THE LEFT, THE 3D DIVISION IN THE CENTER CRACKED THE MAIN LINE OF JAPANESE RESISTANCE.

FOR NEARLY TWO WEEKS MORE, WITH CONTINUOUS SUPPORT BY SEVENTH AIR FORCE AND CARRIER AIRCRAFT AND NAVAL GUNFIRE, THE MARINES PRESSED FORWARD AGAINST A DETERMINED RESISTANCE CONDUCTED BY A WELL-TRAINED, WELL-EQUIPPED ENEMY, FIGHTING FROM THOUSANDS OF DEFENSIVE INSTALLATIONS AND DEEP CAVES. DESPITE HEAVY AND CONTINUOUS LOSSES THE MARINES MAINTAINED THEIR DRIVE UNTIL FINALLY, AFTER 26 DAYS OF BITTER ASSAULT, THE ISLAND WAS SECURED.

THE SEIZURE OF IWO JIMA ENTAILED HEAVY AMERICAN CASUALTIES BUT, EVEN BEFORE THE CAPTURE OF THE ISLAND HAD BEEN COMPLETED, ITS GREAT IMPORTANCE AS AN AIR BASE WAS DEMONSTRATED. THE BOMBARDMENT OF JAPAN WAS INTENSIFIED, COMBAT EFFECTIVENESS WAS INCREASED; UNDOUBTEDLY THE NUMBER OF AMERICANS WHOSE LIVES WERE SAVED BY THE OPERATION OF THIS AIR BASE EXCEEDED THE NUMBER LOST IN ITS CAPTURE.

OKINAWA
26 MARCH–22 JUNE 1945

EARLY IN 1945 THE GREAT CONCENTRATION OF U.S. SEA, LAND, AND AIR POWER IN THE PACIFIC ENABLED OUR FORCES TO CHALLENGE JAPAN IN HER OWN WATERS. FOR MONTHS AIRCRAFT FROM THE NAVY'S FAST CARRIERS, AND ARMY AIR FORCE BOMBERS FROM THE SOUTHWEST PACIFIC AREA AND THE MARIANAS, HAD BOMBED THE IMPORTANT BASES IN THE RYUKYUS. OTHERS IN JAPAN AND FORMOSA WERE ALSO

ATTACKED PRIOR TO THE INVASION. THE AMPHIBIOUS ASSAULT WAS INITIATED WHEN A DIVISION OF THE TENTH ARMY LANDED ON KERAMA RETTO ON 26 MARCH. FIVE DAYS LATER TROOPS LANDED ON THE KEISE ISLETS AND EMPLACED ARTILLERY TO COVER THE LANDING ON THE MAIN ISLAND.

ON 1 APRIL, UNDER COVER OF AN INTENSIVE NAVAL AND AIR BOMBARDMENT BY THE U.S. FIFTH FLEET, TWO DIVISIONS OF THE U.S. ARMY XXIV CORPS AND TWO DIVISIONS OF THE MARINE III AMPHIBIOUS CORPS LANDED ON OKINAWA ITSELF. THE TWO CORPS, ATTACKING ABREAST, PUSHED RAPIDLY ACROSS THE ISLAND, THUS SPLITTING THE JAPANESE FORCES. THE III AMPHIBIOUS CORPS THEN TURNED NORTH, WHILE THE XXIV CORPS TURNED SOUTH TO ATTACK THE JAPANESE MAIN DEFENSIVE POSITIONS. THERE FOLLOWED A DESPERATE THREE MONTHS STRUGGLE ON LAND, ON SEA, AND IN THE AIR.

TO INSURE EARLY WARNING OF THE EXPECTED AIR REACTION FROM ENEMY BASES IN JAPAN, CHINA AND FORMOSA, THE FIFTH FLEET ESTABLISHED A RING OF RADAR PICKET DESTROYERS AND ESCORT VESSELS AROUND OKINAWA. ALTHOUGH SUSTAINING HEAVY LOSSES, THE PICKET SHIPS AND OTHER FIRE-SUPPORT SHIPS FOUGHT OFF INCESSANT AND DESPERATE ATTACKS BY JAPANESE LAND-BASED KAMIKAZE AIRPLANES. MEANWHILE, AIRCRAFT FROM THE U.S. FAST CARRIERS AND ARMY AIR FORCE BOMBERS AND FIGHTERS FROM THE MARIANAS AND THE SOUTHWEST PACIFIC STRUCK HEAVY BLOWS AT ENEMY AIRFIELDS. ON THE NIGHT OF 6–7 APRIL, THE ENEMY SURFACE FLEET MADE ITS LAST SORTIE FROM ITS HOME WATERS. U.S. CARRIER AIRCRAFT ATTACKED THIS FORCE SINKING A BATTLESHIP, A CRUISER AND FOUR DESTROYERS. COMMENCING ON 9 APRIL LAND-BASED AIRCRAFT OF THE U.S. MARINES AND THE ARMY AIR FORCES AUGMENTED THE CARRIER-BASED AIRCRAFT, AND TOGETHER WITH SHIP ANTIAIRCRAFT

FIRE, ULTIMATELY CHECKED THE KAMIKAZES. THE SEIZURE OF IE SHIMA AFTER FOUR DAYS OF BITTER FIGHTING PROVIDED THE SITE FOR AN EXCELLENT AIR BASE WHICH FURTHER STRENGTHENED OUR AIR DEFENSE.

THE MARINE DIVISIONS, WHICH HAD CLEARED THE NORTHERN HALF OF THE ISLAND, JOINED IN THE BATTLE TO THE SOUTH. NAVAL GUNFIRE, MASSED ARTILLERY AND MORTAR FIRE, AND CONTINUOUS STRIKES BY TACTICAL AIRCRAFT SUPPORTED THE ADVANCE OF THESE AND THE ARMY DIVISIONS AS THEY PUSHED SOUTHWARD AGAINST FANATICAL RESISTANCE AND FURIOUS COUNTERATTACKS. THE HIGH GROUND HELD BY THE JAPANESE IN SOUTHERN OKINAWA WAS IDEAL FOR A PROLONGED DEFENSE. THE LIMESTONE HILLS, HONEYCOMBED WITH NATURAL CAVES, AFFORDED EVERY ADVANTAGE OF TERRAIN. EACH SUCCESSIVE ENEMY STRONGPOINT WAS CLEARED ONLY BY PERSISTENT AND HEROIC EFFORT. BY THE MIDDLE OF JUNE OUR GROUND FORCES HAD BATTERED THEIR WAY THROUGH THE FORTIFIED NAHA-SHURI LINE. BY 22 JUNE 1945, THE LAST ORGANIZED UNIT OF THE JAPANESE GARRISON HAD BEEN DESTROYED. OKINAWA THEN BECAME THE FIRST AMERICAN STRATEGIC BASE WITHIN EASY AIR RANGE OF THE JAPANESE HOMELAND.

OPERATIONS AGAINST THE NORTH KOREANS
25 JUNE–23 NOVEMBER 1950

ON 25 JUNE 1950 THE NORTH KOREAN ARMY INVADED THE REPUBLIC OF KOREA. THE UNITED NATIONS DEMAND FOR THE CESSATION OF HOSTILITIES BEING IGNORED, UNITED STATES AIR AND SEA FORCES WERE SENT TO GIVE THE SOUTH KOREAN ARMY COVER AND SUPPORT AND TO PROVIDE AERIAL AND SEA EVACUATION. ON 30 JUNE, THE PRESIDENT AUTHORIZED THE USE OF AMERICAN GROUND TROOPS.

THE FAR EAST AIR FORCES PROMPTLY NULLIFIED AIR OPPOSITION WHILE NAVAL FORCES NEUTRALIZED THE NORTH KOREAN NAVY, MET THE SERIOUS ENEMY MINE THREAT AND ESTABLISHED A BLOCKADE OF THE PENINSULA. NEVERTHELESS, NORTH KOREAN GROUND TROOPS, WHICH HEAVILY OUTNUMBERED AND OUTGUNNED THE REPUBLIC OF KOREA FORCES, CAPTURED THE CAPITAL CITY OF SEOUL AND ADVANCED RAPIDLY SOUTHWARD.

ON 5 JULY ADVANCE ELEMENTS OF THE U.S. 24TH INFANTRY DIVISION FROM THE EIGHTH ARMY IN JAPAN MET THE EMEMY NEAR OSAN; THEN BEGAN A SERIES OF COSTLY DELAYING ACTIONS. THE U.S. 25TH INFANTRY AND 1ST CAVALRY DIVISIONS ARRIVED AND WERE PROMPTLY COMMITTED.

BY 5 AUGUST THE DEFENDERS WERE COMPRESSED INTO A SMALL BEACHHEAD AROUND PUSAN ALTHOUGH THE U.S. FIFTH AIR FORCE AND THE FAR EAST AIR FORCES HAD GREATLY ASSISTED IN SLOWING THE ENEMY'S ADVANCE BY CONTINUOUSLY BOMBING INDUSTRIAL TARGETS AND SUPPLY LINES, AND BY PROVIDING CLOSE SUPPORT. CARRIER-BASED AIRCRAFT AND NAVAL GUNFIRE WERE RENDERING EFFECTIVE INTERDICTION AS WELL AS GROUND SUPPORT. COMMAND OF THE SEAS MADE POSSIBLE A RAPID BUILDUP OF SUPPLIES AND REINFORCEMENTS.

THE U.S. 2D INFANTRY DIVISION AND 1ST MARINE BRIGADE LANDED ON AUGUST 1 AND 2, FOLLOWED BY SEVERAL UNITS FROM OTHER NATIONS. ON 7 AUGUST SOLDIERS AND MARINES LAUNCHED THE FIRST SUSTAINED U.N. COUNTERATTACK IN SOUTHEAST KOREA, STOPPING THE ENEMY DRIVE TOWARD PUSAN. FURTHER COUNTERATTACKS, SUPPORTED BY AIR FORCE, MARINE CORPS AND NAVAL AIRCRAFT, AND AIDED BY NAVAL GUNFIRE, ESTABLISHED A FIRM PERIMETER.

ON 15 SEPTEMBER THE INITIATIVE CHANGED HANDS; PRECEDED BY AIR AND NAVAL BOMBARDMENT THE 1ST MARINE DIVISION WAS LANDED AT INCHON IN A DARING FLANKING OPERA-

TION. THE 7TH INFANTRY DIVISION FOLLOWED AND TOGETHER THEY PRESSED FORWARD TOWARD SEOUL. ON 16 SEPTEMBER THE EIGHTH ARMY BEGAN ITS OFFENSIVE TO BREAK OUT OF THE PUSAN PERIMETER. OPPOSITION WAS STRONG AND THE FIGHTING SEVERE UNTIL THE ENEMY LINE WAS BROKEN AND RESISTANCE COLLAPSED. ON 26 SEPTEMBER ELEMENTS OF THE 1ST CAVALRY DIVISION MET TROOPS OF THE 7TH INFANTRY DIVISION NEAR OSAN; ON THE SAME DAY THE LIBERATION OF SEOUL WAS ANNOUNCED.

PRECEDED BY AIRCRAFT WHOSE ATTACKS HASTENED THE DISORGANIZATION OF THE ENEMY, UNITED NATIONS FORCES CROSSED THE 38TH PARRALLEL, THE BOUNDARY OF NORTH KOREA, WHOSE CAPITAL, PYONGYANG, THEY OCCUPIED ON 21 OCTOBER. AFTER THEIR DEFEATS THE NORTH KOREANS SHOWED LITTLE AGGRESSIVENESS AS U.N. TROOPS ADVANCED TOWARD THE YALU RIVER.

AT THIS MOMENT LARGE CHINESE UNITS ATTACKED UNITED NATIONS FORCES. IN THE WESTERN SECTOR THE EIGHTH ARMY WITHDREW TO A SHORTER LINE AND PREPARED FOR FURTHER OFFENSIVE OPERATIONS. IN THE EASTERN SECTOR U.N. FORCES CONTINUED FORWARD, REACHING A LINE WHICH EXTENDED FROM THE CHOSIN RESERVOIR TO THE CHINESE BORDER AND CHONGJIN.

OPERATIONS AGAINST THE CHINESE INVADERS
24 NOVEMBER 1950–27 JULY 1953

1. ON 24 NOVEMBER 1950 THE U.S. EIGHTH ARMY LAUNCHED AN OFFENSIVE AGAINST THE NORTH KOREANS BUT WAS ABRUPTLY THROWN BACK BY A MASSIVE ATTACK BY CHINESE COMMUNIST FORCES WHICH HAD SECRETLY CROSSED THE YALU RIVER BORDER. THE X CORPS ADVANCE MET A SIMILAR FATE WHEN THE CHINESE CUT OFF MOST OF THE 1ST MARINE DIVISION AND FOUR ARMY BATTALIONS NEAR HAGARU AND KOTO. SURMOUNTING HEAVY ODDS,

BITTERLY COLD WEATHER, AND RUGGED TERRAIN, THE MARINES AND SOLDIERS FOUGHT THEIR WAY TO HUNGNAM WHERE, TOGETHER WITH OTHER TROOPS IN NORTHEAST KOREA, THEY WERE EVACUATED BY SEA AND AIR TO SOUTH KOREA. LAND- AND CARRIER-BASED AIRCRAFT AND SUPPORTING NAVAL GROUPS PROVED INVALUABLE IN THE REDEPLOYMENT.

2. MEANWHILE THE EIGHTH ARMY WITHDREW SOUTH OF PYONGYANG, THEN TO A STRONGER DEFENSIVE POSITION STILL FURTHER SOUTH. ON THE LAST DAY OF DECEMBER 1950 THE ENEMY LAUNCHED A VIGOROUS ATTACK ACROSS THE 38TH PARALLEL INTO SOUTH KOREA, RECAPTURING SEOUL ON 4 JANUARY 1951. THREE WEEKS LATER THE INVADERS WERE HALTED, EXCEPT FOR ONE DIVISION WHICH INFILTRATED ALMOST TO UISONG BEFORE BEING DRIVEN BACK. THIS MARKED THE HIGH TIDE OF THE SECOND INVASION OF SOUTH KOREA.

3. THE EIGHTH ARMY THEN BEGAN A SERIES OF LIMITED-OBJECTIVE ATTACKS; OPPOSITION WAS PARTICULARLY INTENSE SOUTH OF SEOUL AND IN THE CENTER OF THE PENINSULA. IN MARCH U.S. TROOPS CROSSED THE HAN RIVER EAST OF SEOUL, AND, OUTFLANKING THE CITY, FORCED ITS EVACUATION. IN THESE ATTACKS THE TROOPS WERE CONTINUOUSLY ASSISTED BY AIR AND NAVAL FORCES WHICH NOT ONLY PROVIDED CLOSE SUPPORT AND INTERDICTION, BUT ALSO PERFORMED MANY MISSIONS OF AIR SUPPLY AND EVACUATION. SUPPLIES POURED INTO KOREA BY SEA.

4. ON 22 APRIL 1951, THE ENEMY AGAIN ATTACKED IN FORCE BUT WAS HALTED SHORT OF SEOUL AND HONGCHON. IN MID-MAY HE STRUCK ONCE MORE BUT BY THE 22D EXHAUSTION, SUPPLY DIFFICULTIES, AND CASUALTIES FORCED HIM TO ACCEPT FAILURE.

5. ON THE NEXT DAY U.N. TROOPS BEGAN A STEADY DRIVE NORTHWARD. SO HARD HIT WAS THE ENEMY BY EARLY JUNE THAT 10,000 CHINESE SURRENDERED IN A WEEK. ARMISTICE REPRE-

SENTATIVES MET IN JULY BUT CONFER-
ENCES WERE SUSPENDED IN LATE
AUGUST, WHEREUPON U.N. FORCES
RESUMED THE OFFENSIVE AND GAINED
COMMANDING GROUND ALONG THE
WHOLE FRONT. THE NEGOTIATIONS
WERE RESUMED LATE IN OCTOBER 1951.

6. FIGHTING CONTINUED BUT THE
FRONT LINES REMAINED SUBSTAN-
TIALLY UNCHANGED. THE AIR WAR IN-
TENSIFIED DURING THE SUMMER OF
1952 AS U.N. AIRCRAFT STRUCK AT SUP-
PLY CENTERS, TROOP CONCENTRA-
TIONS AND INDUSTRIAL TARGETS
WITHIN NORTH KOREA. GROUND
FIGHTING WAS PARTICULARLY HEAVY
IN OCTOBER AND AGAIN IN THE SPRING
OF 1953. AN ARMISTICE AGREEMENT
WAS FINALLY SIGNED ON 27 JULY 1953,
THUS BRINGING TO A SUCCESSFUL
CONCLUSION THE UNITED NATIONS
DEFENSE OF THE REPUBLIC OF KOREA
AGAINST THE COMMUNIST INVADERS.

The following quotations by General
MacArthur and Admiral Nimitz ap-
pear on scrolls on the maps
"Operations in the Pacific" and
"Victory in the Pacific," respec-
tively:

"THE PROBLEM BASICALLY IS
THEOLOGICAL AND INVOLVES A
SPIRITUAL RECRUDESCENCE AND IM-
PROVEMENT OF HUMAN CHARACTER."

**

"NAMES THAT ARE A CROSS-SECTION
OF DEMOCRACY THEY FOUGHT TO-
GETHER AS BROTHERS-IN-ARMS THEY
DIED TOGETHER AND NOW THEY SLEEP
SIDE-BY-SIDE. TO THEM WE HAVE A
SOLEMN OBLIGATION TO ENSURE THAT
THEIR SACRIFICE WILL HELP TO MAKE A
BETTER AND SAFER WORLD IN WHICH
TO LIVE."

In the spaces between the ex-
tremities of the map galleries and the
adjacent entrances are two sets of
"key" maps, "The War Against
Germany" and "The War Against
Japan." The sets consist of three
maps on enameled metal, each map
covering about one-third of our par-

ticipation in World War II. By these
key maps, each major battle may be
related to the others in time and
space.

THE CHAPEL

The chapel is located behind the
tower between the two map galleries. The two doors leading from
the galleries into the chapel, the
chapel windows and the altar rail are
of bronze grille-work. Inset in the
grilles are colored glass cabochons
designed by Bruce Moore. The
cabochons contain seven different
symbols, two of which are repeated
three times each.

Doors
Liberty . . . .(gold, blue)
The Hero . . . .(gold, blue)
Windows
The Hand of God . . . . . .(blue)
Liberty . . . .(gold)
The Hero . . . .(gold)
The Holy Dove . . . .(gold)
Altar Rail
Liberty . . . .(gold)
The Lamb . . . .(red)
The Shofar . . . .(blue)
The Hero . . . .(gold)

The four cabochons in the bronze
grille of the altar rail are illuminated
electrically.

The United States national flag
stands in each corner of the vestibule
and at each side of the altar. Inscribed upon the southeast wall of
the vestibule is the following dedicatory inscription:

IN PROUD REMEMBRANCE OF THE
ACHIEVEMENTS OF HER SONS AND IN
HUMBLE TRIBUTE TO THEIR SACRIFICES
THIS MEMORIAL HAS BEEN ERECTED BY
THE UNITED STATES OF AMERICA**
1941–1945**1950–1953**1964–1973

The altar, chapel steps and floor
are of Verde (green) Antico marble;
the wall behind the altar is of Rojo
(red) Alicante marble. On the wall

Chapel Tower

behind the altar is a lighted latin cross. It is flanked by a large gold leafed Star of David engraved in the wall to the left and a Buddhist Wheel of Righteousness engraved in the wall to the right.

West Coast Memorial

The West Coast Memorial is situated in the Fort Scott area of the Presidio of San Francisco, California. It stands near the junctions of Washington, Harrison and Lincoln Boulevards on a promontory overlooking the entrance to the Golden Gate, and is accessible by automobile.

THE SITE

Use of the 1½-acre site was granted to the American Battle Monuments Commission by the Department of Defense. It is reached by passing through the Presidio, thence via Park Boulevard and Kobbe Avenue, which leads into Harrison Avenue and the intersection of the latter with Washington Boulevard.

ARCHITECTS

Architects for the memorial were Clark & Beuttler of San Francisco. The landscape architect was Lawrence Halprin, also of San Francisco.

GENERAL LAYOUT

From the parking area at the intersection of Harrison Avenue and Washington Boulevard a path leads southwest to the memorial.

The memorial consists essentially of a curved California Raymond, light gray, granite wall. On the seaward face of this wall are engraved the names, rank, organization and state of 413 men of our Armed Services who lost their lives in the eastern waters of the Pacific Ocean during World War II:

U.S. Army and Army Air Forces[1]	157
U.S. Navy	238
U.S. Marine Corps	7
U.S. Coast Guard	11

---

[1] It will be recalled that during World War II the Air Forces still formed part of the United States Army.

These men gave their lives in the service of their Country, but their remains have not been recovered and identified. The list includes men from every state in the Union except Nevada, Wyoming, Alaska and Hawaii; the District of Columbia and Puerto Rico are also represented.

At the north end of the memorial, surmounted by a relief sculpture panel depicting Pegasus soaring to the heavens from the sea, is the inscription:

1941–1945 ★ ERECTED BY THE UNITED STATES OF AMERICA IN PROUD AND GRATEFUL REMEMBRANCE OF HER SONS WHO GAVE THEIR LIVES IN HER SERVICE AND WHO SLEEP IN THE AMERICAN COASTAL WATERS OF THE PACIFIC OCEAN ★ INTO THY HANDS O LORD.

Standing on a pedestal in front of the pylon terminating the south end of the memorial is a Mount Airy, light gray, granite figure of Columbia mourning the Dead; approximately 8 feet high. The works of sculpture were designed by Jean De-Marco of New York City.

To blend into the natural growth of the area, the memorial is planted with Mesembryanthemum, Ceanothus, Thunberg and Monterey Pines, Monterey Cypress and other plants. In the bed at the base of the memorial are Juniperus sabina.

The memorial was completed in 1960.

CEMETERIES AND MEMORIALS OF OTHER AMERICAN MILITARY EFFORTS:

MEXICO
(The War of 1847)

Mexico City

National

Cemetery

Mexico City National Cemetery is at Virginia Fabregas 31, Colonia San Rafael, about 2 miles west of the cathedral and about 1 mile north of the U.S. Embassy. The cemetery was established in 1851 and contains a small monument over the grave of 750 of our unidentified Dead of the War of 1847. Inscribed on the monument is: "TO THE HONORED MEMORY OF 750 AMERICANS, KNOWN BUT TO GOD, WHOSE BONES, COLLECTED BY THEIR COUNTRY'S ORDER, ARE HERE BURIED." In this 1 acre area there are also 813 remains of Americans and others in wall crypts. The cemetery is closed to burials.

CEMETERIES AND MEMORIALS OF OTHER AMERICAN MILITARY EFFORTS:

PANAMA
(The Building and Defense of the Panama Canal)

Corozal
American
Cemetery
and
Memorial

Corozal American Cemetery is located approximately 3 miles north of Panama City, Republic of Panama, just off Gaillard Highway between the Corozal Railroad and Fort Clayton. To reach the cemetery, follow Gaillard Highway north from Panama City, turn right on Rybicki Road and proceed about one-half mile to the cemetery. Taxi and bus service are available from Panama City. In agreement with the Republic of Panama, care and maintenance of the cemetery in perpetuity were assumed by this Commission on 1 October 1979.

At this cemetery, 16 acres in extent, are interred 4,795 American veterans and others. A small memorial feature sits atop a knoll overlooking the graves area. It consists of a paved plaza with a 12 foot rectangular granite obelisk flanked by two flagpoles from which fly the United States and Panamanian flags. Floral tributes are laid at the obelisk during memorial services. A paved walk leads from the plaza to the chapel at the foot of the knoll. Engraved upon the obelisk is the following inscription: "THIS MEMORIAL HAS BEEN ERECTED BY THE UNITED STATES OF AMERICA IN HUMBLE TRIBUTE TO ALL INTERRED HERE WHO SERVED IN ITS ARMED FORCES OR CONTRIBUTED TO THE CONSTRUCTION, OPERATION AND SECURITY OF THE PANAMA CANAL."

INDEX

Index

Index